CAMPING AND CARAVANNING BRITAIN & IRELAND 1998

CREDITS

Produced by AA Publishing

The directory is generated from the AA's establishment database, Information Research and Control, AA Hotel and Touring Services

Maps prepared by the AA Cartographic Department

The contents of this publication are believed correct at the time of printing. Nevertheless, the publishers cannot be held responsible for any errors or omissions or for changes in the details given in this guide or for the consequences of any reliance on the information provided by the same. Assessments of the campsites are based on the experience of the AA Camping and Caravanning Inspectors on the occasion of their visit(s) and therefore descriptions given in this guide necessarily contain an element of subjective opinion which may not reflect or dictate a reader's own opinion on another occasion. We have tried to ensure accuracy in this guide but things do change and we would be grateful if readers would advise us of any inaccuracies they may encounter.

Advertisements
This guide contains display advertisements in addition to the editorial features and line entries. For further information contact:

Head of Advertisement Sales: Christopher Heard, telephone 01256 491544

Advertisement Production: Karen Weeks, telephone 01256 491545

Filmset/Colour Origination by Avonset, Palace Yard Mews, Bath

Printed and bound in Great Britain by Bemrose Security Printing, Derby

Editor: Denise Laing

Cover Photograph by Julian Dascombe shows Burrowhayes Farm, Porlock, Somerset

A CIP catalogue record for this book is available from the British Library

ISBN 0 7495 1683 6 AA Ref.10025

Published by AA Publishing, a trading name of Automobile Association Developments Limited, whose registered office is Norfolk House, Priestley Road, Basingstoke, Hampshire RG24 9NY. Registered number 1878835

CONTENTS

HOW TO USE THE GUIDE

Whether you are a newcomer to camping and caravanning or an old hand, it is probable that what attracted you in the first place was the 'go-as-you-please' freedom of being able to set off on the merest whim. However, in practice, especially during holiday periods, parks in popular parts of the country get dreadfully crowded, and if you choose somewhere off the beaten track, you may go for miles without finding anywhere.

When you do find somewhere, how do you know that it will have the facilities you need? How do you know whether they will be maintained to an acceptable standard? This is where you will find the AA guide invaluable in helping you to choose the right park. Please also read the section on the Pennant Rating Scheme so that you know what the classification symbols used in this guide mean.

The directory of parks is organised by county in England and Ireland, with locations listed in alphabetical order of location. Scotland and Wales, because of the recent changes to counties and boundaries, are divided into three regions each: in Scotland, Highlands & Islands, Central, Lowlands & Borders; in Wales, North Wales, Mid Wales and South Wales. Channel Islands and Isle of Man appear between England and Scotland. Parks are listed in descending order of pennant rating. There is a location map for every county or region and the map normally appears after the county or regional heading; if it does not, there is a page cross reference.

Explanation of a Directory Entry

(see also The AA Pennant Rating Scheme)

Town name appears in alphabetical order within counties in England, within regions in Scotland and Wales.

Name of park followed by 6-figure Ordnance Survey map reference. If park name is in italic type, details given have not been confirmed by the park. If the words 'Apply to' follow the map ref, this is the contact number for details and bookings.

Pennant Rating or Designation See the section on the AA Pennant Rating scheme for an explanation of pennants. Parks with the highest ratings - four and five pennants - have highlighted entries, and so do Holiday Centres.

ANY TOWN

Pleasant Caravan Park SW8627281
Carnevas Farm PL28 8PN ac 01841 520230 Signposted
Nearby town: Padstow
►►► **Family Park** £5 £8 £5 £8 £5-£8
Open Apr-Oct Ist Apr-Whit & mid Sep-Oct shop closed Booking advisable Jul Aug A rather open site in a rural settng near the North coast. Off B3Z76 Padstow-Newquay road 2m SW of village. A 8 acre site with 195 touring pitches and 74 statics.
A workinq farm site with better than average facilities. The very well converted farm buildings look purpose built. Situated .5 mile offA389 on unclass rd to church. A 3-acre site with 40 touring pitches.

Price Guide For caravans, motor vans and tents. Not every park accepts all three.

Facilities Symbols show amenities on site or (following the arrow) within 3 miles of the site. See the inside back cover for an explanation of symbols.

Credit/Charge Cards See page 6 for the Credit/Charge Card symbols.

Important note. Telephone the park before you travel. In the caravan and camping world there are many restrictions and some categories of visitor are banned altogether. On most sites unaccompanied young people, single-sex groups, single adults, and motorcycle groups will not be accepted. Most parks accept dogs, but some have no suitable areas for exercise, and some will refuse to accept certain large breeds, so you should always check with the park before you set out. On the other hand, some parks cater well for teenagers with magnificent sporting and leisure facilities as well as discos; others have only very simple amenities.

Special Offers In the front of this book you will find a reply-paid card and details of how to enter our prize draw for a relaxing weekend. Please don't forget to fill it in, with your name and address, and return it to us so that we can enter it in one of the draws.

Booking It is advisable to book in advance during peak holiday seasons and at school or public holidays. Where an individual park requires advance booking, 'advance bookings accepted' or 'booking advisable' (followed by dates) appears in the entry. It is also wise to check whether a reservation entitles you to a particular pitch. It does not necessarily follow that an early booking will get you the best pitch; you may just have the choice of what is available at the time you check in.

The words 'Advance bookings not accepted' indicate that a park does not accept reservations. Some parks may require a deposit on booking which may well be non-returnable if you have to cancel your holiday. If you have to cancel, notify the proprietor at once because you may be held legally responsible for partial or full payment unless the pitch can be re-let. Do consider taking out insurance such as AA Travel Insurance to cover lost deposit or compensation. Some parks will not accept overnight bookings unless payment for a full minimum period (e.g. two or three days) is made. If you are not sure whether your camping or caravanning equipment can be used at a park, check beforehand.

Please note: *The AA does not undertake to find accommodation or to make reservations.*

Chemical Closet Disposal Point (CDP) You will usually find one on every park, except those catering only for tents. It must be a specially constructed unit, or a WC permanently set aside for the purpose with adjacent rinsing and soak-away facilities. However, some local authorities are concerned about the effect of chemicals on bacteria in cesspools etc, and may prohibit or restrict provision of cdps in their areas.

Cold Storage A fridge and/or freezer or icepacks for the use of holidaymakers.

Complaints Speak to the park proprietor or supervisor immediately if you have any complaints, so that the matter can be sorted out on the spot. If this personal approach fails, you may decide, if the matter is serious, to approach the local authority or tourist board. AA members may write to:

The Editor,
The AA Camping and Caravanning Guide,
AA Publishing,
Norfolk House,
Priestley Road,
Basingstoke,
Hants RG24 9NY.

The AA will look into any reasonable complaints from members but will not in any circumstances act as negotiator or enter into further correspondence. The AA will not guarantee to take any specific action.

Credit/Charge Cards Most of the larger parks now accept payment by credit or charge card. We use the following symbols at the end of the entry to show which cards are accepted

Access/Mastercharge
Barclaycard/Visa American Express
Switch Connect Delta

Directory if the name of a park is printed in italics this indicates that we have not been able to get details or prices confirmed by the owners.

Electrical Hook-up This is becoming more generally available at parks with three or more pennants, but if it is important to you, you must check before booking. The voltage is generally 240v AC, 50 cycles, although variations between 200v and 250v may still be found. All parks in the AA scheme which provide electrical hook-ups do so in accordance with International Electrotechnical Commission regulations. Outlets are coloured blue and take the form of a lidded plug with recessed contacts, making it impossible to touch a live point by accident. They are also waterproof. A

Appliance			Appliance			Appliance		
Portable black & white TV	50 watts approx.	0.2 amp	**One-bar electric fire**	NB each extra bar rates	1000 watts	**Battery charger**	100 watts approx.	0.4 amp
Small colour TV	90 watts approx.	0.4 amp	**60 watt table lamp**	approx.	0.25 amp	**Small refrigerator**	125 watts approx.	0.4 amp
Small fan heater	1000 (kW) approx.	4.2 amp	**100 watt light bulb**	approx.	0.4 amp	**Domestic microwave**	600 watts approx.	2.5 amp

similar plug, but with protruding contacts which hook into the recessed plug, is on the end of the cable which connects the caravan to the source of supply, and is dead.

These cables can usually be hired on site, or a plug supplied to fit your own cable. You should ask for the male plug; the female plug is the one already fixed to the power supply.

This supply is rated for either 5, 10 or 16 amps and this is usually displayed on a triangular yellow plate attached to source of supply. If it is not, be sure to ask at Reception. This is important because if you overload the circuit, the trip switch will operate to cut off the power supply. The trip switch can only be reset by a park official, who will first have to go round all the hook-ups on park to find the cause of the trip. This can take a long time and will make the culprit distinctly unpopular with all the other caravanners deprived of power, to say nothing of the park official.

It is a relatively simple matter to calculate whether your appliances will overload the circuit. The amperage used by an appliance depends on its wattage and the total amperage used is the total of all the appliances in use at any one time. See the table above.

Last Arrival Unless otherwise stated, parks will usually accept arrivals at any time of the day or night but some have a special 'late arrivals' enclosure where you have to make temporary camp so as not to disturb other people on park. Please note that on some parks access to the toilet block is by key or pass card only, so if you know you will be late, do check what arrangements can be made.

Last Departure As with hotel rooms and self-catering accommodation, most parks will specify their overnight period - e.g. noon to noon. If you overstay the departure time you can be charged for an extra day. Do make sure you know what the regulations are.

Maps A map of each county, highlighting the locations, usually appears as near as possible to the county heading, or if one or more county maps have been grouped together, there will be a cross-reference under the county heading to the appropriate page. These maps will make a good first reference point to show you everything the AA lists in that county. If you have a specific destination in mind you can quickly see if we list any parks there, and if not, what alternatives there may be.

Please note that these are not road maps and have been designed to show you a quick overall picture of the county. When you are driving to a park, you must use a good road atlas - the AA publishes several - or the appropriate Ordnance Survey 1: 50 000 sheet map if the location is really remote. We give you the National Grid map reference (see 'Explanation of a directory entry', page 4) and outline route directions but space in the directory is limited and we cannot go into exhaustive detail.

Motor Caravans At some parks motor caravans are only accepted if they remain static throughout the stay. Also check that there are suitable level pitches at the parks where you plan to stay.

Parking Some park operators insist that cars be put in a parking area separate from the pitches; others will not allow more than one car for each caravan or tent.

Park Rules Most parks display a set of rules which you should read on your arrival. Dogs may or may not be accepted on parks, and this is entirely at the owners' or wardens' discretion. Even when parks say that they accept dogs, it is still discretionary and we most strongly advise that you check when you book. Dogs should always be kept on a lead and under control. Sleeping in cars is not encouraged by most proprietors.

Most parks will not accept the following categories of people: single-sex groups, unsupervised youngsters and motorcyclists whether singly or in groups; even adults travelling on their own are sometimes barred. If you are not a family group or a conventional couple, you would be well advised to make sure what rules apply before you try to book.

Pitches and Charges The number of touring pitches is included in the description. Charges given immediately after the appropriate symbol (caravan, tent, motorvan) are the overnight cost for one tent or caravan, one car and two adults, or one motor caravan and two adults. The price may vary according to the number of people in your party, but some parks have a fixed fee per pitch regardless of the number of people.

Please note that some parks may charge separately for some of the park's facilities, including the showers.

Please note that prices have been supplied to us in good faith by the park operators and are as accurate as possible. They are, however, only a guide and are subject to change at any time during the currency of this book.

When parks have been unable to forecast their 1998 prices, those for 1997 may be quoted, prefixed by an asterisk. See also **Directory** p.6.

Campsites are legally entitled to use an overflow field which is not a normal part of their camping area for up to 28 days in any one year as an emergency method of coping with additional numbers at busy periods.

When this 28 day rule is being invoked site owners should increase the numbers of sanitary facilities accordingly when the permanent facilities become insufficient to cope with extra numbers. In these circumstances the extra facilities are sometimes no more than temporary portacabins.

Rabies Rabies warning: because of quarantine requirements (for instance, six months isolation for dogs and cats) it is not a practical proposition to bring an animal with you from your own or a foreign country on holiday to Britain. Penalties for trying to avoid this regulation are severe, and if you do have to bring an animal into Britain, you must have an import licence, obtainable from Ministry of Agriculture, Fisheries and Food, Hook Rise South, Tolworth, Surbiton, Surrey KT6 7NF.
Tel: 0181-330 4411.

Restricted Service Restricted service means that full amenities and services are not available during the period stated - for example a swimming pool or bar/restaurant may open only in the summer. Restrictions vary greatly from park to park, so you must check before setting off.

Shop The range of food and equipment in shops is usually in proportion to the size of the park. A mobile shop calling several times a week, or a general store within easy distance of the park entrance is acceptable except for 5 Pennant Premier parks and Holiday Centres which must have a well equipped shop.

Signposted This does not refer to AA signs but indicates that there is an International Direction Sign on the nearest main road, showing whether the park accepts caravans, tents or both. These signs have not yet been erected for all parks.

Static Van Pitches We give the number of static van pitches available in the entries in our guide in order to give a picture of the nature and size of the park. The AA pennant rating system is based on an inspection of the touring pitches and facilities only. AA inspectors do not visit or report on the fixed types of accommodation. The AA takes no responsibility for the condition of rented caravans or chalets and can take no action whatsoever about complaints relating to them.

Supervised If this word appears in a directory entry it means that the park has someone in attendance 24 hours a day. Other parks may have less comprehensive cover.

Telephone The telephone authorities are liable to change some telephone numbers during the currency of this guide. If you have difficulty in contacting a park, please check with directory enquiries.

THE NEW AA PENNANT RATING SCHEME

Users of previous editions of our guide who have been familiar with the pennant rating scheme should read the new explanations because we have revised the scheme to incorporate more quality requirements within the pennant rating, especially at the four and five pennant level. We no longer, therefore, use a separate set of symbols to denote quality awards for environment, sanitation and leisure. These are now built in to the requirements for pennant rating at each level.

There is also a new category of Pennanted Holiday Centres - these were previously five pennant parks which were also designated as 'Holiday Centres' - to represent those places with a very high level of leisure and recreation facilities, and able therefore to provide a complete holiday on site. The Pennanted Holiday Centres must achieve a hight level of quality before they are considered for this category. Please see the quick reference list on page 56.

HOW AA PENNANT RATING WORKS

The AA pennant-rating scheme is based on annual inspection by a trained team of experts, and subsequent classification of facilities. The system emphasises quality as much as quantity, and the higher-rated sites are of a very high all-round standard indeed.

The pennant scheme is designed for touring holiday makers who travel with their own caravans, motor caravans, or tents. Our Officers visit camping and caravanning parks to assess their touring facilities, but do not inspect any static caravans, chalets, or ready-erected tents available for hire. All such accommodation is outside the scope of the pennant rating scheme, and outside the scope of this guide.

AA parks are classified on a 4-point scale according to their style and the range of facilities they offer, with a separate category for holiday centres which offer a complete on-site holiday.

As the pennant rating increases, so the quality and variety of facilities and amenities will be greater. The basic requirement for all camping and caravanning parks in the pennant-rating scheme is that they reserve an acceptable number of pitches for the use of touring caravanners and campers, and that the facilities provided for tourers are well maintained and clean, and comply with our standards of classification. All parks receive an annual visit and report, and the pennant rating is based on this report. Many parks in the AA scheme display a yellow and black sign showing their pennant rating, but not all parks choose to have one, and in some areas local authority regulations prohibit the display of signs.

Basic requirements for AA Pennant Rating

All parks must have a local authority site licence (unless specially exempted) and must have satisfied local authority fire regulations. Parks at the higher pennant ratings must also comply with the basic requirements, and offer additional facilities according to their classification.
Please note that campsites are legally entitled to use an overflow field - which is not a normal part of their camping area - for up to 28 days in any one year as an emergency method of coping with additional numbers at busy periods. When this 28-day rule is being invoked, site owners must increase the numbers of sanitary facilities accordingly when these become insufficient to cope with the extra numbers.

Town and Country Pennant Parks

►►

These may offer a simple standard of facilities, and sometimes only drinking water and chemical waste disposal for the really self-contained caravanner. Other parks in this category are well-equipped with toilets, washbasins and showers, and might also have a reception area and dish-washing facilities.

You are advised to check with individual sites at the time of booking to make sure they satisfy your own personal requirements. All Town and Country Pennant Parks should offer the following:

- Maximum 30 pitches per campable acre
- At least 10 feet between units
- Urgent telephone numbers signed
- Whereabouts of an emergency telephone shown
- First aid box

3-Pennant Family Parks

►►►

In addition to the above, 3-Pennant Family Parks guarantee a greater degree of comfort, with modern or modernised toilet blocks offering an ideal minimum of two washbasins and two toilets per 30 pitches per sex. Toilet facilities should include:

- Hot water to washbasins and showers
- Mirrors, shelves and hooks
- Shaver/hairdryer points
- Lidded waste bins in ladies toilets
- Uncracked toilet seats with lids
- Soap and hand dryer/towels
- A reasonable number of modern cubicled showers
- All-night internal lighting.

Family Parks must have evenly surfaced roads and paths, some electric hook-ups, and some level ground suitable for motor caravans. Buildings, facilities, services and park grounds should be cleaned and maintained to a high standard.

In addition to the above, these parks will ideally offer a laundry with drying facilities, separate from the toilets, and a children's playground with some equipment, fenced and away from danger. Details of nearest shops/chemist should be posted.

4-Pennant De-Luxe Parks

►►►►

As well as all of the above, 4-Pennant De-Luxe Parks are of a very high standard, with good landscaping, natural screening and attractive park buildings. Toilets are smartly modern and immaculately maintained, and offer the following:

- Spacious vanitory-style washbasins
- Fully-tiled shower cubicles with dry areas, shelves and hooks, at least one per 30 pitches per sex

Other requirements are:

- Shop on site, or within a reasonable distance
- Warden available 24-hours
- Reception area open during the day
- Internal roads, paths and toilet blocks lit at night
- 25 pitches per campable acre
- Toilet blocks heated October-Easter
- 50% electric hook-ups
- 10% hardstandings where necessary

4-Pennant De-Luxe Parks should also ideally offer a late arrivals enclosure, and some fully-serviced toilet cubicles.

5-Pennant Premier Parks

►►►►►

All parks in this category are of an award-winning standard, and are set in attractive surroundings with superb landscaping. They must offer some fully-serviced pitches or first-class cubicled washing facilities to the ratio of one per 20 pitches per sex; most pitches should also offer electric hook-ups. These top-quality parks will ideally but not necessarily offer, in addition to the above:

- a heated swimming pool (outdoor, indoor or both)
- a clubhouse with some entertainment
- a well-equipped shop
- a cafe or restaurant and a bar
- decent indoor and outdoor leisure facilities for young people
- a designated dog-walking area if dogs accepted.

Pennanted Holiday Centres

In this separate category we distinguish parks which offer a wide range of on-site sports, leisure, entertainment and recreational facilities. Supervision and security are of a very high level, and there is a choice of eating outlets. Any touring facilities must be of equal importance to statics, with a maximum density of 25 pitches per acre; toilets should be of a very good quality. Holiday-makers staying on these parks have no need to look elsewhere for their amusements.

ISLAND CAMPING

SCOTLAND

The Shetland Islands

These are the farthest-flung outpost of the British Isles, taking 14 hours to reach by boat from Aberdeen. The archipelago of Shetland consists of over 100 islands and skerries (reefs of rock), though only 15 are permanently inhabited. At no point on the mainland are you more than three miles from the sea, and the impressively rugged coastline is stunning.

Campers and caravanners are welcome, the only restrictions being on Noss and Fair Isle, and the Tresta Links in Fetlar, where camping is not allowed at all. Elsewhere there are four official campsites, but visitors can stray into the wilds, provided that they seek permission to stay from the owner of the land. Caravans and motor caravans must stick to the public roads. Drivers are strongly advised to check maps and routes carefully so that they don't find themselves in a difficult or dangerous situation.

Camping 'Böds' are a good way of seeing Shetland on a budget as long as you don't mind a unisex dormitory as sleeping accommodation. The böd was traditionally a building for fishermen and their gear during the fishing season, and the idea has been adopted to provide low-cost, basic accommodation, with the emphasis on 'basic'. Some have no electricity, and none has hot water. You need your own sleeping bag and bed roll, camping stove and cooking utensils. What you get is a toilet, table and benches, and a roof over your head.

The Orkney Islands

Closer to the mainland of Scotland, the Orkneys are far less rugged and wild than the Shetlands. There are no restrictions on access for camping and caravanning, and plenty of beautiful spots to pitch camp. Here it is an easy matter to avoid the crowds, although the Orkneys' incredible bird population is never very far away. Only on the tiny island of Fair Isle between Shetland and Orkney is camping not allowed, and there is no car ferry.

The Western Isles (Outer Hebrides)

These are a group of over 200 islands - only 13 of them inhabited - linked by a network of ferries and causeways. Most of the population live on Lewis, with Harris, home of the famous tweed, being another major centre. That leaves miles and miles of spectacular mountains, golden beaches and rolling hills to explore. There are official campsites, but 'wild' camping is allowed within reason, and with the landowner's prior permission.

The Inner Hebrides and Other Scottish Islands

Tucked in against the mainland behind North and South Uist is that most nostalgic of islands, Skye. With its sister isles of Rhum and Eigg, it remains as atmospheric as when Bonnie Prince Charlie fled over the sea. These days he could also take the road bridge from Kyle of Lochalsh, which is less romantic, but there is still a car ferry from Mallaig for those who prefer to make a more traditional crossing. No such ferry goes to Rhum and Eigg, so the only camping possible on these islands is for the backpacker.

The Isle of Bute is tucked into the west coast of Scotland only 30 miles from Glasgow. Official camping is permitted at Rothesay, and wild camping is discouraged.

The islands of Mull, Islay, Coll and Arran have official campsites, and caravan and motor caravans are welcome as are tenters. Offsite camping is also allowed , provided the usual permission is sought. Iona is car-free, and a backpackers' paradise, while Tiree does not accept either caravans or motor caravans, and has no official sites.

Colonsay and Cumbrae allow no camping or caravanning, though organised groups such as the Scouts and Guides may stay with official permission; Jura and Gigha allow no camping or caravanning; Lismore bans caravans but permits camping, although there are no official sites and few suitable places anyway.

THE CHANNEL ISLANDS

The tightest controls are on the Channel Islands, because of the narrowness of the mainly rural roads. On all the Channel Islands you can hire tents on recognised campsites.

Jersey

On this, the largest of the islands, only islanders may own and use towed caravans; visitors are not allowed to bring either caravans or motor caravans, but tents and trailer tents are allowed, as long as you stay on a recognised campsite, and booking is strongly advised during July and August. The AA-approved sites which appear in this guide are attractively located and maintained to a very high standard

Guernsey

The same rules apply as on Jersey, except that motor caravans are allowed under certain strict conditions.

1. You must apply for and receive a permit in advance.
2. You may not use your motor caravan for sleeping but merely as a means of transport.
3. When not being used for transport, the motor caravan must be left under cover on a camping park with prior permission from the owner.

Herm and Sark

These two small islands are traffic-free. Sark is not part of the UK but the smallest independent and feudal state in the commonwealth. Both islands are surrounded by breathtaking stretches of golden sand. Herm is privately owned, with one hotel, a few shops and pubs, a handful of self-catering cottages and a small campsite. You can either hire a tent or pitch your own on a terrace overlooking the sea.

Sark has three campsites and offers a more dramatic landscape. New arrivals are met off the boat by a tractor to carry both themselves and their luggage up the steep hill from the harbour. After that all travel is by foot, on bicycle, or by horse and cart. The island is a natural fortress, being surrounded by cliffs and set high above sea level. There are some excellent beaches, but many of them are a long way down, and a long climb back up again.

Alderney

The third largest Channel Island is the closest to France and small enough to get around on foot for those who relish a slow pace of life. The island is a haven for flora and fauna. The clear seas are ideal for snorkelling, and sailboarding and surfing are popular in the sandy bays. As on Jersey, neither caravans nor motor caravans are allowed and campers must have a confirmed booking on the one official camp site before they arrive.

ISLE OF MAN

Trailer caravans are only allowed on the Isle of Man if they are to be used in connection with trade shows and exhibitions, or for demonstration purposes. They must not be used for living accommodation. Written application for permission should be made to the Secretary, Planning Committee, Isle of Man Local Government Board, The Government Offices, Murray House, Mount Havelock. The shipping line cannot accept a caravan without this written permission. Motor caravans may enter without prior permission.

ISLES OF SCILLY

Caravans and motor caravans are not allowed, and campers must stay at officially licensed sites. Booking is advisable on all sites, especially during school holidays.

For details about licensed sites on St Mary's write to: Mr and Mrs Ted Moulson, Garrison Farm, St Mary's.

For Bryher write to: Mrs J Stedeford, Jenford Bryer.

For St Agnes write to: Mrs S J Hicks, Troy Town, St Agnes.

For St Martin's write to: Mr C A Savill, Middletown, St Martin's.

Please note that strict control is kept on the landing of animals on these islands.

THE DAVID BELLAMY CONSERVATION AWARDS

This innovative new nature conservation scheme, jointly organised by David Bellamy and the British Holiday & Home Parks Association, has made awards to over 60 AA-Pennant Parks out of its 100 or so prize-winning parks. Any small or large project which encourages wildlife to flourish makes parks eligible for an award, and we thought our readers would like to know which AA-recognised parks have been praised for their outstanding contribution to the environment. We list them here, alphabetically by location within county. For full details of the entry, please consult the directory which is organised under country in county (in region in Wales and Scotland) order.

Cornwall
Carbeil Holiday Park, **Downderry**
Maen Valley Holiday Park, **Falmouth**
Silverbow Park, **Goonhavern**
Croft Farm, Luxulyan Hendra Holiday Park, **Newquay**
St Tinney Farm Holidays, **Otterham**
Polruan Holiday Centre, **Polruan**
Trevalgan Family Camping Park, **St Ives**
Kelynack Caravan & Camping Park, **St Just** (near Land's End)

Cumbria
Wild Rose Park, **Appleby-in-Westmorland**
Oakbank Lakes Country Park, **Longtown**
Hillcroft Park, **Pooley Bridge**
Cove Caravan & Camping Park, **Watermillock**

Derbyshire
Darwin Forest Country Park, **Matlock**

Devon
Kennford International Caravan Park, **Kennford**
Channel View Caravan & Camping Park, **Lynton**
Beverley Park, **Paignton**
Widend Touring Park, **Paignton**
Oakdown Touring & Holiday Home Park, **Sidmouth**
Salcombe Regis Camping & Caravan Park, **Sidmouth**
Ramslade Touring Park, **Stoke Gabriel**
Webbers Farm Caravan Park, **Woodbury**

Dorset
Binghams Farm Touring Caravan Park, **Bridport**
Freshwater Beach Holiday Park, **Bridport**
Highlands End Holiday Park, **Bridport**
Bagwell Farm Touring Park, **Chickerell**
Golden Cap Holiday Park, **Chideock**
Beacon Hill Touring Park, **Poole**

Hampshire	Sandy Balls Holiday Centre, **Fordingbridge**
	The Orchards Holiday Caravan & Camping Park, Newbridge, **Isle of Wight**
	Cheverton Farm Camping Park, **Sandown**
Lancashire	Claylands Caravan Park, **Garstang**
	Abbey Farm Caravan Park, **Ormskirk**
	Knepps Farm Holiday Park, **Thornton Cleveleys**
Norfolk	The Old Brick Kilns, **Barney**
	Clippesby Holidays, **Clippesby**
	Searles of Hunstanton
Northumberland	Ord House Caravan Park, **Berwick-on-Tweed**
Somerset	Westermill Farm, **Exford**
	Mendip Heights Caravan & Camping Park, **Priddy**
Shropshire	Stanmore Hall Touring Park, **Bridgnorth**
	Mill Farm Holiday Park, **Hughley**
	Suffolk Cliff House, **Dunwich**
	Peewit Caravans, **Felixstowe**
North Yorkshire	Hawkswick Cote Caravan Park, **Arncliffe**
	High Moor Farm Park, **Harrogate**
	Rudding Holiday Park, **Harrogate**
	Woodhouse Farm Caravan & Camping Park, **Winksley**
	East Yorkshire Far Grange Park, **Skipsea**
Central Scotland	Trossachs Caravan Park, **Aberfoyle**
	The River Tilt Caravan Park, **Blair Atholl**
	Argyll Caravan Park, **Inveraray**
	Craigtoun Meadows Holiday Park, **St Andrews**
Southern Lowlands & Borders	Brighouse Bay Holiday Park, **Brighouse Bay**
	Kippford Caravan Park, **Kippford**

WALES

North Wales	Bryn Cethin Bach Caravan Park, **Abersoch**
	Ty Mawr Holiday Park, **Towyn**
Mid Wales	Pilbach Caravan Park, **Bettws Evan**
	Disserth Caravan & Camping Park, **Llandrindod Wells**
	Cenarth Falls Holiday Park, **Newcastle Emlyn**

AA CAMPSITE OF THE YEAR AWARD 1997-8

Following our annual trawl through a list of sites so impressive that the words 'Award Standard' are permanently stamped all over them, we have narrowed the nominations down to six of the best which we think will take some beating. Three of the parks we recognise as this year's most outstanding best are also winners of the prestigious David Bellamy Conservation Award, (see page 15 for full list of all our winning parks), another two are perfectly placed in the most idyllic countryside where peace and seclusion are part of the package, and our Northern winner, whilst offering a plethora of exciting activities, is also close to the beautiful Solway Firth and Lake District. All six provide modern and luxurious toilet facilities, and all are run by welcoming, friendly and well-organised owners who maintain the highest standards in every department. What more could any camping or caravanning enthusiast ask for?

Campsite of The Year

and Best Campsite for Scotland

Brighouse Bay Holiday Park

Brighouse Bay, Dumfries and Galloway

Given one of the finest natural locations imaginable for a holiday setting, the owners of Brighouse Bay have nevertheless succeeded in improving on even nature's best in creating this leisure activity park. Tucked away within 700 acres on a peaceful, unspoilt peninsula on the Solway Firth, Brighouse Bay Holiday Park enjoys a magnificent coastal setting with its own sandy beach and glorious views over the Irish Sea. Touring pitches have been imaginatively blended into the countryside, and a series of lakes has been recently created for visitors to camp beside. As well as offering a wide range of outdoor activities, including pony trekking, mountain bikes and a farm tour by tractor and trailer, visitors can enjoy the extensive walks, take advantage of the all-tide slipway for launching sailing boats, windsurfers and canoes, and play mini-golf. Indoors there is a superb new leisure centre, with a luxury swimming pool, fitness room, games room, an all-day bistro, and a licensed lounge bar open from midday until late. The warm and welcoming Gillespie Family and their staff are experts at ensuring that their visitors get the best out of their holiday, and their exacting standards guarantee that everywhere is sparkling and manicured even at the most busy times. We unreservedly recommend Brighouse Bay as a shining example of a top quality site, and know that, whatever the weather, a holiday here is always a most enjoyable experience.

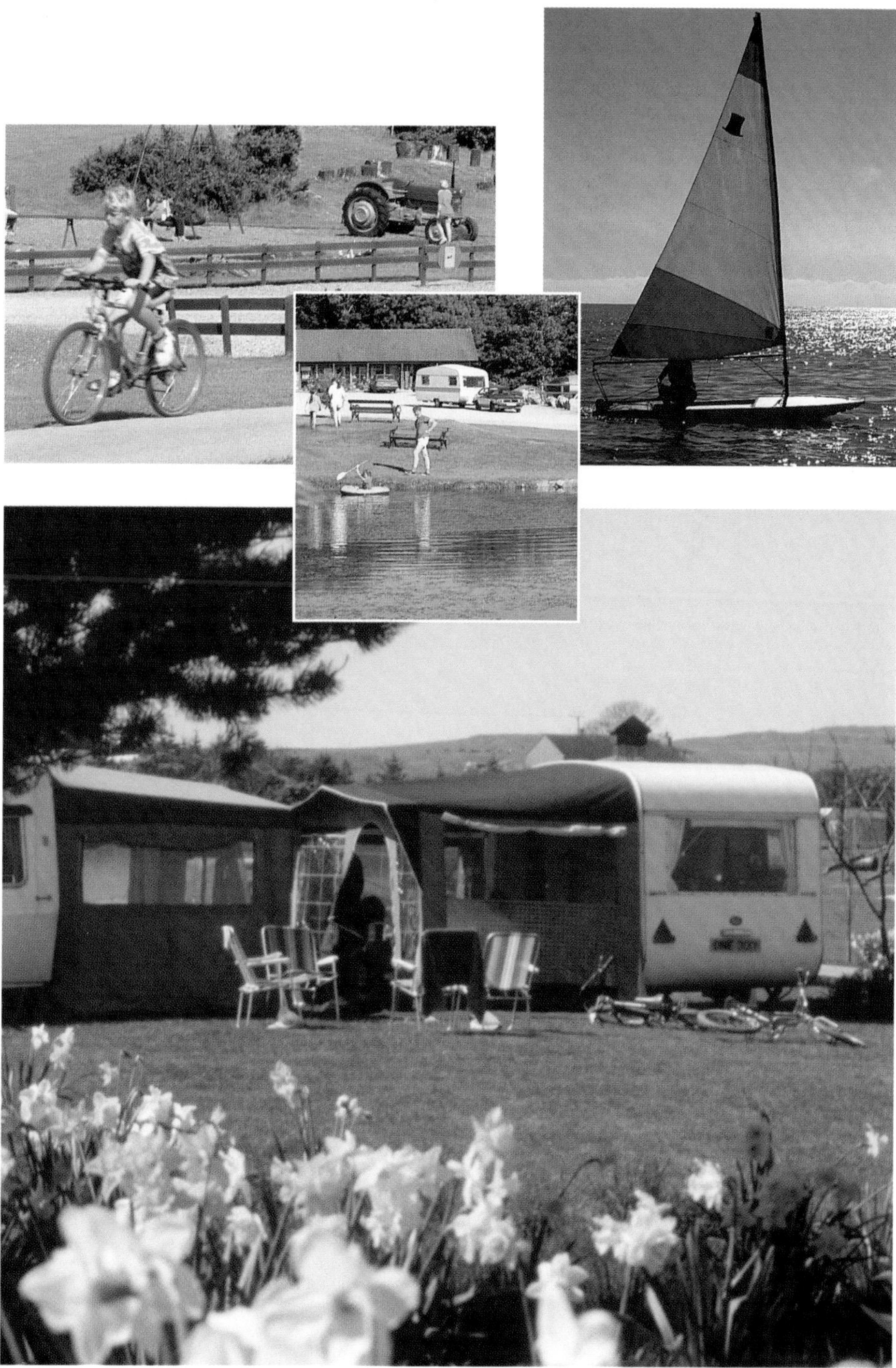

Best Campsite for Wales

Cenarth Falls Holiday Park

Newcastle Emlyn, Mid-Wales

In a spectacular setting overlooking the River Teifi as it cascades through the Cenarth Falls gorge, this beautifully landscaped little park offers the perfect peaceful hideaway amidst verdant hilly countryside. It has been lovingly created on a small plateau high above the village of Cenarth, the work of Yvonne and Howell Davies and their son Darren who are all dedicated to the care and well-being of their visitors. Tucked away between trees and carefully maintained flower beds can be found the park's excellent facilities, which include a heated outdoor swimming pool, and the small Fisherman's Cove country club, which serves meals and provides evening entertainment during the high season. The sanitary facilities have repeatedly brought award status to the park, and the disabled are carefully catered for here. Salmon and trout fishing are available in the nearby river, which tumbles attractively under the 18th-century arched bridge and provides a challenge for even the most experienced fishing fanatic. With plenty to do nearby in an area noted for its scenic coastline and inland beauty, this is the ideal family retreat in a really tranquil setting.

Best Campsite for the North of England

Stanwix Park Holiday Centre

Silloth, Cumbria

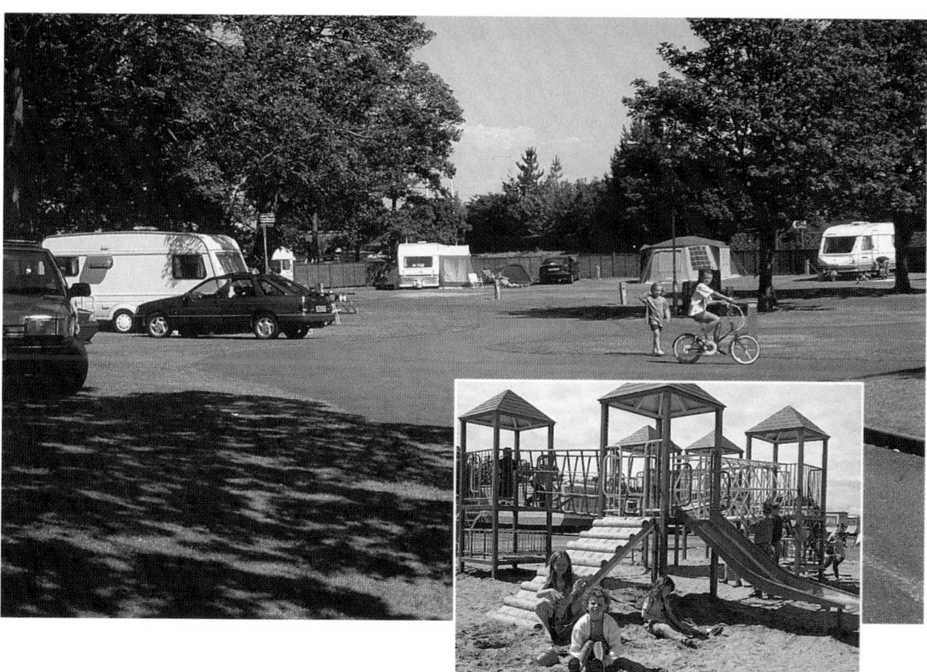

The Stanwix family have been providing camping holidays here since the late 1940s, but what they offer nowadays cannot compare with those early days. This huge holiday centre spread over four acres is packed with enough attractions and leisure activities to keep even the most demanding family happy. Stanwix Park is totally self-contained with every service and amenity within easy reach, and although it is set in the most delightful countryside, visitors need never set foot outside the complex. A major attraction is the huge indoor swimming pool, part of a new leisure centre which contains a restaurant, shop and fitness centre; the pool comes complete with water slide, water cannon, water mushroom, waterfall and air pads - a must for parents and children alike. A children's entertainer organises fun and games for the young ones during the day, whilst in the evening there are talent contests, bingo, discos and professional entertainers. Added to all of this are sanitary facilies of immaculate quality, and touring pitches which are discreetly tucked away in hedged bays. For an action-packed holiday par excellence, take a trip to Stanwix Park without delay.

Best Campsite for Central England

Cliff House

Dunwich, Suffolk

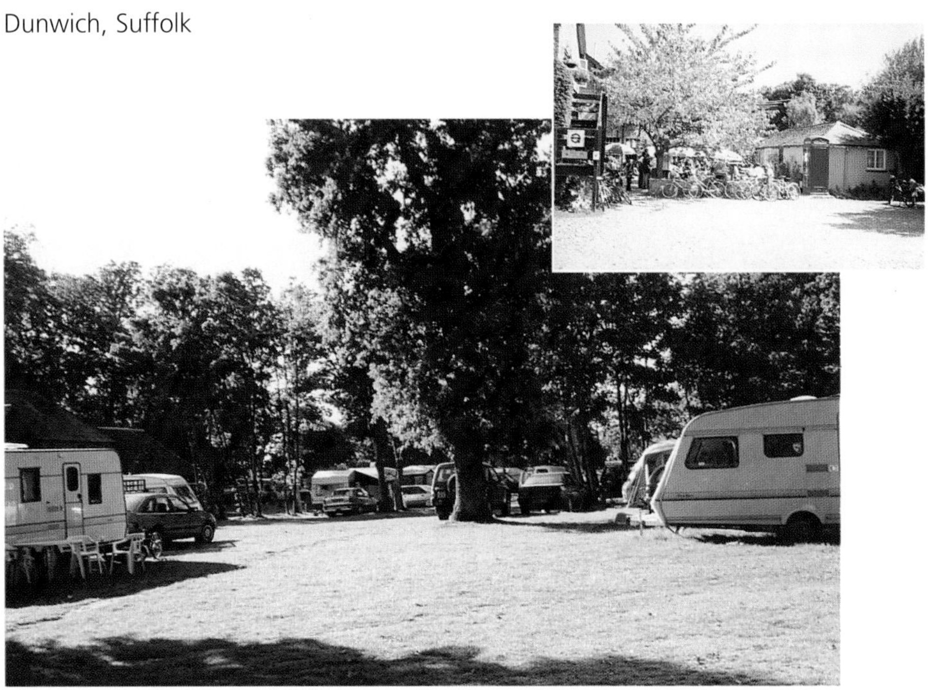

Thirty acres of woodland beside the remote Minsmere Bird Reserve and a great expanse of National Trust land is the enviable setting for this sprawling camping idyll hidden away amongst the trees. The park itself fringes the low cliffs which front the sea between Aldburgh and Southwold, two famous Suffolk towns which attract painters, writers and musicians to their light and spacious coastal surrounds. It was a love of the outdoors that caused Penny and Alan Harris to buy the run down Georgian house and grounds five years ago, and they have succeeded in transforming their purchase into both a delightful holiday centre and a haven for wildlife; their contribution to environmental protection is so impressive that they have won a David Bellamy Conservation Award. The pretty reception area is the centre of the park, where holidaymakers can eat and drink in the sun or inside the bar restaurant, and shop in the self-service store. Two toilet blocks offering facilities of a high standard are well-placed to serve every camping area, and the whole park is criss-crossed with hidden paths leading to the sand and shingle beach, the old sunken garden, and the well-equipped children's play area. A must for country lovers.

Best Campsite for South-East England

Adgestone Camping and Caravan Park

Sandown, Isle of Wight

Gloriously festooned hanging baskets, flower beds and tubs make a delightful first impression on visitors to this beautifully maintained campsite close to the busy resort of Sandown. The contrast between the holiday attractions of the seaside town and this peaceful park could not be more marked, and pitches are carefully sited beside the river which runs along the edge of the park, or hidden amongst the many trees and shrubs. Privacy is part of the attraction, and the Weir and Glover families who own this site are sensitive to the needs of their guests who come here to escape from noise and bustle. New in 1997 is the small lake which has been stocked with fish for visiting anglers, and there are charming nature trails and walks around this 15-acre landscaped park. Children are catered for with two well-stocked play areas and an outdoor swimming pool, and there are facilities for volleyball, table tennis and a net for tennis. This very impressive park also provides excellent sanitary facilities, with some very popular family rooms including showers, wash basins and toilets.

Best Campsite for South West England

Hidden Valley Touring Park

West Down, Devon

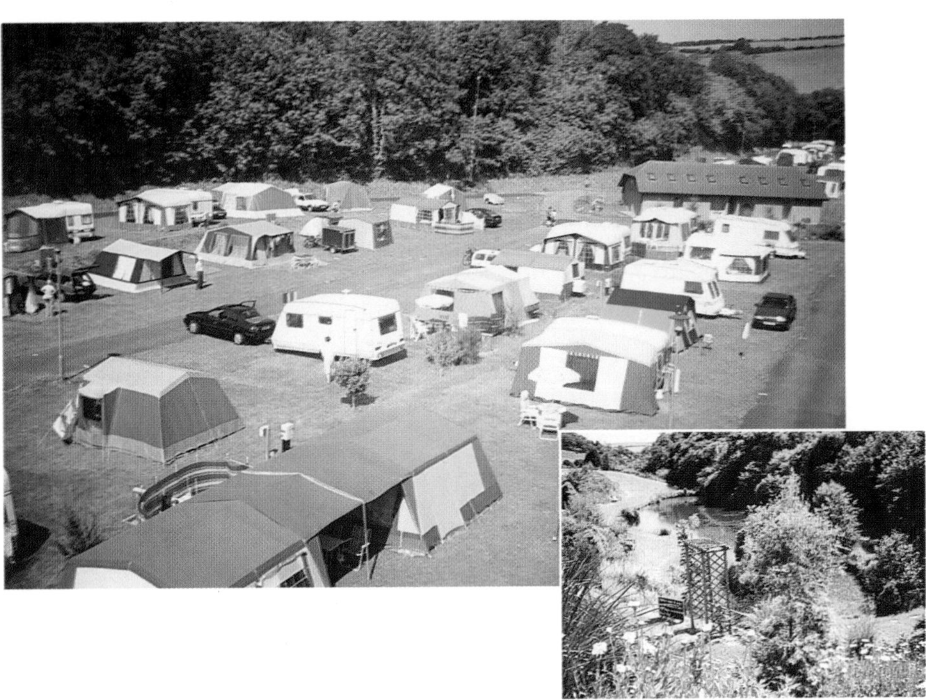

Just how aptly named this delightful touring park is becomes immediately apparent on leaving the road outside and entering its quiet, secluded environs. A haven of tranquility awaits visitors to this - literally - hidden valley where owners Susan and Melvyn Tucker have transformed a disused railway cutting in a steep-sided river valley into an idyllic touring park. The stream which wanders through the park has been dammed to form a lake, bridges have been constructed across the water, and a proliferation of wildlife from buzzards and herons to fat carp and ducks create an endless moving picture which is an entertainment in itself. Two different parks offer contrasting camping experiences, with one set of pitches on hillside terraces in the valley itself, and the other below the lake where the seclusion is deepest. Each park has its own set of superb facilities, and a restaurant/lounge bar makes the best of the views from its position overlooking the lake and the valley below. An adventure playground with aerial glides keeps children happy for hours, and the North Devon countryside is a walker's paradise.

• Ladram Bay • Holiday Centre

OTTERTON • Nr BUDLEIGH SALTERTON EX9 7BX
Tel: Colaton Raleigh (01395) 568398
Fax: (01395) 568338

Ladram Bay lies on the South East Coast of Devon with dramatic red sandstone cliffs and rock stacks it presents a unique setting for a quiet relaxing holiday. Tent and touring sites are on well maintained grass terraces, some with electric hook ups. Showers and hot water are free. On site facilities include private beach, indoor heated pool, pub with free family entertainment, shops, cafe and launderette.

Beautifully situated near Porthmadog towards Black Rock Sands in a soucer shaped valley fully protected by woodland. The site has views across rural countryside and the Moel-y-Gest mountain.

Facilities: Toilets and showers • Children's play area • Games room with TV • Tourist information and shop • Laundry room • Electric hook-ups • Gas and telephone • Touring and camping pitches • Pets welcomed • Dog walking area • Static caravans for sale.

An ideal site from which to tour North Wales and the surrounding area with its many places of interest.

Alun & Lon Roberts, Parc Carafanau, Tyddyn Llwyn, Caravan Park, Marfa Bychan, Porthmadog, Gwynedd LL49 9UR
Tel & Fax: 01766 512205

ADGESTONE

AA

CAMPING PARK
NR. SANDOWN,
ISLE OF WIGHT PO36 0HL

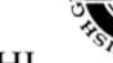

Tel: (01983) 403432/403989

Winners of AA's Best Campsite Award 1997/98 for Southern England.

Superb family run park in beautiful countryside with lovely walks all around, but only 1½ miles to sandy beach. Excellent toilet and disabled facilities include family shower rooms and baby bathing areas. Well stocked shop with off-licence and extensive range of camping/caravan accessories. Pets welcome.

• Heated Swimming Pool • Take-away Food
• Adventure Play Areas • Private River and Pond Fishing
• Package Holidays include Park and Ferry Fees
• Concessions for couples 50 and over •

Rallies are most welcome

Nestling under the beautiful "**Purbeck Hills**", 1 mile from the beach. Ideal for families, walkers, golfers and all watersport enthusiasts.
Open Winter months.

Indoor heated pool • Village Inn & Restaurant • Shop

North West Tourist Board 1996 Award Winner

New toilet & shower block

A secluded, rural, tree lined park, near South East shore of Morecambe Bay, offering easy access to the Fylde Coast, historic Lancaster, Lune Valley and South Lakes.

Crimbles Lane, Cockerham, Lancaster LA2 0ES Telephone: 01524 791041

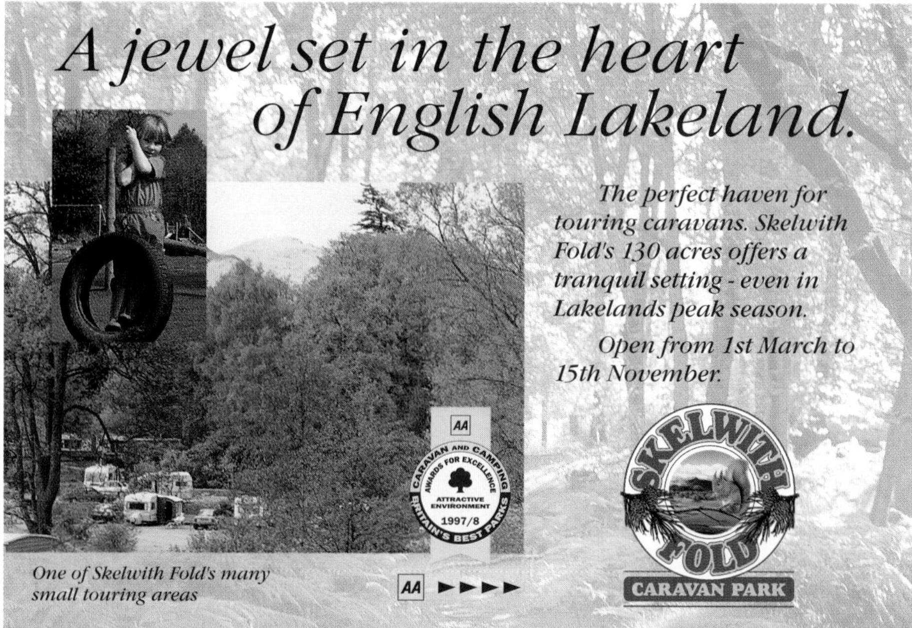

One of Skelwith Fold's many small touring areas

Ambleside, Cumbria LA22 0HX Telephone 015394 32277

2 AWARD WINNING HOLIDAY PARCS IN GLORIOUS DEVON
• Excellent Touring and Pitching Facilities.
• Electrical, Water and Waste Disposal Hook ups.
• Luxury Roman Style Lockable Washing Facilities.
• On Site Shops for all your needs.
• 3 INDOOR AND 2 OUTDOOR HEATED POOLS.
• FLUMES Water Park • Romano Spa Health Club
• Wide Variety of Sporting Facilities.
• FREE Nightly Cabaret and Entertainment.
• FREE Kid's Billy Beachball Club.
• FREE Creche & Qualified Nursery Nurse.
• NEW Luxury Caravans, Villas, Bungalows and Apartments also available. • And Much, Much MORE!
North Devon's only AA 5 Pennant Parc
1996
SILVER
WOOLACOMBE BAY
ROSE AWARD
THE ENGLISH GOLD COAST
GOLDEN COAST & WOOLACOMBE BAY HOLIDAY VILLAGES
WOOLACOMBE • NORTH DEVON • EX34 7HW
BLUE FLAG AWARD
Call now! 01271 870343
AA

See listing under Lincolnshire

See listing under Shropshire

See listing under Central Scotland

PARK OF
BRANDEDLEYS

ADAC 'BEST PARK OF THE YEAR' 1997
CALOR AWARD BEST PARK SCOTLAND 1995

- INDOOR POOL
- OUTDOOR POOL
- GAMES ROOM
- TENNIS COURTS
- BADMINTON
- PLAY AREAS
- PUTTING COURSE
- RESTAURANT/BAR

CROCKETFORD, DUMFRIES DG2 8RG
TELEPHONE 01556 690250

See listing under Southern Lowlands and Borders

Brynich Caravan Park
Brecon, Powys LD3 7SH
Tel/Fax: 01874 623325
BRITISH GRADED HOLIDAY PARKS
THE Best of British CARAVAN & CAMPING PARKS

Situated at the foothills of the Brecon Beacons with panoramic views. Flat site with closely-mown grass. Modern shower facilities, with free hot water including disabled and baby rooms, cleanliness a priority. Shop, telephone, adventure playground and dog exercise field.

See listing under Mid Wales

Winner ~ AA Best holiday park 1997
First for families!
• Indoor Pool
• Toddlers Pool
• Jacuzzi
• Turkish Room
• Sunbed
• Bistro
• Lounge Bar
• Games/TV Room
• Fitness Room
• Golf Course
• Sea Angling
• Sandy Beach
• Licensed Shop
• Launderette
'Brighouse Bay is undoubtedly one of Scotland's finest family parks. Hidden away within 700 acres on a quiet unspoilt peninsula, this wildlife haven has 30 acres of mature woodland adjacent, extensive walks with glorious views over the Irish sea, its own sandy beach, rockpools, all-tide slipway and many aspects of a working farm - yes Brighouse Bay is unique.'
BRITISH GRADED HOLIDAY PARKS
BRIGHOUSE BAY
HOLIDAY PARK
Phone: 01557 870 267 for details.
Thistle
Winner ~ David Bellamy Gold Award for conservation

See listing under Southern Lowlands and Borders

See listing under Devon

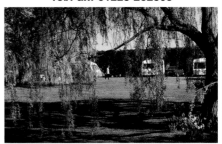

See listing under Dorset

See listing under Oxfordshire

See listing under North Wales

See listing under Dorset

See listing under Cornwall and Isles of Scilly

- Special ferry inclusive package holidays for caravanners and campers
- Holiday caravans to let and for sale
- **Indoor & outdoor swimming pool complex with licensed cafe bar**
- Superb self service shop / takeaway food bar
- Coarse fishing
- Small rallies welcome

or write to the Proprietor
Malcolm A. Peplow
The Orchards, Newbridge,
Yarmouth, Isle of Wight, PO41 0TS

See listing under Wight, Isle of

3 TIMES AA BEST CAMPSITE OF THE YEAR

Seaview International is set in peaceful, beautiful landscaped surroundings renowned for the countless flowering shrubs and close to award winning sandy beaches. All our pitches are large and most are provided with electric hook-ups.

• Fantastic Sea Views • Superb Pool & Large Patio Area • Tennis & Badminton Courts • Putting Green • Crazy Golf • Childrens Play Area • Plenty of FREE Hot Water to the Basins and Dishwashing Areas • FREE Modern Push Button Showers & Hairdryers • Disabled Showers • Large Bathrooms • Shop with Off-licence •

Seaview International, Boswinger, Gorran, St. Austell, Cornwall PL26 6LL Tel: 01726 843425 Fax: 01726 843358

British Graded Holiday Parks

Rose Award Caravan Holiday Park

SEAVIEW INTERNATIONAL

The Best of British Caravan and Camping Parks

Telephone Bookings or Colour Brochure: 01726 843425

See listing under Cornwall and Isles of Scilly

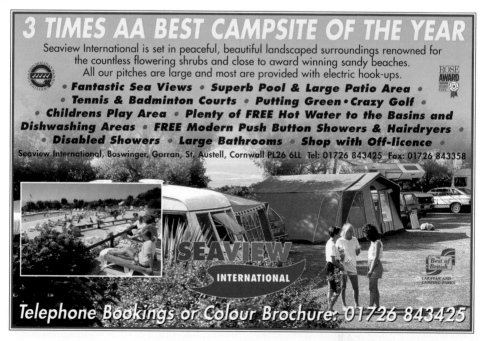

See listing under Sothern Lowlands and Borders

The Grange Country Park is situated on the border of some of the most beautiful countryside in Suffolk. Close to Ipswich & Colchester, it is an easy drive from both London, and the North Sea ferry ports of Harwich and Felixstowe. The amenities are plentiful on the Park and include its own Freehouse Club and restaurant, heated pool and barbecue. It's as pretty as a picture. In the heart of Constable Country.

Tel: 01206 298567 Fax: 01206 298770

See listing under Suffolk

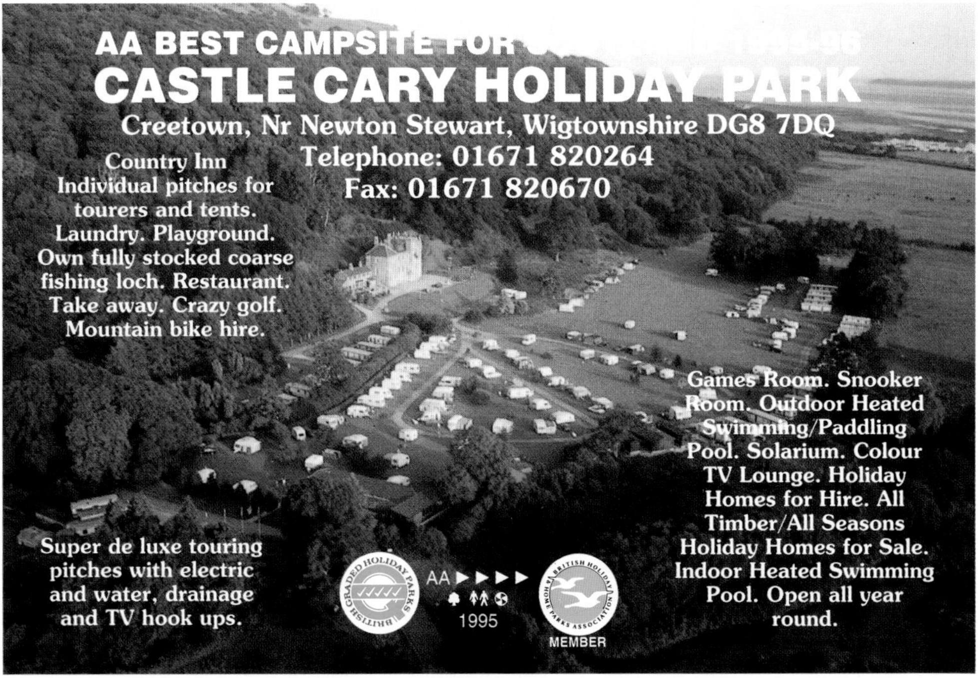

AA BEST CAMPSITE FOR

CASTLE CARY HOLIDAY PARK

Creetown, Nr Newton Stewart, Wigtownshire DG8 7DQ

Telephone: 01671 820264

Fax: 01671 820670

Country Inn
Individual pitches for tourers and tents.
Laundry. Playground.
Own fully stocked coarse fishing loch. Restaurant.
Take away. Crazy golf.
Mountain bike hire.

Games Room. Snooker Room. Outdoor Heated Swimming/Paddling Pool. Solarium. Colour TV Lounge. Holiday Homes for Hire. All Timber/All Seasons Holiday Homes for Sale. Indoor Heated Swimming Pool. Open all year round.

Super de luxe touring pitches with electric and water, drainage and TV hook ups.

British Graded Holiday Parks

AA ▶▶▶▶ 1995

British Holiday Home Parks Association MEMBER

MOON & SIXPENCE

NEAR WOODBRIDGE, SUFFOLK

Secluded tourer sites and good choice of caravan holiday homes for sale owner occupiers, close friends and family. Superb, tranquil, landscaped parkland of 85 acres. Professionally managed lake, fishing Sept & Oct. Sandy beach, woods, meadows. Dog walks, cycle trails. Excellent restaurant serving local specialities. Attractive Lounge and bar. Located unspoilt Coastal Suffolk close Woodbridge and River Deben.

Full colour brochure from:
Moon & Sixpence, Waldringfield Woodbridge, Suffolk IP12 4PP.
Tel: 01473 736 650. Fax: 01473 736 270

AA

Shorefield Country Parks,Shorefield Road
Milford on Sea, Hampshire S041 0LH

Best of both worlds

LYTTON Lawn is the perfect location for a relaxing touring holiday. Only $2^1/_2$ miles from Shorefield Country Park, Lytton Lawn is set in beautiful natural parkland, close to Milford beach and the historic New Forest.

Caravans have individual pitches, with plenty of space for the car, caravan or tent, awning and barbecue. Facilities include: Electricity hook up, showers and purpose-built launderette, 'Premier pitches' and a children's area.

Plus FREE membership of our exclusive Leisure Club with: Indoor/outdoor pools, dance studio, tennis courts, top class restaurant, sauna, solarium, spa bath and nightly entertainment.

For further details telephone

01590 642513

Quoting AA

Fax: 01590 645610
e-mail: holidays@shorefield.co.uk
http://www.shorefield.co.uk

Office open seven days a week

IS YOUR CARAVAN REALLY SAFE?

The AA's Mike Vening, Head of Garage Approvals, talked to Denise Laing, Editor of this Guidebook, about the AA/Caravan Club/National Caravan Council joint scheme for AA-approved specialist Caravan Workshops which was launched in October 1996.

On The Road

Almost by definition, caravanning is a leisure activity pursued by those who want the minimum of fuss and the maximum of adventure, preferably in some unspoilt corner of the country yet within easy reach of entertainment, food supplies and other vital facilities. The temptation, therefore, when the Spring brings warm weather, is to sweep the leaves off the top of that parked caravan, load it with every imaginable holiday item, and tow it away behind your car without further ado. This car will probably have had at least one service in the previous 12 months, and be as reliably road-worthy as possible, while the caravan, sitting outside the house for the past half year doing nothing, will often be presumed to be in tip-top condition. Yet this common assumption is a gravely inaccurate one, and the consequences for some of the many people who tow their caravan away on holiday with no mechanical preparation can be fatal.

The National Scheme

The Automobile Association is acutely aware of the dangers of towing a caravan which has not been serviced for some time, or which has received maintenance from a garage which might not have the necessary expertise in the specialist area of caravan care. In conjunction with The Caravan Club and the National Caravan Council, the AA has devised a scheme which operates nationally, and which offers caravan owners the peace of mind which can enable them to enjoy a trouble-free touring season, at least as far as the caravan is concerned.

Prevention Is Better Than A Cure

Their joint message is this: Before escaping to the freedom of the road and the pleasures of the great outdoors, the emphasis must be on careful planning, meticulous maintenance, and ultimately - safety.
The scheme was launched by these three major organisations in October 1996 with around 70 approved caravan workshops throughout the country, and the number is growing fast. These workshops are carefully monitored and inspected by the AA, and offer a code of practice which protects caravan owners from malpractice, and at the same time guarantees that their unit receives the sort of specialist attention it requires.

Police Attention

Roadside checks conducted by the police and trading standards officers, particularly at the height of the caravanning season, often reveal cases of poorly maintained caravans which subsequently lead to calls for compulsory MOT-type tests on towed vans. This new workshop scheme has been designed to circumvent the need for legislation in this area, by putting the responsibility firmly in the corner of caravan owners, and then providing them with the means to have their vans reliably serviced. Thus owners are protecting themselves and other road users by towing caravans which are in as healthy a condition as possible.

A Code of Practice

All workshops in the scheme must comply with strict standards, and are regularly inspected to ensure that these standards are rigorously maintained. The code of practice under which they operate covers workmanship and engineering, as well as the contents of invoices, and the way that complaints are handled. All AA-approved workshops must offer a collection and delivery service for caravans, and a detailed menu of prices must always be displayed on the premises.

Insurance Matters

The legal requirements for caravans cover speed limits, weight regulations and condition of tyres among several others. New caravan owners are often unaware that some types of work carried out on their unit can cause the warranty to be void, and that poor workmanship can sometimes annul the insurance cover. By choosing to trust their caravans to an AA-approved workshop, owners can be sure that all matters of safety and servicing are carried out by experts who have been carefully selected and are continually monitored. A window sticker issued after completion of work, featuring a different colour each year, is a highly visible sign that the person towing the caravan has taken their responsibilities seriously. Make sure you are one of these!

For further information, *and the address of your nearest AA-approved Caravan Workshop, call 0990 500 600.*

BRITAIN'S & IRELAND'S BEST PARKS

This list has been compiled to give recognition to parks which offer either an outstandingly attractive environment or a notably high standard of quality in the facilities that they provide. They are not necessarily those with greatest number of leisure or recreation facilities - there may be some quite simple parks among them, whose major attraction is peace and quiet in lovely surroundings - so please check the directory entry for full details of the parks.
The directory is organised under country in county (in region in Scotland and Wales) order. Please see the Contents Page for the page references.

CHANNEL ISLANDS

Catel, Guernsey
Fauxquets Valley Farm

St Martin, Jersey
Rozel Camping Park
Beuvelande

ENGLAND

BERKSHIRE

Finchampstead
California Chalet & Touring Park

CAMBRIDGESHIRE

Comberton
Highfield Farm Camping Park

Great Shelford,
Camping & Caravanning Club Site

Houghton
Houghton Mill Caravan
& Camping Park

CORNWALL

Ashton
Boscrege Caravan Park

Bolventor
Colliford Tavern Campsite

Boswinger
Sea View International Caravan & Camping Park

Bude
Budemeadows Touring Holiday Park
Wooda Farm Park

Carlyon Bay
Carlyon Bay Caravan Park

Crantock
Trevella Tourist Park

Goonhavern
Silverbow Park

Trelowarren
Chateau Park

Holywell Bay
Holywell Bay Holiday Park

Leedstown
Calloose Caravan Park

Looe
Polborder House Caravan & Camping Park

Lostwithiel
Powderham Castle

Mawgan Porth
Sun Haven Valley

Pentewan
Sun Valley Holiday Park

Porthtowan
Porthtowan Tourist Park
Rose Hill Park

Rejerrah
Newperran Tourist Park

Relubbus
River Valley Caravan Park

Ruthernbridge
Ruthern Valley Holidays

St Ives
Trevelgan Farm

St Just-in-Roseland
Trethem Mill

Truro
Camping and Caravanning Club Site
Leverton Place
Liskey Touring Park
Summer Valley

CUMBRIA

Ambleside
Skelwith Fold Caravan Park

Appleby in Westmorland
Wild Rose Park

Eskdale
Fisherground Farm Campsite

Kirkby Lonsdale
Wood Close Caravan Park

Lamplugh
Inglenook Caravan Park

Mealsgate
Larches Caravan Park

Milnthorpe
Fell End Caravan Park

Watermillock
Cove Caravan & Camping Park
The Quiet Site

Westward
Clea Hall Holiday Park

Windermere
Fallbarrow Park
Limefitt Park

DERBYSHIRE

Crowden
Camping & Caravanning Club Site

Hayfield
Camping & Caravanning Club Site

Matlock
Darwin Forest Park
Pinegroves Caravan Park

DEVON

Ashburton
Ashburton Caravan Park
River Dart Country Park

Bickington
Dartmoor Halfway
Lemonford Caravan Park

Blackawton
Woodland Leisure Park

Chudleigh
Finlake Leisure Park
Holmans Wood Park

Clifford Bridge
Clifford Bridge Park

Combe Martin
Stowford Farm Meadows

Dartmouth
Little Cotton Caravan Park

Dolton
Dolton Caravan Park

East Worlington
Yeatheridge Farm Caravan Park

Hawkchurch
Hunters Moon Touring Park

Kentisbeare
Forest Glade Holiday Park

Lydford
Camping & Caravanning Club Site

Lynton
Camping & Caravanning Club Site

Modbury
Camping & Caravanning Club Site

Newton Abbot
Dornafield

Paignton
Beverley Park
Widend Camping Park

Plymouth
Riverside Caravan Park

Sidmouth
Oakdown Touring Park

Slapton
Camping & Caravanning Club Site

Stoke Gabriel
Ramslade Touring Park

Tavistock
Higher Longford Farm
Langstone Manor Camping & Caravan Park

West Down
Hidden Valley Coast & Country Park

Whiddon Down
Dartmoor View Caravan & Camping Park

DORSET

Bere Regis
Rowlands Wait Touring Park

Blandford Forum
The Inside Park

Bridport
Binghams Farm Touring Caravan Park
Highlands End Farm Caravan Park

Charmouth
Monkton Wylde Farm Caravan Park

Chickerell
Bagwell Farm Touring Park

Corfe Castle
Woodland Camping Park

Organford
Pear Tree Caravan Park

Wimborne
Merley Court

Wimborne Minster
Wilksworth Farm Caravan Park

ESSEX

Colchester
Colchester Camping

HAMPSHIRE

Bransgore
Harrow Wood Farm Caravan Park

Brockenhurst
Hollands Wood Campsite

Fordingbridge
New Forest Country Holidays

HEREFORD & WORCESTER

Broadway
Leedons Park

Honeybourne
Ranch Caravan Park

ISLE OF WIGHT

Newbridge
Orchards Holiday Caravan Park

Newchurch
Southland Camping Park

Sandown
Adgestone Camping Park

KENT

Ashford
Broad Hembury Holiday Park

Martin Mill
Hawthorn Farm Caravan & Camping Site

Sevenoaks
Camping & Caravanning Club Site

LANCASHIRE

Croston
Royal Umpire Caravan Park

Ormskirk
Abbey Farm Caravan Park

Silverdale
Holgate's Caravan Park

Thornton
Kneps Farm

LINCOLNSHIRE

Boston
Pilgrims Way

Fleet Hargate
Matopos Caravan & Campsite

LONDON

London E4
Lee Valley Leisure Centre Camping & Caravan Site

NORFOLK

Barney
The Old Brick Kilns

Clippesby
Clippesby Holidays

Sandringham
Camping & Caravanning Club Site

Trimingham
Woodlands Caravan Park

West Runton
Camping & Caravanning Club

NORTHUMBERLAND

Bamburgh
Waren Caravan Park

Bellingham
Brown Rigg Caravan & Camping Park

Berwick on Tweed
Ord House Caravan Park

Haltwhistle
Camping & Caravanning Club Site

OXFORDSHIRE

Banbury
Barnstones Caravan
& Camping Site

Charlbury
Cotswold View

Oxford
Oxford Camping International

Standlake
Lincoln Farm Park

SHROPSHIRE

Bridgnorth
Stanmore Hall Touring Park

Haughton
Camping & Caravanning Club Site

Lyneal
Fernwood Caravan Park

SOMERSET

Bath
Newton Mill Caravan
& Camping Park

Bawdrip
Fairways International Touring
Caravan & Camping Park

Bruton
Batcombe Vale Caravan Park

Crowcombe
Quantock Orchard Caravan Park

Exford
Westermill Farm

Glastonbury
Old Oaks Touring Park

Martock
Southfork Caravan Park

Minehead
Camping & Caravanning Club Site

North Wootton
Greenacres Camping

Priddy
Mendip Heights Camping
& Caravan Park

Rodney Stoke
Bucklegrove Caravan
& Camping Park

STAFFORDSHIRE

Cannock Chase
Camping & Caravanning Club Site

SUFFOLK

East Bergholt
Grange Country Park

Wodbridge
Moon & Sixpence

SURREY

East Horsley
Camping and Caravaning Club Site

SUSSEX, EAST

Battle
Senlac Park Caravan
& Camping Site

SUSSEX, WEST

Graffham
Camping & Caravanning Club Site

Littlehampton
White Rose Touring Park

Southbourne
Chichester Camping

WARWICKSHIRE

Aston Cantlow
Island Meadow Caravan Park

WILTSHIRE

Marston Meysey
Second Chance Caravan Park

YORKSHIRE, EAST RIDING

Sproatley
Burton Constable Caravan Park

Rudston
Thorpe Hall Caravan
& Camping Park

Skipsea
Far Grange Park

YORKSHIRE, NORTH

Allerston
Vale of Pickering Caravan Park

Allerton Park
Allerton Park Caravan Site

Aysgarth
Westholme Caravan Park

Cawood
Cawood Holiday Park

Coneysthorpe
Castle Howard Caravan
& Camping Site

Cropton
Spiers House Campsite

Filey
Crows Nest Caravan Park
Flower of May Holiday Park

Fylingdales
Grouse Hill Caravan Park

Guisborough
Tockett's Mill Caravan Park

Harrogate
High Moor
Rudding Holiday Park

Helmsley
Foxholme Caravan Park
Golden Square Touring
Caravan Park

Hunmanby
Orchard Farm Holiday Park

North Stainley
Sleningford Water Mill
Caravan Site

Richmond
Brompton-on-Swale Caravan Park

Ripley
Ripley Caravan Park

Sheriff Hutton
Camping & Caravan Club Site

Snainton
Jasmine Caravan Park

Sutton-on-the-Forest
Goosewood Caravan Park

Threshfield
Wood Nook Caravan Park

Whitby
Northcliffe Holiday Park

Winksley
Woodhouse Farm Caravan &
Camping Park

Wykeham
St Helens Caravan Park

York
Rawcliffe Manor Caravan Site

YORKSHIRE, SOUTH

Worsbrough
Greensprings Touring Park

SCOTLAND

ABERDEENSHIRE

Aboyne
Aboyne Loch Caravan Park

St Cyrus
East Bowstrip Caravan Park

ANGUS

Forfar
Lochside Caravan Park

Kirriemuir
Drumshademuir Caravan Park

ARGYLL & BUTE

Barcaldine
Camping & Caravanning Club Site

Carradale
Carradale Bay

Inveruglas
Loch Lomond Holiday Park

Oban
Oban Divers Caravan Park

Tayinloan
Point Sands Caravan Park

DUMFRIES AND GALLOWAY

Balminnoch
Three Lochs Caravan Park

Brighouse Bay
Brighouse Bay Holiday Park

Creetown
Castle Cary Holiday Park

Crocketford
Park of Brandedleys

Ecclefechan
Cressfield Caravan Park
Hoddom Castle Caravan Park

Gatehouse of Fleet
Auchenlarie Holiday Farm

Glen Trool
Caldons Campsite

Kirkcudbright
Seaward Caravan Park

Lochnaw
Drumlochart

Parton
Loch Ken Holiday Centre

Portpatrick
Galloway Point Holiday Park

Sandhead
Sands of Luce Caravan Park

Sandyhills
Sandyhills Bay Leisure Park

EAST LOTHIAN

Dunbar
Thurston Manor Holiday
Home Park

Musselburgh
Drum Mohr

North Berwick
Tantallon Caravan Park

FIFE

Kirkcaldy
Dunnikier Caravan Park

St Andrews
Craigtoun Meadows Holiday Park

HIGHLAND

Ardmair
Ardmair Point Caravan Park

Aviemore
Glenmore Forest

Balmacara
Balmacara Woodland Campsite
Reraig Caravan Site

Corpach
Linnhe Caravan Park

Dingwall
Camping & Caravanning Club Site

Fort William
Glen Nevis Caravan
& Camping Park

Glencoe
Invercoe Caravan and Campsite

Grantown-on-Spey
Grantown-on-Spey Caravan Park

Invergarry
Faichem Park

Nairn
Spindrift Caravan & Camping Park

Resipole
Resipole Farm

PERTHSHIRE & KINROSS

Auchterarder
Auchterarder Caravan Park

Blair Atholl
Blair Castle Caravan Park
River Tilt Caravan Park

Bridge of Cally
Corriefodly Holiday Park

Inchture
Inchmartine Caravan Park
& Nurseries

Perth
Cleeve Caravan Park

SCOTTISH BORDERS

Kelso
Springwood Caravan Park

Peebles
Crossburn Caravan Park

SOUTH AYRSHIRE

Maybole
Camping & Caravanning Club Site

Tarbolton
Middlemuir Park

STIRLING

Aberfoyle
Trossachs Holiday Park

Callander
Callander Holiday Park
Gart Caravan Park

Luib
Glendochart Caravan Park

WALES

ANGLESEY

Brynteg
Nant Newydd Caravan Park

Dulas
Tyddyn Isaaf Caravan Park

Marianglas
Home Farm Caravan Park

CEREDIGION

Cross Inn
Camping & Caravan Club Site

Llandre
Riverside Park

New Quay
Cei Bach Country Clut

CARMARTHENSHIRE

Newcastle Emlyn
Afon Teifi Caravan
& Camping Park
Cenarth Falls Holiday Park

Rhandirmwyn
Camping & Caravanning Club Site

CONWY

Betws-yn-Rhos
Hunters' Hamlet Caravan Park

Conwy
Conwy Touring Park

Llanddulas
Bron Y Wendon Caravan Park

Llanrwst
Bodnant Caravan Site

DENBIGHSHIRE

Llandrillo
Hendwr Caravan Park

Llangollen
Ty-Ucha Caravan Park

GWYNEDD

Abersoch
Bryn Cethin Bach Caravan Park

Bala
Camping & Caravanning Club Site

Barmouth
Hendre Mynach

Beddgelert
Beddgelert Forest Campsite

Betws Garmon
Bryn Gloch Caravan

Caernarfon
Bryn Teg Holiday Park
Glan Gwna Holiday Park

Llandwrog
White Towers Park

Llanystumdwy
Camping & Caravanning Club Site

Porthmadog
Camping & Caravanning Club Site

Talsarnau
Barcdy Touring Caravan
& Camping Park

MONMOUTHSHIRE

Dingestow
Bridge Caravan Park

PEMBROKESHIRE

Tenby
Rowston Holiday Park

Trefalun
Well Park Caravan & Camping Site

POWYS

Brecon
Brynich Caravan Park

Builth Wells
Forest Fields Caravan
& Camping Park

Presteigne
Rock Bridge Park

NORTHERN IRELAND

CO DOWN

Castlewellan
Castlewellan Forest Park

REPUBLIC OF IRELAND

CO. CLARE

Killaloe
Lough Derg Caravan
& Camping Park

Kilrush
Aylevarroo Caravan Park

Lahinch
Lahinch Camping & Caravan Park

O'Brien's Bridge
Shannon Cottage Caravan
& Camping Park

CO. CORK

Ballylickey
Eagle Point Caravan
& Camping Park

Crookhaven
Barley Cove Caravan Park

Glandore
Meadow Camping Park

CO. KERRY

Castlegregory
Anchor Caravan Park

Killarney
Fleming's White Bridge
Caravan Park
Flesk Caravan & Campsite

CO. ROSCOMMON

Boyle
Lough Key Forest Park

CO. TIPPERARY

Aherlow
Ballinacourty House Camping
& Caravan Park

CO. WATERFORD

Clonea
Casey's Caravan Park

CO. WEXFORD

Wexford
Ferry Bank Caravan Park

CO. WICKLOW

Donard
Moat Farm Caravan
& Camping Park

Redcross
River Valley Caravan Park

Roundwood
Roundwood Caravan Park

PENNANTED HOLIDAY CENTRES

These parks are in a class on their own, and must achieve levels of quality for their touring facilities equivalent to which are at least those for their static vans before we can consider giving them this separate designation. Additionally, they will have high levels of supervision and security as well as the range of leisure and recreational facilities that enable them to offer a completely self-contained holiday experience on site.

We should like to make it clear, however, that we only inspect them and classify them for their facilities and standards of environment and maintenance, and not for their static holiday vans or self-catering chalets, which are outside the scope of our classification.

ENGLAND

CORNWALL

Hayle
St Ives Holiday Park

Holywell Bay
Trevornick Holiday Park

Mullion
Mullion Holiday Park

Newquay
Hendra Holiday Park
Newquay Holiday Park

Polperro
Killigarth Manor Holiday Estate

Rejerrah
Newperran Tourist Park

Whitecross
White Acres Holiday Park

CUMBRIA

Silloth
Stanwix Park Holiday Centre

DEVON

Chudleigh
Finlake Holiday Park

Dawlish
Golden Sands Holiday Park

Paignton
Beverley Parks Caravan & Camping Park
Grange Court Holiday Centre

Woolacombe
Golden Coast Holiday Village

GLOUCESTERSHIRE

South Cerney
Cotswold Hoburne

LANCASHIRE

Blackpool
Marton Mere Holiday Village

LINCOLNSHIRE

Cleethorpes
Thorpe Park Holiday Centre

Woodhall Spa
Bainland Country Park

NORFOLK

Gt Yarmouth
Vauxhall Holiday Park

Hunstanton
Searles of Hunstanton

NORTHUMBERLAND

Berwick-upon-Tweed
Berwick Holiday Centre
Haggerston Castle

SUSSEX, WEST

Selsey
Warner Farm Touring Park

YORKSHIRE, EAST RIDING OF

Skipsea
Far Grange Park

YORKSHIRE, NORTH

Filey
Flower of May Holiday Park

SCOTLAND

CENTRAL SCOTLAND

Longniddry
Seton Sands Holiday Village

WALES

MID WALES

Tenby
Kiln Park

REPUBLIC OF IRELAND

CO. KERRY

Killarney
Fossa Caravan Park

Follow the Country Code

Enjoy the countryside and respect its life and work.

Guard against all risks of fire.

Fasten all gates.

Keep your dogs under close control.

Use gates and stiles to cross fences, hedges and walls.

Leave livestock, crops and machinery alone.

Take your litter home.

Help keep all water clean.

Protect wildlife, plants and trees.

Take special care on country roads.

Directory

ENGLAND

FORESTRY COMMISSION CARAVAN AND CAMPSITES

Forestry Commission sites which come within the scope of the Automobile Association's Caravan and Campsite classification scheme are listed in this guide. For a Forestry Commission brochure telephone 0131 334 0066. In addition there are entries for minimum-facility sites suitable for the camper or caravanner who prefers to be self-sufficient and carries his own chemical toilet.

ISLE OF

Places incorporating the words 'Isle of' or 'Isle' will be found under the actual name, eg Isle of Wight is listed under Wight, Isle of. Channel Islands and Isle of Man, however, are between England and Scotland.

BERKSHIRE

For the map of this county, see page 60

FINCHAMPSTEAD

California Chalet & Touring Park (SU785650)
Nine Mile Ride RG40 3HU ☎ 01734 733928 Signposted
Nearby town: Wokingham
►►► **Family Park** ★ fr £9 fr £9 fr £9
Open Mar-Oct Booking advisable bank & school hols & Ascot wk Last arrival 22.00hrs Last departure noon
A secluded site in a delightful country park, with well-spaced pitches giving a good degree of privacy. From A321 to Sandhurst turn right on B3016, and after .75m turn right onto Nine Mile Ride. Signposted. A 5.5-acre site with 35 touring pitches.
Fishing on site.

NEWBURY

Oakley Farm Caravan & Camping Park (SU458628)
Andover Rd, Washwater RG20 0LP ☎ 01635 36581 (2.5m S off A343)
Town & Country Pennant Park ★ fr £6 fr £6 fr £6
Open Mar-Oct Booking advisable bank hols
An open farmland site, well maintained and clean, S of Newbury. From rndbt S of Newbury on A34, take A343 Andover rd. About 300yds past Hants/Berks boundary bridge, turn left at car sales garage into Penwood Rd. Site on L. A 3-acre site with 30 touring pitches.

BUCKINGHAMSHIRE

For the map of this county, see page 60

CHALFONT ST GILES

Highclere Farm Country Touring Park (SU977927)
Highclere Farm, Newbarn Ln, Seer Green HP9 2QZ
☎ 01494 874505 & 875665 (1.25m SW) Signposted
Nearby town: Beaconsfield
►►► **Family Park** £8.50-£10 £8.50-£10 £7.50-£10
Open Mar-Jan Booking advisable Last departure noon
A small, level touring park situated between Chalfont St Giles and Seer Green. Toilets immaculate. A 2.5-acre site with 60 touring pitches.

Credit Cards

CAMBRIDGESHIRE

BURWELL

Stanford Park (TL578675)
Weirs Rd CB5 0BP ☎ 01638 741547
Nearby town: Cambridge
Town & Country Pennant Park ★ £7.50-£8 £7.50-£8 £6.50-£9
Open all year Booking advisable bank hols Last arrival 20.30hrs Last departure noon
A secluded site on outskirts of Burwell with modern amenities including purpose-built disabled facilities. Signed from B1102. A 14-acre site with 100 touring pitches and 3 statics.
See advertisement under CAMBRIDGE

CAMBRIDGE

See **Burwell & Comberton**

COMBERTON

Highfield Farm Camping Park (TL389572)
Long Rd CB3 7DG ☎ 01223 262308 Signposted
Nearby town: Cambridge

►►►► **De-Luxe Park** ★ £6.75-£8.25 £6.50-£8 £6.50-£8
Open Apr-Oct Booking advisable bank hols wknds Last arrival 22.00hrs Last departure 14.00hrs

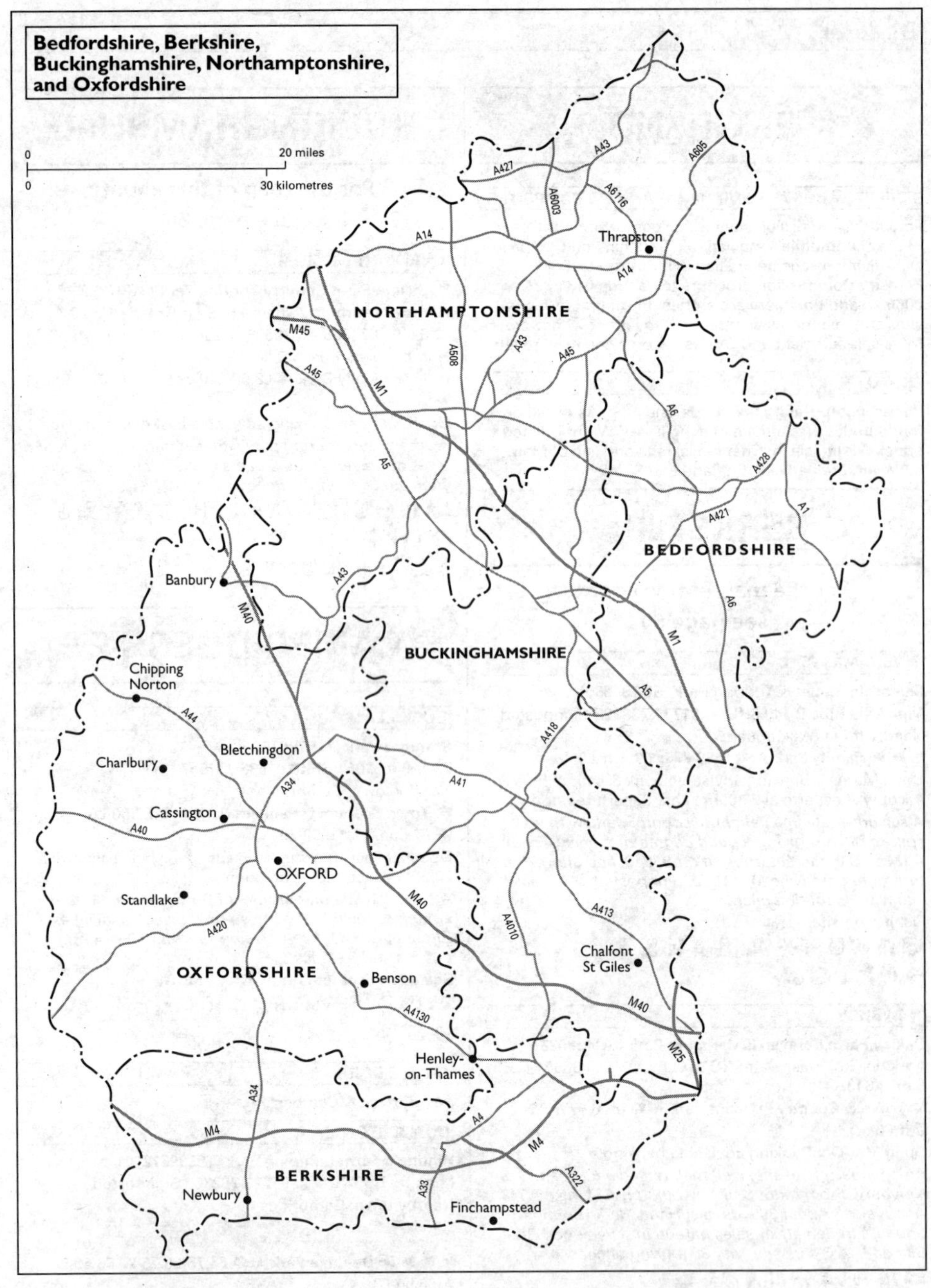
Bedfordshire, Berkshire, Buckinghamshire, Northamptonshire, and Oxfordshire
0
20 miles
0
30 kilometres
NORTHAMPTONSHIRE
BEDFORDSHIRE
BUCKINGHAMSHIRE
OXFORDSHIRE
BERKSHIRE
Thrapston
Banbury
Chipping Norton
Charlbury
Bletchingdon
Cassington
OXFORD
Standlake
Benson
Chalfont St Giles
Henley-on-Thames
Newbury
Finchampstead
A427
A43
A605
A6003
A6116
A14
M45
A508
A45
M1
A5
A6
A428
A421
A1
M40
A44
A34
A41
A418
A40
A420
A4010
A413
A4130
M25
M4
A4
A33
A322

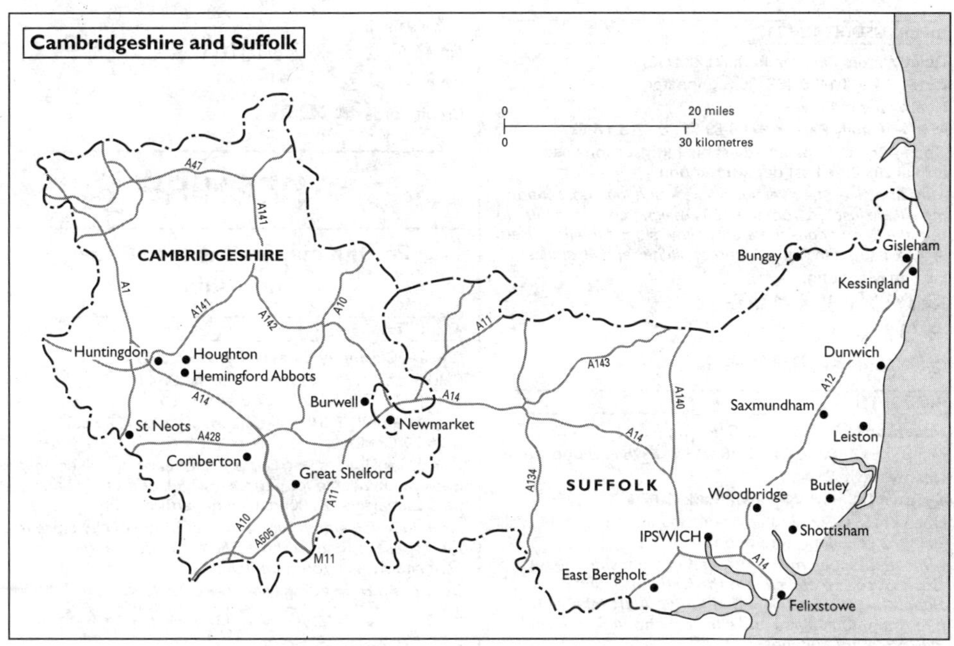

A first class site with good quality facilities, set in farmland and screened by conifers and hedges. 3m W of Cambridge between A45 and A603. From junc 12 of M11 take A603 Sandy road for .5m, then B1046 to Comberton. An 8-acre site with 120 touring pitches.

Dishwashing facility, postbox & hardstanding.

See advertisement under Colour Section

GREAT SHELFORD

Camping & Caravanning Club Site (TL455539)

19 Cabbage Moor CB2 5NB ☎ 01223 841185 (in season) & 01203 694995 Signposted

Nearby town: Cambridge

►►► **Family Park** ★ £9.10-£12.10 £9.10-£12.10 £9.10-£12.10

Open end Mar-early Nov Booking advisable bank hols & Jul-Aug Last arrival 21.00hrs Last departure noon

An attractive site with good landscaping and excellent toilet blocks. From junc 11 of M11 take A1309, then R at traffic lights on to A1301; site .5m on L. Please see the advertisement on page 27 for details of Club Members' benefits. A 12-acre site with 130 touring pitches.

Credit Cards

HEMINGFORD ABBOTS

Quiet Waters Caravan Park (TL283712)
PE18 9AJ ☎ 01480 463405 Signposted
Nearby town: St Ives
►►► **Family Park** ★ £8-£9 £8-£9 £8-£9
Open Apr-Oct Booking advisable high season Last arrival 20.00hrs Last departure noon
This attractive little riverside site is found in a most charming village just 1m from the A604 making an ideal centre to tour the Cambridgeshire area. Follow signs for village from A14. A 1-acre site with 20 touring pitches and 40 statics.
Fishing & boating.

Credit Cards

HOUGHTON

Houghton Mill Caravan & Camping Park (TL284721)
Mill St PE17 2BJ ☎ 01480 462413 & 492811 Signposted
Nearby town: St Ives
Town & Country Pennant Park
Open Etr-Sep Booking advisable at all times Last arrival 20.00hrs Last departure noon
A most attractive meadow location alongside the River Great Ouse and adjacent to the National Trust's Houghton Mill. From Huntingdon on A604 take A1123 into Houghton village and site is at end. A 5-acre site with 65 touring pitches.
Boating & fishing.

HUNTINGDON

Park Lane Touring Park (TL245709)
Godmanchester PE18 8AF ☎ 01480 453740 Signposted
►►► **Family Park** ★ fr £8 fr £8 fr £8
Open Mar-Oct Booking advisable bank hols Last arrival 22.00hrs
Attractive little site with good facilities and a high standard of maintenance. Situated just off the A14 Huntingdon bypass. Follow signs into Godmanchester along Cambridge Rd then Post St, and turn into Park Lane by the Black Bull Inn. A 3-acre site with 50 touring pitches.
Enclosed dishwashing & preparation area.

ST NEOTS

Camping & Caravanning Club Site (TL182598)
Rush Meadow PE19 2UD ☎ 01480 474404 (in season) & 01203 694995 (signed from B1043) Signposted
►►► **Family Park** ★ £9.10-£12.10 £9.10-£12.10 £9.10-£12.10
Open end Mar-early Nov Booking advisable bank hols & peak periods Last arrival 21.00hrs Last departure noon
A level meadowland site adjacent to the River Ouse on the outskirts of St Neots, well maintained and with helpful, attentive staff. Take B1043 N, crossing A428 into Eynesbury, cross small rndbt, then take first left. Please see the advertisement on page 27 for details of Club Members' benefits. A 10-acre site with 202 touring pitches.
Coarse fishing.

Credit Cards

CHESHIRE

For the map of this county, see Shropshire

CHESTER

Chester Southerly Caravan Park (SJ385624)
Balderton Ln, Marlston-Cum-Lache CH4 9LB
☎ 01829 270791 & 270697 Signposted
►►► **Family Park** ★ £6.20-£8.80 £6.20-£8.80 £6.20-£8.80
Open Mar-Nov (rs Dec-Feb open for caravan rallies only) Booking advisable for periods of 1 wk or more & bank hols Last arrival 23.00hrs Last departure noon
A well-tended site in rural area, on S side of city close to the bypass, and just off the A55/A483 roundabout. A 6-acre site with 90 touring pitches.
Duck pond & breeding cage.

MACCLESFIELD

Capesthorne Hall (SJ840727)
Siddington SK11 9JY ☎ 01625 861779 & 861221 Signposted
Town & Country Pennant Park
Open Mar-Oct Booking advisable public hols Last arrival dusk Last departure noon
Set in grounds and gardens of Capesthorne Hall in the heart of the Cheshire countryside. The pitches are on level ground close to the Hall, off the A34. Immaculate toilets in old stable block. A 5.5-acre site with 50 touring pitches.
Capesthorne Hall, gardens, fishing. Laundry room.

RIXTON

Holly Bank Caravan Park (SJ693904)
Warburton Bridge Rd WA3 6HU ☎ 0161 775 2842 Signposted
Nearby town: Warrington
►►► **Family Park** £10-£12 £10-£12 £9-£11
Open all year Booking advisable bank hols & wknds Apr-Oct Last arrival 21.00hrs Last departure noon
Attractive site with spotlessly clean facilities. Just off A57 close to the Manchester Ship Canal and convenient to M6 and Manchester. From junc 21 of M6 turn E on A57 to Irlam, in 2m turn right at traffic lights, and site immediately on left. A 9-acre site with 70 touring pitches.
Lending library.

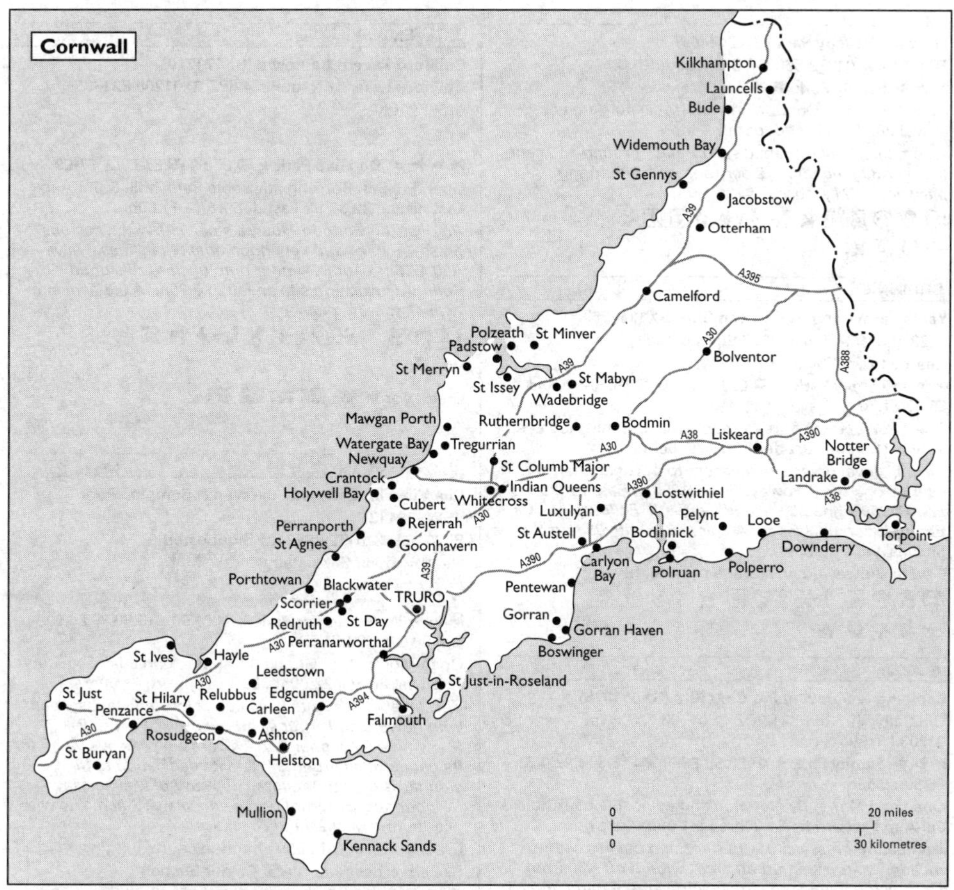

CORNWALL & ISLES OF SCILLY

ASHTON

Boscrege Caravan Park (SW595305)

TR13 9TG ☎ 01736 762231

Nearby town: Helston

►►► **Family Park** ★ £5.75-£9.50 £5.75-£9.50 £5.75-£9.50

Open Apr-Oct Booking advisable Jul-Aug Last arrival 22.00hrs Last departure 11.00hrs

A much improved site in an isolated rural area with very good screening. From Helston take A394 signed Penzance, turn right in Ashton on unclass rd, and follow signs to Boscreage. A 4-acre site with 50 touring pitches and 26 statics.

Recreation field. Microwave facility.

Credit Cards

BLACKWATER

Chiverton Caravan & Touring Park (SW743468)

East Hill TR4 8HS ☎ 01872 560667 (jct A30/A390) Signposted

Nearby town: Truro

►►► **Family Park** ★ £4-£6 £4-£6 £4-£6

Open Good Fri/Apr-Oct (rs Apr-May & mid Sep-Oct limited stock kept in shop) Booking advisable mid Jul-Aug Last arrival 22.00hrs Last departure noon

A small, well maintained, level, grassy site recently laid out and run by enthusiastic owners. Leave A30 at Three Burrows/Chiverton rndbt onto unclass rd (3rd exit) signed Blackwater. Take 1st right and site in 300yds. A 4-acre site with 30 touring pitches and 30 statics.

Covered sink area, drying lines.

Trevarth Holiday Park (SW744468)
TR4 8HR ☎ 01872 560266 Signposted
►►► **Family Park**
Open Etr or Apr-Oct Booking advisable Jul-Aug Last arrival 20.00hrs Last departure noon
A compact, well screened site on high ground adjacent to A30/A39 junction. A 2-acre site with 30 touring pitches and 21 statics.

BODINNICK

Yeate Farm Camp & Caravan Site (SX134526)
PL23 1LZ ☎ 01726 870256 Signposted
Nearby town: Fowey
►►► **Family Park** ★ £5.50-£7.50 £5.50-£7.50 £5.50-£7.50
Open Apr-Oct Booking advisable mid Jul-mid Aug Last arrival 21.30hrs Last departure 11.00hrs
A small, level grass site adjacent to a working farm overlooking the R Fowey. From A390 at East Taphouse take B3359 signed Looe and Lanreath. Follow signs for Bodinnick on unclass rd. A 1-acre site with 33 touring pitches and 2 statics.
Private slipway/quay, storage of small boats.

BODMIN

Camping & Caravanning Club Site (SX081676)
Old Callywith Rd PL31 2DZ ☎ 01208 73834 (in season) & 01203 694995 Signposted
►►► **Family Park** ★ £6.60-£9.50 £6.60-£9.50 £6.60-£9.50
Open end Mar-early Nov Booking advisable bank hols & Jul-Aug Last arrival 21.00hrs Last departure noon
Undulating grassy site with trees and bushes set in meadowland within urban area. Signed off A30 from Launceston. Please see the advertisement on page 27 for details of Club Members' benefits. A 10.75-acre site with 175 touring pitches.
Credit Cards

Glenmorris Park (SX053733)
Longstone Rd, St Mabyn PL30 3BY ☎ 01208 841677 Signposted
►►► **Family Park**
Open Etr-Oct Booking advisable Last arrival 22.30hrs Last departure noon
A refurbished site in a peaceful area close to the village. Signed on unclass rd off B3266 towards St Mabyn village at Longstone. A 5-acre site with 100 touring pitches and 6 statics.
Off-licence.

BOLVENTOR

Colliford Tavern Campsite (SX171740)
Colliford Lake, St Neot PL14 6PZ ☎ 01208 821335 Signposted
►►►► **De-Luxe Park** ★ £7-£9 £7-£9 £7-£9
Open Etr-Sep Booking advisable Bank hols & Jul-Aug Last arrival 22.30hrs Last departure 11.00hrs
An oasis on Bodmin Moor, a small site with spacious grassy pitches and very good quality facilities. Leave A30 1.25m W of Bolventor onto unclass rd signed Colliford Lake, and site on left in 0.25m. A 3.5-acre site with 40 touring pitches.
Credit Cards

BOSWINGER

Sea View International Caravan & Camping Park (SW990412)
PL26 6LL ☎ 01726 843425 Signposted
Nearby town: St Austell
►►►►► **Premier Park** ★ £6.90-£15.90 £6.90-£15.90 £6.90-£15.90
Open Mon before Good Fri-Sep Booking advisable Jul-Aug Last arrival 22.00hrs Last departure 11.00hrs
This level, grassy site has been colourfully landscaped with flowers and shrubs and overlooks Veryan Bay. Many times a winner of AA awards in previous years for its beautiful environment and its dedication to high standards of maintenance. 3.5m SW of Mevagissey harbour and .5m from beach and sea. A 7-acre site with 165 touring pitches and 38 statics.
Crazy golf, volleyball, badminton courts, putting.
See advertisement under Colour Section
Credit Cards

BUDE

Wooda Farm Park (SS229080)
Poughill EX23 9HJ ☎ 01288 352069 (2m E) Signposted
►►►►► **Premier Park** £6.50-£10 £6.50-£10 £6.50-£10
Open Apr-Oct (rs Apr-end May & mid Sep-end Oct shop hrs, laundrette/restaurant limited) Booking advisable Jul-Aug Last arrival 20.00hrs Last departure noon

Have you completed and returned the prize draw card inside the front cover of this guide? If not, do so today for the chance of a weekend break.

There are sea views from this site set on raised grounds overlooking Bude Bay. From the A39 at the edge of Stratton follow the unclassified Coombe Valley road. A 12-acre site with 160 touring pitches and 52 statics.

Coarse fishing, clay pigeon shoots, pets corner.

Credit Cards

Budemeadows Touring Holiday Park (SS215012)
EX23 0NA ☎ 01288 361646 (3m S of Bude on A39)
Signposted

►►►► **De-Luxe Park** ★ £7.20-£10 £7.20-£10 £7.20-£10

Open all year (rs Oct-Spring bank hol shop & pool closed) Booking advisable Jul-Aug Last arrival 21.00hrs Last departure noon

A very well kept site of distinction, with good quality facilities. A 9-acre site with 100 touring pitches and 1 static.

Outdoor table tennis & giant chess. Baby changing.

Credit Cards

CAMELFORD

Juliot's Well Holiday Park (SX095829)
PL32 9RF ☎ 01840 213302 Signposted
Nearby town: Tintagel

►►►► **De-Luxe Park** ★ £5-£10 £5-£10 ▲ £5-£10
Open Mar-Oct (rs Mar-Apr & Oct swimming pool closed) Booking advisable bank hols & Jul-Aug Last arrival 21.30hrs Last departure 11.00hrs
A quiet site in the grounds of an old manor house. From A39 in Camelford turn right onto B3266, at T junc turn left and site on right in 300 yds. An 8-acre site with 60 touring pitches and 50 statics.
Skittle alley, boules.volley ball, tennis, badminton.

Credit Cards

Lakefield Caravan Park (SX095853)
Lower Pendavey Farm PL32 9TX ☎ 01840 213279 (1.5m N on B3266) Signposted
►►► **Family Park** ★ £5-£8 £5-£8 ▲ £5-£8
Open Etr or Apr-Oct Booking advisable Jul-Aug Last arrival 22.00hrs Last departure noon
Set in a rural location, this friendly park is part of a specialist equestrian centre, and offers good quality services. From A39 in Camelford turn right onto B3266, turn right at T junc, and site on left in 1.5m. A 5-acre site with 30 touring pitches.
Own lake & full Equestrian Centre.

CARLEEN

Lower Polladras Camping (SW617308)
TR13 9NX ☎ 01736 762220 Signposted
Nearby town: Helston
►►► **Family Park** ▲
Open Apr-Oct Booking advisable Jul-Aug Last arrival 22.00hrs Last departure noon
A very rural farm site with good facilities. From A394 turn onto B3302 Hayle road at Hilltop Garage, then take 2nd turning on L to Carleen for site, about 2m on R. A 4-acre site with 60 touring pitches.

Poldown Caravan Park (SW629298)
Poldown TR13 9NN ☎ 01326 574560 Signposted
Nearby town: Helston
►►► **Family Park** ★ £4.50-£9 £4.50-£9 ▲ £4.50-£9
Open Apr-Oct Booking advisable Jul-Aug Last arrival 22.00hrs Last departure noon
A small, quiet site set in attractive countryside. From A394 turn off onto the B3302 Hayle road at Hilltop Garage, then take second left to Carleen for site which is .75m on right. A 2-acre site with 10 touring pitches and 7 statics.

CARLYON BAY

Carlyon Bay Caravan & Camping Park (SX052526)
Bethesda, Cypress Av PL25 3RE ☎ 01726 812735 Signposted
Nearby town: St Austell

►►►► **De-Luxe Park** ★ £6-£14 £5-£13 ▲ £6-£14
Open Etr-3 Oct (rs Etr-mid May & mid Sep-3 Oct swimming pool/take-away/shop closed) Booking advisable mid Jul-mid Aug Last arrival anytime Last departure 11.00hrs
An attractive, secluded site set amongst a belt of trees with background woodland. Off A390 W of St Blazey, turn left on A3092 for Par, and right again in .5m. On private rd to Carlyon Bay. A 35-acre site with 180 touring pitches.
Crazy golf, childrens entertainment in Jul & Aug.

Credit Cards

CRANTOCK (NEAR NEWQUAY)

Trevella Tourist Park (SW801599)
TR8 5EW ☎ 01637 830308 Signposted
Nearby town: Newquay

►►►► **De-Luxe Park**
Open Etr-Oct Booking advisable bank hols & Jul-Aug
A well established and very well run family site, with outstanding floral displays. Set in rural area close to Newquay between Crantock and A3075. A 15-acre site with 295 touring pitches and 50 statics.
Crazy golf, fishing & badminton.
See advertisement on page 80

Credit Cards

Crantock Plains Touring Park (SW805589)
TR8 5PH ☎ 01637 830955 & 831273
Nearby town: Newquay
►►► **Family Park** ★ £5.50-£8.50 £5.50-£8.50 £5.50-£8.50
Open Etr/Apr-Sep Booking advisable Jul-Aug Last arrival 22.00hrs Last departure noon
A small farm site with level grassy touring pitches. From A3075 take 3rd turning right signed Crantock. Site on left along narrow lane. A 6-acre site with 40 touring pitches.

Treago Farm Caravan Site (SW782601)
TR8 5QS ☎ 01637 830277 Signposted
Nearby town: Newquay
►►► **Family Park** ★ £6-£9 £6-£9 £6-£9
Open mid May-mid Sep (rs Apr-mid May & Oct no shop or bar) Booking advisable Jun-Aug Last arrival 22.00hrs Last departure 18.00hrs
Grass site in open farmland in a south-facing sheltered valley; direct access to Crantock and Polly Joke beaches, National Trust Land and many natural beauty spots. From A3075 W of Newquay turn right for Crantock. Site signed beyond village. A 4-acre site with 92 touring pitches and 7 statics.

CUBERT

Cottage Farm (SW786589)
Treworgans TR8 5WW ☎ 01637 831083
►►► **Family Park**
Open Apr-Sep
A small grassy touring park nestling in the tiny hamlet of Treworgans, in sheltered open countryside close to a lovely beach. Leave A30 onto A392 towards Newquay, turn left onto A3075 towards Redruth, and in 2m turn right signed Holywell, Cubert and Penhalt Camp. Turn right in 1.5m signed Crantock, and left in 0.5m past school. Site in 300yds. A 2-acre site with 45 touring pitches and 1 static.

Trebellan Park (SW789571)
TR8 5PY ☎ 01637 830552
►►► **Family Park**
Open Etr-Oct
Terraced grassy rural park within picturesque valley with views of Cubert common and adjacent to the Smugglers Den, a 16th century thatched Inn. 4m S of Newquay, turn W off A3075, at signpost to Cubert in 0.75m turn left onto unclassified minor road signed to park and Smugglars Inn. A 20-acre site with 150 touring pitches.
Coarse fishing lake.

DOWNDERRY

Carbeil Caravan & Camping Park (SX318544)
Treliddon Ln PL11 3LS ☎ 01503 250636 Signposted
Nearby town: Looe
►►► **Family Park**
Open 31 Mar-Oct Booking advisable all year Last arrival 21.00hrs Last departure noon
A compact park in a sheltered valley with pitches tiered into grass paddocks. Site at end of Downderry, up narrow lane and signed. A 1.25-acre site with 20 touring pitches and 8 statics.

EDGCUMBE

Retanna Holiday Park (SW711327)
TR13 OEJ ☎ 01326 340643 (10Om off A394) Signposted
►►► **Family Park** ★ £6-£7 £6-£7 £6-£7
Open May-Sep (rs Apr & Oct limited shop facilities) Booking advisable Jul & Aug Last arrival 22.00hrs Last departure 11.00hrs
A small rural site with limited amenities but central for touring and 5m from Falmouth. Signed off the A394 4m E of Helston. A 4-acre site with 24 touring pitches and 34 statics.

Credit Cards

FALMOUTH

Maen Valley Holiday Park (SW789311)
Roscarrick Rd TR11 5BJ ☎ 01326 312190 Signposted

►►►► **De-Luxe Park** ★ £6-£12 £6-£12 £6-£12
Open Etr-Oct Booking advisable Jul & Aug Last arrival 22.00hrs
Set in a picturesque valley with a stream, this site offers rural tranquility and well-kept facilities. 1.5m SW of Falmouth but within walking distance of Swanpool beach. Leave A39 at Hillhead rndbt on Penryn by-pass and follow signs to Maenporth and industrial estate. Site in 1.5m. A 4-acre site with 90 touring pitches and 94 statics.

contd.

Crazy golf.

→ U

Credit Cards

Tremorvah Tent Park (SW798313)

Swanpool TR11 5BA ☎ 01326 312103 Signposted

►►► **Family Park** ★ £6.50-£7.10 £6.50-£7.10

Open mid May-Oct Booking advisable Jul-Aug Last arrival 22.00hrs Last departure 10.00hrs

A secluded tent park in a meadowland setting overlooking Swanpool Beach. No towed caravans. In Falmouth follow signs to 'Beaches', and on to Swanpool; site signed on right. A 3-acre site with 72 touring pitches.

Dishwashing sinks & electric cooking hob.

→ U

GOONHAVERN

Silverbow Park (SW782531)

Perranwell TR4 9NX ☎ 01872 572347 Signposted

►►►► **De-Luxe Park**

Open mid May-mid Sep (rs mid Sep-Oct & Etr-mid May swimming pool & shop closed) Booking advisable Jul-Aug Last arrival 22.00hrs Last departure noon

A very well kept park in a rural setting, thoughtfully laid out and screened by mature shrubs and trees. Adjacent to A3075 .5m S of village. A 14-acre site with 100 touring pitches and 15 statics.

Badminton courts, short mat bowls rink.

See advertisement under PERRANPORTH

→ U

Perran Springs Touring Park (SW796535)

Bodmin Rd TR4 9QG ☎ 01872 540568 Signposted

Nearby town: Newquay

►►► **Family Park**

Open Etr or Apr-Oct Booking advisable Jul-Aug Last arrival anytime Last departure 10.00hrs

A brand new site with quality buildings and a good standard of facilities. Turn R off A30 on to B3285, signed Perranporth. Site on R in 1m. An 8-acre site with 120 touring pitches.

→ U

Rosehill Farm Tourist Park (SW787540)

TR4 9LA ☎ 01872 572448 Signposted

Nearby town: Perranporth

►►► **Family Park**

Open Whit-Oct (rs Etr-Whit shop) Booking advisable Jul-Aug Last arrival 21.30hrs Last departure 11.00hrs

A small, well-kept site set in hilly meadowland, .5m W of village on B3285. A 7-acre site with 65 touring pitches.

Off-licence in shop.

See advertisement under PERRANPORTH

→ U

GORRAN

Tregarton Park (SW984437)

PL26 6NF ☎ 01726 843666 Signposted

Nearby town: St Austell

►►► **Family Park** ★ £7.50-£10.50 £7.50-£10.50 £7.50-£10.50

Open Etr-Sep Booking advisable Jul-Aug Last arrival 22.00hrs Last departure 11.00hrs

A sheltered park set in lovely countryside lying 2m from the sea and off minor road to Gorran Haven. From St Austell bypass turn left on B3273 for Mevagissey. At crossroads signed 'No caravans beyond this point', turn right on to unclass. road for Gorran. Site on right in 2.5m. An 8-acre site with 150 touring pitches.

Camping equipment for sale, Off Licence.

See advertisement under MEVAGISSEY

→ U

Credit Cards

Treveor Farm Caravan & Camping Site (SW988418)
PL26 6LW ☎ 01726 842387 Signposted
Nearby town: St Austell
►►► **Family Park** ★ £6.50-£12 £6.50-£12 ▲ £6.50-£12
Open Apr-Oct Booking advisable Jan Last arrival 20.00hrs Last departure 11.00hrs
A small family run camping park with good facilities, situated on a working farm. From St Austell bypass turn left onto B3273 for Mevagissey. On hilltop before descent to village turn right on unclass rd for Gorran; in 3.5m fork right, and site signed on right. A 4-acre site with 50 touring pitches.
Coarse fishing.

GORRAN HAVEN

Trelispen Caravan & Camping Park (SX008421)
PL26 6HT ☎ 01726 843501 Signposted
Nearby town: St Austell
► **Town & Country Pennant Park** ★ £8-£12 £7-£10 ▲ £7-£10
Open Etr & Apr-Oct Booking advisable Last arrival 22.00hrs Last departure noon
A very basic site in a beautiful, quiet location within easy reach of beaches. From St Austell bypass take B3273 for Mevagissey. At crossroads signed 'No caravans beyond this point', turn right on unclass. rd, continue through Gorran, and site on left towards Gorran Haven. A 2-acre site with 40 touring pitches.
A 30 acre nature reserve may be visited.

HAYLE

St Ives Bay Holiday Park (SW577398)
73 Loggans Rd, Upton Towans TR27 5BH
☎ 01736 752274
Signposted

★ £5-£19 £5-£19 ▲ £5-£19
Open 3 May-27 Sep (rs Etr-3 May & 27 Sep-25 Oct no entertainment, pool, food & bar service) Booking advisable Jan-Mar Last arrival 23.00hrs Last departure 09.00hrs
An excellently maintained holiday park with a relaxed atmosphere, built on sand dunes adjacent to a three-mile long beach. The touring section forms a number of separate locations in amongst the statics. Leave A30 at first Hayle rndbt towards town centre, and in .25m turn right at double rndbt signed Gwithian. Site on left. A 13-acre site with 240 touring pitches and 250 statics.
Crazy golf, video room.
See advertisement under Colour Section

Credit Cards

Higher Trevaskis Caravan Park (SW611381)
Gwinear Rd, Conner Downs TR27 5JQ ☎ 01209 831736 Signposted
►►► **Family Park** ★ £5-£9 £5-£9 ▲ £5-£9
Open mid Apr-mid Oct Booking advisable May-Sep Last arrival 20.00hrs Last departure 11.00hrs
Rural grassy park divided into sheltered paddocks, and with views towards St Ives. Fluent German and Swedish spoken. At Hayle rndbt on A30 take 1st exit signed Connor Downs, in 1m turn right signed Carnhell Green, and site is in 0.75m just past level crossing. A 6.5-acre site with 82 touring pitches.

Parbola Holiday Park (SW612366)
Wall TR27 5LE ☎ 01209 831503 Signposted
Nearby town: St Ives
►►► **Family Park** ▲
Open Etr-Oct (rs Etr-spring bank hol & Sep-Oct takeaway closed) Booking advisable Jul-Aug Last arrival 22.00hrs Last departure noon
A level grassy site in Cornish downland, with pitches in both woodland and open grassy areas. Follow old A30 to Connor Downs, turn left on unclass rd for Wall, and site in village on right. A 17.5-acre site with 110 touring pitches and 20 statics.
Crazy golf & bike hire.

Credit Cards

HELSTON

Trelowarren Chateau Park (SW721238)
Mawgan TR12 6AF ☎ 01326 221637 (3m S off B3293 to St Keverne) Signposted
►►► **Family Park** ▲
Open Apr-16 Oct Booking advisable bank hols & Jul-Aug Last departure noon
A very attractive setting in the extensive park of Trelowarren House. From Helston on A3083 turn left past Culdrose Naval Air Station on to B3293. Signed on left in 1.5m. A 20-acre site with 225 touring pitches.

HOLYWELL BAY

Trevornick Holiday Park (SW776586)
TR8 5PW ☎ 01637 830531
Signposted
Nearby town: Newquay

★ £6.40-£11 £11 ▲ £6.40-£11
Open Etr & mid May-mid Sep (limited entertainment at certain times) Booking advisable Jul-Aug Last arrival anytime Last departure 10.00hrs

contd.

A large seaside holiday complex with excellent facilities and amenities. From A3075 turn right near Rejerrah for Holywell Bay, and site on right. A 20-acre site with 450 touring pitches and 50 statics.
Fishing, golf course, entertainment.
See advertisement under NEWQUAY

Credit Cards

Holywell Bay Holiday Park (SW773582)
TR8 5PR ☎ 01637 871111 Signposted

►►►► **De-Luxe Park** £7-£12.10 £7-£12.10 ▲ £7-£12.10
Open Etr-25 Oct Booking advisable Jun-Aug Last arrival 21.00hrs Last departure 10.00hrs
Close to lovely local beaches in a rural location, this level grassy park borders on National Trust land, and is only a short distance from the Cornish Coastal Path. A 2.5-acre site with 75 touring pitches and 149 statics.

Credit Cards

INDIAN QUEENS

Gnome World Touring Park (SW890599)
Moorland Rd TR9 6HN ☎ 01726 860812 Signposted
►**Town & Country Pennant Park** ★ £4-£7 £4-£7 ▲ £4-£7
Open Etr-Oct Booking advisable Jul-Aug Last arrival 22.00hrs Last departure noon
A level grassy park set in extensive farmland. Signed from slip road at A30 and A39 rndbt at village of Indian Queens - park is on old A30, now unclassified. A 4.5-acre site with 50 touring pitches.
Nature trail.

JACOBSTOW

Edmore Tourist Park (SX187955)
Edgarrd, Wainhouse Corner EX23 0BJ ☎ 01840 230467 Signposted
Nearby town: Bude
►►► **Family Park** ★ £5-£6 £5-£6 ▲ £5-£6
Open Etr-Oct Booking advisable peak periods Last departure noon
Small, family run, rural campsite in good location, just off main A39 at Wainhouse Corner, and signed. A 3-acre site with 28 touring pitches and 2 statics.

KENNACK SANDS

Gwendreath Farm Caravan Park (SW738168)
TR12 7LZ ☎ 01326 290666
Nearby town: Helston
►►► **Family Park** ▲
Open Etr-Oct Booking advisable all times Last departure 10.00hrs
A grassy park in elevated position with extensive sea and coastal views. A short walk through woods to the beach. From Helston on A3083 turn left past Culdrose Naval Air Station on to B3293, turn right past Goonhilly earth satellite station, signed Kennack Sands. Turn left in 1m. A 5-acre site with 10 touring pitches and 30 statics.

Silver Sands Holiday Park (SW727166)
Gwendreath TR12 7LZ ☎ 01326 290631 Signposted
Nearby town: Helston
►►► **Family Park** ▲
Open May-Sep Booking advisable Jul-Aug Last arrival 22.00hrs Last departure 11.00hrs
A small, remote site adjacent to a beach and well maintained. Take A3083 from Helston, at Culdrose naval air station turn left on B3293 to Goonhilly earth station, and right at crossrds onto unclass rd. Site signed on left in 1m. A 4-acre site with 34 touring pitches and 16 statics.

KILKHAMPTON

East Thorne Caravan & Camping Park (SS260110)
EX23 9RY ☎ 01288 321618 Signposted
►►► **Family Park** ▲
Open Apr-Oct Booking advisable Last arrival 22.00hrs Last departure 11.00hrs
Small rural campsite situated adjacent to non-working farm, ideally positioned for touring Devon and Cornwall. In village centre follow B3254 Launceston road for approx .75m. A 2-acre site with 29 touring pitches and 1 static.

LANDRAKE

Dolbeare Caravan & Camping Park (SX363616)
St Ive Rd PL12 5AF ☎ 01752 851332 Signposted
Nearby town: Plymouth
►►► **Family Park** £7.50-£8.50 £7.50-£8.50 ▲ £5.50-£8.50
Open all year Booking advisable peak periods only Last arrival 23.00hrs
A mainly level grass site with trees and bushes set in meadowland. Cross Tamar Bridge, stay on A38 for 4m, turn right immed after footbridge in Landrake village, and follow site signs for .75m. A 4-acre site with 60 touring pitches.
Volley ball pitch, Boules pitch, Info Centre.

LAUNCELLS

Red Post Holiday Park (SS264052)
EX23 9NW ☎ 01288 381305 Signposted
Nearby town: Bude
►►► **Family Park** ★ £4-£7.50 £4-£7.50 £3-£6
Open 31 Mar-Oct Booking advisable Jul & Aug Last arrival 23.00hrs Last departure 11.00hrs
A basic site at rear of a country inn, midway between Bude and Holmsworthy on the A3072 at the junction with the B3254. A 4-acre site with 50 touring pitches.

LEEDSTOWN (NEAR HAYLE)

Calloose Caravan & Camping Park (SW597352)
TR27 5ET ☎ 01736 850431 Signposted
Nearby town: St Ives

►►►► **De-Luxe Park** ★ £6.50-£11 £6.50-£11 £6.50-£11
Open Apr-Sep (rs Apr-mid May & late Sep swimming pool) Booking advisable Etr, May bank hols & Jun-Aug Last arrival 22.00hrs Last departure 11.00hrs
A comprehensively equipped leisure park in a remote rural setting in a small river valley. Follow B3302 from 'Duke of Leeds' public house in town centre for 0.5m. Winner of the Best Campsite for South-West England 1996/7. A 12.5-acre site with 120 touring pitches and 17 statics.
Crazy golf, skittle alley & fishing
See advertisement under ST IVES

Credit Cards

LISKEARD

Pine Green Caravan & Camping Sitr (SX195646)
Doublebois PL14 6LE ☎ 01579 320183 & 01271 328981 Signposted
►►► **Family Park** ★ £5-£9 £5-£9 £4-£8
Open Jan-Nov Booking advisable high season Last arrival 22.00hrs Last departure noon
A well-kept terraced site in a good touring location with scenic views over surrounding countryside and Fowey River Valley. Follow A38 through Dobwalls traffic lights, and take 1st left in 0.5m; site signed. A 3-acre site with 50 touring pitches and 1 static.

LOOE

Tencreek Caravan & Camping Park (SX233525)
PL13 2JR ☎ 01503 262447 & 01831 411843 (take A387 1.75m from Looe site on left) Signposted

►►►► **De-Luxe Park** ★ £7-£11.50 £7-£11.50 £7-£11.50
contd.

Open all year Booking advisable Jul & Aug Last arrival 23.00hrs Last departure 10.00hrs

A mainly level grass site with good views. Signed off A387 W of Looe. A 14-acre site with 254 touring pitches and 62 statics.

Nightly entertainment & solarium. 45m Flume in Poo

Credit Cards

Polborder House Caravan & Camping Park (SX283557)

Bucklawren Rd, St Martins PL13 1QR ☎ 01503 240265 (2.5m E, off B3253) Signposted

►►► **Family Park** ★ £6-£8 £6-£8 £6-£8

Open Etr or Apr-Oct Booking advisable Jul-Aug Last arrival 22.00hrs Last departure noon

A very neat and well-kept small grassy site on high ground above Looe in a peaceful rural setting. Friendly and enthusiastic owners. Site signed from A387. A 3-acre site with 36 touring pitches and 5 statics.

Washing up/food preparation sinks. Off-licence.

Tregoad Farm Touring Caravan & Camping Park (SX272560)

St Martin's PL13 1PB ☎ 01503 262718 Signposted

►►► **Family Park**

Open Apr-Oct Booking advisable Jul & Aug

A terraced grassy site with fine sea and rural views, approx 1.5m from Looe. Signed with direct access from B3253, or approaching Looe from E on A387 follow B3253 for 1.75m towards Looe, and site on left. A 10-acre site with 150 touring pitches and 3 statics.

Fishing lake.

LOSTWITHIEL

Powderham Castle Tourist Park (SX083593)

PL30 5BU ☎ 01208 872277 (1.5m SW on A390 turn right at signpost Lanlivery Luxulyan) Signposted

Nearby town: Fowey

►►► **Family Park** ★ £6.70-£8.90 £6.70-£8.90 £6.70-£8.90

Open Apr-Oct Booking advisable peak periods Last arrival 22.00hrs Last departure 11.30hrs

A very quiet and well-run site in a good touring location, set in mature parkland and well screened. 1.5m SW of Lostwithiel, signed off A390 towards St Austell. A 12-acre site with 70 touring pitches and 38 statics.

Badminton, soft tennis, boat hire & paddling pool.

LUXULYAN

Croft Farm Touring Park (SX044568)

PL30 5EQ ☎ 01726 850228

Nearby town: St Austell

►►► **Family Park** ★ £5.15-£9.30 £5.15-£9.30 £5.15-£9.30

Open Apr-Oct Booking advisable Last departure noon

A peaceful, picturesque setting at the edge of a wooded valley. From A390 turn right past St Blazey level crossing signed Luxulyan, turn right at T-junc, and right again at next T-junc. From A30 turn left off Bodmin by-pass onto A391, turn left at traffic lights at Bugle onto B3374, turn left at Penwithick signed Trethurgy/Luxulyan. In 1.75m turn left at T-junc, and site on left in .5m. Do not take any other routes signed Luxulyan or Luxulyan Valley. A 5-acre site with 46 touring pitches and 6 statics.

Credit Cards

MAWGAN

See **Helston**

MAWGAN PORTH

Sun Haven Valley Caravan & Camping Site (SW861669)

TR8 4BQ ☎ 01637 860373 Signposted

Nearby town: Newquay

►►►► **De-Luxe Park** ★ £7.50-£9 £7.50-£9 £7.50-£9

Open May-Sep (rs Etr & mid Sep no laundry or disabled facilities) Booking advisable Jul-Aug Last arrival 22.00hrs Last departure 11.00hrs

An attractive site set on the side of a river valley with a camping area alongside the river. Exceptional floral landscape and very high quality facilities. Situated .75m from sea and fine sandy beach. Winner of the 1995 Campsite of the Year Award for the South West. From B3276 at Mawgan Porth take unclass rd up Vale of Lanherne for 1m. Site on left. A 5-acre site with 118 touring pitches and 36 statics.

See advertisement on page 74

Credit Cards

Trevarrian Holiday Park (SW853661)

TR8 4AQ ☎ 01637 860381 Signposted

Nearby town: Newquay

►►► **Family Park**

Open Etr-Sep Booking advisable Jun-Aug Last arrival 22.00hrs Last departure 11.00hrs

A well-established and well-run holiday park overlooking Mawgan Porth beach. From A39 at St Columb rndbt turn right onto A3059 towards Newquay. Fork left in approx 2m for St Mawgan to join B3276 coast road. Turn right and site on left. A 7-acre site with 185 touring pitches.

contd.

Sports field & pitch n putt.

MEVAGISSEY

See **Gorran, Boswinger & Pentewan**

MULLION

Mullion Holiday Park (SW699182)
Lizard Peninsula, A3083 TR12 7LJ
☎ 01326 240000 & 240428

Signposted
Nearby town: Helston

Open Etr & May-Sep Booking advisable Jul-Aug Last arrival 21.00hrs Last departure noon

A comprehensively equipped leisure park geared mainly for self-catering holidays, set in rugged moorland on the Lizard peninsula, adjacent to A3083 Helston road. A 10-acre site with 150 touring pitches and 347 statics.
Adventure playgrounds, sandpit, amusement & arcade.

See advertisement on page 73

Credit Cards

'Franchis' Holiday Park (SW698203)
Cury Cross Lanes TR12 7AZ ☎ 01326 240301 Signposted
Nearby town: Helston
►►► **Family Park** ★ £6.50-£7.50 £6.50-£7.50 £6.50-£7.50
Open Wed before Etr-Sep (rs low season shop open on request) Booking advisable end Jul-Aug Last arrival 22.00hrs Last departure noon
This site is surrounded by hedges and coppices situated on the A3083 between Helston and The Lizard, an ideal position for exploring the Peninsula. A 4-acre site with 70 touring pitches and 12 statics.
Dive air to 3500 P.S.I. Dishwashing, Licensed shop

Criggan Mill (SW670179)
Mullion Cove TR12 7EU ☎ 01326 240496
Nearby town: Helston
►**Town & Country Pennant Park** ★ £6.50-£8.50 £6.50-£8.50 £6.50-£8.50
Open Apr-Oct Booking advisable Jul-Aug Last arrival 22.00hrs Last departure 10.00hrs
A secluded site with level pitches in a combe near to Mullion Cove. From the A3083 Helston road take B3296 to Mullion. A 1-acre site with 10 touring pitches and 30 statics.

Credit Cards

NEWQUAY

Hendra Holiday Park (SW833601)
TR8 4NY ☎ 01637 875778 (2m SE)
Signposted

Open Etr or Apr-Oct (rs Apr-Spring bank hol) Booking advisable Jul-Aug Last arrival dusk Last departure noon
A large, long-established complex with mature trees and bushes set in downland, with superb leisure facilities. Situated 2m SE of Newquay, off Lane-Quintrel Down road. A 46-acre site with 600 touring pitches and 160 statics.
Solarium, fish bar, sauna & kids club.
See advertisement on page 75.

Credit Cards

Newquay Holiday Park (SW853626)
TR8 4HS ☎ 01637 871111 (on A3059)
Signposted

★ £7-£11.80 £7-£11.80 £7-£11.80
Open 13 May-15 Sep Booking advisable Jun-Aug Last arrival 21.00hrs Last departure 10.00hrs

contd.

EXCELLENT
AA
ROSE AWARD

A well-managed and maintained site with a wide range of indoor and outdoor activities. Signed on B3059, 3m E of Newquay. A 14-acre site with 259 touring pitches and 124 statics.

Snooker/Pool tables,9hole pitch & putt, crazy golf.

See advertisement on page 77.

Credit Cards

Roseclistion Park (SW815594)

Trevemper TR8 5JT ☎ 01637 830326 (2m S on A3075) Signposted

►►►► De-Luxe Park ★ £6.60-£10 £6.60-£10 £6.60-£10

Open Whit-Oct Booking advisable Jul-Aug Last arrival 22.00hrs Last departure 14.00hrs

Small, well-organised site with attractively arranged pitches. From N on A3075 signed Redruth. On left in .5m. An 8-acre site with 130 touring pitches.

Sauna & solarium.

Credit Cards

Trencreek Holiday Park (SW828609)

Higher Trencreek TR8 4NS ☎ 01637 874210 (A392 to Quintrell Downs, turn right in direction of Newquay, turn left at 2 mini rdbts into Trevenson rd to Trencreek) Signposted

►►►► De-Luxe Park ★ £6.50-£9.90 £6.50-£9.90 £6.50-£9.90

Open Whit-mid Sep (rs Etr, Apr-May & late Sep swimming pool, cafe & bar closed) Booking advisable Jul-Aug Last arrival 22.00hrs Last departure noon

Slightly sloping grassy site with excellent facilities, set in meadowland in the village of Trencreek, 1.5m from Newquay town centre. A 10-acre site with 194 touring pitches and 6 statics.

Coarse fishing on site.

Gwills Holiday Park (SW829592)

Ln TR8 4PE ☎ 01637 873617 (2m SE) Signposted

►►► Family Park ★ £5.20-£9 £4.60-£8 £5.20-£9

Open Etr-Oct (rs Etr-Whitsun takeaway closed) Booking advisable Jul-Aug Last arrival 21.00hrs Last departure 10.00hrs

A lightly wooded, riverside site with level and sloping pitches. From A30 turn R at Indian Queens to A392 then follow unclass road between Lane and Newlyn East. An 11-acre site with 140 touring pitches and 30 statics.

Fishing.

Credit Cards

Porth Beach Tourist Park (SW834629)

Porth TR7 3NH ☎ 01637 876531 (1m NE) Signposted

►►► Family Park ★ £4.20-£22.65 £4.20-£22.65 £4.20-£22.65

Open Apr-Oct Booking advisable Jul-Aug Last arrival 21.00hrs Last departure 10.00hrs

A well-run site set in meadowland adjacent to sea and a fine sandy beach. Off B3276. A 6-acre site with 200 touring pitches and 12 statics.

Credit Cards

Trebellan Park (SW790571)

Cubert TR8 5PY ☎ 01637 830522

►►► Family Park

Open Etr-Oct

A terraced grassy rural park within a picturesque valley with views of Cubert Common, and adjacent to the Smuggler's Den, a 16th-century thatched inn. 4m S of Newquay, turn W off A3075 at Cubert signpost, and turn

contd.

left in .75m onto unclass minor rd. An 8-acre site with 150 touring pitches.
Three well stocked coarse fishing lakes.

Treloy Tourist Park (SW858625)
TR8 4JN ☎ 01637 872063 & 876279 (just off A3059) Signposted
►►► **Family Park** ★ £5-£9 £5-£9 ▲ £5-£9
Open Apr-Oct (rs Apr swimming pool & bar closed) Booking advisable Jul-Aug Last arrival mdnt Last departure 11.00hrs
Attractive site with fine countryside views, within easy reach of resorts and beaches. From A3058 take A3059, and site signed on left. A 12-acre site with 119 touring pitches.
Golf, entertainment, childs club, fishing nearby.

Credit Cards

Trenance Caravan & Chalet Park (SW818612)
Edgcumbe Av TR7 2JY ☎ 01637 873447 Signposted
►►► **Family Park** ★ £6-£10 £6-£10 ▲ £6-£10
Open 26 May-Oct (rs Apr-25 May no showers or take-away restaurant) Booking advisable Jul-Aug Last arrival 22.00hrs Last departure 10.00hrs
Principally a static park with a small, upgraded touring area on high ground, set within the urban confines of Newquay. Off A3075 near viaduct. Entrance by boating lake rndbt. A 2-acre site with 50 touring pitches and 190 statics.
Hairdressing salon, dishwashing facilities.

Credit Cards

Trethiggey Touring Park (SW846596)
Quintrell Downs TR8 4LG ☎ 01637 877672 (2m SE A392) Signposted
►►► **Family Park** ★ £5.95-£8.45 £5-£7.50 ▲ £5.95-£8.45
Open Mar-Dec Booking advisable Jul-Aug
A pleasant, improving site divided into paddocks with maturing trees and shrubs. On the A3058 3m from Newquay. A 15-acre site with 120 touring pitches and 12 statics.
Off licence & dishwashing sinks, recreation field.

Credit Cards

NOTTER BRIDGE

Notter Bridge Caravan & Camping Park (SX384608)
PL12 4RW ☎ 01752 842318 Signposted
Nearby town: Plymouth
►►► **Family Park** ▲

Open Apr-Oct Booking advisable peak periods Last arrival 23.00hrs Last departure 11.00hrs

Small, level grassy riverside site in wooded Lynner Valley, adjacent to A38, 2m W of Saltash. Fishing licences available. A 5-acre site with 55 touring pitches and 20 statics.

Salmon & trout fishing, canoeing.

OTTERHAM

St Tinney Farm Holidays (SX169906)

PL32 PTA ☎ 01840 261274 (1m off A39) Signposted

►►► **Family Park** ★ £4-£7.50 £4-£7.50 £4-£7.50

Open all year Booking advisable Spring bank hol & Jul-Aug Last arrival 21.00hrs Last departure 11.00hrs

A family-run farm site in a rural area, with nature trails, lakes, valleys and complete seclusion. Take unclass rd off A39 signed Otterham, and site signed. A 5-acre site with 20 touring pitches and 9 statics.

Coarse fishing, horse & donkey rides, farm animals

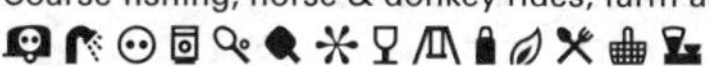

PADSTOW

Dennis Cove Camping (SW918743)

Dennis Farm, Dennis Cove PL28 8DR ☎ 01841 532349 Signposted

►►► **Family Park**

Open Whitsun-Sep (rs Etr-Whitsun & Sep onwards

contd.

swimming pool & club closed) Booking advisable before Jun Last arrival 23.00hrs Last departure noon
Level and slightly sloping site with mature trees set in meadowland, overlooking Padstow Bay with access to River Camel estuary and Padstow Bay beach. Approach Padstow on A389 and turn right into Sarah's Lane. A 4.5-acre site with 63 touring pitches.

Trerethern Touring Park (SW913738)
PL28 8LE ☎ 01841 532061 (on A389 1m SSW town) Signposted
►►► **Family Park** ★ £5.60-£8.50 £5.60-£8.50 ▲ £5.60-£8.50
Open Apr-mid Oct Booking advisable Jul-Aug Last arrival 19.00hrs Last departure 16.00hrs
A rather open site situated 2m S of Padstow on eastern side of A389 Padstow-Wadebridge road. A 13.5-acre site with 90 touring pitches.
Motorvan hardstanding, electric & pumpout.

PELYNT

Camping Caradon (SX218539)
Trelawne PL13 2NA ☎ 01503 272388 Signposted
Nearby town: Looe
►►► **Family Park** ★ £5-£8.50 £5-£8 ▲ £5-£8.50
Open Etr-Oct Booking advisable Jul-Aug Last arrival 20.00hrs Last departure 11.00hrs
Established residential site with a level grass touring park in rural setting. Off B3359, between Looe and Polperro. A 4-acre site with 85 touring pitches and 1 static.
See advertisement under POLPERRO

Trelay Farmpark (SX219545)
PL13 2JX ☎ 01503 220900 & 220993 (on B3359 towards Pelynt, 1m on right) Signposted
Nearby town: Liskeard
►►► **Family Park** £7-£8.50 £7-£8.50 ▲ £7-£8.50
Open Apr-Oct Booking advisable Jul & Aug Last arrival 21.00hrs
A slightly sloping, grass site in a rural area with extensive views. Signed off B3359, .5m S of Pelynt (on the Looe side). 3m from Looe and Polperro. A 3-acre site with 55 touring pitches and 20 statics.

PENTEWAN

Sun Valley Holiday Park (SX005486)
Pentewan Rd PL26 6DJ ☎ 01726 843266 Signposted
Nearby town: St Austell

►►►►► **Premier Park** ★ £7-£18 £7-£18 ▲ £7-£18
Open Apr (or Etr if earlier)-Oct Booking advisable May-Sep Last arrival 23.00hrs Last departure noon
A mainly static park in a woodland setting with a neat and well-maintained touring park. Sanitary facilities are outstanding. Situated 1m from sea, beach and river on B3273 St Austell-Mevagissey road. A 4-acre site with 22 touring pitches and 75 statics.

Credit Cards

Penhaven Touring Park (SX008481)
PL26 6DL ☎ 01726 843687 Signposted
Nearby town: St Austell
►►► **Family Park** ★ £7.50-£16 £7.50-£16 ▲ £7.50-£16
Open Etr or Apr-Oct Booking advisable public hols & end Jul-Aug Last arrival 22.00hrs Last departure 10.00hrs
Level, landscaped site in wooded valley, with river running by and 1m from sandy beach at Pentewan. Situated on B3273. A 13-acre site with 105 touring pitches.
Off-licence.

Credit Cards

Pentewan Sands Holiday Park (SX018468)
PL26 6BT ☎ 01726 843485 Signposted
Nearby town: Mevagissey
►►► **Family Park** ★ £5.60-£14 £5.60-£14 ▲ £5.60-£14
Open 21 Mar-1 Nov (rs 5 Apr-20 May & 16 Sep-Oct shop, snacks, pool, clubhouse ltd or closed) Booking advisable Jul-Aug Last arrival 22.00hrs Last departure 10.30hrs
A large camping site on the dunes adjacent to a private beach, well equipped for aquatic activities. 4m S of St Austell on B3273. A 32-acre site with 480 touring pitches and 105 statics.
Mini golf, cycle hire, boat launching, water sports.

Credit Cards

PENZANCE

Bone Valley Caravan Park (SW472316)
Heamoor TR20 8UJ ☎ 01736 60313 due to change to 360313 Signposted
►►► **Family Park** ★ £8-£9 £7-£8 ▲ £8-£9
Open Mar-7 Jan (rs Oct-Dec & Mar shop closed) Booking advisable Jul-Aug Last arrival 22.00hrs Last departure 11.00hrs
A compact grassy riverside site on the outskirts of Penzance, with well maintained facilities. Follow A30 to west Penzance and signs to Heamoor. At 1st crossroads

turn right, then 1st left; signed. A 1-acre site with 17 touring pitches and 1 static.

PERRANARWORTHAL

Cosawes Caravan Park (SW768376)
TR3 7QS ☎ 01872 863724 & 863717 Signposted
Nearby town: Truro
►►► **Family Park** ★ £7.50-£9.50 fr £7 ▲ £6-£8
Open all year Booking advisable mid Jul-mid Aug
A small touring park in a peaceful wooded valley, midway between Truro and Falmouth. 6m W of Truro on A39. A 2-acre site with 40 touring pitches and 100 statics.
Squash court.

PERRANPORTH

Perranporth Camping & Touring Site (SW768542)
Budnick Rd TR6 0DB
☎ 01872 572174 Signposted

►►►► **De-Luxe Park** ★ £8-£11 £8-£11
▲ £8-£11
Open Whit-Sep (rs Etr-Whitsun & mid Sep-end Sep shop & club facilities) Booking advisable Jul-Aug Last arrival 23.00hrs Last departure noon

contd.

A mainly tenting site with few level pitches but adjacent to a fine sandy beach. .5m E off B3285. A 6-acre site with 180 touring pitches and 9 statics.

Credit Cards

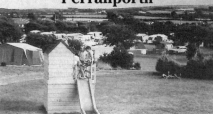

POLPERRO

Killigarth Manor Holiday Estate (SX214519)
PL13 2JQ ☎ 01503 272216 & 272409
Signposted
Nearby town: Looe

★ £8.40-£11.60 fr £8.20 fr £8.40
Open Etr-Oct Booking advisable 3rd wk Jul-Aug Last arrival 20.00hrs Last departure noon

A well-ordered site on high ground on the approach to a historic fishing village on the A 387. A large touring and holiday complex with many amenities and facilities. A 7-acre site with 202 touring pitches and 147 statics.
Amusement arcade, pool table & table tennis.

Credit Cards

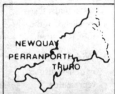

POLRUAN

Polruan Holiday Centre (SX133509)
Polruan-by-Fowey PL23 1QH ☎ 01726 870263
Signposted
Nearby town: Looe
►►► **Family Park** £5.50-£8.50 £5.50-£8.50
£4-£8.50
Open Etr-Sep Booking advisable Jul, Aug & bank hols
Last arrival 21.00hrs Last departure noon
A very rural and quiet site in a lovely elevated position above the village, with good views. River Fowey passenger ferry close by. Leave A390 at East Taphouse and turn left onto B3359 after 4m. Turn right onto unclass rd signed Polruan, and site signed. A 3-acre site with 32 touring pitches and 11 statics.
Tourist information.

POLZEATH

South Winds Caravan & Camping Park (SW948790)
Polzeath Rd PL27 6QU ☎ 01208 863267 & 862646
Signposted
Nearby town: Wadebridge
►►► **Family Park** ★ £8-£15 £8-£15 £6-£15
Open Mar-Oct Booking advisable Jul & Aug Last arrival 23.00hrs Last departure 11.00hrs
A peaceful site with beautiful sea and panoramic rural views, within walking distance of new golf complex, and 0.75m from beach and village. Leave B3314 on unclassified road signed Polzeath, and park is on right just past turn to New Polzeath. A 6-acre site with 50 touring pitches.
Credit Cards

Tristram Caravan Park (SW936790)
PL27 6SR ☎ 01208 862215 & 863267 Signposted
Nearby town: Wadebridge
►►► **Family Park** ★ £10-£20 £10-£20 £8-£15
Open Mar-Oct Booking advisable Jul & Aug Last arrival 23.00hrs Last departure 10.00hrs
An ideal family site, positioned on a gently-sloping cliff with grassy pitches and glorious sea views. Direct gated access to the beach, where surfing is very popular. From B3314 take unclassified road signed Polzeath, go through the village and up the hill, and site is 2nd turning on right. A 10-acre site with 100 touring pitches.
Credit Cards

PORTHTOWAN

Porthtowan Tourist Park (SW693473)
Mile Hill TR4 8TY ☎ 01209 890256 Signposted
Nearby town: Redruth
►►► **Family Park** ★ £5-£8.50 £5-£8.50
£5-£8.50
Open Etr-Oct Booking advisable Jul-Aug Last departure noon *contd.*

A neat, level grassy site on high ground above Porthtowan, with maturing landscape providing shelter from winds. Leave A30 at Redruth onto unclass rd signed Portreath, and in 3m at T junc turn right for Porthtowan. Site on left. A 5.5-acre site with 50 touring pitches.

Rose Hill Park (SW693466)
Rose Hill TR4 8AR ☎ 01209 890802
Nearby town: St Agnes
►►► **Family Park**
Open end Mar-end Oct Booking advisable Jun-Aug Last arrival 22.00hrs Last departure 11.00hrs
A small, well-kept park in an attractive position, set into the hillside and terraced. Site at bottom of descent to port. A 2.5-acre site with 40 touring pitches.
Tourist information.
See advertisement on page 84

REDRUTH

Cambrose Touring Park (SW684453)
Portreath Rd TR16 4HT ☎ 01209 890747 (take B3300 towards Portreath pass Gold Centre on left 1st rd on rght (Porthtowan Rd). Entrance to site 100yds on left)
Signposted
Nearby town: Portreath
►►► **Family Park** ★ £7-£9 £7-£9 £7-£9
Open Apr-Oct Booking advisable Jul-Aug Last arrival 22.00hrs Last departure 11.30hrs
A mature park in a rural setting with trees and bushes. 2m from Redruth off B3300 (signposted 'Porthtowan and Portreath' from A30). A 6-acre site with 60 touring pitches.

Lanyon Park (SW684387)
Loscombe Ln, Four Lanes TR16 6LP ☎ 01209 313474
►►► **Family Park**
Open mid Feb-mid Jan
Small, friendly rural park in elevated position with fine views to distant St Ives Bay. Signed 0.5m off B2397 on Helston side of Four Lanes village. A 10-acre site with 25 touring pitches and 49 statics.

REJERRAH

Monkey Tree Touring Park (SW803545)
TR8 5QL ☎ 01872 572032 Signposted
Nearby town: Newquay

►►►► **De-Luxe Park**
Open all year (rs Apr swimming pool weather permitting, shop) Booking advisable main season Last arrival 22.00hrs Last departure from 10.00
A quiet, open moorland setting, well-screened by mature hedges on high ground near the N Cornwall coast. Access from Rejerrah-Zelah road off A3075. A 12-acre site with 295 touring pitches and 6 statics.
Sauna, solarium, mountain bike hire & football pitch
See advertisement in Colour Section

Credit Cards

Newperran Tourist Park (SW801555)
TR8 5QJ ☎ 01872 572407 in season & 01637 830308
Signposted Nearby town: Newquay

►►►► **De-Luxe Park**
Open mid May-mid Sep Booking advisable Jul-Aug
A very good family site in a lovely rural position, central for several beaches and bays. In an airy location, but with some screening from wind. 4m SE of Newquay and 1m S of Rejerrah on A3075. A 25-acre site with 270 touring pitches.
Crazy golf, adventure playground, pool & badminton.
See advertisement on page 81

Credit Cards

RELUBBUS

River Valley Caravan Park (SW565326)
TR20 9ER ☎ 01736 763398 (from A30 signpost Helston A394, next rbdt 1st left signposted Relubbus)
Signposted Nearby town: St Ives

►►►► **De-Luxe Park** ★ £8.50-£10 £8.50-£10 £8.50-£10
Open Mar-5 Jan (rs Nov-4 Jan hardstanding only, restricted facilities) Booking advisable Jul-Aug Last arrival 20.00hrs Last departure 11.00hrs
A quiet, attractive, family-run site of quality in a picturesque river valley with direct access to shallow trout stream. Situated 4m from N and S coast sandy beaches, 3m from Marazion on B3280. An 18-acre site with 90 touring pitches and 15 statics.
Washing up sinks, fishing.
See advertisement under Colour Section

Credit Cards

ROSUDGEON

Kenneggy Cove Holiday Park (SW562287)
Higher Kenneggy TR20 9AU ☎ 01736 763453
Signposted
Nearby town: Penzance
►►► **Family Park** ★ £4.30-£7.50 £4.30-£7.50 £4.30-£7.50

Open Apr-Nov Booking advisable Jul-Aug Last arrival 21.00hrs Last departure 11.00hrs

An attractive and neatly-kept site within a short walk of a sheltered, sandy beach and with lovely sea views. 6m W of Helston and 6m E of Penzance off A394, overlooking Mount's Bay. A 4-acre site with 60 touring pitches and 9 statics.

RUTHERNBRIDGE

Ruthern Valley Holidays (SX014665)

PL30 5LU ☎ 01208 831395 Signposted

Nearby town: Bodmin

►►► **Family Park**

Open Apr-Oct Booking advisable high season Last arrival 21.00hrs Last departure noon

An attractive woodland site in remote, small river valley S of Bodmin Moor. From A30 just past W end of Bodmin bypass, site signed on right on unclass rd to Ruthernbridge. A 2-acre site with 29 touring pitches and 6 statics.

Off-licence.

ST AGNES

Beacon Cottage Farm Touring Park (SW705502)

Beacon Dr TR5 0NU ☎ 01872 552347 (left after St Agnes museum & follow signs)

Nearby town: Truro

►►► **Family Park** £5-£12 £5-£12 £5-£12

Open end May-Oct (rs Etr-Whitsun shop closed) Booking advisable Jul-Aug Last arrival 20.00hrs Last departure noon

A neat and compact site utilizing a cottage and outhouses, an old orchard and adjoining walled paddock. Unique location on a headland looking NE along the coast. From A30 at Threeburrows rndbt take B3277 to St Agnes, then Beacon Rd left. A 4-acre site with 50 touring pitches and 1 static.

ST AUSTELL

Trencreek Farm Holiday Park (SW966485)

Hewas Water PL26 7JG ☎ 01726 882540 Signposted

►►► **Family Park**

Open Spring bank hol-13 Sep (rs Etr-Spring bank hol & 14 Sep-Oct restricted shop hours & pool closed) Booking advisable Jul-Aug Last arrival 21.00hrs Last departure noon

A working farm site with mature trees and bushes, close to river and lake. Off B3287, 1m from junction with A390. An 8-acre site with 140 touring pitches and 37 statics.

Fishing, fitness & agility course & mini golf.

Credit Cards

Trewhiddle Holiday Estate (SX005512)

Trewhiddle PL26 7AD ☎ 01726 67011 Signposted

►►► **Family Park** ★ £6-£11 £6-£11 £6-£11

Open all year Booking advisable

Secluded wooded site with well-kept gardens, lawns and flower beds, set in the grounds of a mature estate, and with country club facilities. From St Austell rndbt on A390 take B3273 towards Mevagissey, and site on right in 0.75m. A 10.5-acre site with 105 touring pitches and 74 statics.

Credit Cards

ST BURYAN

Camping & Caravanning Club Site (SW378276)

Higher Tregiffian Farm TR19 6JB ☎ 01736 871588 (in season) & 01203 694995 (off B3306) Signposted

Nearby town: Penzance

►►► **Family Park** ★ £8.10-£10.30 £8.10-£10.30 £8.10-£10.30

Open end Mar-Sep Booking advisable bank hols & Jul-Aug Last arrival 21.00hrs Last departure noon

A level grassy park in a rural area with distant views of Carn Brae and the coast, situated just 2m from Land's End. Follow A30 from Penzance to Land's End, and site is signed off B3306 (St Just Airport road). Please see the advertisement on page 27 for details of Club Members' benefits. A 4-acre site with 75 touring pitches.

Credit Cards

Cardinney Caravan & Camping Park (SW401278)
Crows an Wra, Main A30 TR19 6HX ☎ 01736 810880 Signposted
►►► **Family Park**
Open Etr-Oct Booking advisable Jul & Aug Last departure noon
A pleasant grassy park set in farmland with an open aspect, midway between Penzance and Land' End. Site has direct access from A30, 4m from Penzance. A 4.5-acre site with 105 touring pitches and 2 statics.
See advertisement under PENZANCE

Lower Treave Caravan Park (SW388272)
Crows-an-Wra TR19 6HZ ☎ 01736 810559 Signposted
Nearby town: Penzance
►►► **Family Park** £6-£8 £6-£8 £6-£8
Open Apr-Oct Booking advisable Jul-Aug Last arrival 22.30hrs Last departure noon
Terraced, grass site with trees and bushes, set in meadowland, 4m NE of Land's End off A30. A 5-acre site with 80 touring pitches and 5 statics.
See advertisement under PENZANCE

Tower Park Caravans & Camping (SW406263)
TR19 6BZ ☎ 01736 810286 Signposted
Nearby town: Penzance
►►► **Family Park** £6-£8 £6-£8 £5-£8
Open Mar-Oct (rs Mar-Whitsun shop & cafe closed) Booking advisable Jul-Aug Last arrival 22.00hrs Last departure noon
A rural site sheltered by mature trees, and close to village amenities, near Land's End and 4m from Sennen Cove and Porthcurno. Off A30 and B3283. A 6-acre site with 102 touring pitches and 5 statics.

Treverven Touring Caravan & Camping Site (SW410237)
Treverven Farm TR19 6DL ☎ 01736 810221 (on B3315) Signposted
Nearby town: Penzance
►►► **Family Park** ★ £6-£9.50 £6-£9.50 £6-£9.50
Open Etr-Oct Booking advisable Jul-Aug Last departure noon
An isolated but well-maintained farm site set off B3315 with panoramic views and in sight of the sea. A 6-acre site with 115 touring pitches.

The AA pennant classification has been revised for 1998. Please read the explanation of the scheme on page 10.

ST COLUMB MAJOR

Southleigh Manor Tourist Park (SW918623)
TR9 6HY ☎ 01637 880938 Signposted
►►► **Family Park** ★ £10-£11.30 £10-£11.30 £10-£11.30
Open mid Apr-mid Sep Booking advisable Jul & Aug Last arrival 20.00hrs Last departure noon
A very well maintained naturist park in the heart of the Cornish countryside, catering for families and couples only. Seclusion and security are very well planned, and the lovely gardens provide a calm setting. Leave A30 at sign to RAF St Mawgan and St Columb onto A3059, and park 3m on left. A 2.5-acre site with 50 touring pitches.
Sauna, Spa bath & croquet lawn.

ST DAY

Tresaddern Holiday Park (SW733422)
TR16 5JR ☎ 01209 820459 Signposted
Nearby town: Redruth
►►► **Family Park** ★ £5-£6 £5-£6 £5-£6
Open Etr & Apr-Oct Booking advisable Jul-Aug
A very friendly park in a good location. 2m NE of Redruth on B3298. A 2-acre site with 15 touring pitches and 17 statics.

ST GENNYS

Camping & Caravanning Club Site (SX176943)
Gillards Moor EX23 0BG ☎ 01840 230650 (in season) & 01203 694995 Signposted
Nearby town: Bude
►►► **Family Park** ★ £8.70-£11.30 £8.70-£11.30 £8.70-£11.30
Open end Mar-Sep Booking advisable bank hols & Jul-Aug Last arrival 21.00hrs Last departure noon
A well-kept, level grass site with good quality facilities. Signed off A39 1m S of Wainhouse Corner. Please see the advertisement on page 27 for details of Club Members' benefits. A 6-acre site with 100 touring pitches.
Credit Cards

ST HILARY

Wayfarers Caravan & Camping Park (SW558314)
Relebbus Ln TR20 9EF ☎ 01736 763326 (on B3280) Signposted
►►► **Family Park** ★ £6-£8 £6-£8 £6-£8
Open Etr/Mar-Oct Booking advisable Jul & Aug Last arrival 23.00hrs Last departure noon
A quiet family park in a peaceful rural setting within 2.5m of St Michael's Mount. Turn left off A30 onto A394 towards Helston, turn left at rndbt onto B3280 in 2 miles, and site is 1.5miles on left. A 4.75-acre site with 54 touring pitches and 6 statics.

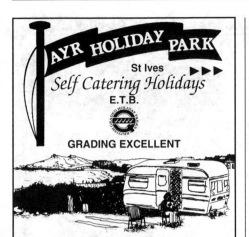

ST ISSEY

Trewince Farm Holiday Park (SW937715)
PL27 7RL ☎ 01208 812830 Signposted
Nearby town: Wadebridge

►►►► **De-Luxe Park**
Open Etr-Oct Booking advisable anytime Last departure 11.00hrs
A family-owned park run to high standards amongst rolling farmland close to the coast. From Wadebridge on A39 towards St Columb take A389 signed Padstow, and site on left in 2m. A 6-acre site with 120 touring pitches and 35 statics.
Crazy golf, farm rides in summer, near Camel trail

Credit Cards

ST IVES

Polmanter Tourist Park (SW510388)
Halsetown TR26 3LX ☎ 01736 795640 (on holiday route into St Ives B3311) Signposted

►►►► **De-Luxe Park** ★ £6.50-£13 £6.50-£13 £6.50-£13
Open Whit-10 Sep (rs Etr-Whit & 12 Sep-Oct shop, pool, bar & takeaway food closed) Booking advisable Jul-Aug Last arrival 21.00hrs Last departure 10.00hrs
A well-developed touring park on high ground, with distant views of the sea in St Ives Bay. Signed off B3311 at Halestown. A 13-acre site with 240 touring pitches.
Putting, sports field, two family shower rooms.

Credit Cards

Ayr Holiday Park (SW509408)
TR26 1EJ ☎ 01736 795855 Signposted
►►► **Family Park**
Open Apr-Oct (rs Apr-mid May & Oct shop closed) Booking advisable Jul-Aug Last arrival 22.00hrs Last departure 10.00hrs
A well-established park on a cliffside overlooking St Ives Bay. From town centre follow Penzance signs , turn right at 1st rndbt, and left at T junc. Signed ahead. A 2-acre site with 40 touring pitches and 43 statics.

Credit Cards

Trevalgan Family Camping Park (SW490402)
Trevalgan TR26 3BJ ☎ 01736 796433 Signposted
►►► **Family Park** £6-£10 £6-£10 £6-£10
Open May-Sep Booking advisable mid Jul-mid Aug Last arrival 23.30hrs Last departure noon
An open, level grass site on a working farm with very good facilities. From St Ives take B3306; site signed on right. A 4.75-acre site with 120 touring pitches.
Farm trail, pets corner.

Credit Cards

ST JUST (NEAR LAND'S END)

Kelynack Caravan & Camping Park (SW374301)
TR19 7RE ☎ 01736 787633 Signposted
Nearby town: Penzance
►►► **Family Park** £5 £5 £5
Open Apr-Oct Booking advisable Jul-Aug Last arrival 22.00hrs Last departure noon
A small, secluded site in the grounds of an old walled garden, surrounded by open countryside. 1m from town on B3306 Land's End road. A 2-acre site with 20 touring pitches and 13 statics.
Wash-up room.

Bosavern House Caravan Park (SW370305)
TR19 7RD ☎ 01736 788301 Signposted
Nearby town: Penzance
Town & Country Pennant Park ★ £5.50-£7.50 £5.50-£7.50
Open Mar-Oct Booking advisable Jul-Aug Last arrival 22.00hrs Last departure 14.00hrs
A small, neat site in a walled garden behind a guest house. Turn off A3071 near St Just onto B3306 Land's End Rd, and park on left in 0.5m. A 2-acre site with 12 touring pitches.

Credit Cards

Roselands Caravan Park (SW387305)
Dowran TR19 7RS
☎ 01736 788571 (1.25m E on unclass rd, off A3071) Signposted
Nearby town: Penzance
Town & Country Pennant Park ★ £5-£7 £5-£7 £5-£7
Open Feb-Oct (rs Jan & Oct) Booking advisable Jun-Sep Last arrival 23.00hrs Last departure noon
A small site in an isolated rural setting with well-kept facilities and friendly owners. A 2-acre site with 12 touring pitches and 15 statics.

ST JUST-IN-ROSELAND

Trethem Mill Touring Park (SW860365)
TR2 5JF ☎ 01872 580504 Signposted
Family Park ★ £6-£9 £6-£9 £6-£9
Open Apr-Oct Booking advisable Jul-Aug Last arrival 22.00hrs Last departure 11.00hrs
A carefully tended and sheltered park in a rural setting. Take A3078 for St Mawes, and site signed on right 3m N of St Mawes. A 4-acre site with 80 touring pitches.
Mountain bike hire & info centre.

Credit Cards

ST MABYN

Glenmorris Park (SX058733)
Glenmorris PL30 3BY ☎ 01208 841677
Signposted
Nearby town: Bodmin
Family Park ★ £5-£7 £5-£7 £5-£7
Open Etr-Oct Booking advisable bank hols & Jul-Aug Last arrival 10.00hrs Last departure 13.00hrs
A very good park in a peaceful rural setting. Signed on unclass. road off B3266 towards St Mabyn Village at Longsshore. A 10-acre site with 80 touring pitches and 80 statics.

Credit Cards

ST MERRYN (NEAR PADSTOW)

Carnevas Farm Holiday Park (SW862728)
Carnevas Farm PL28 8PN ☎ 01841 520230 & 521209 (take B3276 towards Porthlothan Bay, 2m) Signposted
Nearby town: Padstow
►►► **Family Park** ★ £5-£8.25 £5-£8.25 £5-£8.25
Open Apr-Oct (rs Apr-Whit & mid Sep-Oct shop closed) Booking advisable Jul-Aug
A rather open site in a rural setting near the North coast. Off B3276 Padstow-Newquay road 2m SW of village. An 8-acre site with 195 touring pitches and 14 statics.

Tregavone Touring Park (SW898732)
Tregavone Farm PL28 8JZ
☎ 01841 520148 (1m off A389)
Nearby town: Padstow
► **Town & Country Pennant Park** ★ £5-£6 £5-£6 £5-£6
Open Mar-Oct Booking advisable end Jul-beg Aug
A working farm site with better than average facilities. The very well converted farm buildings look purpose built. Situated .5 mile off A389 on unclass rd to church. A 3-acre site with 40 touring pitches.

Trevean Caravan & Camping Park (SW875724)
Trevean Ln PL28 8PR ☎ 01841 520772
Signposted
Nearby town: Padstow
► **Town & Country Pennant Park** ★ £5.50 £5.50 £5.50
Open Apr-Oct Booking advisable mid Jul-Aug Last arrival 22.30hrs Last departure noon
A small working farm site with level grassy pitches in rather open countryside. Signed on left off B3276, 1.5m S of St Merryn. A 1.5-acre site with 36 touring pitches and 3 statics.

ST MINVER

Gunvenna Touring Caravan & Camping Park (SW969782)
PL27 6QN ☎ 01208 862405
►►► **Family Park**
Open Apr-Oct Booking advisable Jul-Aug Last arrival mdnt Last departure 11.00hrs
Attractive site offering good facilities located 4m NE of Wadebridge on the B3314. Ideal position for touring North Cornwall. A 10-acre site with 75 touring pitches.
Swimming lessons.

St Minver Holiday Park (SW965772)
PL27 6RR ☎ 01208 862305 Signposted
Nearby town: Wadebridge
►►► **Family Park**
Open Etr-5 Oct Booking advisable Jul-Sep Last arrival mdnt Last departure 10.00hrs
A large, mainly static holiday park set around St Minver House in sylvan surroundings. From A39 N of Wadebridge take Port Isaac rd B3314; site signed on left in 3m. A 5-acre site with 120 touring pitches and 99 statics.
Crazy golf, free evening entertainment, amusements.

Credit Cards

SCILLY, ISLES

(No map) No sites on the island hold AA classification. See Island Camping on page 13

SCORRIER

Wheal Rose Caravan & Camping Park (SW717449)
TR16 5DD ☎ 01209 891496 Signposted
►►► **Family Park** ★ £6-£9 £6-£9 £6-£9
Open Mar-Oct/Nov Booking advisable Aug
A quiet, peaceful park in secluded valley setting, central for beaches and countryside. Leave A30 dual carriageway signed Scorrier, follow signs on unclass rd to Wheal Rose, and park in 0.5m on left. A 4-acre site with 50 touring pitches.

TINTAGEL

See **Camelford**

TORPOINT

Whitsand Bay Holiday Park (SX410515)
Millbrook PL10 1JZ ☎ 01752 822597 Signposted
►►► **Family Park**
Open all year Booking advisable Last departure 10.00hrs
A very well-equipped site with panoramic views from its tiered pitches, and plenty of on-site entertainment. Leave Torpoint on A374 and turn left at Anthony onto B3247 for 1.25m to T-junc. Turn left for .25m then right onto Cliff Rd, and site is 2m on left. A 6-acre site with 100 touring pitches and 40 statics.
Sauna, sunbed, entertainment.

Credit Cards

TREGURRIAN

Camping & Caravanning Club Site (SW853654)
TR8 4AE ☎ 01637 860448 (in season) & 01203 694995
Signposted
Nearby town: Newquay
►►► **Family Park** ★ £8.10-£10.30 £8.10-£10.30 £8.10-£10.30

contd.

Open end Mar-end Sep Booking advisable bank hols & Jul-Aug Last arrival 21.00hrs Last departure noon

A very well-kept older type club site with fairly basic essentials. From A3059 fork right for St Mawgan, then join B3276 coast road and turn left for Watergate Bay. Please see the advertisement on page 27 for details of Club Members' benefits. A 4.25-acre site with 106 touring pitches.

Credit Cards

TRURO

Leverton Place (SW774453)

Greenbottom, Chacewater TR4 8QW ☎ 01872 560462 Signposted

►►►► **De-Luxe Park** ★ £7.50-£14.50 £7.50-£14.50 ▲ £7.50-£14.50

Open all year (rs Oct-May not all facilities open all year round) Booking advisable Spring bank hol & Jun-early Sep Last arrival 22.00hrs Last departure noon

An attractive park divided into paddocks, close to Truro yet in a pleasant rural area 3.5m W of city, off A390 at Threemilestone Roundabout. A 9.75-acre site with 107 touring pitches and 15 statics.

Hairdrying room, childrens heated pool.

Credit Cards

Ringwell Valley Holiday Park (SW805408)

Bissoe Road, Carnon Downs TR3 6LQ

☎ 01872 862194 & 865409 (3m SW off A39) Signposted

►►►► **De-Luxe Park** ★ £7-£11 £6-£10 ▲ £5-£8

Open Etr-Oct Booking advisable Jul & Aug Last arrival 21.30hrs Last departure noon

A well-run park nestling in a tranquil valley with open countryside views. Turn off A39 at rndbt signed Carnon Downs, then right onto Bissoe Rd in the village. Park 0.75m on right. A 4-acre site with 30 touring pitches and 30 statics.

Credit Cards

Camping & Caravanning Club Site (SW935445)

Tretheake Manor, Veryon TR2 5PP ☎ 01203 694995 (from A390 turn onto A3078 signed St Mawes, site 6m on left) Signposted

►►► **Family Park** ★ £8.70-£11.30 £8.70-£11.30 ▲ £8.70-£11.30

Open 24 Mar-3 Nov Booking advisable Jul-Aug Last arrival 21.00hrs Last departure noon

A quiet park situated on slightly undulating land with pleasant views of the surrounding countryside. Turn left off A3078 at filling stn, signed Veryan and Portloe, on unclass road, and site signed on left. A 17-acre site with 130 touring pitches.

Carnon Downs Caravan & Camping Park (SW805406)

Carnon Downs TR3 6JJ ☎ 01872 862283 (3m off A39) Signposted

►►► **Family Park** ★ £6.50-£10.50 £6.50-£10.50 ▲ £6.50-£10.50

Open Etr or Apr-Oct Booking advisable Jul-Aug Last arrival 23.00hrs Last departure 11.00hrs

A mature park with a high standard of landscaping set in meadowland and woodland just outside the urban area, adjacent to A39 Falmouth-Truro road. An 11-acre site with 150 touring pitches.

Baby & children bathroom.

Credit Cards

Chacewater Park (SW740438)

Coxhill, Chacewater TR4 8LY ☎ 01209 820762 Signposted

►►► **Family Park** ★ £8.50 £8.50 ▲ £8.50

Open May-Sep Booking advisable May-Sep Last arrival 23.00hrs Last departure noon

A level grassy site with young trees set in meadowland. Along A30 towards Penzance, take A3047 to Scorrier, 400yds turn left at Crossroads Motel, continue to join B3298 for 1.25m, at next crossroads turn left to Chacewater & continue for 0.75m. A 4-acre site with 87 touring pitches and 12 statics.

Family shower rooms.

Credit Cards

Liskey Touring Park (SW772452)

Greenbottom TR4 8QN

☎ 01872 560274 (3m W off A390) Signposted

►►► **Family Park** £5.60-£9.30 £5.60-£9.30 ▲ £5.60-£9.30

Open Apr-Sep Booking advisable Jul-Aug Last arrival 20.00hrs Last departure noon

Small, south facing park, neat and well-maintained with quality facilities, and enjoying a friendly relaxed atmosphere. Off A390 at Threemilestone rndbt on to unclass rd towards Chacewater. Signed on left in .5m. A 4.5-acre site with 68 touring pitches.

Serviced pitches, dish washing, undercover playbarn.

Credit Cards

Summer Valley (SW800479)
Shortlanesend TR4 9DW ☎ 01872 277878 (3m NW off B3284) Signposted
►►► **Family Park** ★ £6-£8 £6-£8 £6-£8
Open Apr-Oct Booking advisable Jul-Aug Last arrival 22.00hrs Last departure noon
A very attractive and secluded site in a rural setting, and very well-maintained. From A30 take B3284 signed Truro. Site on right in 1.5m. A 3-acre site with 60 touring pitches.
Campers lounge.

WADEBRIDGE

Little Bodieve Holiday Park (SW995734)
Bodieve Rd PL27 6EG ☎ 01208 812323 Signposted
►►► **Family Park**
Open Mar-Oct (rs early & late season pool closed) Booking advisable Jul-Aug Last arrival 20.00hrs Last departure 11.00hrs
An established and well-organised level grassy site 1m from centre of Wadebridge on B3314 in quiet rural area, with good touring facilities. Signed Rock and Port Isaac. A 20-acre site with 195 touring pitches and 75 statics.
Crazy golf, water shute/splash pool & pets corner.
Credit Cards

WATERGATE BAY

Watergate Bay Tourist Park (SW850653)
Tregurrian TR8 4AD ☎ 01637 860387 Signposted
Nearby town: Newquay
►►► **Family Park** ★ £6.50-£10.50 £6.50-£10.50 £6.50-£10.50
Open 22 May-12 Sep (rs Mar-21 May & 13 Sep-Nov restricted bar, cafe, shop & swimming pool) Booking advisable Jul-Aug Last arrival 22.00hrs Last departure noon
A well-established park on high ground above Watergate Bay. Situated on B3276 .5m from Watergate beach. A 24-acre site with 171 touring pitches.
Entertainment, free minibus to beach.
See advertisement under NEWQUAY
Credit Cards

WHITECROSS

White Acres Holiday Park (SW890599)
TR8 4LW ☎ 01726 860220 & 860999 Signposted
Nearby town: Newquay
★ £6.50-£9.60 £6.50-£9.60 £6.50-£9.60
Open Etr-Sep Booking advisable Jul-Aug Last arrival 22.00hrs Last departure 10.00hrs
A large holiday complex, partially terraced, in a rural setting, with one of the best coarse fishing centres in the South West on site. From A30 at Indian Queen take A392 signed Newquay. Site on right in 3m. A 44-acre site with 200 touring pitches and 100 statics.
Entertainment, sauna, solarium, fishing lakes, gym.
See advertisement under NEWQUAY

Summer Lodge Holiday Park (SW890597)
TR8 4LW ☎ 01726 860415 Signposted
Nearby town: Newquay
►►► **Family Park** ★ £6-£15 £6-£15 £6-£15
Open Whitsun-Oct (rs Etr-Whitsun & Sep-Oct shop cafe & disco closed) Booking advisable Jul-Aug Last arrival 20.00hrs Last departure noon
Small holiday complex offering use of good facilities. From Indian Queens on A30 take A392 signed Newquay, and site on left at Whitecross in 2.5m. A 10-acre site with 50 touring pitches and 126 statics.
Credit Cards

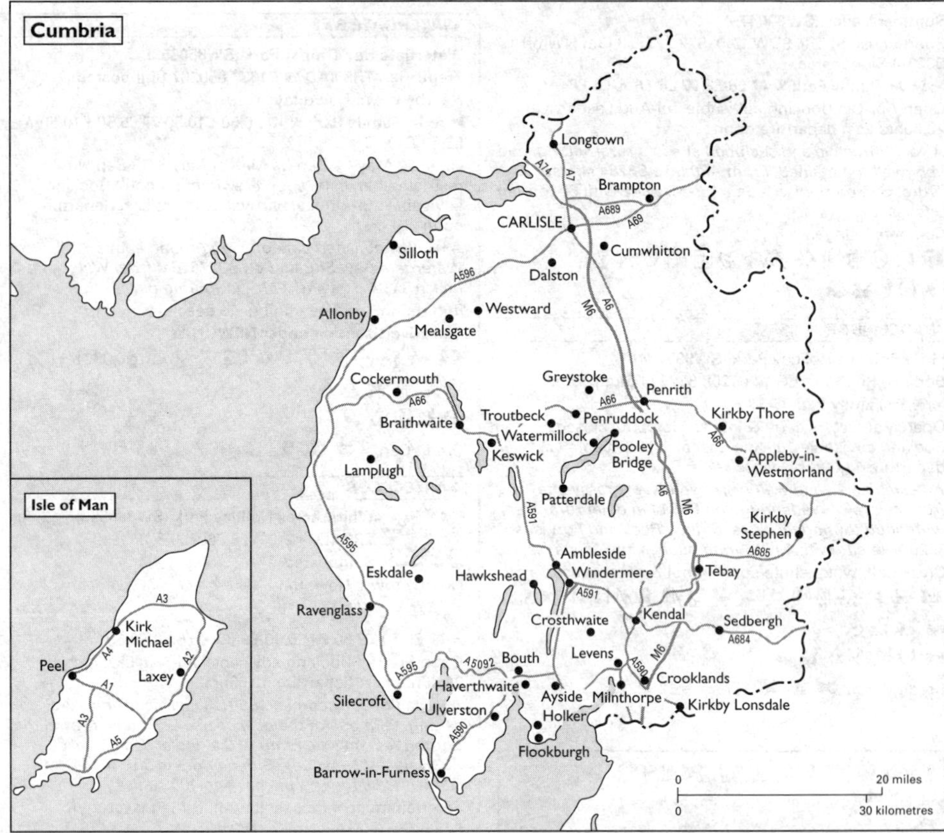

WIDEMOUTH BAY

Penhalt Farm Holiday Park (SS194003)

EX23 0DG ☎ 01288 361210 Signposted

►►► Family Park

Open Etr-Oct Booking advisable Jul & Aug

Splendid views of the sea and coast can be enjoyed from all pitches on this sloping but partly level site, set in a rural area on a working farm. From Bude take Widemouth Bay road off A39 4m S of town, turn left at end of road signed Millook onto Cornish coastal footpath, and site on left in .75m. An 8-acre site with 100 touring pitches and 3 statics.

Pool table.

Widemouth Bay Caravan Park (SS199008)

EX23 ODF ☎ 01288 361208 Signposted

►►► Family Park

Open Mar-Oct Booking advisable Last arrival mdnt Last departure 10.00hrs

A partly sloping rural site set in countryside overlooking the sea and one of Cornwall's finest beaches. Nightly entertainment in high season. Leave A39 at Widemouth Bay sign, join coast road and turn left. Park on left, 3m from Bude. A 10-acre site with 100 touring pitches and 150 statics.

Paddling pool.

See advertisement under BUDE

CUMBRIA

ALLONBY

Spring Lea Caravan Park (NY084434)

CA15 6QF ☎ 01900 881331 Signposted

►►► Family Park

Open Mar-Oct Booking advisable high season

Flat grassy park close to the seashore and village amenities, with its own leisure complex and wide range of facilities. Signed on unclass rd directly off B3500 in centre of village. A 2-acre site with 35 touring pitches and 96 statics.

AMBLESIDE

Skelwith Fold Caravan Park (NY355029)
LA22 0HX ☎ 015394 32277 Signposted

►►►► **De-Luxe Park**
Open Mar-15 Nov Booking advisable public hols & Jul-Aug Last departure noon
In grounds of old mansion, this park is in a beautiful setting close to Lake Windermere. On the B5286, 2m from Ambleside. A 10-acre site with 150 touring pitches and 300 statics.
Family recreation area.

Low Wray National Trust Campsite (NY372013)
Low Wray LA22 0JA ☎ 015394 32810 Signposted
►►► **Family Park** ★ fr £8
Open 1 wk before Etr-Oct Last arrival 23.00hrs
A site for tenters on banks of Lake Windermere, divided naturally into areas for families and for young people. 3m SW via A583 to Clappersgate, then B5286 and unclass road. A 10-acre site with 200 touring pitches and 6 statics.
Launching for sailing.

APPLEBY-IN-WESTMORLAND

Wild Rose Park (NY698165)
Ormside CA16 6EJ ☎ 017683 51077 Signposted

►►►►► **Premier Park** £7.25-£11.50 £7.25-£11.50 £7.25-£11.50
Open all year (rs Nov-Mar shop, swimming pool & restaurant closed) Booking advisable bank & school hols Last arrival 22.00hrs Last departure noon
An excellent, well-maintained site with good views of surrounding countryside. Facilities are of a high standard. Site signed on unclass road to Great Ormside off B6260 from Appleby-in-Westmorland. A 40-acre site with 240 touring pitches and 240 statics.
Tourist Information, bike hire & pitch and putt.

Credit Cards

Hawkrigg Farm (NY659203)
Colby CA16 6BB ☎ 017683 51046 Signposted
► **Town & Country Pennant Park** ★ £3 £3 £1.50-£3
Open all year Booking advisable Jul-Aug Last arrival 23.30hrs
Attractive level farm site in a pleasant and quiet location on the edge of the small village of Colby. On entering

contd.

village from Appleby turn left signed Kings Meadburn and Newby, and site on right in 800 yards. A 1-acre site with 15 touring pitches and 4 statics.

AYSIDE

Oak Head Caravan Park (SD389839)
LA11 6JA ☎ 015395 31475 Signposted
Nearby town: Grange-over-Sands
►►► **Family Park** £8.50 £8.50 £7
Open Mar-Oct Booking advisable bank hols Last departure noon
A tiered grassy site with some hardstandings set in hilly country with woodland, close to A590. A 3-acre site with 60 touring pitches and 71 statics.

BARROW-IN-FURNESS

South End Caravan Park (SD208628)
Walney Island LA14 3YQ
☎ 01229 472823 & 471556
Signposted
►►► **Family Park**
Open Mar-Oct Booking advisable Jul-Aug Last arrival 22.00hrs Last departure noon
Mainly level grass site adjacent to sea, and close to a nature reserve, on southern end of Walney Island. From Barrow cross bridge onto island and turn L into council estate and L again just before new private estate. Signed. A 7-acre site with 60 touring pitches and 100 statics.
Bowling green.

BASSENTHWAITE LAKE

See map for locations of sites in the vicinity

BOUTH

Black Beck Caravan Park (SD335855)
LA12 8JN ☎ 01229 861274 Signposted
Nearby town: Newby Bridge
►►► **Family Park**
Open Mar-Nov Booking advisable bank hols Last arrival 20.00hrs Last departure 13.00hrs
A quiet site surrounded by woods and fields close to S Cumbria and the Lake District. N of A590. A 2-acre site with 75 touring pitches and 235 statics.

BOWNESS-ON-WINDERMERE

Sites are listed under **Windermere**

BRAITHWAITE

Scotgate Caravan Park (NY235235)
CA12 5TJ ☎ 017687 78343 Signposted
Nearby town: Keswick
►►► **Family Park**
Open Mar-Oct Last arrival 22.00hrs Last departure 11.00hrs
A pleasant rural site with dramatic views towards Skiddaw. Situated at junction of A66 and B5292, 2m from Keswick. An 8-acre site with 165 touring pitches and 35 statics.

BRAMPTON

Irthing Vale Holiday Park (NY522613)
Old Church Ln CA8 2AA ☎ 016977 3600 Signposted
►►► **Family Park**
Open Mar-Oct Booking advisable public hols & Jul-Aug Last arrival 23.30hrs Last departure noon
A grassy site on the outskirts of the market town on the A6071. Brampton now bypassed, so leave A69 into town to join A6071, and site .5m outside. A 4.5-acre site with 30 touring pitches and 26 statics.

CARLISLE

Dandy Dinmont Caravan & Camping Park (NY399620)
Blackford CA6 4EA ☎ 01228 74611 (4m N on A7)
Signposted
►►► **Family Park** £7-£7.25 £7-£7.25 £5.75-£6.25
Open Etr-Oct (rs Mar showers not available) Booking advisable high season Last arrival anytime Last departure 15.00hrs
A level, sheltered site, screened on two sides by hedgerows. Situated alongside A7 about 1m N of junction 44 of M6. A 4-acre site with 47 touring pitches and 15 statics.

Orton Grange Caravan & Camping Park (NY355519)
Orton Grange, Wigton Rd CA5 6LA ☎ 01228 710252
Signposted
►►► **Family Park** ★
Open all year Booking advisable bank hols & Jul-Aug Last arrival 22.00hrs Last departure noon
Mainly grassy site in rural surroundings close to A595, 4m from Carlisle. A 6-acre site with 50 touring pitches and 22 statics.
Cafe & Fast food facilities in Apr-Sep only.

Credit Cards

COCKERMOUTH

Violet Bank Holiday Home Park (NY126295)
Simonscales Ln, Off Lorton Rd CA13 9TG
☎ 01900 822169 Signposted
►►► **Family Park** £4.90-£6.50 £4.90-£6.50 £4.90-£6.50
Open Mar-15 Nov Booking advisable Spring bank hol & Jul-Aug Last arrival mdnt Last departure noon
Well-maintained site in a pleasant rural setting affording

excellent views of Buttermere Hills. Approach by way of A5292 Lorton Road, via town centre. An 8.5-acre site with 30 touring pitches and 86 statics.

CROOKLANDS

Waters Edge Caravan Park (SD533838)
LA7 7NN ☎ 015395 67708 & 67414
Nearby town: Kendal
►►► **Family Park** ★ £9.95-£13.50 £9.95-£13.50 £4.50-£12.50
Open Mar-14 Nov Booking advisable bank hols
A small rural site, close to junc 36 of M6 yet in a very peaceful setting. From M6 follow signs for Kirkby Lonsdale A65, at second roundabout follow signs for Crooklands/Endmoor. Site 1m on right. A 3-acre site with 30 touring pitches and 9 statics.

Credit Cards

CROSTHWAITE

Lambhowe Caravan Park (SD422914)
LA8 8JE ☎ 015395 68483 & 01539 723339 Signposted
Nearby town: Kendal
►►► **Family Park** £9-£11 £9-£11
Open Mar-Oct Booking advisable Etr, Spring bank hol & Jul-Aug Last arrival 21.00hrs Last departure noon
A secluded wooded site on A5074 between Lancaster and Windermere, ideal for touring the Lake District National Park. No tents. A 1-acre site with 14 touring pitches and 112 statics.

CUMWHITTON

Cairndale Caravan Park (NY518523)
CA4 9BZ ☎ 01768 896280
Nearby town: Carlisle
►►► **Family Park** ★ £4.50-£5 £4.50-£5
Open Mar-Oct Booking advisable school & public hols Last arrival 22.00hrs
Lovely grass site set in tranquil Eden Valley with good views. Off A69 at Warwick Bridge on unclass road through Great Corby to Cumwhitton, turn left at village sign, then site in 1m. A 2-acre site with 5 touring pitches and 15 statics.

DALSTON

Dalston Hall Caravan Park (NY378519)
Dalston Hall Estate CA5 7JX ☎ 01228 710165 Signposted
Nearby town: Carlisle
►►► **Family Park** £7-£7.50 £7-£7.50 £6-£6.50
Open Mar-Oct Booking advisable Jul-Aug Last arrival 21.00hrs Last departure 13.00hrs
A neat, well-maintained site, on level grassy ground, situated in grounds of estate located between Carlisle and Dalston on B5299. Ideal position for touring northern Lake District, Carlisle and surrounding country. A 3-acre site with 60 touring pitches and 17 statics.
9 hole golf course & fly fishing.

ESKDALE

Fisherground Farm Campsite (NY152002)
Fisherground CA19 1TF ☎ 019467 23319
►►► **Family Park** £7-£8 £7-£8
Open 8 Mar-14 Nov
A mainly level grassy site on farmland amidst beautiful scenery, in Eskdale Valley below Hardknott Pass, between Eskdale and Boot. Own railway halt on the Eskdale-Ravenglass railway, 'The Ratty'. A 3-acre site with 30 touring pitches and 5 statics.
Adventure playground and miniature railway.

FLOOKBURGH

Lakeland Leisure Park (SD372743)
Moor Ln LA11 7LT ☎ 015395 58556
►►► **Family Park**
Open late Mar-early Nov (rs 15 Nov-3 Jan open wknds only for static plots) Booking advisable May-Oct Last arrival 21.00hrs Last departure 11.00hrs
A complete leisure park with full range of activities and entertainments, making this flat, grassy site ideal for families. Approach on B5277 through Grange over Sands to Flookburgh, turn left at village square, and park is in 1 mile. A 105-acre site with 120 touring pitches and 740 statics.
Horse riding.

GREYSTOKE

Hopkinsons Whitbarrow Hall Caravan Park (NY405289)
Berrier CA11 0XB ☎ 01768 483456 Signposted
Nearby town: Penrith
►►► **Family Park** ★ fr £8 fr £8 fr £8
Open Mar-Oct Booking advisable bank hols & for electric hook up Last arrival 23.00hrs Last departure 23.00hrs
A level grassy site, an ideal base for touring the Lake District National Park. Leave M6 at junc 40 onto A66 towards Keswick. Turn right in 8m at Sportsman's Inn onto unclass rd, signed Hutton Roof. Site in .5m. An 8-acre site with 81 touring pitches and 167 statics.
Table tennis, pool table & video games.

The AA pennant classification has been revised for 1998. Please read the explanation of the scheme on page 10.

Thanet Well Caravan Park (NY398349)
CA11 OXX ☎ 017684 84262 Signposted
Nearby town: Penrith
►►► **Family Park**
Open Mar-Oct Booking advisable bank hols & Jul-Aug Last arrival 21.30hrs
A very isolated site in lovely rolling countryside. Approach from M6 at junction 41 and follow B5305 for 6m towards Wigtown. Turn left at sign for Lamonby and follow signs. A 3-acre site with 20 touring pitches and 60 statics.

HAVERTHWAITE

Bigland Hall Caravan Park (SD344833)
LA12 8PJ ☎ 01539 531702 Signposted
Nearby town: Grange-over-Sands
►►► **Family Park**
Open Mar-Oct Booking advisable public hols Last arrival 22.30hrs Last departure 13.00hrs
A wooded site in lovely countryside with direct access from B5278. 3m from the southern end of Lake Windermere and near the Haverthwaite Steam Railway. A 30-acre site with 86 touring pitches and 29 statics.
Off-licence on site.

→

HAWKSHEAD

Camping & Caravanning Club Site (SD337943)
Grizedale Hall LA22 0GL ☎ 01229 860257(in season) & 01203 694995
Nearby town: Ambleside
► **Town & Country Pennant Park** ★ £8.10-£10.30 £8.10-£10.30
Open end Mar-Sep Booking advisable Spring bank hol & Jul-Aug Last arrival 21.00hrs Last departure noon
A peaceful, sloping site with level pitches set in Grizedale Forest, with lots of marked walks. Close to the famous theatre in the forest with its live shows. Take A590 from Newby Bridge via Greenodd, then minor road to right at Penny Bridge. Please see the advertisement on page 27 for details of Club Members' benefits. A 4-acre site with 59 touring pitches.

→

Credit Cards

HOLKER

Old Park Wood Caravan Park (SD335784)
LA11 7PP ☎ 015395 58266
►►► **Family Park**
Open Mar-Oct
Terraced park gently sloping towards the River Leven estuary, surrounded on three sides by woodland; very well maintained and with good facilities. 2m N of Cark in Cartmel, off B5278; follow signs for Holker Hall. A 4-acre site with 50 touring pitches and 325 statics.
Sauna, solarium

→

KENDAL

Camping & Caravanning Club Site (SD526948)
Millcrest, Skelsmergh, Shap Rd LA9 6NY ☎ 01539 741363 (in season) & 01203 694995 (on A6, 1.5m N) Signposted
►►► **Family Park** ★ £8.70-£11.30 £8.70-£11.30 £8.70-£11.30
Open end Mar-early Nov Booking advisable bank hols & high season Last arrival 21.00hrs Last departure noon
Sloping grass site, set in hilly wood and meadowland. Situated on the A6, 1.5m N of Kendal. Please see advertisement on page 27 for details of Club Members' benefits. A 3-acre site with 55 touring pitches.

→

Credit Cards

KESWICK

Camping & Caravanning Club Site (NY258234)
Derwentwater CA12 5EP ☎ 01768 772392 (in season) & 01203 694995 Signposted
►►► **Family Park** ★ £9.10-£12.10 £9.10-£12.10 £9.10-£12.10
Open early Feb-Nov Booking advisable all season Last arrival 21.00hrs Last departure noon
A well-situated lakeside site within walking distance of the town centre. Please see advertisement on page 27 for details of Club Members' benefits. An 11-acre site with 250 touring pitches.

→

Credit Cards

Castlerigg Hall Caravan & Camping Park (NY282227)
Castlerigg Hall CA12 4TE ☎ 017687 72437 Signposted
►►► **Family Park**
Open Etr-mid Nov Last arrival 21.00hrs Last departure 11.30hrs
A family-run site with tiered pitches and spectacular views over Derwent Water to the mountains beyond. Situated about 300yds along unclass rd off A591, about 1.5m SE of Keswick in Ambleside direction, signed towards Heights Hotel. An 8-acre site with 173 touring pitches and 30 statics.

→

Derwentwater Caravan Park (NY257234)
Crowe Park Rd CA12 5EN ☎ 017687 72579 Signposted
►►► **Family Park** ★ £8.40-£9.20 £8.40-£9.20
Open Mar-14 Nov Booking advisable at all times Last arrival 22.00hrs Last departure noon
A very well managed and maintained site which is divided into two areas for tourers. Signed off B5289 in town centre. A 4-acre site with 50 touring pitches and 160 statics.

→

Gill Head (NY380269)
Troutbeck CA11 0ST ☎ 017687 79652 Signposted
►►► **Family Park** ★ £7-£9 £7-£9 fr £7
Open Apr-Oct Booking advisable bank hols
An attractive and well-maintained site, with spacious and comfortable facilities, set against a backdrop of Blencathra and the northern fells. From junc 40 of M6 avoiding Kirkstone Pass, site 200yds from A66/A5091. A 5.5-acre site with 42 touring pitches and 17 statics.

KIRKBY LONSDALE

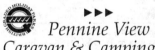

Woodclose Caravan Park (SD618786)
Casterton LA6 2SE ☎ 01524 271597 Signposted
►►►► **De-Luxe Park** ★ £8.50-£10.50 £8.50-£10.50 £5.50-£10.50
Open Mar-Oct Booking advisable bank hols, Jul-Aug & Sep Last arrival 22.00hrs Last departure 16.00hrs
A pleasant site in a quiet, rural area. Situated off the A65, .5m SE of the town. A 9-acre site with 70 touring pitches and 50 statics.

KIRKBY STEPHEN

Pennine View Caravan & Camping Park (NY772076)
Pennine View, Station Rd CA17 4SZ ☎ 01768 371717
Nearby town: Kendal
►►► **Family Park**
Open Mar-Oct Booking advisable bank hols & Jul-Aug Last arrival 22.00hrs Last departure 12.30hrs
Once a railway goods yard on a now disused line, this is an attractive, level, well-maintained site with river walks, situated on the coast to coast path. 100 metres off A685 on the B6270. A 2.5-acre site with 43 touring pitches.

KIRKBY THORE

Low Moor Caravan Site (NY624259)
CA10 1XQ ☎ 017683 61231
Nearby town: Appleby-in-Westmorland
►►► **Family Park**
Open Apr-Oct Booking advisable high season Last arrival 23.00hrs
A small farm site with well cared for grounds and clean sanitary facilities. 7m SE of Penrith on A66. A 2-acre site with 25 touring pitches and 25 statics.

LAMPLUGH

Inglenook Caravan Park (NY084206)
Fitzbridge CA14 4SH ☎ 01946 861240 Signposted
Nearby town: Cockermouth
►►► **Family Park** ★ £7.50-£8.50 £7.50-£8.50 £6.50-£8.50
Open all year Booking advisable bank hols Last arrival 20.00hrs Last departure noon
An ideal touring site, well-maintained and situated in beautiful surroundings just off A5086. A 3-acre site with 36 touring pitches and 22 statics.

LEVENS

Sampool Caravan Park (SD479844)
LA8 8EQ ☎ 015395 52265 Signposted
►►► **Family Park** ★ £6-£9 £6-£9
Open 15 Mar-Oct Booking advisable Bank hols & Jul-Aug
A pleasantly landscaped park adjacent to the River Kent. Turn off A6 at Levens Bridge onto A590, then left on unclassified lane to park in 1m. A 1.5-acre site with 20 touring pitches and 200 statics.

LONGTOWN

Camelot Caravan Park (NY391666)
CA6 5SZ ☎ 01228 791248 Signposted
Nearby town: Carlisle
►►► **Family Park** ★ fr £6.70 fr £6.70 fr £5.70
Open Mar-Oct Booking advisable Jul-Aug Last arrival 22.00hrs Last departure noon

contd.

Very pleasant level grassy site near junction 44 of M6. Ideal stopover site. A 1.5-acre site with 20 touring pitches and 1 static.

Oakbank Lakes Country Park (NY369700)
CA6 5NA ☎ 01228 791108
Town & Country Pennant Park
Open all year
Set alongside three fishing lakes, and adjacent to the River Esk, this park has many established and newly planted trees, and a bird sanctuary with a game bird breeding unit. Leave Longtown on A7 towards Langholm/Galashiels, turn left in 1m signed Corries Mill Chapelknowe, and site in 200yards. A 2-acre site with 20 touring pitches and 2 statics.
Fishing.

MEALSGATE

Larches Caravan Park (NY205415)
☎ 016973 71379 Signposted
Nearby town: Wigton

►►►► **De-Luxe Park**
Open Mar-Oct (rs early & late season) Booking advisable Etr Spring bank hol & Jul-Aug Last arrival 21.30hrs Last departure noon
Set in wooded rural surroundings on the fringe of the Lake District National Park. Situated on A595 Carlisle-Cockermouth road. A 5-acre site with 73 touring pitches and 100 statics.
Ensuite units with toilets, shower, washbasin.

MILNTHORPE

Fell End Caravan Park (SD505780)
Slackhead Rd, Hale LA7 7BS ☎ 015395 62122
Signposted
Nearby town: Kendal

►►►► **De-Luxe Park** ★ £11.50 £11.50 £9.50-£11.50
Open all year Booking advisable school & bank hols
Well-kept site, constantly improving and with high standards being continually maintained. Pleasantly situated in a very picturesque natural setting surrounded by woodland. Within easy reach of the lakes and South Cumbria. 4.75m from junction 35 of M6. An 8-acre site with 68 touring pitches and 215 statics.
Off-licence, TV aerial hook ups, kitchen facility.

Credit Cards

PATTERDALE

Sykeside Camping Park (NY403119)
Brotherswater CA11 0NZ ☎ 017684 82239
Nearby town: Windermere
►►► **Family Park** ★ fr £6.90 fr £9.40
Open all year Booking advisable bank hols & Jul-Aug Last arrival 22.30hrs Last departure 14.00hrs
A camper's delight, this family-run park is situated halfway up Kirkstone Pass, under the 2000ft Hartsop Dodd in a spectacular area with breathtaking views. Off A592 Windermere to Ullswater Road; not suitable for caravans. A 5-acre site with 86 touring pitches.

Credit Cards

PENRITH

Lowther Caravan Park (NY527265)
Eamont Bridge CA10 2JB ☎ 01768 863631
Signposted

►►►► **De-Luxe Park** ★ £10-£11 £10-£11 £10-£11
Open mid Mar-mid Nov Booking advisable bank hols Last arrival 21.00hrs
A secluded natural woodland site with lovely on-site riverside walks and glorious surrounding countryside. From Penrith site is 3m S of Penrith on A6. A 10-acre site with 150 touring pitches and 407 statics.

Thacka Lea Caravan Site (NY509310)
Thacka Ln CA11 9HX ☎ 01768 863319 Signposted
►►► **Family Park** ★ fr £6 fr £6
Open Mar-Oct Booking advisable public hols
A good, spotlessly clean site in urban area at the edge of town, just off A6 and signed. A 2-acre site with 25 touring pitches.

PENRUDDOCK

Beckses Caravan Park (NY419278)
CA11 0RX ☎ 01768 483224 Signposted
►►► **Family Park** ★ fr £6 fr £6 fr £4.50
Open Etr-Oct Booking advisable public hols Last arrival 20.00hrs Last departure 11.00hrs
A small site on sloping ground with level pitches and views of distant fells, on edge of National Park. From A66 towards Keswick turn right onto B5288. A 4-acre site with 23 touring pitches and 18 statics.

POOLEY BRIDGE

Park Foot Caravan & Camping Park (NY469235)
Howtown Rd CA10 2NA ☎ 017684 86309 Signposted
Nearby town: Penrith

►►►► **De-Luxe Park** ★ £12-£15 £7-£10.50
£7-£10.50
Open Mar-Oct Booking advisable Last arrival 22.00hrs
Last departure noon
A mainly tenting park on gently sloping ground, with access to Lake Ullswater and lovely views. Leave M6 junc 40 onto A66 towards Keswick, then take A592 to Ullswater. Turn left for Pooley Bridge, turn right at church, and right at crossrds signed Howtown. Site 1m on left. An 18-acre site with 323 touring pitches and 131 statics.
Lake access with boat launching.

Hillcroft Caravan & Camping Site (NY478241)
Roe Head Ln CA10 2LT ☎ 017684 86363 Signposted
Nearby town: Penrith
►►► **Family Park** £8-£11.50 £8-£11.50 £8
Open 7 Mar-14 Nov Booking advisable bank hols
A pleasant rural site close to the village and Ullswater; an ideal touring base. From A592 fork L just before Pooley Bridge, and site is signed on L. A 10-acre site with 125 touring pitches and 200 statics.

RAVENGLASS

Walls Caravan & Camping Park (SD087964)
CA18 1SR ☎ 01229 717250 Signposted
Nearby town: Whitehaven
►►► **Family Park** £7.50 £7 £3.50-£7.50
Open Mar-15 Nov Booking advisable bank hols & summer Last arrival 22.00hrs Last departure noon
A well-maintained site in a woodland park with all hardstandings. Situated off A595 close to Ravenglass-Eskdale narrow railway service. A 5-acre site with 50 touring pitches.
Washing up sinks with free hot water.

SEDBERGH

Pinfold Caravan Park (SD665921)
Garsdale Rd LA10 5JL ☎ 01539 620576 Signposted
►►► **Family Park** £8.50 £8.50 £8.50
Open Mar-Oct Booking advisable bank hols & Jul-Aug
Last arrival 21.30hrs Last departure 13.30hrs
A mature site amongst beautiful scenery on a river bank; at edge of village on the Hawes road. A 4-acre site with 40 touring pitches and 56 statics.

SILECROFT

Silecroft Caravan Site (SD124811)
LA18 4NX ☎ 01229 772659 Signposted
Nearby town: Millom
►►► **Family Park** ★ £9-£10 £8.50-£9.50 £8.50-£9.50
Open Mar-15 Nov Booking advisable
Quietly situated close to the shore 4m N of Millom, in a beautiful, little-known area of the Lake District with lovely beach nearby. A 5-acre site with 60 touring pitches and 124 statics.
Sauna, gym & Jacuzzi.

SILLOTH

Stanwix Park Holiday Centre (NY108527)
Green Row CA5 4HH
☎ 016973 32666 (1m SW on B5300)
Signposted
★ £11-£14.50 £11-£14.50 £11-£14.50
Open Mar-Oct (rs Nov-Feb no mid week entertainment) Booking advisable Etr, Spring bank hol & Jul-Aug Last arrival 21.00hrs Last departure 11.00hrs
A large well-run family park within easy reach of the Lake District. Attractively laid-out, with lots of amenities to ensure a lively holiday. On outskirts of Silloth on B5300. Winner of the Campsite of the Year Award for the North of England, 1997/8. A 4-acre site with 121 touring pitches and 212 statics.

Pony trekking & entertainment.

Credit Cards

Tanglewood Caravan Park (NY131534)
Causewayhead CA5 4PE ☎ 016973 31253 Signposted
►►► **Family Park** £6 £6 £6
Open Mar-Oct Booking advisable Etr, Whit & Jul-Aug Last arrival 23.00hrs Last departure 10.00hrs
Mainly level grass site sheltered by a variety of trees and bushes, and set in meadowland adjacent to B5302 Wigton-Silloth road. A 2-acre site with 31 touring pitches and 58 statics.

TEBAY

Tebay Caravan Site (NY609060)
Orton CA10 3SB ☎ 015396 24511 Signposted
Nearby town: Kendal
►►► **Family Park** ★ £6.95 £6.95
Open 14 Mar-Oct Booking advisable Jul-Aug Last departure noon
An ideal stopover site and good for touring the Lake District. Screened by high grass banks, bushes and trees. Site is adjacent to M6 at Tebay Service area .75m N of exit 38 for northbound traffic. Southbound traffic join northbound at junction 38, and can easily rejoin motorway with site warden's instructions. A 4-acre site with 70 touring pitches.

TROUTBECK (NEAR KESWICK)

Troutbeck Head Caravan Park (NY383254)
CA11 0SS ☎ 017684 83521 Signposted
Nearby town: Keswick
►►► **Family Park** ★ £7 £7
Open Mar-mid Jan Booking advisable bank & school hols Last arrival 21.00hrs Last departure 11.00hrs
A natural, unspoilt site surrounded by towering fells. Off A5091, 1m from A66. A 12-acre site with 54 touring pitches and 75 statics.

Credit Cards

ULLSWATER

ULVERSTON

Bardsea Leisure Park (SD292765)
Priory Rd LA12 9QE ☎ 01229 584712 Signposted
►►► **Family Park**
Open all year Booking advisable bank hols & Jul-Aug Last arrival 21.00hrs Last departure 18.00hrs
Attractively landscaped former quarry making a quiet

and very sheltered site. On southern edge of town off the A5087, convenient for both the coast and the Lake District. A 5-acre site with 83 touring pitches and 73 statics.

WATERMILLOCK

Cove Caravan & Camping Park (NY431236)
Ullswater CA11 0LS ☎ 017684 86549 (A592 to Ullswater, approx 4m to T jct, turn rught then rigth at Brackenrigg Inn, park 1.5m on left) Signposted
Nearby town: Penrith
►►► **Family Park** ★ £8-£8.50 £6.40-£6.80 £6.40-£8.50
Open Etr-Oct Booking advisable bank & school hols Last arrival 21.00hrs Last departure noon
A family site in attractive rural setting amidst fells with views over the lake. Leave M6 at junction 40, turn W following signs for Ullswater (A592). Turn right at lake junction, then right at Brackenrigg Hotel. Site is 1.5m on left. A 3-acre site with 50 touring pitches and 38 statics.
Dishwashing area, drinks machine.

The Quiet Site (NY431236)
Ullswater CA11 0LS ☎ 01768 486337 Signposted
Nearby town: Penrith
►►► **Family Park** ★ £8.50-£10 £7.50-£9 £7.50-£9
Open Mar-Oct Booking advisable bank hols & Jul-Aug Last arrival 22.00hrs Last departure noon
A well-maintained site in a lovely, peaceful location, with very good facilities, including a charming olde-worlde bar. Leave M6 at junction 40, turn W following signs for Ullswater (A592). Turn right at lake junction, then right at Brackenrigg Hotel. Site is 1.5m on right. A 6-acre site with 60 touring pitches and 23 statics.
Pets corner. Pool & darts (adults only).

Ullswater Caravan Camping Site & Marine Park (NY438232)
High Longthwaite CA11 0LR ☎ 01768 486666 Signposted
Nearby town: Ullswater/Penrith
►►► **Family Park** ★ fr £10 fr £9 fr £9
Open Mar-Nov Booking advisable public hols Last arrival 21.00hrs Last departure noon
A pleasant rural site with own nearby boat launching and marine storage facility. Leave M6 at junction 40, and W following signs for Ullswater (A592) for 5 miles. Turn right alongside Ullswater for 2 miles, then turn right at telephone box signposted Longthwaite and Watermillock Church. Site .5 mile on right. A 9-acre site with 155 touring pitches and 55 statics.
Boat launching & moorings.
Credit Cards

WESTWARD

Clea Hall Holiday Park (NY279425)
CA7 8NQ ☎ 016973 42880 Signposted
Nearby town: Wigton

►►►► **De-Luxe Park** ★ £10-£12 £10-£12
£10-£12
Open Mar-Nov Booking advisable bank hols & Jul-Aug Last departure noon
A slightly sloping grassy site surrounded by woods, moorland and hills. 3.5m S of A595 from Red Dial, signed in 3.5m.. A 10-acre site with 16 touring pitches and 83 statics.

See advertisement on page 103

WINDERMERE

Fallbarrow Park (SD401973)
Rayrigg Rd LA23 3DL ☎ 015394 44428 Signposted

►►►►► **Premier Park** ★ £10.60-£16.70
£10.60-£16.70
Open mid Mar-Oct Booking advisable bank hols & Jul-Aug Last arrival 23.00hrs Last departure 13.00hrs
A well-organised site with many facilities, a few minutes' walk from Bowness on shore of Lake Windermere. Winner of the 1996/97 Campsite of the Year Award. A 32-acre site with 83 touring pitches and 248 statics.
Boat launching facilities.
See advertisement under Colour Section

Credit Cards

Limefitt Park (NY416032)
LA23 1PA ☎ 015394 32300 ext 41

►►►►► **Premier Park** ★ £9.50-£12.50
£9.50-£12.50 £9-£12
Open 1 wk prior Etr-Oct Booking advisable bank hols & Jun-Sep Last arrival 22.30hrs Last departure noon
A lovely family site with superb facilities in a beautiful location in the Lake District National Park. Direct access off A592 approach from Windermere but do not enter Troutbeck village. A 12-acre site with 165 touring pitches and 45 statics.
See advertisement under Colour Section

Credit Cards

Ashes Lane Caravan & Camping Park (SD478962)
Ashes Ln LA8 9JS
☎ 01539 821119 Signposted

►►►► **De-Luxe Park** ★ £10-£13 £10-£13
£6-£13
Open mid Mar-mid Jan Booking advisable bank hols Last arrival 22.00hrs Last departure noon
Large, well-equipped park in naturally secluded Lake District area with level grassy pitches. Signed off A591, .75m from rndbt with B5284 towards Windermere. A 22-acre site with 200 touring pitches and 68 statics.

Credit Cards

Park Cliffe Farm Camping & Caravan Estate (SD391912)
Birks Rd, Tower Wood LA23 3PG
☎ 01539 531344
Signposted
►►► **Family Park** ★ £10-£11.20 £10-£11.20
£8.80-£11.20
Open 21 Mar-Oct Booking advisable bank hols & Aug Last arrival 22.00hrs Last departure noon
A lovely hillside site on level and sloping ground with

trees, bushes, rocks and mountain stream. 3m S of Windermere off A592. A 25-acre site with 250 touring pitches and 50 statics.
Off-licence.

Credit Cards

DERBYSHIRE

For the map of this county, see Staffordshire

ASHBOURNE

Sandybrook Hall Holiday Park (SK179481)
Buxton Rd DE6 2AQ ☎ 01335 342679 (1m N of Ashbourne on A515) Signposted
Nearby town: Derby
Town & Country Pennant Park ★ £7-£8.50 £7-£8.50 ▲ £7-£8.50
Open 26 Mar-Oct Booking advisable public hols & Jul-Aug
A family-run touring site on mostly sloping grass. Leave Ashbourne on A515 Buxton rd, and site on right in 2m opp sign for Thorpe and Dovedale. An 8-acre site with 70 touring pitches and 25 statics.
Bar meals, sand pit.

BAKEWELL

Greenhills Caravan Park (SK202693)
Crow Hill Ln DE45 1PX ☎ 01629 813467 & 813052 (on A6, 2km NW) Signposted
► ► ► Family Park ★ £9-£14 £9-£12 ▲ £9-£10
Open all year (rs Oct-Apr bar & shop closed) Booking advisable school & bank hols Last arrival 23.00hrs Last departure noon
Nicely kept and run site. Tenting field well cut with path of shorter grass to facilities block. 1 mile NW of Bakewell on A6, and site signed before Ashford in the Water, 50yds up unclass rd on right. An 8-acre site with 90 touring pitches and 60 statics.

BUXTON

Limetree Holiday Park (SK070725)
Dukes Dr SK17 9RP ☎ 01298 22988 Signposted
► ► ► ► De-Luxe Park ▲
Open Mar-Oct Booking advisable bank hols & Jul-Aug Last arrival 21.00hrs Last departure noon
A most attractive and well-designed site, set on the side of a narrow valley in an elevated situation of gently sloping land with views. Leaving Buxton on A515 S, turn L after hospital and site is .25m on R. A 10.5-acre site with 65 touring pitches and 43 statics.

Credit Cards

Thornheyes Farm Campsite (SK084761)
Thornheyes Farm, Longridge Ln, Peak Dale SK17 8AD ☎ 01298 26421
Town & Country Pennant Park ★ fr £4.50 fr £3.75 ▲ £2-£4.50
Open Etr-Oct Booking advisable bank hols & high season Last arrival 21.30hrs Last departure evenings
A pleasant farm site run by a friendly family team, in the central Peak District. 1.5m N of Buxton on A6 turn east for Peak Dale, and after .5m south at crossroads, site is on right up Longridge Lane. A 2-acre site with 10 touring pitches.

CROWDEN

Camping & Caravanning Club Site (SK072992)
SK14 7HZ ☎ 01457 866057 (in season) & 01203 694995 (off A628) Signposted
Nearby town: Hyde
Town & Country Pennant Park ★ ▲ £5.60-£8.60
Open end Mar-early Nov Booking advisable bank hols & Jun-Aug Last arrival 21.00hrs Last departure noon
A beautifully located moorland site, overlooking the reservoirs and surrounded by hills. Tents only, with backpackers' dining room. Off the A628. .5m from Glossop take B6105. Please see the advertisement on

contd.

page 27 for details of Club Members' benefits. A 2.5-acre site with 46 touring pitches.

Credit Cards

EDALE

Coopers Caravan Site (SK121859)
Newfold Farm, Edale Village S30 2ZD ☎ 01433 670372
Town & Country Pennant Park
Open all year Booking advisable bank hols Last arrival 23.30hrs Last departure 15.00hrs
Rising grassland behind a working farm, divided by a wall into two fields, culminating in the 2062ft Edale Moor. Facilities converted from original farm buildings. Only 15 vans accepted. From A625 at Hope take minor rd for 4m to Edale, and site 800yds on the right. A 6-acre site with 135 touring pitches and 11 statics.

FENNY BENTLEY

Bank Top Farm (SK181498)
DE6 1LF ☎ 01335 350250 (leave Ashbourne on A515 fro 2m, take B5056, 200yds on right)
Nearby town: Ashbourne
Family Park ★ £5-£5.50 £5-£5.50 £5-£5.50
Open Mar/Etr-Sep Booking advisable peak periods Last arrival 22.00hrs Last departure 14.00hrs
Gently sloping grass site with some level pitches on working dairy farm, just off B5056. A 2-acre site with 36 touring pitches and 15 statics.
Working dairy farm with viewing gallery.

HAYFIELD

Camping & Caravanning Club Site (SK048868)
Kinder Rd SK12 5LE ☎ 01663 745394 (in season) & 01203 694995 (off A624) Signposted
Nearby town: Stockport
Town & Country Pennant Park ★ £8.70-£11.30 £8.70-£11.30
Open end Mar-early Nov Booking advisable bank hols & peak periods Last arrival 21.00hrs Last departure noon
Pleasant site bordered by trees near the River Sett, off A624. Please see advertisement on page 27 for details of Club Members' benefits. A 7-acre site with 90 touring pitches.

Credit Cards

MATLOCK

Darwin Forest Country Park (SK302649)
Darley Moor, Two Dales DE4 5LN ☎ 01629 732428 (3m NW off B5057) Signposted

Premier Park £10-£12 £10-£12
Open Mar-Dec Booking advisable bank hols & Jul-Aug Last arrival 21.00hrs Last departure 10.00hrs
A mostly level woodland site set amongst tall pines in the heart of the Derbyshire Dales. 3m NW off B5057. A 44-acre site with 50 touring pitches.

Credit Cards

Packhorse Farm (SK323617)
Tansley DE4 5LF ☎ 01629 582781
Town & Country Pennant Park
Open all year Booking advisable bank hols Last arrival 22.30hrs Last departure noon
A pleasant, well-run farm site in quiet situation with good views. 2m NE of Matlock off A632 at the Tansley signpost. A 2-acre site with 30 touring pitches.

Pinegroves Caravan Park (SK345585)
High Ln, Tansley DE4 5GS ☎ 01629 534815 & 534670
Town & Country Pennant Park ★ fr £6.50 fr £6.50 £6.50-£8
Open Apr or Etr-Oct Booking advisable bank hols & Jul-Aug Last arrival 21.00hrs Last departure 16.00hrs
A beautiful hilltop location overlooking Matlock and Riber Castle. Very secluded site in a former plant nursery. From Matlock take A615 for 3m, then 2nd right at crossroads and site 400yds on left. A 23-acre site with 60 touring pitches and 14 statics.
Area of woodland for walks.

Sycamore Caravan & Camping Park (SK329615)
Lant Ln, nr Tansley DE4 5LF ☎ 01629 55760 (2.5m NE off A632)
Town & Country Pennant Park ★ £6-£7 £6-£7 £7-£8
Open 15 Mar-Oct Booking advisable bank hols & summer hols Last arrival 21.00hrs Last departure noon
An open grassland site with mainly level touring pitches in two fields. 2.5m NE of Matlock off A632. A 6.5-acre site with 80 touring pitches and 35 statics.

Credit Cards

Wayside Farm Caravan Park (SK361620)
Chesterfield Rd, Matlock Moor DE4 5LF
☎ 01629 582967
Town & Country Pennant Park
Open all year (rs winter) Booking advisable Last arrival anytime Last departure flexible
A small hilltop farm overlooking Matlock with two camping fields and good facilities. From Matlock on

A632 to Chesterfield, site on right in 2m opposite golf course. A 1.5-acre site with 30 touring pitches.

NEWHAVEN

Newhaven Holiday Camping & Caravan Park (SK167602)
SK17 0DT ☎ 01298 84300 (on A515 at Jct with A5012) Signposted
Nearby town: Buxton
▶ ▶ ▶ **Family Park** ★ £6.75-£7.75 £6.75-£7.75 ▲ £6.75-£7.75
Open Mar-Oct Booking advisable public hols Last arrival 23.00hrs Last departure anytime
Pleasantly situated within the Peak District National Park, between Ashbourne-Buxton on A515 at junction with A5012. Well-maintained and immaculate site. A 30-acre site with 95 touring pitches and 45 statics.

ROWSLEY

Grouse & Claret (SK258660)
Station Rd DE4 2EL ☎ 01629 733233 Signposted
▶ ▶ ▶ **Family Park** ▲
Open all year Booking advisable wknds, bank hols & peak periods Last arrival 20.00hrs Last departure noon
A well-designed site behind an eating house on A6 between Bakewell and Chatsworth. A flat grassy area running down to the river. A 2.5-acre site with 29 touring pitches.

Credit Cards

SHARDLOW

Shardlow Marina Caravan Park (SK444303)
London Rd DE72 2GL ☎ 01332 792832 Signposted
Nearby town: Derby
▶ ▶ ▶ **Family Park** ★ £7-£10.75 £7-£10.75 ▲ £7-£8
Open Apr-Oct Booking advisable bank hols Last arrival 20.00hrs Last departure 14.00hrs
A steadily improving pleasant site with modern facilities, part of a marina complex on the Trent/Mersey Canal. Situated near the A6 close to its junction with the M1. From junc 24 take turning for Shardlow. A 25-acre site with 70 touring pitches.

YOULGREAVE

Camping & Caravanning Club Site (SK206632)
c/o Hopping Farm DE45 1NA ☎ 01629 636555 (in season) & 01203 694995 Signposted
Nearby town: Bakewell
▶ **Town & Country Pennant Park** ★ £6.70-£8.30 £6.70-£8.30 ▲ £6.70-£8.30
Open end Mar-end Sep Booking advisable bank hols & peak periods Last arrival 21.00hrs Last departure noon
Ideal for touring and walking in the Peak District National Park, this gently sloping grass site is accessed through narrow streets and along unadopted hardcore. Own sanitary facilities essential. Please see the advertisement on page 27 for details of Club Members' benefits. An 11.75-acre site with 100 touring pitches.

Credit Cards

DEVON

ASHBURTON

Ashburton Caravan Park (SX753723)
Waterleat TQ13 7HU ☎ 01364 652552 (1.5m N towards moor) Signposted
Nearby town: Newton Abbot
▶ ▶ ▶ ▶ **De-Luxe Park** ▲
Open Etr-Sep Booking advisable bank hols & Jul-Aug Last arrival 22.30hrs Last departure noon
A secluded park set in an attractive location amongst the trees in Dartmoor National Park, offering quality facilities. From A38 in village centre turn right at T junc for Buckland on the Moor on unclass rd. Fork right at river bridge, and site 1.5m on left. A 2-acre site with 35 touring pitches and 40 statics.

Parkers Farm Holidays (SX779713)
Higher Mead Farm TQ13 7LJ ☎ 01364 652598 Signposted

►►►► **De-Luxe Park** ★ £4.50-£8.50 £4.50-£8.50 £4-£8.50
Open Etr-end Oct Booking advisable Whitsun & school hols
A well-developed site terraced into rising ground, with maturing shrubs. Signed off A38, .75m E of Ashburton. An 8-acre site with 60 touring pitches and 25 statics.

Credit Cards

See advertisement on page 107

The AA pennant classification has been revised for 1998. Please read the explanation of the scheme on page 10.

River Dart Country Park (SX734700)
Holne Park TQ13 7NP ☎ 01364 652511 Signposted
Nearby town: Totnes

►►►► **De-Luxe Park** ★ £8.60-£11.40 £8.60-£11.40 £8.60-£11.40
Open May-Aug (rs Apr & Sep no evening facilities ie bar) Booking advisable Spring Bank Hol & Jul-Aug Last arrival 21.00hrs Last departure 10.00hrs
Mainly level site in a very attractive and quiet location in Holne Country Park just off the B3357. A 7-acre site with 117 touring pitches.

Credit Cards

AXMINSTER

Andrewshayes Caravan Park (SY248088)
Dalwood EX13 7DY ☎ 01404 831225 (on A35)
Signposted
►►► **Family Park** ★ £8-£9.50 £7-£9.50 ▲ fr £8
Open Mar-Jan (rs Apr-21 May & Oct shop hours restricted, pool closed) Booking advisable Spring bank hol & Jul-Aug Last arrival 22.00hrs Last departure noon
Slightly sloping site within easy reach of Lyme Regis, Seaton, Branscombe and Sidmouth. From Axminster take A35 W, and site on right 3m from town. A 4-acre site with 90 touring pitches and 80 statics.
Fast food/takeaway & cafe in high season.

Credit Cards

BERRYNARBOR

Napps Camping Site (SS561477)
Old Coast Rd EX34 9SW ☎ 01271 882557 & 882778
Signposted
Nearby town: Combe Martin
►►► **Family Park** ★ £5-£9.80 £5-£9 ▲ £5-£9
Open Etr-Oct (rs Etr-Whitsun & Sep-Nov shop closed) Booking advisable always for caravans Last arrival 22.00hrs Last departure noon
Seclusion is guaranteed at this cliff top site adjacent to Combe Martin.Turn north off A399 W of Combe Martin at bottom of hill. An 11-acre site with 250 touring pitches and 2 statics.
Childrens paddling pool & slide.

Credit Cards

BICKINGTON (NEAR ASHBURTON)

Halfway House Caravan Site (SX804719)
TQ12 6JW ☎ 01626 821270

►►►► **De-Luxe Park** ★ £5-£8.30 £5-£8.30
Open 8 Mar-8 Jan Booking advisable high season & bank hols Last departure 10.00hrs
A recently developed site tucked away on the edge of Dartmoor, beside the River Lemon and adjacent to the Halfway Inn. Direct access off A383, 1m from A38 Exeter-Plymouth Rd. A 2-acre site with 22 touring pitches.

Credit Cards

Many parks in this guide may exclude some categories of people from staying. Please check before you book, and see the important note on page 4.

Lemonford Caravan Park (SX793723)
TQ12 6JR ☎ 01626 821242 Signposted
Nearby town: Ashburton

►►►► **De-Luxe Park** ★ £5-£8 £5-£8 ▲ £5-£8
Open Etr-Oct Booking advisable Whit & last wk Jul-1st wk Aug Last arrival 22.30hrs Last departure 11.00hrs
Small, secluded and well-maintained site. From Exeter along A38 take A382 turnoff, take 3rd exit on roundabout and follow site signs to Bickington. From Plymouth take A383 signed Newton Abbot, then turn left in 500m signed Bickington Camp on right hand turn. A 7-acre site with 70 touring pitches and 15 statics.
Clothes drying area.
See advertisement under NEWTON ABBOT

BLACKAWTON

Woodland Leisure Park (SX813522)
TQ9 7DQ ☎ 01803 712598 (signposted from A38)
Signposted
Nearby town: Dartmouth

►►►► **De-Luxe Park** ★ £5.75-£12.50 £5.75-£12.50 ▲ £5.75-£12.50
Open 15 Mar-15 Nov Booking advisable anytime Last departure 11.00hrs
An extensive woodland park with a terraced grass camping area, and facilities of a very high standard. A wildlife park is attached, with entry free to campers. Signed off A381 at Halwell. An 8-acre site with 80 touring pitches.
60 acre leisure park with animal farm complex.

Credit Cards

BRATTON FLEMING

Greenacres Farm Touring Caravan Park (SS658414)
EX31 4SG ☎ 01598 763334 (2.5m N) Signposted
Nearby town: Barnstaple
►►► **Family Park** £4.50-£6.50 £4.50-£6.50
Open Apr-Oct Booking advisable all times Last arrival 23.00hrs Last departure 11.00hrs
New site with well-appointed facilities and enthusiastic owners. On farmland, with good views over North Devon. From A361 Tiverton/Barnstaple rd take B3226 at 2nd rndbt N of South Molton, signed Blackmoor Gate. Ignore all signs to Bratton Fleming. Turn left at Stowfall crossrds, and site on left. A 4-acre site with 30 touring pitches.

BRAUNTON

Lobb Fields Caravan & Camping Park (SS475378)
Saunton Rd EX33 1EB ☎ 01271 812090 Signposted
Nearby town: Barnstaple
►►► **Family Park** ★ £5-£8 £4-£6.50 £4-£6.50
Open 28 Mar-Oct Booking advisable Jul-Aug Last arrival 21.00hrs Last departure 10.30hrs
Gently sloping grassy site on outskirts of Braunton, with good wide entrance. Follow signs to Croyde Bay from crossrds in Braunton, and site on right in 1m. A 14-acre site with 180 touring pitches.

BRIDESTOWE

Bridestowe Caravan Park (SX519893)
EX20 4ER ☎ 01837 861261 Signposted
Nearby town: Okehampton
►►► **Family Park** ★ £6 £6 £6
Open Mar-Dec Booking advisable Last arrival 22.30hrs Last departure noon
A small, well-established mainly static park in a rural setting close to Dartmoor National Park. Leave A30 at Sourton Down junc with A386, join old A30 (now B3278) signed Bridestowe, and turn left in 5m. At village centre turn left down unclass rd and site 1m on left. A 1-acre site with 13 touring pitches and 40 statics.

BRIDGERULE

Hedleywood Caravan & Camping Park (SS262013)
EX22 7ED ☎ 01288 381404 Signposted
Nearby town: Bude
►►► **Family Park** ★ £5.50-£7.50 £5.50-£7.50 £5.50-£7.50
Open all year Booking advisable public hols & Jul-Aug Last arrival anytime Last departure anytime
An isolated site in a good location, with a considerable amount of landscaping work in progress. From B3254 take Widemouth road (unclass) at the Devon/Cornwall boundary. A 16.5-acre site with 120 touring pitches and 12 statics.
Dog kennels, Nature Trail.

BRIXHAM

Galmpton Touring Park (SX885558)
Greenway Rd TQ5 0EP ☎ 01803 842066 Signposted
►►► **Family Park**
Open May-Sep (rs Apr shop closed) Booking advisable Jul-Aug Last arrival 22.00hrs Last departure 11.00hrs
An excellent location on high ground overlooking the River Dart, with outstanding views of the river and anchorage. Signed off A3022 Torbay/Brixham road at Churston. A 10-acre site with 120 touring pitches.

Hillhead Holiday Camp (SX903535)
TQ5 0HH ☎ 01803 853204 (2.5m SW)
►►► **Family Park**
Open Etr-Oct
Attractive, well laid out site with screening and landscaping to each pitch. Good views all around of countryside and sea. Amenities block well screened from touring park. On B3205 between Brixham and Kingswear. A 12.5-acre site with 330 touring pitches.

BRIXTON

Brixton Caravan & Camping Park (SX550520)
Venn Farm PL8 2AX ☎ 01752 880378 Signposted
Nearby town: Plymouth
► **Town & Country Pennant Park**
Open 15 Mar-14 Oct (rs 15 Mar-Jun & Sep-14 Oct no warden) Booking advisable Jul-Aug Last arrival 23.00hrs Last departure noon
A small site adjacent to a farm in the village, on A379. A 2-acre site with 43 touring pitches.

The AA pennant classification has been revised for 1998. Please read the explanation of the scheme on page 10.

BUCKFASTLEIGH

Beara Farm Caravan & Camping Site (SX751645)
Colston Rd TQ11 0LW ☎ 01364 642234 Signposted
Town & Country Pennant Park ★ £5.50-£6 fr £5 fr £5
Open all year Booking advisable peak periods Jul-Aug
Last arrival anytime Last departure anytime
Level site, close to the River Dart and the Dart Valley steam railway line, within easy reach of sea and moors. Approach is narrow with passing places and needs care. Leave A38 at Buckfast A384 junc, and take B3380 (old A38) towards Buckfastleigh. Turn left on Old Totnes Rd in .25m after passing under bridge. Turn right into Colston Rd, and follow single track for 2m. A 4-acre site with 30 touring pitches.

Churchill Farm Campsite (SX743664)
TQ11 0EZ ☎ 01364 642844
Nearby town: Totnes
Town & Country Pennant Park
Open Mar-Nov
A working family farm in a relaxed and peaceful setting with panoramic views. From A38 Dart Bridge exit for Buckfastleigh/Totnes head towards Buckfast Abbey. Turn left at mini rndbt, turn left at crossroads (Round Cross), and site opp Holy Trinity church. A 3-acre site with 25 touring pitches.

BUDLEIGH SALTERTON

See **Ladram Bay**

CHUDLEIGH

Finlake Holiday Park (SX855786)
TQ13 0EJ ☎ 01626 853833
Signposted
Nearby town: Newton Abbot

Open all year Booking advisable bank hols & Jul-Aug
Last arrival 22.00hrs Last departure 11.00hrs
A very well-appointed holiday centre situated in a wooded valley surrounded by 110 acres of wooded parkland. A wide range of leisure facilities and entertainment is available. Signed off A38 at Chudleigh exit. A 130-acre site with 450 touring pitches.
Fishing, horseriding & golf.

Credit Cards

The AA pennant classification has been revised for 1998. Please read the explanation of the scheme on page 10.

Holmans Wood Tourist Park (SX881812)
Harcombe Cross TQ12 5TX ☎ 01626 853785 Signposted
Family Park
Open Mar-Nov Booking advisable bank hols & Jul-Aug
Last arrival 22.00hrs Last departure 11.00hrs
Delightful small, personally-managed touring site, set back in secluded wooded area off A38. Convenient location for touring South Devon and Dartmoor National Park. An 11-acre site with 144 touring pitches.
Caravan storage facilities.

Credit Cards

CLIFFORD BRIDGE

Clifford Bridge Park (SX780897)
EX6 6QE ☎ 01647 24226 Signposted
Nearby town: Moretonhampstead
Family Park £7.15-£10.95 £6.50-£9.95 £7.15-£10.95
Open Etr-Sep Booking advisable school & bank hols
Last arrival 22.00hrs Last departure 11.00hrs
A very attractive location in a deep wooded valley in the Dartmoor National Park. The approach roads are narrow and steep in parts, and care is needed in towing large units. Site signed from Cheriton Biship. Turn near Old Thatch Inn and follow brown signs for 2m. Turn right at crossrd signed Clifford Bridge, follow very narrow lane for 1m, go straight across junc, and over bridge to site

contd.

on left. A 6-acre site with 65 touring pitches and 5 statics.
Fly fishing on site.

COLYTON

Leacroft Touring Park (SY217925)
Colyton Hill EX13 6HY ☎ 01297 552823 Signposted
Nearby town: Seaton
►►► **Family Park** ★ £6-£9 £6-£9 ▲ £5-£8
Open 15 Mar-Oct Booking advisable Jul-Aug & Spring bank hol Last arrival 22.00hrs Last departure noon
A mostly level site with enthusiastic owners, offering good sanitary facilities. 1m from Stafford Cross on A3052 towards Colyton. A 10-acre site with 138 touring pitches.
Off-licence.

COMBE MARTIN

Stowford Farm Meadows (SS560427)
Berry Down EX34 0PW ☎ 01271 882476 Signposted
►►►► **De-Luxe Park** ★ £3.75-£9 £3.75-£9 ▲ £3.75-£9
Open Etr-Oct (rs Etr-Spring bank hol & Oct some amenities may be available ltd hrs) Booking advisable bank hols & Jul-Aug Last arrival 20.00hrs Last departure 10.00hrs
Very gently sloping, grassy, sheltered and south-facing site approached down a wide, well-kept driveway. From A399 turn left onto B3343 to T-junc. Turn left then right, and site in .5m. A 100-acre site with 570 touring pitches.
Horse rides, fun golf, mini zoo, snooker, cycle hire.
See advertisement in Colour Section
Credit Cards

CROCKERNWELL

Barley Meadow Caravan & Camping Park (SX757925)
EX6 6NR ☎ 01647 281629 Signposted
►►► **Family Park** ▲
Open 15 Mar-15 Nov Booking advisable bank hols & Jul-Aug Last arrival mdnt Last departure noon
A small, very well-maintained site set on high ground in the National Park with easy access. Off the old A30, now bypassed, and isolated. From M5 take A30, leave by exit for Tedburn; turn left through Cheriton Bishop and Crockernwell, and site on left. A 4-acre site with 40 touring pitches.
Picnic tables.

DARTMOUTH

Little Cotton Caravan Park (SX858508)
Little Cotton TQ6 0LB ☎ 01803 832558

►►►► **De-Luxe Park**
Open 15 Mar-Oct Booking advisable Jul & Aug Last arrival 22.00hrs Last departure noon
A small, well-kept farm site on high ground above Dartmouth, with quality facilities and park and ride to the town from the gate. From Totnes take A381 signed Kingsbridge, at Halwell take B3207 for Dartmouth, and site on right before town. A 7.5-acre site with 95 touring pitches.

Deer Park Holiday Estate (SX864493)
Stoke Fleming TQ6 0RF ☎ 01803 770253 (Stoke Fleming 2m S A379) Signposted
►►► **Family Park**
Open 15 Mar-Oct Booking advisable Jul-Aug Last arrival anytime Last departure 10.00hrs
A rather open, mainly level grass site on high ground overlooking Start Bay. Direct access from A379 from Dartmouth before Stoke Fleming. A 6-acre site with 160 touring pitches and 43 statics.

Credit Cards

DAWLISH

Golden Sands Holiday Park (SX968784)
Week Ln EX7 0LZ ☎ 01626 863099
Signposted

★ £5.50-£14.50 £5.50-£14.50
Open Etr-Oct Booking advisable May-Sep Last arrival 22.00hrs Last departure 10.00hrs
A mainly static park with a small touring area set amongst trees, offering full family entertainment. Signed off A379 Exeter/Dawlish road, 1m N of Dawlish. A 2.5-acre site with 60 touring pitches and 188 statics.

Credit Cards

Cofton Country Holiday Park (SX967801)
Starcross EX6 8RP ☎ 01626 890111

►►►► **De-Luxe Park**
Open Etr-Oct (rs Etr-Spring bank hol & mid Sep-Oct swimming pool closed) Booking advisable bank hols & Jul-Aug Last arrival 20.00hrs Last departure noon
A well-ordered grass site in a good holiday location 1m S of Starcross on A379. A 16-acre site with 450 touring pitches and 62 statics.

contd.

Coarse fishing, pub with family room.

Credit Cards

Lady's Mile Touring & Caravan Park (SX968784)
EX7 0LX ☎ 01626 863411

►►►► De-Luxe Park
Open 17 Mar-27 Oct Booking advisable bank hols & Jul-Aug Last arrival 20.00hrs Last departure 11.00hrs
A well-ordered, clean and tidy site, with all grass pitches, and indoor and outdoor pools with chutes. Fairly central for the surrounding beaches, and 1m N of Dawlish on A379. A 16-acre site with 286 touring pitches and 1 static.
See advertisement in Colour Section

Credit Cards

Peppermint Park (SX978788)
Warren Rd EX7 0PQ ☎ 01626 863436 & 862211 Signposted

►►►► De-Luxe Park
Open Etr-Oct Booking advisable Spring bank hol & Jul-Aug Last arrival 20.00hrs Last departure 10.00hrs
Well-managed attractive site close to the coast, with excellent facilities including club and bar which are well away from pitches. From A379 at Dawlish follow signs for Dawlish Warren. Site on left in 1m. A 17-acre site with 250 touring pitches and 35 statics.
Licensed club & free entertainment.
See advertisement on page 113

Credit Cards

DOLTON

Dolton Caravan Park (SS573122)
EX19 8QF ☎ 01805 804536 Signposted
Nearby town: Great Torrington
► Town & Country Pennant Park £5-£7 £5-£7 £5-£7
Open Etr-15 Nov Booking advisable Jul-Aug Last arrival 22.00hrs Last departure noon
A well-maintained, landscaped paddock with wide countryside views, at the rear of the Royal Oak Inn in the centre of Dolton. Take B3217 south at its junc with B3220 at Dolton Beacon. Site signed from Dolton. A 2-acre site with 25 touring pitches.

DREWSTEIGNTON

Woodland Springs Touring Park (SX695912)
Venton EX6 6PG ☎ 01647 231695 Signposted
►►► Family Park
Open all year Booking advisable Last arrival 22.30hrs Last departure 11.00hrs
A brand new site in a rural area within Dartmoor National Park. Leave A30 at Merrymeet rndbt, turn left onto A382 towards Mortonhampstead, and site 2m on left. A 4-acre site with 85 touring pitches.

EAST WORLINGTON

Yeatheridge Farm Caravan Park (SS768110)
EX17 4TN ☎ 01884 860330
Nearby town: Witheridge
►►► Family Park
Open Etr-Sep Booking advisable Etr, Spring bank hol & school hols Last arrival 22.00hrs Last departure 22.00hrs
Gently sloping grass site with young trees set in meadowland in rural Devon. On B3042 1.5m W of Thelbridge Arms Inn. Site is NOT in East Worlington village which is unsuitable for caravans. A 9-acre site with 85 touring pitches and 2 statics.
Horse riding, fishing & pool table.
See advertisement under TIVERTON

Credit Cards

EXETER

See **Kennford**

HAWKCHURCH

Hunters Moon Touring Park (SY345988)
EX13 5UL ☎ 01297 678402 Signposted
Nearby town: Axminster
►►► **Family Park** ★ £5.85-£8.95 £5.85-£8.95 £5.85-£8.95
Open 15 Mar-Oct Booking advisable Whitsun & Jul-Aug Last arrival 23.00hrs Last departure noon
An attractive site in wooded area with panoramic country views. From Charmouth take A35 W to B3165. Site on left in 1.5m. An 11-acre site with 150 touring pitches.
All weather bowling green & putting green.

Credit Cards

See advertisement on page 130

HONITON

See also **Kentisbeare**

Camping & Caravanning Club Site (ST176015)
Otter Valley Park, Northcote EX14 8SP
☎ 01404 44546 & 01203 694995 Signposted
► **Town & Country Pennant Park** ★ £8.70-£11.30 £8.70-£11.30 £8.70-£11.30
Open Mar-Nov Booking advisable bank hols & Jul-Aug Last arrival 21.00hrs Last departure noon
A well run site just a short walk from the town. From Yeovil leave A30 at sign for A35 Dorchester, then turn left. Please see the advertisement on page 27 for details of Club Members' benefits. A 6-acre site with 90 touring pitches.
Dish washing sinks.

Credit Cards

ILFRACOMBE

Watermouth Cove Holiday Park (SS558477)
Berrynarbor EX34 9SJ
☎ 01271 862504 (towards Berrynarbor 2.5m E A361)

►►►► **De-Luxe Park**
Open Etr-Oct (rs Etr-Whit & Sep-Nov pool, takeaway, club & shop) Booking advisable Whit & Jul-Aug Last arrival anytime Last departure 11.00hrs
A popular site in very attractive surroundings, set amidst trees and bushes in meadowland with access to sea, beach and main road. On A399 from Combe Martin, past Berrynarbor, A 6-acre site with 90 touring pitches.
Coastal headland fishing.

Mullacott Cross Caravan Park (SS511446)
Mullacott Cross EX34 8NB ☎ 01271 862212 & 862200 (Mullacott Cross 2.5m S A361) Signposted
►►► **Family Park** ★ £6-£12 £5-£11 £5-£11
Open Etr-Sep (rs Etr-Whit & Oct restaurant restricted) Booking advisable Whit & Jul-Aug Last arrival 21.00hrs Last departure noon
This meadowland site is on gentle grass slopes with views over the Atlantic coastline, 2m S of Ilfracombe and 3m E of the sandy beach at Woolacombe. Located adjacent to A361 Braunton-Ilfracombe road. An 8-acre site with 115 touring pitches and 160 statics.
Caravan accessory shop.

Credit Cards

KENNFORD

Kennford International Caravan Park (SX912857)
EX6 7YN ☎ 01392 833046 Signposted
Nearby town: Exeter

►►►► **De-Luxe Park** ★ fr £9 fr £9 fr £9
Open all year Booking advisable public hols & Jul-Aug Last arrival mdnt Last departure noon
A well-kept touring site on the A38, with mature

landscaping. Mainly a transit site. An 8-acre site with 120 touring pitches.

Credit Cards

KENTISBEARE

Forest Glade Holiday Park (ST100075)
Cullompton EX15 2DT ☎ 01404 841381 Signposted
Nearby town: Honiton

►►►► **De-Luxe Park** £6-£11.50 £6-£11.50 £6-£11.50
Open 2 wks before Etr-Oct (rs low season pool closed) Booking advisable school hols Last arrival 21.00hrs
A quiet, attractive site in a forest clearing with well-kept gardens and beech hedge screening, on top of the Black Down Hills. Tent traffic from A373 signed at Keepers Cottage Inn, 2.5m E of M5 junc 28. Touring caravans via Honiton/Dunkeswell road. Please telephone for route details. There is no need to enter Kentisbeare Village. A 10-acre site with 80 touring pitches and 57 statics.
Adventure play area & childrens paddling pool.
See advertisement in Colour Section

Credit Cards

LADRAM BAY

Ladram Bay Holiday Centre (SY096853)
EX9 7BX ☎ 01395 568398 Signposted
Nearby town: Budleigh Salterton
► **Town & Country Pennant Park** ★ £8-£16 £7-£14 £7-£16
Open Spring bank hol-Sep (rs Etr-Spring Bank Hol pool closed no boat hire & entertainment) Booking advisable for caravans, school & Spring bank hols Last arrival 18.00hrs Last departure 10.00hrs
A large caravan site with many static vans and a separate camping area, set on terraced ground in wooded surroundings, overlooking rocky, shingle beach. A 5-acre site with 255 touring pitches and 369 statics.
Boat & canoe hire.
See advertisement in Colour Section

Credit Cards

LYDFORD

Camping & Caravanning Club Site (SX512853)
EX20 4BE ☎ 01822 820275 (in season) & 01203 694995 Signposted
Nearby town: Okehampton
►►► **Family Park** ★ £8.70-£11.30 £8.70-£11.30 £8.70-£11.30
Open end Mar-end Sep Booking advisable bank hols & peak periods Last arrival 21.00hrs Last departure noon
Site on mainly level ground looking towards the western slopes of Dartmoor at the edge of the village, near the spectacular gorge. Leave A386 towards Lydford village centre. Site signed on right. Please see advertisement on page 27 for details of Club Members' benefits. A 4-acre site with 70 touring pitches.

Credit Cards

LYNTON

Camping & Caravanning Club Site (SS700484)
Caffyns Cross EX35 6JS ☎ 01598 752379 (in season) & 01203 694995 Signposted
►►► **Family Park** ★ £8.70-£11.30 £8.70-£11.30 £8.70-£11.30
Open end Mar-early Nov Booking advisable bank hols & peak periods Last arrival 21.00hrs Last departure noon
A level grassy site, with bushes, set below hill in well-wooded countryside. 2m SW of Lynton off A39 Barnstaple-Minehead road. Please see the advertisement on page 27 for details of Club Members' benefits. A 5.5-acre site with 105 touring pitches.

Credit Cards

NEWTON ABBOT

Dornafield (SX838683)
Dornafield Farm, Two Mile Oak TQ12 6DD
☎ 01803 812732 Signposted

▶▶▶▶ **De-Luxe Park** ★ £8-£12.50 £8-£12.50 Ã £8-£12.50

Open Mar-Oct Booking advisable bank hols & Jul-Aug Last arrival 22.30hrs Last departure 11.00hrs

A quiet, very attractive and well-laid out site in a secluded wooded valley setting. Take A381 (Newton Abbot-Totnes) for 2m and at Two Mile Oak Inn turn right, then in .5m at cross roads turn left for site on right. A 30-acre site with 135 touring pitches.

Wet weather room.

Credit Cards

Stover International Caravan Park (SX823745)
Lower Staple Hill TQ12 6JD ☎ 01626 821446 Signposted

▶▶▶▶ **De-Luxe Park** ★ £4.25-£8.75 £4.25-£8.75 Ã £4.25-£8.75

Open Etr & Spring Bank-mid Sep (rs mid Sep-last Sat in

Oct shop, cafe, bar & pool reduced hours) Booking advisable Jun-Aug Last arrival 21.00hrs Last departure noon

A very well-equipped site set in a good touring location, adjacent to the famous Trago Mills shopping centre and theme park. Leave A38 at junc with A382, go towards Newton Abbot for 600yds, turn right at Trago Mills sign, and site on left past petrol stn.. A 15-acre site with 200 touring pitches and 20 statics.

Credit Cards

OKEHAMPTON

See also **Whiddon Down**

Moorcroft Leisure Park (SX603954)

Exeter Rd EX20 1QF ☎ 01837 55116 Signposted

►►► **Family Park**

Open all year Booking advisable Jul & Aug

A level grassy field behind Moorcroft Inn with adequate facilities. Leave A30 at sign for Belstone Services, and follow signs for Okehampton. Site on left in 1m. A 3-acre site with 35 touring pitches.

PAIGNTON

Beverley Parks Caravan & Camping Park (SX886582)

Goodrington Rd TQ4 7JE

☎ 01803 843887 (along A380/A3022, 2m S) Signposted

★

Open Etr-Oct Booking advisable Jun-Sep Last arrival 22.00hrs Last departure 10.00hrs

A well-ordered and well-established holiday park on raised ground adjacent to residential area south of town. A 12-acre site with 194 touring pitches and 198 statics.

Table tennis, pool, spa bath, crazy golf, sauna.

See advertisement in Colour Section

Credit Cards

Grange Court Holiday Centre (SX888588)

Grange Rd TQ4 7JP ☎ 01803 558010 Signposted

★ £8-£20 £8-£20

Open 23 May-19 Sep (rs 15 Feb-22 May & 20 Sep-15 Jan club, entertainment & swimming pool) Booking advisable public hols & Jul-Aug Last arrival 22.00hrs Last departure 10.00hrs

Large grassy site situated amidst woodland near to sea, very well-equipped and maintained. 1.5m from Paignton on Brixham road. A 10-acre site with 157 touring pitches and 520 statics.

Crazy golf, sauna, steam room & snooker.

Credit Cards

Byslades Camping Park (SX853603)

Totnes Rd TQ4 7PY ☎ 01803 555072 (2m W on A385) Signposted

►►►► **De-Luxe Park** £6-£11 £5.50-£10 £5.50-£11

Open Jun-Sep (rs Mar-May & Oct bar & swimming pool closed) Booking advisable Jul-Aug Last arrival 22.00hrs Last departure 10.00hrs

A well-kept terraced site set in beautiful countryside only 2 miles from Paignton. Signed off A385 at entry to town. A 23-acre site with 170 touring pitches.

Ornamental lake, crazy golf.

Widend Camping Park (SX852619)

Berry Pomeroy Rd, Marldon TQ3 1RT
☎ 01803 550116 Signposted

►►►► **De-Luxe Park**

Open Apr-Oct (rs Apr-mid May & mid Sep-Oct swimmimg pool, Club house May-Oct & Etr) Booking advisable Jul-Aug & Whit Last arrival 21.00hrs Last departure 10.00hrs

A terraced grass site paddocked and screened on high ground overlooking Torbay with views of Dartmoor. A well laid out and equipped site with high standards of maintenance. Signed off Torbay ring road. A 10-acre site with 207 touring pitches.

Credit Cards

Marine Park Holiday Centre (SX886587)

Grange Rd TQ4 7JR ☎ 01803 843887 (2m S on A3022) Signposted

►►► **Family Park** ★ £7-£12 £7-£12

Open Etr-Oct Booking advisable Jul-Aug Last arrival 22.00hrs Last departure 10.00hrs

A mainly static site catering for those who prefer peace and quiet. Next door to sister site Beverley Park whose amenities are available. Signed from ring road A3022 and B3198. A 2-acre site with 30 touring pitches and 66 statics.

Credit Cards

PLYMOUTH

Riverside Caravan Park (SX515575)

Longbridge Rd, Marsh Mills, Plympton PL6 8LD
☎ 01752 344122 (.5m E off A38) Signposted

►►►► **De-Luxe Park** £6.50-£10.25 £6.50-£10.25 £6.50-£10.25

Open Etr-Sep (rs Oct-Etr Bar, Restaurant & Take-away closed) Booking advisable Jun-Aug Last arrival 22.00hrs Last departure 10.00hrs

A well-groomed site on the outskirts of Plymouth on the banks of the R Plym. Approach by way of Longbridge road, which is E of Marsh Mills roundabout. An 11-acre site with 293 touring pitches.

Credit Cards

RATTERY

Edeswell Farm Country Caravan Park (SX731606)

Edeswell Farm TQ10 9LN ☎ 01364 72177 Signposted
Nearby town: Totnes

►►► **Family Park** ★ £7.50-£9.50 £7.50-£9.50 £7.50-£9.50

Open Etr-Sep Booking advisable school hols Last arrival 20.30hrs Last departure noon

Gently sloping, terraced grass site with mature trees, in hilly country and near river, off A385. A 3-acre site with 46 touring pitches and 18 statics.

Badminton, table tennis, adventure playground.

SALCOMBE

Karrageen Caravan & Camping Park (SX686395)

Malborough TQ7 3EN ☎ 01548 561230 (from Kingsbridge take A351 towards Salcombe, at Malborough turn sharp right following signs to Bolberry) Signposted

►►► **Family Park** ★ £7-£9.50 £7-£8 £6-£8.50

Open 15 Mar-15 Nov Booking advisable bank & school hols Last departure 11.30hrs

A small, friendly, family-run park with terraced grassy pitches giving extensive sea and country views. One mile from the beach in the pretty hamlet of Hope Cove. At Malborough on A381, turn sharp right through village, follow Bolberry signs for 0.5 miles. Turn right to Bolberry and the park is one mile on right. A 7.5-acre site with 75 touring pitches and 20 statics.

Bolberry House Farm Caravan & Camping Park (SX687395)

Bolberry TQ7 3DY ☎ 01548 561251 & 560926

Nearby town: Kingsbridge

►► **Town & Country Pennant Park** ★ £6.50-£8.50 £6.50-£8.50 £5-£7.50

Open Etr-Oct Booking advisable Jul & Aug Last arrival 22.00hrs Last departure noon

A level well maintained family run park in peaceful setting on coastal farm with sea views. At Malborough on A381 turn R signed Hope Cove & Bolberry. Take L fork after village signed Soar & Bolberry, and site signed in .5m. Discount in low season for senior citizens. A 6-acre site with 70 touring pitches and 4 statics.

Childrens play area & play barn.

SEATON

See **Colyton**

SIDMOUTH

Kings Down Tail Caravan & Camping Park (SY173907)

Salcombe Regis EX10 0PD

☎ 01297 680313 (off A3052 3m E of junc with A375) Signposted

►►► **Family Park** ★ £5.85-£8 £5.60-£6.95 £5.85-£8

Open 15 Mar-15 Nov Booking advisable Whit, bank hols & mid Jul-Sep Last arrival 22.00hrs Last departure noon

A well-kept site on level ground on east side of Sid Valley in tree-sheltered position. Opposite Branscombe water tower on A3052. A 5-acre site with 100 touring pitches and 2 statics.

Off licence.

Credit Cards

Oakdown Touring & Holiday Home Park (SY168901)

Weston EX10 0PH ☎ 01297 680387 (off A3052,2.5m E of junc with A375) Signposted

►►► **Family Park** ★ £6.75-£10.30 £6.75-£10.30 £6.75-£10.30

Open Apr-Oct Booking advisable Spring bank hol & Jul-Aug Last arrival 22.00hrs Last departure 10.30hrs

Friendly, well-maintained, level site with good landscaping. Reached by a short approach road off A3052, between Seaton and Sidmouth. A 13-acre site with 120 touring pitches and 46 statics.

Dishwashing sinks.

Credit Cards

Salcombe Regis Caravan & Camping Park (SY153892)

Salcombe Regis EX10 0JH ☎ 01395 514303 (off A3052 3m E of junc with A375) Signposted

►►► **Family Park**

Open Etr-15 Oct Booking advisable bank hols & Jul-Aug

contd.

Last arrival 22.00hrs Last departure 10.00hrs

Spacious level park with well-maintained facilities, on the coastal path 1.5m from Sidmouth and .5m from the sea. A 16-acre site with 110 touring pitches and 10 statics.

Off licence, bike hire, putting & barbecue hire.

Credit Cards

SLAPTON

Camping & Caravanning Club Site (SX825450)

Middle Grounds TQ7 1QW ☎ 01548 580538 (in season) & 01203 694995 Signposted

Nearby town: Kingsbridge

►►► **Family Park** ★ £9.10-£12.10 ▲ £9.10-£12.10

Open end Mar-early Nov Booking advisable bank hols & Jul-Aug Last arrival 21.00hrs Last departure noon

A very attractive location and well-run site open to non-members. The site overlooks Start Bay within a few minutes' walk of the beach. Take A379 coast road signed Dartmouth, after Tor Cross village turn left at American War Memorial for Slapton. Site on right. Please see the advertisement on page 27 for details of Club Members' benefits. A 5.5-acre site with 115 touring pitches.

Credit Cards

SOURTON CROSS

Bundu Camping & Caravan Park (SX546916)

EX20 4HT ☎ 01837 861611 Signposted

►►► **Family Park** ★ £6.50 £6.50 ▲ £4-£6.50

Open 15 Mar-15 Nov Booking advisable Jul & Aug

A level grassy site in an ideal location, on the border of the Dartmoor National Park and offering fine views. Leave A30 at A386 signed Tavistock/Plymouth, and site up first road on left. A 4-acre site with 38 touring pitches.

SOUTH BRENT

Webland Farm Holiday Park (SX715594)

Avonwick TQ10 9EX ☎ 01364 73273 (1m S of A38) Signposted

Nearby town: Totnes

► **Town & Country Pennant Park** ★ £5-£6.50 £5-£6.50 ▲ £5-£6.50

Open Etr-15 Nov Booking advisable school hols Last arrival 22.00hrs Last departure noon

A very rural park with extensive views, surrounded by farmland, with sloping pitches mainly for tents. For towed caravans, access can be awkward. Leave A38 at junc with A385 signed Marley Head, and site in 1m on unclass single track rd. A 5-acre site with 35 touring pitches and 50 statics.

STARCROSS

See **Dawlish**

STICKLEPATH

Olditch Caravan & Camping Park (SX645935)
EX20 2NT ☎ 01837 840734 Signposted
Nearby town: Okehampton
► Town & Country Pennant Park ★ £6 £6 £6
Open 14 Mar-14 Nov Booking advisable bank hols & Jul-Aug Last arrival 22.00hrs Last departure 16.00hrs
A basic farm site with trees and bushes set in Dartmoor National Park. Some pitches are now tiered. .5m E of village on A30, and 3m from Okehampton; follow signs for Sticklepath and South Zeal, and site 300 metres past garage at bottom of hill.. A 3-acre site with 32 touring pitches and 20 statics.
Small tourist information area

STOKE GABRIEL

Ramslade Touring Park (SX861592)
Stoke Rd TQ9 6QB ☎ 01803 782575 Signposted
Nearby town: Paignton

►►►► De-Luxe Park ★ £8-£11.50 £8-£11.50 £8-£11.50
Open mid Mar-Oct Booking advisable Jul-Aug also Etr & Spring bank hol Last arrival 20.00hrs Last departure 11.00hrs
A high quality park in a rural setting next to the Dart Valley. Situated between Paignton and the picturesque village of Stoke Gabriel on the River Dart, .75 miles from Stoke Gabriel. An 8-acre site with 135 touring pitches.
Paddling pool and dishwashing room.

Credit Cards

TAVISTOCK

Higher Longford Farm Caravan Site (SX520747)
Moorshop PL19 9JU ☎ 01822 613360 & 0585 166632 (2.5m from town along B3357) Signposted

►►►► De-Luxe Park £7-£8.50 £7-£8.50 £5.50-£8.50
Open all year Booking advisable Jun-Aug Last arrival 22.30hrs Last departure noon
A very pleasant small park on an isolated working farm in a moorland location. Adjacent to B3357 between Ashburton and Tavistock in the Dartmoor National Park. A 6-acre site with 52 touring pitches and 24 statics.
Farm animals.

Langstone Manor Camping & Caravan Park (SX524738)
Moortown PL19 9JZ ☎ 01822 613371 (2.5m W off B3357) Signposted

►►►► De-Luxe Park ★ £6-£7 £6-£7 £6-£7
Open 15 Mar-15 Nov Booking advisable bank hols & Jul-Aug Last arrival 23.00hrs Last departure 11.00hrs
A secluded site set in the well-maintained grounds of a manor house, within the National Park. Signed off B3357 Tavistock to Princetown road. A 3-acre site with 40 touring pitches and 25 statics.

Harford Bridge Holiday Park (SX504768)
PL19 9LS ☎ 01822 810349 (off A386) Signposted
►►► Family Park ★ £6-£9 £6-£9 £6-£9
Open 22 Mar-4 Nov Booking advisable Aug Last arrival 21.00hrs Last departure noon
Level, grassy site with mature trees, set in Dartmoor National Park, beside the River Tavy. 2m N of Tavistock on A386. A 10-acre site with 120 touring pitches and 80 statics.
Fly fishing.

Credit Cards

Woodovis Holiday Park (SX432744)
PL19 8NY ☎ 01822 832968 Signposted
►►► Family Park ★ £7-£8 £7-£8 £7-£8
Open Mar-Jan Booking advisable Jul-Aug Last arrival 22.00hrs Last departure noon
A well-kept small park in a remote woodland setting. Take A390 Tavistock-Liskeard road, after 2m at Gulworthy crossroads turn right, for site in 1.5m. A 14.5-acre site with 54 touring pitches and 23 statics.
Mini-golf & boules court.

Credit Cards

TEDBURN ST MARY

Springfield Holiday Park (SX788935)
Tedburn Rd EX6 6EW
☎ 01647 24242 (1.5m E of village off A30)
Signposted
Nearby town: Exeter
►►► Family Park
Open 15 Mar-15 Nov Booking advisable Jul-Aug Last arrival 22.00hrs Last departure 14.00hrs
This terraced site offers panoramic views of the surrounding countryside, a tranquil atmosphere and useful facilities. Leave A30 at Tedburn St Mary exit, turn left onto old A30 towards Cheriton Bishop, and signed on right. A 9-acre site with 88 touring pitches and 12 statics.
Licensed shop.

contd.

See advertisement under EXETER

See advertisement on page 115

TIVERTON

See **East Worlington**

TORQUAY

See also **Newton Abbot**

Widdicombe Farm Tourist Park (SX880650)
Compton TQ3 1ST ☎ 01803 558325 Signposted

►►►► **De-Luxe Park** ★ £6-£9.50 £6-£9.50
£6-£9.50
Open Mar-mid Nov Booking advisable Whitsun & Jul-Aug Last arrival 21.30hrs Last departure 11.00hrs
Family-owned and run park on a working farm, with good quality facilities and extensive views. On A380 dual carriageway, midway between two rndbts on N-bound lane from Compton Castle, and signed. An 8-acre site with 200 touring pitches and 3 statics.

Credit Cards

UMBERLEIGH

Camping & Caravanning Club Site (SS606242)
Over Weir EX37 9DU
☎ 01769 560009 (in season) & 01203 694995 Signposted
►►► **Family Park** ★ £8.70-£11.30 £8.70-£11.30
£8.70-£11.30
Open end Mar-early Nov Booking advisable bank hols & Jul-Aug Last arrival 21.00hrs Last departure noon
A compact site on high ground with fine country views adjacent to wooded area. Approached by metalled road, with wide entrance. Situated on the B3227, 200yds from the A377 at Umberleigh. Please see the advertisement on page 27 for details of Club Members' benefits. A 4-acre site with 60 touring pitches.
Fishing & tennis.

Credit Cards

WEST DOWN

Hidden Valley Coast & Country Park (SS499408)
EX34 8NU ☎ 01271 813837 (1m SW off A361)
Signposted
Nearby town: Ilfracombe

►►►► **De-Luxe Park** ★ £3.50-£10.50
£3.50-£10.50 £3.50-£10.50
Open 15 Mar-15 Nov Booking advisable high season
Last departure 11.00hrs

A delightful, well-appointed family site set in a wooded valley, with superb facilities and a restaurant. Winner of the Best Campsite for the South West of England, 1997/8. 5m SW of Ilfracombe off A361. A 25-acre site with 135 touring pitches.

Lounge/bar.

See advertisement in Colour Section

Credit Cards

WHIDDON DOWN

Dartmoor View Holiday Park (SX685928)

EX20 2QL ☎ 01647 231545 Signposted

Nearby town: Okehampton

►►►► **De-Luxe Park** ★ £6.30-£8.60 £6.30-£8.60 £6.30-£8.60

Open Mar-Oct Booking advisable Etr, Whitsun & Jul-Aug Last arrival 22.30hrs Last departure 10-12.00hrs

A pleasant, informal site with modern facilities on high ground within the National Park. In rural location yet near to the main A30 West Country road, .5m from Whiddon Down. A 5-acre site with 75 touring pitches and 40 statics.

Off licence, cycle/hire service, games room, putting.

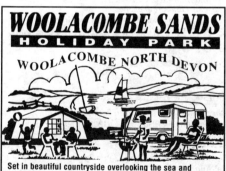

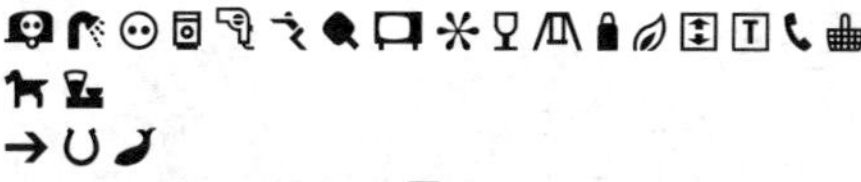

Credit Cards

WOODBURY Map 03 SY08

Webbers Farm Caravan Park (SY029878)

Castle Ln EX5 1EA ☎ 01395 232276 Signposted

Nearby town: Exmouth

►►► **Family Park** £6.90-£9.50 £6.90-£9.50 £6.90-£9.50

Open Etr-Sep Booking advisable all times Last arrival 22.00hrs Last departure 11.00hrs

Unspoilt farm site in two parts, with a fine view over River Exe towards Dartmoor. 4m from junction 30 of M5. Take the A376, then the B3179 to Woodbury Village, site is 500yds E of village. An 8-acre site with 115 touring pitches.

Pets corner, caravan storage facilities.

Credit Cards

WOOLACOMBE

Golden Coast Holiday Village (SS482436)

Station Rd EX34 7HW ☎ 01271 870343 Signposted

Nearby town: Barnstaple

★ £10.70-£26.45 £10.70-£26.45 £7.20-£16.90

Open Etr-Nov Booking advisable Whitsun & mid Jul-end Aug Last arrival 23.30hrs Last departure 10.00hrs

This holiday village includes villas and static caravans as well as the camping site. Woolacombe is surrounded by National Trust land. Follow road to Woolacombe Bay from Mullacott, and site in 1.5m on left. A 10-acre site with 231 touring pitches.

Sauna, solarium, jacuzzi, tennis squash, entertainment

See advertisement in Colour Section

Credit Cards

Woolacombe Sands Holiday Park (SS471434)

Beach Rd EX34 7AF ☎ 01271 870569 Signposted

►►► **Family Park** ★ £6.75-£16.50 £6.75-£16.50 £5.75-£15.50

Open Apr-Sep Booking advisable 18 Jul-30 Aug & 23-30 May Last arrival 22.00hrs Last departure 10.00hrs

A terraced site with level pitches and good facilities. From Woolacombe Bay go uphill towards Mullacott, and site in .25m on right. A 20-acre site with 200 touring pitches and 63 statics.

Credit Cards

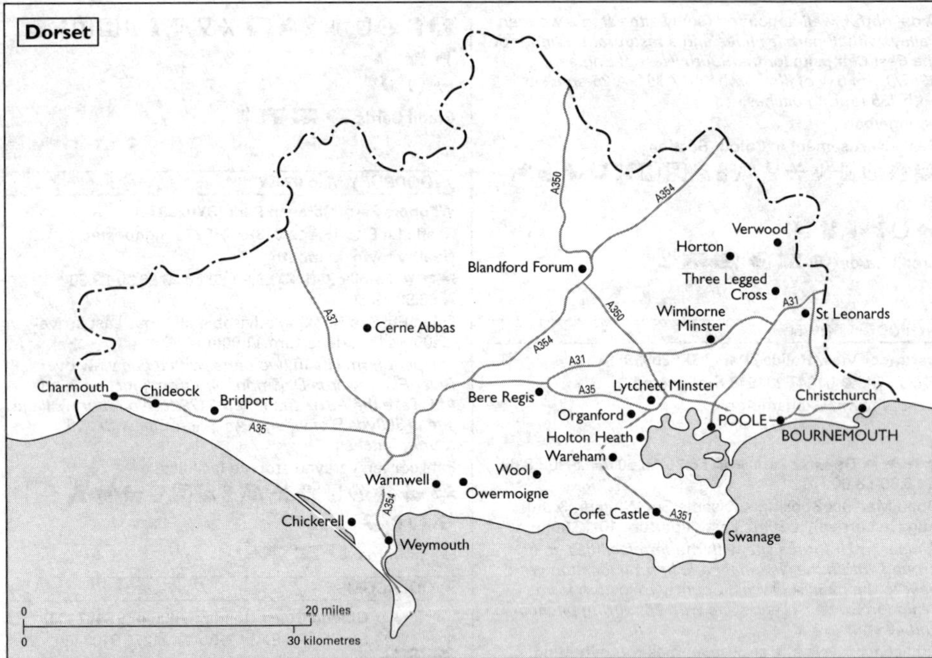

DORSET

BERE REGIS

Rowlands Wait Touring Park (SY842933)

Rye Hill BH20 7LP ☎ 01929 471958 (at Bere Regis take rd signposted to Wool/Bovington, about .75m at top of Rye Hill, turn right. Site about 200yds. Signposted

Nearby town: Dorchester

►►► **Family Park** ★ £5.60-£8.60 £5.60-£8.60 £5.60-£8.60

Open Mar-Oct Booking advisable bank hols & Jul-Aug Last arrival 21.30hrs Last departure noon

This park lies in a really attractive setting overlooking Bere and the Dorset countryside, set amongst undulating areas of trees and shrubs. At the A35 roundabout E of village exit left for village. At the next roundabout exit left for Bovington Camp. Do not enter village. Site signed on right approx 1.5m. An 8-acre site with 71 touring pitches.

BLANDFORD FORUM

The Inside Park (ST869046)

Down House Estate DT11 0HG ☎ 01258 453719 Signposted

►►►► **De-Luxe Park**

Open Etr-Oct Booking advisable bank hols & Jul-Aug Last arrival 22.00hrs Last departure noon

An attractive, well-sheltered and quiet site with some level pitches, in an isolated valley of woods and pasturelands. From town cross R Stour and follow signs to Winterbourne Stickland and site in 1.5m. A 12-acre site with 125 touring pitches.

Farm trips (main season). Kennels for hire.

Credit Cards

BOURNEMOUTH

Chesildene Touring Caravan Park (SZ107951)

2 Chesildene Av BH8 0DS ☎ 01202 513238 Signposted

►►► **Family Park**

Open Apr-Oct Booking advisable Spring bank hol & Jul-Aug

A well-maintained, level site in a quiet residential area close to the town centre and convenient for Poole. From Ringwood direction: 1m SW leave A31 and A338 signposted Bournemouth. In 7m at roundabout turn right onto A3060 then in 1m turn right at signpost. A 3-acre site with 70 touring pitches.

BRIDPORT

Binghams Farm Touring Caravan Park (SY478963)

Melplash DT6 3TT ☎ 01308 488234

►►► **Family Park** ★ £8-£10.50 £8-£10.50 £8-£10.50

Open all year Booking advisable bank hols Last arrival 22.00hrs Last departure 11.00hrs

A very good site with good quality buildings, fittings and services, in a lovely rural setting. Take A3066 signed Beaminster, then left into farm road after 1.5m. A 5-acre site with 60 touring pitches.

Washing-up facilities.

Freshwater Beach Holiday Park (SY493892)

Burton Bradstock DT6 4PT ☎ 01308 897317 (take B3517 towards Weymouth, park 1.5m on right)

►►► **Family Park** ★ £6.50-£16 £6.50-£16 £6.50-£16

Open 15 Mar-10 Nov Booking advisable Jul-Aug Last arrival 23.30hrs Last departure 10.00hrs

A well-maintained, typical holiday site with newly-built toilet block. On B3157, 1.5m E of Bridport. A 13-acre site with 400 touring pitches and 250 statics.

See advertisement in Colour Section

Credit Cards

Highlands End Farm Caravan Park (SY454913)

Eype DT6 6AR ☎ 01308 422139 (Eype, 1m W of A35) Signposted

►►► **Family Park** ★ £7.50-£11.75 £7.50-£11.75 £7.50-£11.75

Open mid Mar-early Nov Booking advisable public hols & Jul-Aug Last arrival 22.00hrs Last departure 11.00hrs

A well-screened site with clifftop views over Channel and Dorset coast. Adjacent to National Trust land and overlooking Lyme Bay. From Bridport take A35 Lyme rd, and site on left in 2m. A 9-acre site with 195 touring pitches and 160 statics.

Solarium, Gym & snooker room.

See advertisement in Colour Section

Credit Cards

CERNE ABBAS

Giant's Head Caravan & Camping Park (ST675029)

Giants Head Farm, Old Sherborne Rd DT2 7TR ☎ 01300 341242 Signposted

Nearby town: Dorchester

► **Town & Country Pennant Park** ★ £5-£6.50 £5-£6.50 £5-£6.50

Open Etr-Oct (rs Etr shop closed, Bar Jun-Aug only) Booking advisable Aug Last arrival anytime Last departure 13.00hrs

Part-level, part-sloping, grassy site set in Dorset downland near Cerne Giant (a figure cut into the chalk). A good stopover site ideal for tenters and back-packers on the Ridgeway route. Go into Dorchester avoiding by-pass. Take Sherborne road at town roundabout, after 500 yards take right fork at garage. A 4-acre site with 50 touring pitches.

Two holiday chalets.

CHARMOUTH

Wood Farm Caravan & Camping Park (SY356940)

Axminster Rd DT6 6BT ☎ 01297 560697 Signposted

Nearby town: Lyme Regis

►►►► **De-Luxe Park** ★ £7.50-£12.50 £7.50-£12.50 £7.50-£12.50

Open Etr-Oct Booking advisable school hols Last arrival 19.00hrs Last departure noon

A pleasant, well-maintained terraced site adjoining the A35. From village centre travel W to A35 rndbt, and site entrance signed here. A 13-acre site with 216 touring pitches and 83 statics.

Coarse fishing lake.

Credit Cards

Monkton Wylde Farm Caravan Park (SY336964)

DT6 6DB ☎ 01297 34525 Signposted

Nearby town: Lyme Regis

►►► **Family Park** ★ £6.25-£9 £6.25-£9 £6.25-£9

Open Etr-Oct (rs low & mid season site gate will be locked at 22.30hrs) Booking advisable after Xmas Last arrival 22.00hrs Last departure 11.00hrs

A pleasant family site in a secluded location yet central for Charmouth, Lyme and the coast. Situated on a 200 acre sheep and cereals farm. Leave A35 3m NW of Charmouth, and take B3165 signposted Marshwood. Site .25m on left. A 6-acre site with 60 touring pitches.

Family shower room.

CHICKERELL (NEAR WEYMOUTH)

Bagwell Farm Touring Park (SY627816)

DT3 4EA ☎ 01305 782575 Signposted

Nearby town: Weymouth

►►► **Family Park** £5.50-£10 £5.50-£10 £4.50-£9

Open all year Booking advisable Jul-Aug Last arrival 21.30hrs Last departure 11.00hrs

Attractive terraced site set in hillside and valley leading to sea, with good views of Dorset downland. Situated 4m W of Weymouth on the B3157 Abbotsbury-Bridport road, 500yds past the 'Victoria Inn' public house. A 14-acre site with 320 touring pitches.

Wet suit shower, campers shelter.

CHIDEOCK

Golden Cap Caravan Park (SY422919)

Seatown DT6 6JX ☎ 01297 489341 Signposted

►►► **Family Park** ★ £7.50-£11.75 £7.50-£11.75 £7.50-£11.75

Open mid Mar-early Nov Booking advisable public hols & Jul-Aug Last arrival 22.00hrs Last departure 11.00hrs

contd.

POOLE

Beacon Hill Touring Park (SY977945)
Blandford Rd North BH16 6AB ☎ 01202 631631 (off A350, NW of junc A35) Signposted

►►►► **De-Luxe Park** ★ £7.40-£15 £6.60-£15 ▲ £6.60-£15

Open Etr-Sep (rs low & mid season bar/take-away/coffee shop, swimming pool) Booking advisable Etr, Whit & Jul-Aug Last arrival 23.00hrs Last departure 11.00hrs

Set in attractive, wooded area with conservation very much in mind. Two large ponds are within the grounds and the terraced pitches offer some fine views. From Upton Cross rndbt take bridge over A35 towards Blandford on A350. Site on right in 250yds. A 30-acre site with 170 touring pitches.

Fishing & view point.

See advertisement on page 119

Rockley Park (SY982909)
Hamworthy BH15 4LZ ☎ 01202 679393

►►► **Family Park** ★ £5-£12 £5-£12 ▲ £5-£12

Open Mar-Oct Booking advisable Last arrival 20.00hrs Last departure noon

A touring park within a static site, with all the advantages of a holiday centre. Take A31 off M27 to Poole centre, then follow signs to park. A 4.25-acre site with 112 touring pitches.

Credit Cards

ST LEONARDS

Camping International Holiday Park (SU104024)
Athol Lodge, 229 Ringwood Rd BH24 2SD ☎ 01202 872817 & 872742 (on A31) Signposted

Nearby town: Ringwood

►►►► **De-Luxe Park** ★ £7.70-£11.30 £7.40-£11.30 ▲ £7.40-£11.30

Open Mar-Oct (rs Mar-May & Sep-Oct (ex bank hols) restaurant/take-away food not available) Booking advisable school & bank hols Last arrival 22.30hrs Last departure 10.30hrs

Small, well-equipped, level camping site surrounded by trees adjacent to A31. Travel W on A31 from Ringwood through underpass to 2nd rndbt, turn left, and site on left. An 8-acre site with 200 touring pitches.

Football/basketball park.

See advertisement on page 143, Hampshire.

Credit Cards

Oakdene (SZ095023)
BH24 2RZ ☎ 01202 875422
►►► **Family Park**
Open Mar-5 Jan Booking advisable
An open site surrounded by forest, with good on-site facilities. Travel W on A31(T) from Ringwood, and site entrance next to hospital entrance, and signed. A 20-acre site with 388 touring pitches and 207 statics.

Shamba Holiday Park (SU105029)
230 Ringwood Rd BH24 2SB ☎ 01202 873302 Signposted
Nearby town: Ringwood
►►► **Family Park**
Open Mar-Oct Booking advisable bank hols & Jul-Aug Last arrival 23.30hrs Last departure 11.00hrs
Level grassy site in hilly wooded country. 3m W of Ringwood off A31. A 7-acre site with 150 touring pitches.

SWANAGE

Ulwell Cottage Caravan Park (SZ019809)
Ulwell Cottage, Ulwell BH19 3DG ☎ 01929 422823 & 424931 Signposted
►►► **Family Park** ★ £10-£18 £10-£18 £10-£18
Open Mar-7 Jan (rs Mar-spring bank hol & mid Sep-early Jan takeaway closed, shop open variable hours) Booking advisable bank hols & Jul-Aug Last arrival 23.00hrs Last departure 11.00hrs
Nestling under the Purbeck Hills surrounded by scenic walks and only 2m away from the beach. A 13-acre site with 77 touring pitches and 140 statics.
See advertisement under Colour Section
Credit Cards

THREE LEGGED CROSS

Woolsbridge Manor Farm Caravan Park (SZ103050)
Three Legged Cross BH21 6RA ☎ 01202 826369 (2m off A31,3m W of Ringwood)
Nearby town: Ringwood
►►► **Family Park** ★ £6-£8 £6-£8 £6-£8
Open Etr-Oct Booking advisable bank hols & Aug Last arrival 22.00hrs Last departure 13.00hrs
A flat quiet site with a very low density and clean, well-maintained toilets. Situated 2m off A31, 3m W of Ringwood. From Three Legged Cross continue S to Woolsbridge, and site on left in 1.75m. A 6.75-acre site with 60 touring pitches.
See advertisement under RINGWOOD

The AA pennant classification has been revised for 1998. Please read the explanation of the scheme on page 10.

VERWOOD

Camping & Caravanning Club Site (SU069098)
Sutton Hill, Woodlands BH21 6LF
☎ 01202 822763 & 01203 694995 Signposted
►►► **Family Park** ★ £9.10-£12.10 £9.10-£12.10 £9.10-£12.10
Open end Mar-early Nov Booking advisable Jul-Aug & bank hols Last arrival 21.00hrs Last departure noon
A popular site with pleasant wardens and staff. 7m from Ringwood on B3081, 1.5m past Verwood on R. Please see the advertisement on page 27 for details of Club Members' benefits. A 12.75-acre site with 150 touring pitches.
Recreation room, pool table, table tennis.
Credit Cards

WAREHAM

Birchwood Tourist Park (SY917883)
Bere Rd, North Trigon BH20 7PA ☎ 01929 554763 Signposted
Nearby town: Poole
►►► **Family Park** ★ fr £6 fr £6 fr £6
Open Mar-Oct Booking advisable bank hols & Jul-Aug Last arrival 22.00hrs Last departure noon
A well-maintained site which is maturing into a very attractive park. Situated 3m N of Wareham on road linking A351 at Wareham and Bere Regis. A 25-acre site with 175 touring pitches.

Riding stables, bike hire, pitch & putt, table tennis

Credit Cards

Lookout Holiday Park (SY927858)
Stoborough BH20 5AZ ☎ 01929 552546 Signposted
►►► **Family Park**
Open Mar-Dec Booking advisable bank hols & Jul-Aug Last arrival 22.00hrs Last departure noon
Ideal family touring site on main road to Swanage 2m from Wareham. The touring pitches are set well back from the road. Turn right at exit for Wareham, and site in 1.5 miles. A 15-acre site with 150 touring pitches and 90 statics.
9 hole crazy golf.

Manor Farm Caravan Park (SY872866)
1 Manor Farm Cottage, East Stoke BH20 6AW
☎ 01929 462870
►►► **Family Park** ★ £6.50-£8.50 £6.50-£8.50 £6.50-£8.50
Open Etr-Sep Booking advisable school hols Last arrival 22.00hrs Last departure 11.00hrs
An attractive, mainly touring site in a quiet rural setting. From Wareham follow Dorchester road (A352) for 2m then turn left onto B3070, at first crossroads turn right, then next crossroads turn right; site is on the left. From Wool take B3071 and follow Bindon Lane unclass, in 1.75m turn left. A 2.5-acre site with 40 touring pitches.

WARMWELL

Warmwell Country Touring Park (SY764878)
DT2 8JD ☎ 01305 852313 Signposted
Nearby town: Dorchester

►►►► **De-Luxe Park**
Open mid Mar-Jan Booking advisable Etr-Sep & Xmas Last arrival dusk Last departure 11.00hrs
A landscaped terraced site 5m from the Lulworth beaches. Take B3390 1m N of Warmwell. A 15-acre site with 190 touring pitches.

Credit Cards

WEYMOUTH

Pebble Bank Caravan Park (SY659775)
Camp Rd, Wyke Regis DT4 9HF ☎ 01305 774844
► **Town & Country Pennant Park**
Open Etr- mid Oct bar open high season & wknds only Booking advisable peak times Last arrival 21.00hrs Last departure 11.00hrs

contd.

A sloping, mainly static site overlooking Lyme Bay and Chesil Beach. From Weymouth take Portland Rd, and at last rndbt turn right then 1st left to Army Tent Camp. Site opposite. A 4-acre site with 40 touring pitches and 80 statics.

WIMBORNE MINSTER

Merley Court Touring Park (SZ008984)
Merley BH21 3AA ☎ 01202 881488 (1m S A349)
Signposted
Nearby town: Wimborne

►►►►► **Premier Park** ★ £6-£11.50 £6-£11.50 £6-£11.50

Open Mar-7 Jan (rs low season pool closed & bar/shop open limited hrs) Booking advisable bank hols & Jun-Sep Last arrival 22.00hrs Last departure 11.00hrs

A superb site in a quiet, rural position on the edge of Wimborne, with woodland on two sides and good access roads. From Wimborne take B3073 to rndbt, turn left to next rndbt with A31, turn right, and site signed. An 11-acre site with 160 touring pitches.

Badminton, mini football, table tennis, crazy golf.

See advertisement under Colour Section

Credit Cards

Wilksworth Farm Caravan Park (SU004018)
Cranborne Rd BH21 4HW ☎ 01202 885467
Signposted
Nearby town: Wimborne

►►►► **De-Luxe Park** ★ £6-£11 £6-£11 £6-£11

Open Mar-30 Oct (rs Mar no shop/coffee shop) Booking advisable Spring bank hol & Jul-Aug Last arrival 21.30hrs Last departure 11.00hrs

This popular and attractive site lies in the heart of Dorset, 1m N of the town on the B3078. It is well-maintained with good facilities. An 11-acre site with 85 touring pitches and 77 statics.

Paddling pool, volley ball, mini football pitch.

Charris Camping & Caravan Park (SY991988)
Candy's Lane, Corfe Mullen BH21 3EF
☎ 01202 885970 (2m W off A31) Signposted

►►► **Family Park**

Open Mar-Oct Booking advisable bank hols & Jul-Aug Last arrival 22.30hrs Last departure 13.00hrs

A neat, clean, simple site enjoying a rural situation, with views of surrounding countryside. From Wimborne turn S on B3073 to rndbt, turn right onto A31, and site on left. A 3-acre site with 45 touring pitches.

Springfield Touring Park (SY987989)
Candys Ln, Corfe Mullen BH21 3EF
☎ 01202 881719
Signposted
Nearby town: Wimborne

►►► **Family Park** £7-£8 £7-£8 £5-£8

Open mid Mar-Oct Booking advisable bank hols & Jul-Aug Last arrival 22.00hrs Last departure 11.00hrs

A small touring site with good facilities and hardworking owners. A quiet site overlooking the Stour Valley. Turn left off A31 at rndbt at W end of Wimborne bypass signed Corfe Mullen. Within .25m turn right into Candys Lane, and entrance 300yds past farm. A 3.5-acre site with 45 touring pitches.

WOOL

Whitemead Caravan Park (SY841869)
East Burton Rd BH20 6HG ☎ 01929 462241
Signposted
Nearby town: Wareham

►►► **Family Park** ★ £4.50-£8.50 £4.50-£8.50 £4.50-£8.50

Open mid Mar-Oct Booking advisable public hols & mid Jul-Aug Last arrival 22.00hrs Last departure noon

Well laid-out level site in valley of River Frome, 300yds W off A352. A 5-acre site with 95 touring pitches.

CO DURHAM

For the map of this county see Northumberland

BARNARD CASTLE

Camping & Caravanning Club Site (NZ025168)
Dockenflatts Ln DL12 9DG
☎ 01833 630228 & 01203 694995
Signposted

►►► Family Park ★ £3.90-£5.20 £3.90-£5.20 £3.90-£5.20

Open end Mar-beg Nov Booking advisable Jan-Mar Last arrival 21.00hrs Last departure noon

A peaceful site surrounded by mature woodland and meadowland, with first class facilities. Leave A66 by B6277 if approaching from S to avoid Barnard Castle. Park off B6277, 1.5m from junc with A67. A 10-acre site with 90 touring pitches.

Credit Cards

BEAMISH

Bobby Shafto Caravan Park (NZ218541)
Cranberry Plantation DH9 0RY
☎ 0191 370 1776
Signposted

►►► Family Park

Open Mar-Oct Booking advisable school hols Last arrival 11.00hrs Last departure 11.00hrs

A tranquil rural site surrounded by mature trees, with well-organised facilities. Leave A1(M) at junc 63, follow A1693 signed Beamish, and after 2 rndbts turn right in 1.25m. Turn immed left, then right onto unclass rd. After .75m take left fork, and after .75m turn left. Site in 500 metres on left. A 9-acre site with 20 touring pitches and 35 statics.

CASTLESIDE

Allensford Caravan & Camping Park (NZ083505)
DH8 9BA ☎ 01207 591043 Signposted

►►► Family Park

Open Mar-Oct Booking advisable Whit wknd Last arrival 22.00hrs Last departure noon

Level parkland with mature trees, in hilly moor and woodland country near the urban area adjacent to River Derwent and A68. Situated approx 2m SW of Consett, N on A68 for 1 mile then right at Allensford Bridge. A 2-acre site with 40 touring pitches and 46 statics.

Tourist information centre.

WYCLIFFE (NEAR BARNARD CASTLE)

Thorpe Hall (NZ105141)
DL12 9TW ☎ 01833 627230 (off unclass between Wycliffe & Greta Bridge) Signposted
Nearby town: Barnard Castle

Town & Country Pennant Park ★ £7.50 £7.50

Open Apr-Oct (rs Mar no showers restricted parking) Booking advisable bank hols & Jul-Aug Last arrival 21.00hrs Last departure 13.00hrs

A very pleasant site with good facilities in the grounds of a large country house. Lies S of River Tees and 5m from Barnard Castle. From A66 1m SE of Greta Bridge take unclassified road (signed Wycliffe). A 2-acre site with 12 touring pitches and 16 statics.

ESSEX

BRENTWOOD

Camping & Caravanning Club Site (TQ577976)
Warren Ln, Frog St, Kelvedon Hatch CM15 0JG
☎ 01277 372773

►►► Family Park

Open end Mar-early Oct

A very pretty rural site with many separate areas amongst the trees, and a secluded field for campers. Head N on A128 out of Brentwood, and turn right at Kelvedon Hatch. Signed. A 12-acre site with 120 touring pitches.

CANEWDON

Riverside Village Holiday Park (TQ929951)
Creeksea Ferry Rd, Wallasea Island SS4 2EY
☎ 01702 258297 Signposted
Nearby town: Southend-on-Sea

►►► Family Park ★ £7-£9 £7-£9 £2.50-£5

Open Mar-Oct Booking advisable public hols Last arrival 22.00hrs Last departure 17.00hrs

A pleasant and popular riverside site, well laid out and very neat. An 8-acre site with 60 touring pitches and 180 statics.

Boule pitch.

COLCHESTER

Colchester Camping Caravan Park (TL971252)
Cymbeline Way, Lexden CO3 4AG ☎ 01206 545551
Signposted

►►►► De-Luxe Park

Open all year Booking advisable public hols Last arrival

contd.

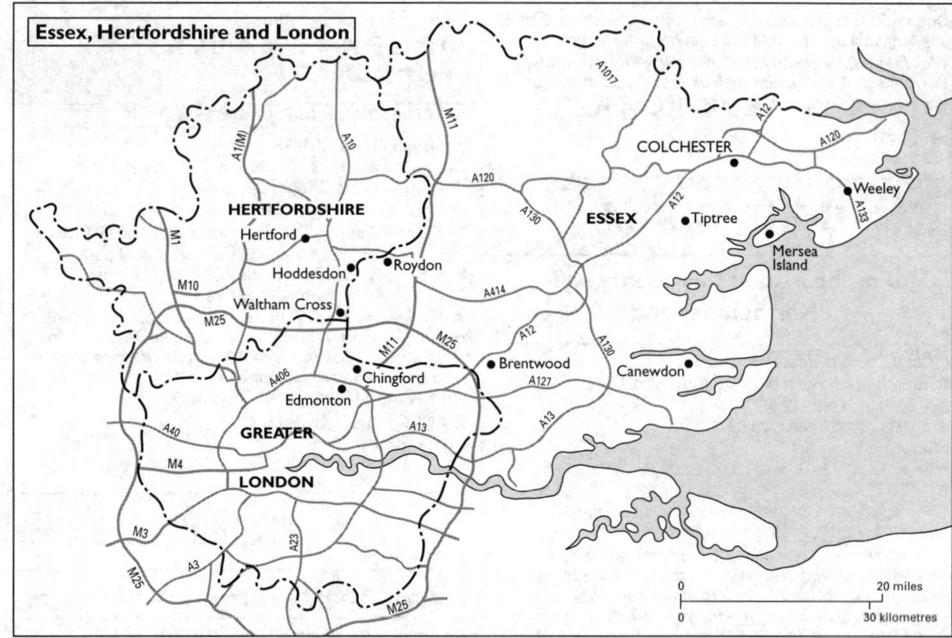

20.00hrs Last departure noon

A well-designed campsite on level grassland, on the west side of Colchester near the town centre. Close to main routes to London (A12) and east coast. A 12-acre site with 251 touring pitches.

Badminton court & putting green on site.

Credit Cards

MERSEA ISLAND

Waldegraves Holiday Park (TM033133)

West Mersea, Mersea Island CO5 8SE ☎ 01206 382898 Signposted

►►► **Family Park** ★ £8-£12 £8-£12 ▲ £8-£12

Open Mar-Oct Booking advisable bank hols Last arrival 22.00hrs Last departure noon

A spacious and pleasant site, located between farmland and its own private beach on the Blackwater Estuary. Facilities include two fresh water fishing lakes. Signed from Colchester. Follow signs through town to Mersey and military barracks. A 15-acre site with 60 touring pitches and 205 statics.

Boating and fishing on site.

Credit Cards

ROYDON

Roydon Mill Leisure Park (TL403104)

CM19 5EJ ☎ 01279 792777 Signposted

►►► **Family Park** £9.50-£10.70 £9.50-£10.70 ▲ £9.50-£10.70

Open all year Booking advisable bank hols Last arrival 23.00hrs Last departure 23.00hrs

A busy complex with caravan sales and water sports. Facilities have recently been upgraded. Signed from A414 between A10 and Harlow. An 11-acre site with 120 touring pitches and 149 statics.

Large lake, clay pigeon shooting, waterski school.

Credit Cards

TIPTREE

Villa Farm (TL881155)

West End Rd CO5 0QN ☎ 01621 815217

Nearby town: Colchester

► **Town & Country Pennant Park** ★ £3-£6 £3-£6 ▲ £2-£4

Open Apr-Sep Booking advisable mid Jun-mid Jul Last arrival 23.00hrs Last departure anytime

Grassland site on fruit farm, quiet except mid-June to mid-July which is picking season (when booking is advisable). From Tiptree follow B1022, at pub fork right into West End Road. A 7-acre site with 5 touring pitches.

WEELEY

Weeley Bridge Caravan Park (TM145219)
CO16 9DH ☎ 01255 830403 (off A133) Signposted
Nearby town: Clacton-on-Sea
Town & Country Pennant Park ★ £15 £15
Open Mar-Oct (rs Nov-Feb open wknds only & 10 days Xmas) Booking advisable Last arrival 22.00hrs Last departure 10.00hrs no cars by caravans
Level grass touring area at far end of large static park beside Weeley Station and freight depot. Signed from A133 to Clacton. A 16-acre site with 26 touring pitches and 290 statics.
Private fishing lake, live entertainment wknds.

Credit Cards

GLOUCESTERSHIRE

For the map of this county, see Wiltshire

CHELTENHAM

Caravan Club Site (SO954245)
Cheltenham Racecourse GL50 4SH ☎ 01242 523102 Signposted
►►► Family Park
Open 2 Apr-mid Oct Booking advisable bank hols & for awning pitches Last arrival 20.00hrs Last departure noon
A mainly level site on Cheltenham Racecourse in hilly country with nearby downland 1.5m N of town on A435 Evesham road. A 4-acre site with 84 touring pitches.
Two sinks for veg prep & dish washing.

Credit Cards

Longwillows Caravan & Camping Park (SO967278)
Station Rd, Woodmancote GL52 4HN
☎ 01242 674113 (3.5m N) Signposted
►►► Family Park ★ £5.50-£6 £5.50-£6
£5.50-£6
Open Mar-Oct Booking advisable bank hols & Jul-Aug Last arrival 23.00hrs Last departure 18.00hrs
Mostly level site with good quality, clean toilet facilities in a remote situation. From Cheltenham take A438 to Bishop Cleave, turn right for Woodmancote and follow signs. A 4-acre site with 80 touring pitches.
Separate games area.

CIRENCESTER

Mayfield Touring Park (SP020055)
Cheltenham Rd, Perrott's Brook GL7 7BH
☎ 01285 831301 (2m N on A435) Signposted
►►► Family Park £6.80-£9.40 £5.80-£9.40
£5.40-£9.40
Open all year Booking advisable public hols & Jun-Aug Last arrival 22.30hrs Last departure noon
Part-level, part-sloping grass site, in hilly meadowland in the Cotswolds, an area of outstanding natural beauty. Situated off A435, 2m from Cirencester. A 4-acre site with 72 touring pitches.
Dishwashing area.

COLEFORD

Christchurch Forest Park Camping Ground (SO568129)
GL16 8BA ☎ 01594 833376 (site) (1m N) Signposted
►►► Family Park ★ £5.20-£9.40 £5.20-£9.40
£5.20-£9.40
Open Mar-Oct Booking advisable all times Last arrival 22.00hrs Last departure noon
A well-appointed site in open forest with good amenities. A good base for walking. From Coleford follow signs for Symonds Yat to Berry Hill where site is signed. A 20-acre site with 280 touring pitches.

Credit Cards

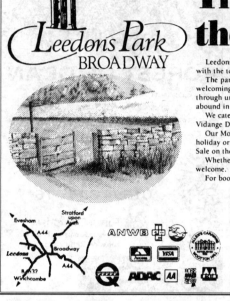

GLOUCESTER

Red Lion Camping & Caravan Park (SO849258)
Wainlode Hill, Norton GL2 9LW ☎ 01452 730251 Signposted
►►► **Family Park**

Open all year Booking advisable spring bank hol Last arrival 22.00hrs Last departure 11.00hrs

An attractive meadowland site opposite River Severn. Ideal fishing centre and touring base. Turn off A38 at Norton and follow road to river. A 13-acre site with 60 touring pitches and 20 statics.

Bar snacks, hot & cold food.

SEVERN BEACH

Salthouse Farm Caravan & Camping Park (ST543854)
BS12 3NH ☎ 01454 632274 & 632699 Signposted
Nearby town: Bristol
►►► **Family Park** ★ £7-£7.50 £7-£7.50 £7-£7.50

Open Apr-Oct Booking advisable public hols Last arrival 22.00hrs Last departure 14.00hrs

Level, grassy site in meadowland adjacent to Severn Estuary and beach, and well-protected from winds. From M5 (London) from junc 17 take B4055 to Pilning. At crossrds turn left, cross mini rndbt in 0.25m, and in 0.5m take 1st right (signed). From M4 (London) change to M48 at junc 1, take A403 to Pilning, then as above. A 3-acre site with 40 touring pitches and 50 statics.

SLIMBRIDGE

Tudor Caravan & Camping (SO728040)
Shepherds Patch GL2 7BP
☎ 01453 890483 (from M5 Jct 13/14. Follow signs to Wildfowl Trust Site at rear of Tudor Arms PH 10yds before canal) Signposted
Nearby town: Dursley
►►► **Family Park** £6.75-£7 £6.75-£7 £5.25-£7

Open all year Booking advisable bank & school hols Last arrival 21.00hrs Last departure 18.00hrs

Level grass and gravel site with trees and bushes, set in meadow by canal, off A38. Nearby is the Wildlife Trust. Access through pub car park. An 8-acre site with 75 touring pitches.

SOUTH CERNEY

Cotswold Hoburne (SU055958)
Broadway Ln GL7 5UQ ☎ 01285 860216 Signposted
Nearby town: Cirencester

Open Good Fri-Oct Booking advisable public hols & high season Last arrival 21.00hrs Last departure 10.00hrs

A large holiday centre on flat grassy ground and adjoining the Cotswold Water Park. From Cirencester take A419 for 3m. Turn right at sign, and right again in

1m. Site on left. A 70-acre site with 302 touring pitches and 211 statics.
Crazy golf, fishing & pedal-boat hire.

Credit Cards

GREATER MANCHESTER

For the map of this county, see Shropshire

ROCHDALE

Gelder Wood Country Park (SD852127)
Ashworth Rd OL11 5UP ☎ 01706 364858 & 620300 Signposted
Nearby town: Heywood
►►► **Family Park** ★ £6-£7 £6-£7 £6-£7
Open Mar-Oct Booking advisable Etr Last departure 22.00hrs
A very rural site in a peaceful private country park with excellent facilities. All pitches have extensive views of the moor. Signed off B6222 midway between Bury and Rochdale. A 10-acre site with 34 touring pitches.

HAMPSHIRE

NEW FOREST

The New Forest covers 144 square miles and is composed of broadleaf and coniferous woodland, open commonland and heath. This unique area was originally a royal hunting forest and there are long established rights of access. It is not a 'Forest Park' but similar facilities for visitors are maintained by the Forestry Commission; these include caravan and camp sites, picnic sites, car parks, way-marked walks and an ornamental drive. The camp sites are open from the Friday before Easter until the end of September (two sites remain open in October). Information and camping leaflet available from the Forestry Commission, 231 Corstorphine Road, Edinburgh EH12 7AT. Telephone 0131 334 0066. Information also available from the Tourist Information Centre at Lyndhurst Car Park. Telephone Lyndhurst (01703) 282269. See Ashurst, Bransgore, Brokenhurst, Fritham, Lyndhurst and Sway for AA pennant classified sites.

Many parks in this guide may exclude some categories of people from staying. Please check before you book, and see the important note on page 4.

ASHURST

Ashurst Campsite (SU332099)
Lyndhurst Rd SO4 2AA ☎ 0131 314 6100 (on A35) Signposted
Nearby town: Lyndhurst
►►► **Family Park** ★ £6.50-£10 £6.50-£10 £6.50-£10
Open Etr-Oct Booking advisable all times Last arrival 23.30hrs Last departure noon
Situated just off the A35 Southampton-Bournemouth road, this quiet, secluded Forestry Commission site is set amongst woodlands and heathland on the fringe of the New Forest. See under 'Forestry Commission' for further information. A 23-acre site with 280 touring pitches.
Lightweight camping area.

Credit Cards

BRANSGORE

Harrow Wood Farm Caravan Park (SZ194978)
Harrow Wood Farm, Poplar Ln BH23 8JE
☎ 01425 672487
Nearby town: Christchurch

►►►► **De-Luxe Park** £9-£12.75 £9-£12.75
Open Mar-6 Jan Booking advisable bank & school hols Last arrival 22.00hrs Last departure noon
A very well laid out site in a pleasant rural position with adjoining woodland and fields. Leave village from S, and take last turning on left past shops. Site at top of lane. A 6-acre site with 60 touring pitches.
Washing up facilities.

Credit Cards

Holmsley Campsite (SZ215991)
Forest Rd, Holmsley BH23 7EQ
☎ 0131 314 6100 (off A35) Signposted
Nearby town: New Milton
►►► **Family Park** ★ £6.50-£10 £6.50-£10 £6.50-£10
Open Etr-Sep Booking advisable all times Last departure noon
A large Forestry Commission site, in rural surroundings on the fringe of the New Forest. See under Forestry Commission for further information. From A35 S take Bransgore turn on right, and right again in 1m. Site signed. An 89-acre site with 700 touring pitches.

Credit Cards

BROCKENHURST

Hollands Wood Campsite (SU303038)
Lyndhurst Rd SO42 7QH

contd.

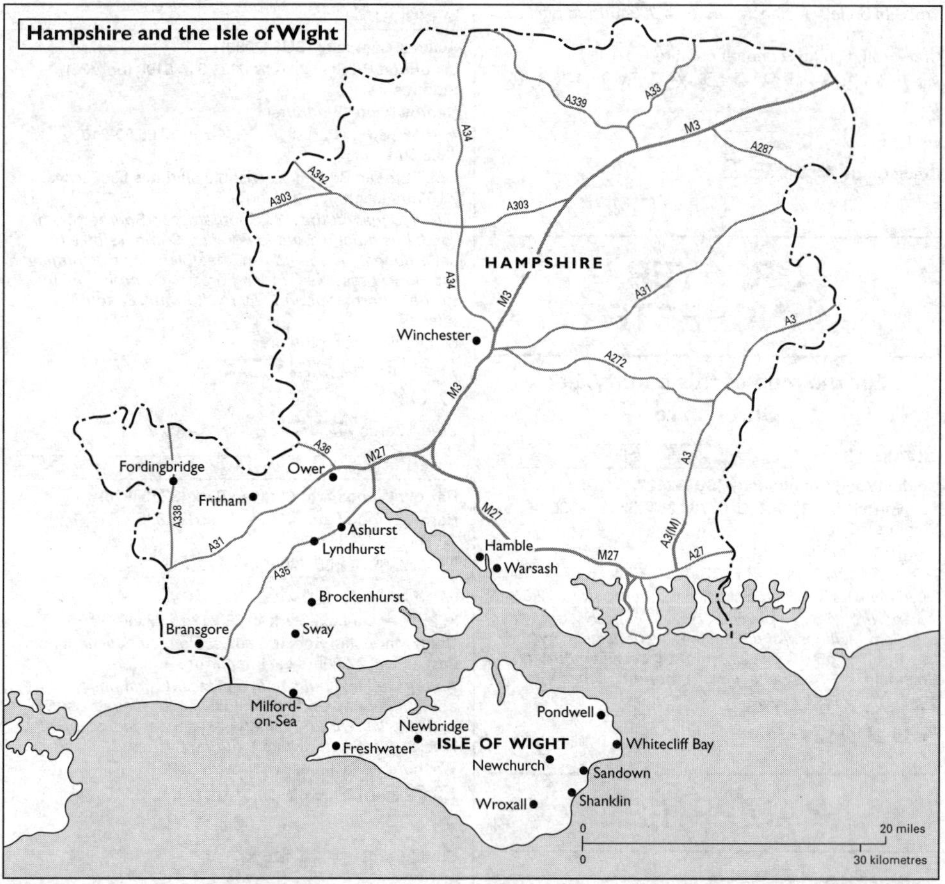

Hampshire and the Isle of Wight

☎ 0131 314 6100 (off A337) Signposted

►►► **Family Park** ★ £7.50-£11 £7.50-£11 £7.50-£11

Open Etr-Sep Booking advisable Spring bank hol & peak season Last arrival 23.30hrs Last departure noon

Large and very popular secluded site, set amongst oak and woodland, within the New Forest adjoining Balmer Lawn. Take A337 Lyndhurst rd from Brockenhurst, and site on right in .5m. See under 'Forestry Commission' for further information. A 168-acre site with 600 touring pitches.

Credit Cards

Roundhill Campsite (SU332021)

Beaulieu Rd SO42 7QL

☎ 0131 314 6100 (off B3055, 2m E) Signposted

►**Town & Country Pennant Park** ★ £6-£8.50 £6-£8.50 £6-£8.50

Open Etr-Sep Booking advisable all times Last departure noon

Large secluded site amongst gorse and birch within the New Forest, offering a separate area for motorcyclists and also a lightweight camping area. Take A3055 from Brockenhurst, and site on right and signed in 2m. A 156-acre site with 500 touring pitches.

Motorcyclists camp, Rally site. Dishwashing rooms.

Credit Cards

FORDINGBRIDGE

Sandy Balls Holiday Centre (SU167148)

Sandy Balls Estate Ltd, Godshill SP6 2JY

☎ 01425 653042 (take B3078 for Cadnam, 1.25m E) Signposted. Nearby town: Salisbury

►►►►► **Premier Park** ★ £12-£21 £12-£20 £10.50-£18.50

Open all year Booking advisable public hols & Jul-Aug Last arrival 20.00hrs Last departure 11.00hrs

A mostly wooded New Forest site with open fields, river walks and fishing. Facilities and amenities constantly

contd.

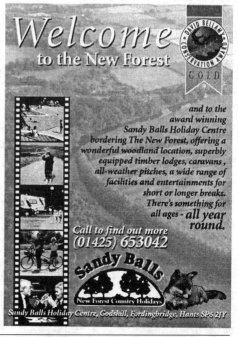

improving. Cross bridge towards Godshill from Fordingbridge, and site on left in 1m. A 30-acre site with 350 touring pitches and 250 statics.

Jacuzzi, steam room, sauna, sunbeds, gym, fitness suite

Credit Cards

FRITHAM

Longbeech Campsite (SU255128)

SO43 7HH ☎ 0131 314 6100 (take B3079 off A31 at Badnam) Signposted

Nearby town: Lyndhurst

Town & Country Pennant Park ★ £6-£8.50 £6-£8.50 ▲ £6-£8.50

Open Etr-Sep Booking advisable Spring bank hol Last arrival 23.30hrs Last departure noon

Large site set attractively amongst trees and close to a disused airfield bordering the New Forest. Own sanitary facilities essential. Turn off A37 at signs for Ocknell and Longbeach, 4m E of Ringwood. A 20-acre site with 180 touring pitches.

Lightweight camping area.

Credit Cards

Ocknell Camp Site (SU251119)

SO43 7HH ☎ 0131 314 6100 (take B3079 off A31 at Cadnam, through Brook & Fritham) Signposted

Nearby town: Lyndhurst

Town & Country Pennant Park ▲

Open Etr-Sep Booking advisable all time Last arrival 23.00hrs Last departure noon

An open New Forest site amid trees, shrubs and open heath. Turn off A37 at signs for Ocknell and Longbeach, 4m E of Ringwood. A 28-acre site with 300 touring pitches.

Credit Cards

HAMBLE

Riverside Park (SU481081)

Satchell Ln SO31 4RH ☎ 01703 453220 Signposted

Nearby town: Southampton

Town & Country Pennant Park ▲

Open Mar-Oct (rs Nov-Feb open wknds & bank hols for statics only) Booking advisable bank hols & peak season Last arrival 21.00hrs Last departure 14.00hrs

A slightly sloping, pleasant and peaceful site overlooking the R. Hamble. Located 1m north of Hamble just off the B3397. A 6-acre site with 60 touring pitches and 86 statics.

Credit Cards

LYNDHURST

Denny Wood Campsite (SU334069)

Beaulieu Rd SO43 7FZ ☎ 0131 314 6100 (2m E off B3056) Signposted

Town & Country Pennant Park ★ £5.50-£6.50 £5.50-£6.50 ▲ £5.50-£6.50

Open Etr-Sep Booking advisable all times Last departure noon

Quiet site in pleasant surroundings of mixed woodland, grass and gravel surface. Own sanitary facilities essential. From Lyndhurst take B3056, and site on right on bend in 2m. A 20-acre site with 170 touring pitches.

Credit Cards

Matley Wood Campsite (SU332075)

Beaulieu Rd SO43 7FZ

☎ 0131 314 6100 (2m E off B3056) Signposted

Town & Country Pennant Park ★ £5.50-£6.50 £5.50-£6.50 ▲ £5.50-£6.50

Open Etr-Sep Booking advisable all times Last departure noon

Clearings in pleasant partially wooded area. Own sanitary facilities essential. From Lyndhurst take B3056, and site on left in 1.5m. An 8-acre site with 70 touring pitches.

Credit Cards

MILFORD ON SEA

Lytton Lawn (SZ293937)

Lymore Ln, Everton SO41 0TX

☎ 01590 642513 & 643339 (A337 from Lymington, turn left onto B3058) Signposted

Nearby town: Lymington

►►►► **De-Luxe Park** ★ £9-£22 £9-£22 ▲ £9-£22

Open Mar-5 Jan Booking advisable at all times Last arrival 22.00hrs Last departure 10.00hrs

An ideal family site with refurbished facilities and plans for future improvements. From Lymington take A337 towards Christchurch for 2.5m, turn left on B3058 towards Milfod-on-Sea. After .25m turn left into Lymore Lane. A 9.5-acre site with 126 touring pitches.

Dishwashing facilities.

See advertisement under Colour Section

Credit Cards

OWER

Green Pastures Farm (SU321158)

SO51 6AJ ☎ 01703 814444 Signposted

Nearby town: Romsey

►►► **Family Park** ★ fr £7.50 fr £7.50 ▲ fr £7.50

Open 15 Mar-Oct Booking advisable bank hols & peak periods

Open, level, grassy site in rural surroundings. Situated on edge of New Forest W of Ower and off A31 between Romsey and Cadnam. Take exit 2 off M27. A 5-acre site with 45 touring pitches.

RINGWOOD

Camping International Holiday Park

See advertisement on page 143.

SWAY

Setthorns (SU262004)

Wootton BH25 5UA ☎ 0131 314 6100 Signposted

Nearby town: New Milton

► **Town & Country Pennant Park** ★ £5.50-£8 £5.50-£8 ▲ £5.50-£8

Open all year Booking advisable Spring bank hol & peak season Last departure noon

Pleasant level site in woodland with no sanitary facilities. Take Sway rd from Brockenhurst to crossroads, turn left and site 1.5m on left. A 60-acre site with 320 touring pitches.

Credit Cards

WARSASH

Dibles Park (SU505060)

Dibles Rd SO31 9SA ☎ 01489 575232 Signposted

Nearby town: Fareham

►►► **Family Park** ★ £6.70 £6.70 ▲ £5-£6

Open Mar-Nov Booking advisable bank hols & Jul-Aug Last arrival 20.30hrs Last departure 13.00hrs

Level, grass site with young trees and bushes, near River Hamble and the Solent. Immaculate toilets. From M27 junc 8 onto A27 signed Bursledon. Cross river bridge and follow signs on right. A 0.75-acre site with 14 touring pitches and 46 statics.

WINCHESTER

Morn Hill Caravan Club Site (SU522295)

Morn Hill SO21 1HL ☎ 01962 869877

►►► **Family Park** ▲

Open Mar-Nov Booking advisable bank hols & Jul-Aug Last arrival 20.00hrs Last departure noon

A beautifully maintained large site divided into two areas, and well broken up by trees and shrubs. The site lies 1.5m E of Winchester off the A31 at Morn Hill rndbt. A 9-acre site with 150 touring pitches.

Veg prep area.

Credit Cards

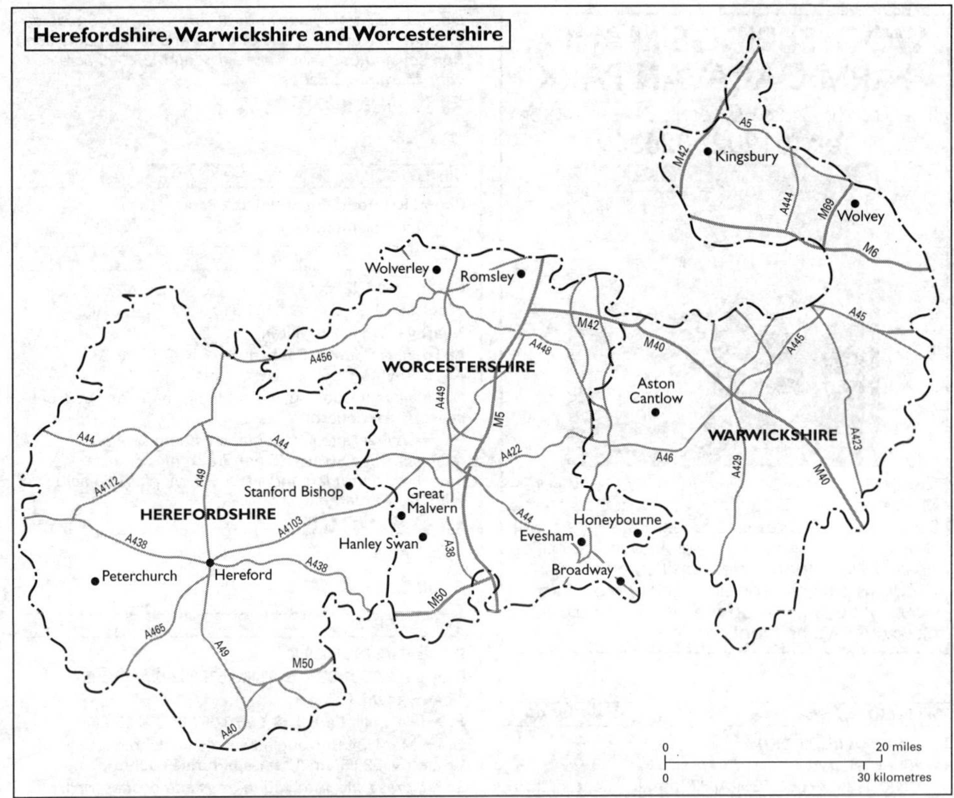

HEREFORDSHIRE

HEREFORD

Hereford Racecourse Campsite (SO501420)
Hereford Racecourse, Roman Rd HR4 9QN ☎ 01432 272364 Signposted
▶ Town & Country Pennant Park
Open early Apr-mid Sep Booking advisable bank hols Last arrival 20.00hrs Last departure noon
Quiet, well-maintained sloping grass site with pitches on the perimeter of the racecourse. Visitors must move their units to adjacent pitches on racedays. Adjacent to A49 Leominster road and A4103. A 5-acre site with 60 touring pitches.
Free access to racing on race days.

Credit Cards

PETERCHURCH

Poston Mill Caravan & Camping Park (SO355373)
HR2 OSF ☎ 01981 550225 & 01584 711280
Nearby town: Hereford
► ► ► Family Park ★ £6.50-£7.50 £6.50-£7.50 £4.75-£8.50
Open all year Booking advisable bank & summer hols Last departure noon
A level, grassy site with mature trees in hilly country near River Dore, 11m W of Hereford on B4348. A 10-acre site with 72 touring pitches and 40 statics.

STANDFORD BISHOP

Boyce Caravan Park (SO692528)
WR6 5UB ☎ 01885 483439 Signposted
Nearby town: Bromyard
► ► ► Family Park ★ fr £7.50 fr £7.50 fr £7.50
Open Mar-Oct Booking advisable bank hols Last arrival 18.00hrs Last departure noon
A pleasant site on an Elizabethan farm with good facilities. From B4220 Malvern road take sharp turn opposite Herefordshire House Pub, R in .25m. A 10-acre

site with 30 touring pitches and 80 statics.
Course fishing available.

HERTFORDSHIRE

For the map of this county, see Essex

HERTFORD

Camping & Caravanning Club Site (TL334113)
Mangrove Ln SG13 8QF ☎ 01992 586696 Signposted

►►►► **De-Luxe Park**
Open 24 Mar-3 Nov Booking advisable
A well-landscaped site with immaculate new toilet facilities, peacefully located off A414 S of Hertford. A 32-acre site with 250 touring pitches.

HODDESDON

Lee Valley Caravan Park (TL383082)
Dobbs Weir, Essex Rd EN11 OAS ☎ 01992 462090 Signposted
Town & Country Pennant Park ★ £9.20 £9.20 £9.20
Open Etr-Oct Booking advisable public hols Last arrival 21.30hrs Last departure noon
Neat, well kept site on level ground near river. An 8-acre site with 100 touring pitches and 100 statics.
Fishing.

Credit Cards

See advertisement on page 160

WALTHAM CROSS

Camping & Caravanning Club Site (TL344005)
Theobands Park, Bulls Cross Ride EN7 5HS ☎ 01992 620604 Signposted
Town & Country Pennant Park
Open end Mar-beg Nov Booking advisable
Lovely open site surrounded by mature trees, and set in parkland at Theobalds Hall. From M25 take A10 S, then 1st right towards Crews Hill, and site signed in 0.5m. A 14-acre site with 100 touring pitches.

KENT

ASHFORD

Broad Hembury Holiday Park (TR009387)
Steeds Ln, Kingsnorth TN26 1NQ ☎ 01233 620859 Signposted
Nearby town: Canterbury

►►►► **De-Luxe Park** ★ £10-£12 £10-£12 £6-£12
Open all year Booking advisable Jul-Aug Last departure noon
Well-run and maintained small farm site surrounded by open pasture, with pitches sheltered by mature hedges, and all neatly landscaped. From junc 10 on M20 take A2070 for 2m, then continue on A2042, following camping signs to Kingsnorth. Turn left at 2nd crossrds in village. A 5-acre site with 60 touring pitches and 25 statics.
Sports field with football & volley ball.

Credit Cards

BIDDENDEN

Woodlands Park (TQ867372)
Tenterden Rd TN27 8BT ☎ 01580 291216 Signposted
Nearby town: Tenterden
►►► **Family Park** ★ £8.50-£10 £8.50-£10 £8.50-£10
Open Mar-Oct (rs Mar-Apr weather permitting) Booking advisable bank hols & Jul-Aug Last arrival anytime Last departure anytime
A site of level grassland bordered by hedges and trees, with two ponds and a new toilet block. 1.5m S of Biddenden on northern side of A262. Ideal centre for Kent, Sussex and Channel ports. A 9-acre site with 100 touring pitches and 205 statics.
Camping accessory sales. Small site shop.

BIRCHINGTON

Quex Caravan Park (TR321685)
Park Rd CT7 0BL ☎ 01843 841273 Signposted

►►►► **De-Luxe Park** ★ £8.40-£9.75 £8.40-£9.75
Open Mar-Nov Booking advisable bank hols Last arrival anytime Last departure noon
Small parkland site, quiet and secluded, with very good sanitary facilities. From Birchington (A28) turn SE into Park Road, site in 1m. An 11-acre site with 88 touring pitches and 120 statics.

Credit Cards

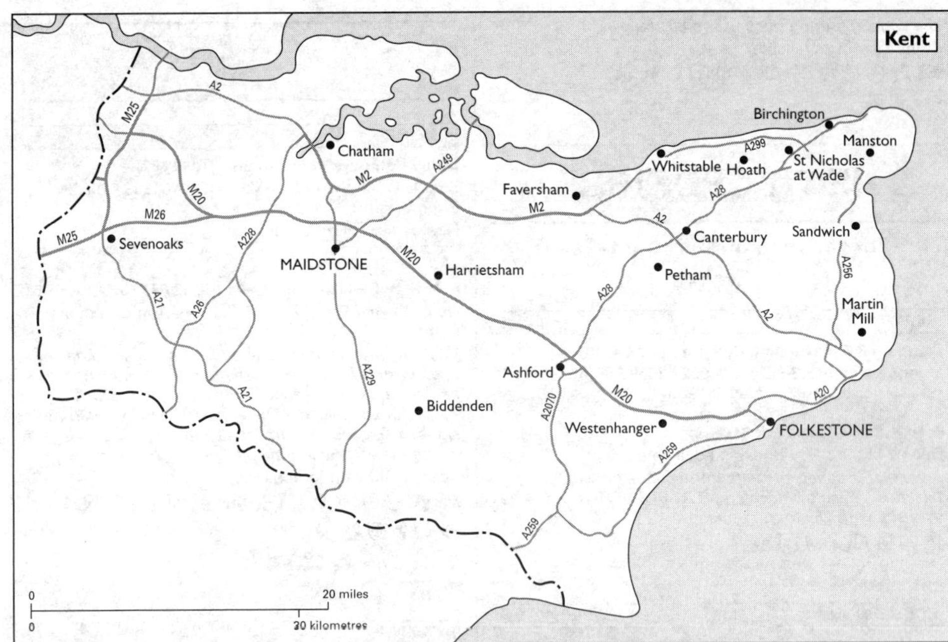

Two Chimneys Caravan Park (TR320684)
Shottendane Rd CT7 OHD ☎ 01843 841068 & 843157 Signposted
Nearby town: Margate
►►► **Family Park** ★ £6.50-£14 £6.50-£14 ▲ £6.50-£14
Open Mar-Oct (rs Mar-May & Sep-Oct shop/bar/pool/takeaway restricted) Booking advisable bank & school hols Last arrival 23.00hrs Last departure noon
A good, well-managed site with a swimming pool and well-tended grounds. From A28 in Birchington turn right by church along Park Lane (B2048). Turn left at Manston Rd along Shottendane Rd, and site on R. A 9-acre site with 75 touring pitches and 65 statics.
Sauna, spa bath, solarium, amusement arcade.

Credit Cards

CANTERBURY

Camping & Caravanning Club Site (TR172577)
Bekesbourne Ln CT3 4AB ☎ 01227 463216 (in season) & 01203 694995 (off A257) Signposted

►►►► **De-Luxe Park** ★ £9.10-£12.10 £9.10-£12.10 ▲ £9.10-£12.10
Open all year Booking advisable bank hols & peak periods Last arrival 21.00hrs Last departure noon
An attractive tree-screened site in pleasant rural surroundings. Off A257 Canterbury-Sandwich road. Please see the advertisement on page 27 for details of Club Members' benefits. A 20-acre site with 210 touring pitches.

Credit Cards

CHATHAM

Woolmans Wood Caravan Park (TQ746638)
Bridgewood ME5 9SB ☎ 01634 867685 Signposted
►►► **Family Park** ▲
Open all year Last departure 14.00hrs
Small site alongside the city airport and close to the London-Dover road. 3.25m S of Rochester. From M2 motorway leave at junction 3, then via A229 and B2097, .75m from junction 3. A 5-acre site with 60 touring pitches.
Caravan servicing, washing & valeting.

DOVER

See **Martin Mill**

FAVERSHAM

Painters Farm Caravan & Camping Site (TQ990591)
Painters Forstal ME13 0EG ☎ 01795 532995 Signposted
► **Town & Country Pennant Park** ★ £6.50-£8.50 £6.50-£8.50 ▲ £5.20-£8.50
Open Mar-Oct Booking advisable bank hols Last arrival 23.59hrs

Delightful simple farm site in immaculately kept cherry orchard, with spotless toilets in converted farm buildings. Signed from A2 at Faversham. A 3-acre site with 45 touring pitches.

FOLKESTONE

Little Satmar Holiday Park (TR260390)
Winehouse Ln, Capel Le Ferne CT18 7JF
01303 251188 (2m W off A20 onto B2011)
Signposted
► ► ► **Family Park** £7.50-£8.50 £7.50-£8.50 £7.50-£8.50
Open Apr-Oct Booking advisable bank hols & Jul-Aug Last arrival 23.00hrs Last departure 14.00hrs
A quiet, well-screened site well away from the road. A useful base for touring Dover/Folkestone area, signed off B2011. A 5-acre site with 46 touring pitches and 80 statics.

Camping & Caravanning Club Site (TR246376)
The Warren CT19 6PT 01303 255093 (in season) & 01203 694995 (signed from A20 rbdt)
Signposted
► **Town & Country Pennant Park** ★ £8.10-£10.30 £8.10-£10.30 £8.10-£10.30
Open end Mar-end Sep Booking advisable bank hols & peak periods Last arrival 21.00hrs Last departure noon
This site commands marvellous views across the Strait of Dover and is well located for the channel ports. It nestles on the side of the cliff and is tiered in some areas. Signed from A20 roundabout. Please see the advertisement on page 27 for details of Club Members' benefits. A 4-acre site with 82 touring pitches.

Credit Cards

Little Switzerland Camping & Caravan Site (TR248380)
Wear Bay Rd CT19 6PS 01303 252168 Signposted
► **Town & Country Pennant Park** ★ £7.50-£9.50 £7.50-£9.50 fr £4
Open Mar-Oct Booking advisable from Mar Last arrival mdnt Last departure noon
A small site perched on the cliffs overlooking the Dover Straits, with cosy, sheltered pitches. Signed from A2 and A20 E of Folkestone. A 4-acre site with 18 touring pitches and 12 statics.

HARRIETSHAM

Hogbarn Caravan Park (TQ885550)
Hogbarn Ln, Stede Hill ME17 1NZ
01622 859648 Signposted
Nearby town: Maidstone
► ► ► **Family Park** ★ £2.25-£5.75 £4 £2.25-£5.75
Open Apr-Oct Booking advisable bank hols & Jul-Aug Last arrival 22.00hrs Last departure noon
A very good country site, with mainly large, fenced in pitches. Situated off A20, between Ashford and Maidstone, along a narrow lane at top of N Downs. A 5-acre site with 60 touring pitches and 70 statics.
Coffee bar & Sauna.

HOATH

South View (TR205648)
Maypole Ln CT3 4LL 01227 860280
Signposted
Nearby town: Canterbury
► ► ► **Family Park**
Open all year Booking advisable bank hols Last arrival 23.00hrs Last departure 22.00hrs
A small rural site, level and well secluded. Off A299 or A28. A 3-acre site with 45 touring pitches.

MAIDSTONE

Pine Lodge Touring Park (TQ815549)
Ashford Rd, Nr Bearsted, Hollingbourne ME17 1XH
01622 730018 (2m NW on A20, from junc 8 M20)
Signposted
► ► ► **Family Park** ★ £8.50-£9.50 £8.50-£9.50 £8.50-£9.50
Open all year Booking advisable bank hols Last arrival 22.00hrs Last departure 14.00hrs
A very well laid out site close to Leeds Castle and the A20. Much planting of trees will result in good screening. A 7-acre site with 100 touring pitches.
Waste disposal points.

Credit Cards

MANSTON

Manston Caravan & Camping Park (TR348662)
Manston Court Rd CT12 5AU
01843 823442 (follow signs to Kent Int Airport. After passing entrance, turn left, opp garage, into Manston Court rd. Entrance 400yds on right)
Signposted
Nearby town: Margate/Ramsgate
► ► ► **Family Park** ★ £7-£9 £7-£10 £4.50-£10.50
Open Etr-Oct (rs Apr shop open weekends only (off-peak)) Booking advisable bank hols & Jul-Aug Last arrival 23.55hrs Last departure 11.00hrs
A level grassy site with mature trees situated near Manston Airport and convenient for the seaside resorts on the Isle of Thanet. Signed off B2150 in village. A 5-acre site with 100 touring pitches and 46 statics.

Credit Cards

Pine Meadows Tourer Park (TR357662)
Spratling Court Farm, Spratling St CT12 5AN
☎ 01843 587770
Town & Country Pennant Park
Open Apr-Sep
A quiet family site screened by high hedges, on a working farm on the Isle of Thanet. Generous pitches and a pleasant atmosphere. Just off B2050, .5m E of Manston, opp Greensole Golf Range. A 3.5-acre site with 40 touring pitches.

MARTIN MILL

Hawthorn Farm Caravan Park (TR342464)
Station Rd CT15 5LA ☎ 01304 852658 & 852914 Signposted
Nearby town: Dover

►►►► **De-Luxe Park** ★ £8.55-£10.80 £8.55-£10.80 £8.55-£10.80
Open Mar-mid Dec (water off if weather cold) Booking advisable bank hols & Jul-Aug Last arrival anytime Last departure noon
This pleasant rural site is screened by young trees and hedgerows, in grounds which include a rose garden and woods. Signed from A258. A 15-acre site with 160 touring pitches and 176 statics.

Credit Cards

PETHAM

Ashfield Farm (TR138508)
Waddenhall CT4 5PX ☎ 01227 700624 Signposted
Nearby town: Canterbruy
Town & Country Pennant Park £6-£8.50 £6-£8.50 £6-£8.50
Open Apr-Oct Booking advisable Jul & Aug Last arrival anytime Last departure noon
Small rural site with new toilet block and well-drained pitches, located S of Canterbury. Signed off B2068. A 4.5-acre site with 20 touring pitches and 1 static.
Mini golf, short term kennelling.

ST NICHOLAS AT WADE

St Nicholas at Wade Camping Site (TR254672)
Court Rd CT7 0NH ☎ 01843 847245 Signposted
Nearby town: Margate
Town & Country Pennant Park ★ £6.50-£8.50 fr £6.50 £7-£9
Open Etr-Oct Booking advisable Jul-Aug Last arrival 22.00hrs Last departure 16.00hrs

A small field with a toilet block, close to village and shop, off A299 and A28. A 3-acre site with 75 touring pitches.

SANDWICH

Sandwich Leisure Park (TR326581)
Woodnesborough Rd CT13 0AA
☎ 01304 612681 & 01227 771777 Signposted
► ► ► **Family Park** £6.80-£10.50 £6.80-£10.50
£4.50-£10.50
Open Mar-Oct Booking advisable Etr, Spring bank hol & Jul-Aug Last arrival 20.00hrs Last departure 11.00hrs
A useful touring site on the edge of Sandwich, with well laid out pitches and temporary toilets. Signed from A256 at Sandwich. A 5.5-acre site with 100 touring pitches and 103 statics.
Washing-up area.

SEVENOAKS

Camping & Caravanning Club Site (TQ577564)
Styants Bottom Rd, Styants Bottom, Nr Seal TN15 0ET
☎ 01732 762728 (in season) & 01203 694995 Signposted
► ► ► **Family Park**
Open end Mar-early Nov Booking advisable bank hols & peak periods Last arrival 21.00hrs Last departure noon
A quiet park in the centre of NT woodlands, with buildings blending well into the surroundings. Please see the advertisement on page 27 for details of Club Members' benefits. A 4-acre site with 60 touring pitches.
Credit Cards

WESTENHANGER

Caravan Club Site (TR128371)
Mr David Benge, Folkestone Racecourse CT21 4HX
☎ 01303 261761 & 266407 Signposted
Nearby town: Folkestone
Town & Country Pennant Park
Open Mar-mid Oct Booking advisable Jul-Aug Last arrival 20.00hrs Last departure noon
Situated in rural surroundings 7m W of Folkestone and 3m from nearest beach. Conveniently positioned for Channel ports. From junc 11 of M20 onto A261 at roundabout with A20, signed Sellinge. A 4-acre site with 60 touring pitches.
Credit Cards

WHITSTABLE

Sea View Caravan Park (TR145675)
St John's Rd CT5 2RY ☎ 01227 792246 Signposted
Nearby town: Herne Bay
► ► ► **Family Park** ★ £8-£10 £8-£10 £8-£10
Open Etr-Oct Booking advisable all times Last arrival 21.30hrs
Pleasant open site on the edge of Whitstable, set well away from the static site. Signed off A229, 0.5m E of Whitstable. A 12-acre site with 20 touring pitches and 452 statics.
Amusements in games room & adventure trail.

LANCASHIRE

BLACKPOOL

Marton Mere Holiday Village (SD347349)
Mythop Rd FY4 4XN
☎ 01253 767544
★ £4-£10 £4-£10
Open Mar-Oct Booking advisable Last arrival 22.00hrs Last departure noon
A large holiday centre with plenty of on-site entertainment, and a regular bus service into Blackpool. Leave M55 at junc 4 onto A583 towards Blackpool, turn right past windmill at 1st traffic lights into Mythop Rd, and park is 150yds on left. A 30-acre site with 431 touring pitches and 921 statics.
Credit Cards

Mariclough Hampsfield Camping Site (SD356329)
Preston New Rd, Peel Corner FY4 5JR
☎ 01253 761034 (on A583 0.5m S of M55 Jct 4)
Town & Country Pennant Park ★ fr £6 fr £4.40
fr £4.40
Open Etr-Nov Booking advisable high season bank hols (for caravans) Last arrival 22.30hrs Last departure noon
A small, tidy, family camping site located on A583 and on the outskirts of Blackpool, set in open countryside. A 2-acre site with 50 touring pitches and 2 statics.

BOLTON-LE-SANDS

Sandside Caravan & Camping Park (SD472681)
The Shore LA5 8JS ☎ 01524 822311
Signposted
Nearby town: Lancaster
► ► ► **Family Park**
Open Mar-Oct Booking advisable bank hols & Jul-Aug Last arrival 21.00hrs
A well-maintained site on pleasant sloping ground overlooking Morecambe Bay, with distant views of the Lake District. Leave junction 35 of M6; A6 through

contd.

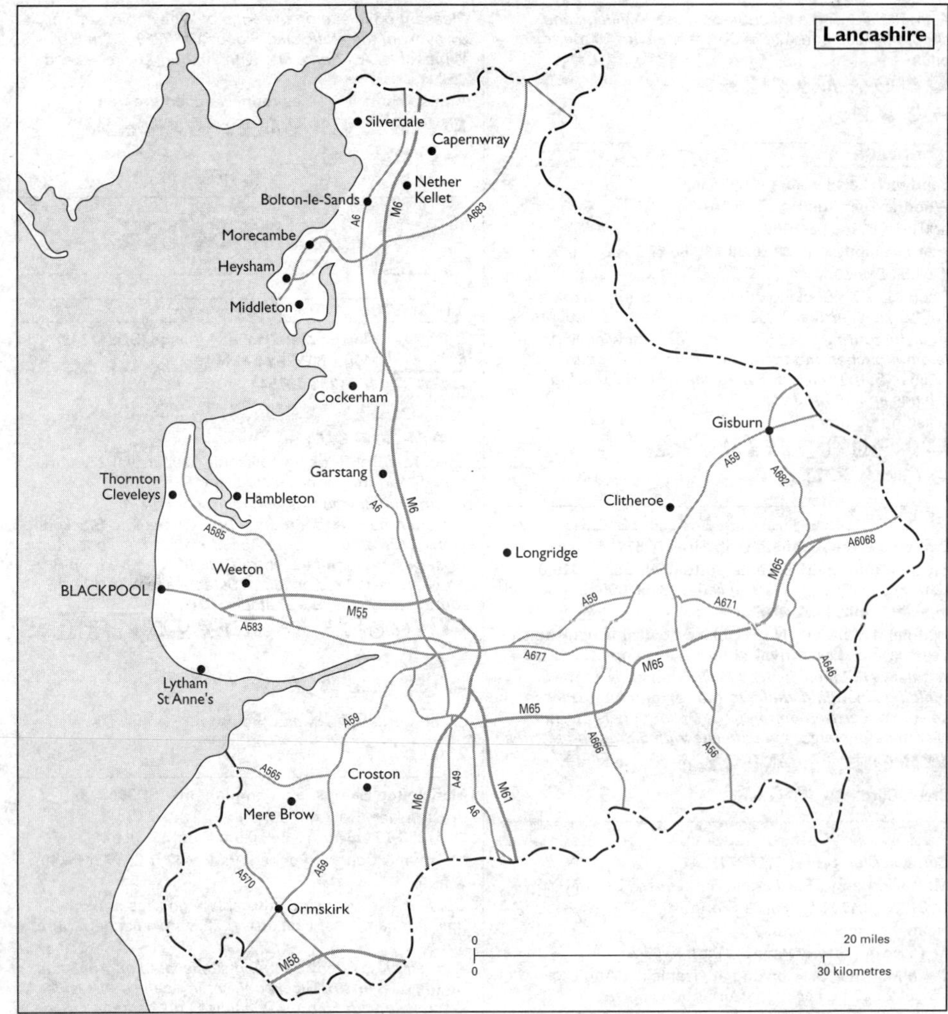

Carnforth, turn right at Little Chef in Bolton-le-Sands, over level-crossing to site. A 6-acre site with 130 touring pitches and 35 statics.

Credit Cards

Detron Gate Farm (SD478683)

LA5 9TN ☎ 01524 732842 & 733617 (night) Signposted

►Town & Country Pennant Park £6-£7 £6-£7 ▲ £4.50-£5.50

Open Mar-Oct (rs Mar-May shop hours restricted) Booking advisable bank hols Last arrival 22.00hrs Last departure 18.00hrs

Rural grassy site overlooking Morecambe Bay off A6. A popular site on sloping ground with a small farm adjacent. A 10-acre site with 100 touring pitches and 42 statics.

Bolton Holmes Farm (SD481693)

off Mill Ln LA5 8ES ☎ 01524 732854

Nearby town: Lancaster

►Town & Country Pennant Park ★ fr £4 fr £4 ▲ fr £4

Open Apr-Sep Booking advisable peak periods

A gently sloping site forming part of a farm complex, offering good views across Morecambe Bay and to the hills of the Lake District. Site is signed off A6 between Morecambe and Carnforth. A 5-acre site with 30 touring pitches and 45 statics.

CAPERNWRAY

Old Hall Caravan Park (SD533716)
LA6 1AD ☎ 01524 733276 & 735996
Nearby town: Carnforth
►►► **Family Park** £8.50-£10
Open Mar-10 Jan Booking advisable bank hols & Jul-Aug
Set in a clearing in lovely secluded woods in a natural setting with marked walks. Off M6 at junc 35, towards Over Kellet, turn left at village green, and site on right in 1.5m. A 3-acre site with 38 touring pitches and 128 statics.

CLITHEROE

Camping & Caravanning Club Site (SD727413)
Edisford Bridge, Edisford Rd BB7 3LA ☎ 01200 25294 (in season) & 01203 694995 (1m W off B6243) Signposted
►►► **Family Park** ★ £8.10-£10.30 £8.10-£10.30 £8.10-£10.30
Open end Mar-early Nov Booking advisable bank hols & peak periods Last arrival 21.00hrs Last departure noon
Set on the banks of the River Ribble, this site is ideal for fishing and walking as well as enjoying the adjacent park. Situated 1m out of town on the B6243. Please see the advertisement on page 27 for details of Club Members' benefits. A 6-acre site with 80 touring pitches.

Credit Cards

COCKERHAM

Mosswood Caravan Park (SD456497)
Crimbles Ln LA2 0ES ☎ 01524 791041 (1m W along A588) Signposted
Nearby town: Lancaster
►►► **Family Park** ★ £8-£8.50 £8-£8.50 £8-£8.50
Open Mar-Oct Booking advisable bank hols & Jul-Sep Last arrival 20.00hrs Last departure 16.00hrs
A tree-lined grassy park with sheltered, level pitches, located on peaceful Cockerham Moss. Situated about 4m from A6/M6 junc 33, 1m W of Cockerham on A588. A 3-acre site with 25 touring pitches and 143 statics.
See advertisement in Colour Section

Credit Cards

CROSTON

Royal Umpire Touring Park (SD504190)
Southport Rd PR5 7HP ☎ 01772 600257 (on the A581, between A59 & A49) Signposted
Nearby town: Chorley
►►►► **De-Luxe Park** ★ £5.50-£15.40 £5.50-£15.40 £4-£10
Open all year (rs 7 Nov-21 Dec only serviced pitches available) Booking advisable bank hols & peak season Last arrival 22.00hrs Last departure noon
A pleasant, level site with good facilities and high standard of maintenance, set in open countryside, and signed off A581 from Chorley. A 10-acre site with 200 touring pitches.
Assault course, five a side football pitch.
See advertisement in Colour Section

Credit Cards

GARSTANG

Claylands Caravan Park (SD496485)
Cabus PR3 1AJ ☎ 01524 791242 (2m N, off A6) Signposted
►►►► **De-Luxe Park** ★ fr £8.75 fr £8.75 fr £8.75
Open Mar-4 Jan (rs Jan & Feb) Booking advisable bank hols & Jul-Aug Last arrival 23.00hrs Last departure 14.00hrs
A well-maintained site with lovely river and woodland walks and good views, convenient for A6 and M6 between junctions 32 and 33. Signed off A6 down private rd on Lancaster side of Garstang. A 14-acre site with 64 touring pitches and 22 statics.
Fishing.

Credit Cards

Bridge House Marina & Caravan Park (SD483457)
Nateby Crossing Ln, Nateby PR3 0JJ ☎ 01995 603207 (1m W on unclass rd) Signposted
Nearby town: Preston
►►► **Family Park** ★ £6.50-£8 £6.50-£8
Open Mar-4 Jan Booking advisable bank hols Last arrival 22.00hrs Last departure 13.00hrs
A well-maintained site in attractive countryside by the Lancaster Canal, with good views towards the Trough of Bowland. Just off A6, on unclass rd signed Knott End. A 4-acre site with 50 touring pitches and 20 statics.

Credit Cards

GISBURN

Rimington Caravan Park (SD825469)
Hardacre Lane, Rimington BB7 4DS
☎ 01200 445355 (off A682 1m S of Gisburn) Signposted
Nearby town: Clitheroe
►►► **Family Park** ★ £7-£10 £7-£10 fr £7
Open Apr-Oct (rs Mar hardstanding available only) Booking advisable bank hols & Jul-3 Sep Last arrival 20.00hrs Last departure noon
A well-cared for site set in an attractive rural valley close to the Pendle Hills and situated just off A682 Gisburn-Nelson road 1m from town centre. A 4-acre site with 30 touring pitches and 150 statics.

Todber Caravan Park (SD835469)
BB7 4JJ ☎ 01200 445322 Signposted
Nearby town: Nelson
►►► **Family Park** ★ £8 £8 £8
Open Mar-Oct (rs Mar-Etr clubhouse open wknds only) Booking advisable public hols & for electric hook-up Last arrival 20.00hrs Last departure 18.00hrs
A popular rural site on sloping ground with good views all round, off A682. A 5-acre site with 100 touring pitches and 257 statics.
Indoor playroom & games field.

HAMBLETON

Sunset Adventure Park (SD375437)
Sower Carr Ln FY6 9EQ ☎ 01253 700222 & 701888 Signposted
►►► **Family Park** ★ £10 £10 £10
Open Mar-Oct Booking advisable wknds & bank hols Last departure noon
A pleasant rural park with plenty of children's entertainment on site. Take A588 turning off A585, cross Chard bridge, and site 1m on right through village. A 4-acre site with 40 touring pitches and 53 statics.
Pool table.

Credit Cards

HEYSHAM

Ocean Edge Caravan Park (SD407591)
Moneyclose Ln LA3 2XA ☎ 01524 855657
►►► **Family Park**
Open Mar-Oct
A newly developed touring area of a large holiday complex adjacent to the sea. From junc 34 of M6, follow A683 to Heysham, and site signed at Heysham before ferry pont. A 10-acre site with 100 touring pitches and 629 statics.

The AA pennant classification has been revised for 1998. Please read the explanation of the scheme on page 10.

LONGRIDGE

Beacon Fell View Caravan Park (SD618382)
110 Higher Rd PR3 2TF ☎ 01772 785434
►►► **Family Park** ★ £7-£13.50 £7-£13.50 £7-£13.50
Open 8 Apr-28 Oct Booking advisable bank & school hols Last arrival 21.00hrs Last departure 18.00hrs
An elevated site with views over Beacon Fell. Leave A6 at Broughton on B5269 into Longridge and follow B6243 out of town centre, then take L fork signed Jeffrey Hill; site is .75m on R. A 7-acre site with 97 touring pitches and 397 statics.
Free evening entertainment, pool tables, darts.

Credit Cards

LYTHAM ST ANNES

Eastham Hall Caravan Site (SD379291)
Saltcotes Rd FY8 4LS
☎ 01253 737907 Signposted
►►► **Family Park** ★ £9-£10 £9-£10
Open Mar-Oct Booking advisable bank hols & Jul Last arrival 22.00hrs Last departure 14.00hrs
A level, secluded site with trees and hedgerows, in rural surroundings. From Preston on A584, turn right onto B5259 to site in .75m. A 15-acre site with 200 touring pitches and 200 statics.

MERE BROW

Leisure Lakes (SD408176)
PR4 6JX ☎ 01772 813446 & 814502 (from Southport, Take A565 for 3.5m, right turn on B5246 to site) Signposted
Nearby town: Southport
►►► **Family Park** ★ £9.50 £9.50
Open all year Booking advisable bank hols, Jun-Aug & wknds Last arrival 21.00hrs Last departure 16.30hrs
A level grassy site in spacious parkland with ample amenities including watersports, fishing and walking. Site is just off A565 Preston-Southport road approx 5 miles from Southport. A 9-acre site with 86 touring pitches.
Windsurfing, canoe hire, golf range, cycle hire.

MIDDLETON (NEAR MORECAMBE)

Melbreak Caravan Park (SD415584)
Carr Ln LA3 3LH ☎ 01524 852430 (in village turn right at church, signed Middleton Sands, site .5m on left) Signposted
Nearby town: Morecambe
►►► **Family Park** £6.50-£7.50 £6.50-£7.50 £6-£6.50
Open Mar-Oct Booking advisable Jul-Aug Last arrival 22.00hrs Last departure noon
Small, well run, tidy site in open countryside S of Morecambe. Site on unclass rd from Heysham towards

Middleton Sands. A 2-acre site with 22 touring pitches and 10 statics.

MORECAMBE

Riverside Caravan Park (SD448615)
Snatchems LA3 3ER ☎ 01524 844193 (take unclass road S off B5273) Signposted
Nearby town: Lancaster
►►► **Family Park** ★ £6 £6 £6
Open Mar-Oct Booking advisable public hols & high season Last arrival 22.00hrs Last departure noon
A nice level grassy site with views over River Lune and Morecambe Bay. On unclass road off B5273 near Heaton. A 2-acre site with 50 touring pitches.

Credit Cards

Venture Caravan Park (SD436633)
Langridge Way, Westgate LA4 4TQ ☎ 01524 412986 & 412585 Signposted
Nearby town: Lancaster
►►► **Family Park** ★ £7-£8 £7-£8 £8
Open Mar-Oct (rs Nov-Feb touring vans only, one toilet block open) Booking advisable bank hols & peak periods Last arrival 22.00hrs Last departure noon
Large, mainly static site off the A589, close to the centre of town. A 5-acre site with 56 touring pitches and 304 statics.
Amusement arcade & off licence.

NETHER KELLET

Hawthorns Caravan & Camping Park (SD514686)
LA6 1EA ☎ 01524 732079 Signposted
Nearby town: Carnforth
►►► **Family Park** ★ £11.50 £11.50 £8-£10
Open Mar-Oct Booking advisable bank hols Last arrival 22.00hrs Last departure noon
A very well-kept and planned site in a rural setting on the edge of the village. From junc 35 of M6 take B6254 towards Kirkby Lonsdale through village. A 10-acre site with 25 touring pitches and 62 statics.
Putting green, library, table tennis & darts.

ORMSKIRK

Abbey Farm Caravan Park (SD434098)
Dark Ln L40 5TX ☎ 01695 572686 Signposted
Nearby town: Liverpool

►►►► **De-Luxe Park** ★ £7-£8.50 £7-£8.50 £5-£8.50
Open all year Booking advisable public hols & Jul-Aug Last arrival 22.00hrs Last departure 13.00hrs
A well-maintained rural site with level, grassy pitches close to town. In the grounds of Burscough Abbey, signed from the town centre on unclass rd to A5209 to Burscough. A 6-acre site with 56 touring pitches and 44 statics.
Undercover washing up area. Off-licence.

Credit Cards

ROCHDALE

See **Greater Manchester**

SILVERDALE

Holgate's Caravan Park (SD455762)
Cove Rd LA5 0SH ☎ 01524 701508 Signposted
Nearby town: Lancaster

►►►►► **Premier Park** ★ £14.25-£15.75 £14.25-£15.75 £14.25-£15.75
Open mid Feb-2 Nov (rs 22 Dec-mid Feb) Booking advisable school & public hols & wknds Last arrival 22.00hrs Last departure 14.00hrs
A superb family holiday centre set in wooded countryside adjacent to the sea, this was the Regional Winner for Northern England of the AA's 1996 Campsite of the Year Award. From Carnforth centre take unclass Silverdale rd & follow tourist signs after Warton. A 10-acre site with 70 touring pitches and 350 statics.
Sauna, spa bath, steam room & mini-golf.

Credit Cards

SOUTHPORT

See **Merseyside**

THORNTON CLEVELEYS

Kneps Farm Holiday Park (SD353429)
River Rd FY5 5LR ☎ 01253 823632 Signposted
Nearby town: Blackpool

►►►► **De-Luxe Park** £8-£10.50 £8-£10.50 £8-£10.50
Open Mar-mid Nov Booking advisable at all times Last arrival 20.00hrs Last departure noon
A level stony and grassy site with mature trees near a river and with good facilities. 5m N of Blackpool. Leave A585 at roundabout onto B5412 to Little Thornton. Turn right at St Johns Church into Stanah Road, leading to River Road. A 10-acre site with 70 touring pitches and 90 statics.
Bird watching hide.

Credit Cards

WEETON

High Moor Farm Caravan Park (SD388365)
PR4 3JJ ☎ 01253 836273 (opposite Weeton Barracks)
Signposted
Nearby town: Blackpool
Town & Country Pennant Park ★ £10-£12
£4-£5
Open Mar-Oct Booking advisable bank hols & Jul-Aug Last arrival 21.00hrs Last departure 14.00hrs
A small site in open farmland about 6m from Blackpool. Situated N of M55 (exit 3) off A585 Fleetwood road on B5260. A 4-acre site with 60 touring pitches.

LEICESTERSHIRE

For the map of this county, see Nottinghamshire

CASTLE DONINGTON

Donington Park Farmhouse Hotel (SK414254)
Melbourne Rd, Isley Walton DE74 2RN
☎ 01332 862409
Signposted
Town & Country Pennant Park £7-£10 £7-£10
£5-£8
Open Mar-Dec (rs winter months hardstanding only) Booking advisable summer season Last arrival 20.00hrs Last departure noon
A developing site at rear of hotel beside Donington Park racecourse, .5m off A453 towards Melbourne. Booking essential on race days, but a quiet rural site at other times. A 6-acre site with 4034 touring pitches.

Credit Cards

NORTH KILWORTH

Kilworth Caravan Park (SP605838)
Lutterworth Rd LE17 6JE ☎ 01858 880597
Family Park £5-£7 £5-£7
Open Etr/Apr-Oct Booking advisable bank hols Last arrival 22.00hrs Last departure noon
Set in 12-acres of beautiful wooded estate with fishing lake and newly modernised facilities. On A4304, 3m from junc 20 of M1, and 1m W of North Kilworth. A 14-acre site with 40 touring pitches and 100 statics.
Lake for fishing.

ULLESTHORPE

Ullesthorpe Garden Centre (SP515872)
Lutterworth Rd LE17 5DR ☎ 01455 202144
Town & Country Pennant Park
Open Mar-Oct
A pleasant site next to the garden centre, ideal for the self-contained caravanner, with nature walk and fishing on site. From M1 junc 20 take A427 through Lutterworth, then B577 for 2m, and site just SE of Ullesthorpe village. A 1-acre site with 16 touring pitches.
Fishing & Nature Walks.

LINCOLNSHIRE

BARTON-UPON-HUMBER

Silver Birches Tourist Park (TA028232)
Waterside Rd DN18 5BA
☎ 01652 632509 (follow Bridge Viewing Point signs to Waterside rd, site just past Sloop pub)
Signposted
Family Park ★ £5.50 £5.50 £5.50
Open Apr-Oct Booking advisable bank hols Last arrival 23.00hrs Last departure 20.00hrs
A very pleasant, well-screened site, convenient for Humber Bridge as well as Humberside and Lincolnshire. Situated S of bridge. Take A15 into Barton and site is clearly signed. A 2-acre site with 24 touring pitches.
Putting green.

BOSTON

Pilgrims Way (TF358434)
Church Green Rd, Fishtoft PE21 0QY
☎ 01205 366646

De-Luxe Park
Open Apr-Oct
A very attractive site in the gardens of the Grange, with individually screened pitches and new purpose-built toilet facilities. From Boston travel N on A16(T), turn right onto A52, and right again at Ball House pub to Fishtoft 1m on left. A 1-acre site with 22 touring pitches.

Midville Caravan Park (TF386578)
Stickney PE22 8HW ☎ 01205 270316
Family Park
Open Mar-Nov
A pleasant touring site in a quiet area. From A16(T) at Stickney travel E to Midville, turn left at bridge (Hobhole Drain), and site clearly signed. A 3-acre site with 24 touring pitches and 40 statics.

The AA pennant classification has been revised for 1998. Please read the explanation of the scheme on page 10.

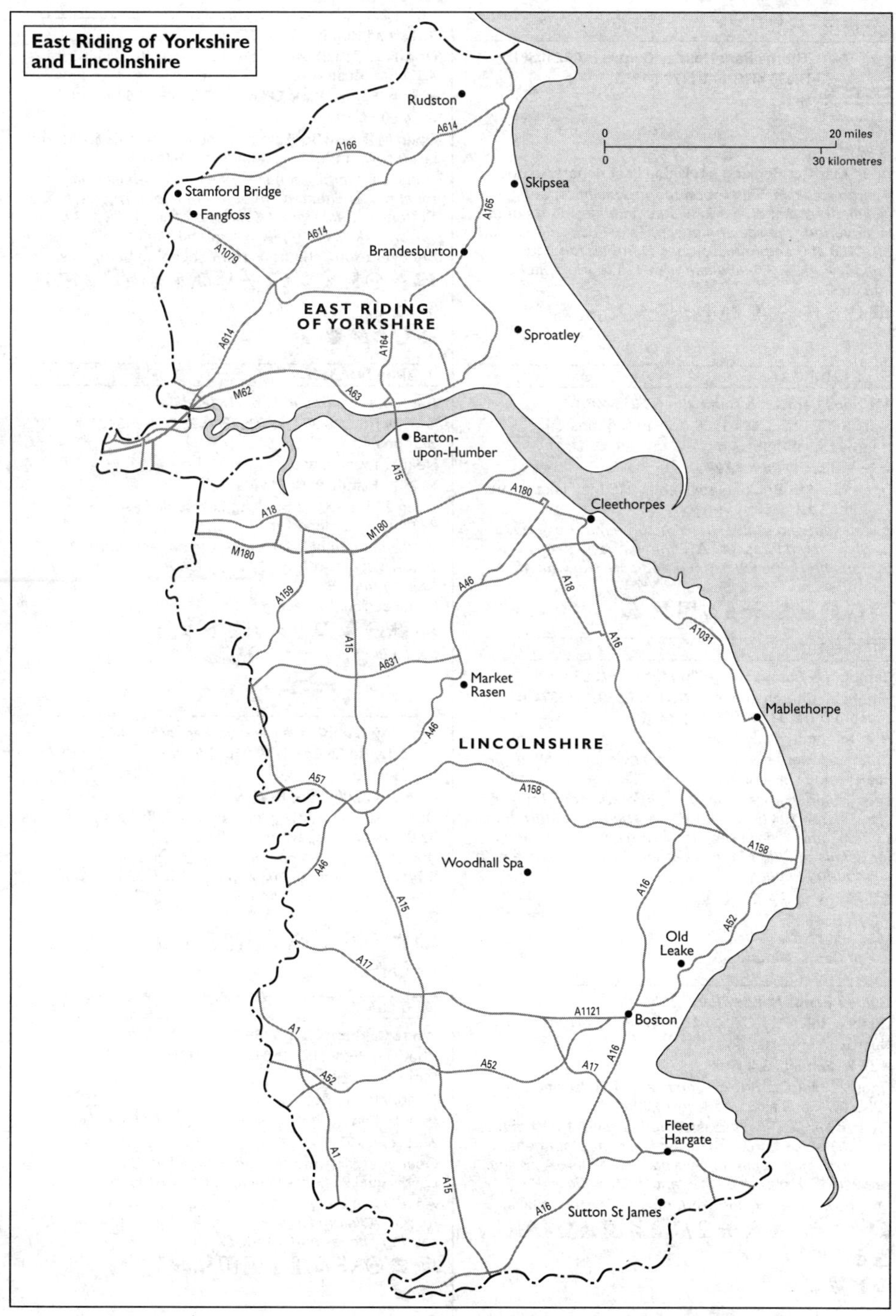
East Riding of Yorkshire and Lincolnshire
0
20 miles
0
30 kilometres
Rudston
Stamford Bridge
Fangfoss
Skipsea
Brandesburton
EAST RIDING OF YORKSHIRE
Sproatley
Barton-upon-Humber
Cleethorpes
Market Rasen
Mablethorpe
LINCOLNSHIRE
Woodhall Spa
Old Leake
Boston
Fleet Hargate
Sutton St James
A614
A166
A1079
A165
A164
A63
M62
A15
A180
A18
M180
A46
A16
A159
A631
A1031
A57
A158
A17
A52
A1121
A1

CLEETHORPES

Thorpe Park Holiday Centre (TA321035)
DN36 4HG ☎ 01472 813395
Signposted

Open Mar-Oct Booking advisable Last departure noon
A large static site with good touring facilities, and excellent recreational and leisure activities. Parts of the site overlook the sea and beach. Take unclassified road off A180 at Cleethorpes, signed Humberston and holiday Park. A 3.5-acre site with 115 touring pitches and 80 statics.

FLEET HARGATE

Matopos Caravan & Campsite (TF388248)
Main St PE12 8LL ☎ 01406 422910 Signposted
Nearby town: Holbeach
►►► **Family Park**
Open Mar-Oct Booking advisable 1-10 May Last arrival 22.30hrs Last departure noon
A well-kept and pretty site with some mature and many newly-planted trees. Off A17 midway between Long Sutton and Holbeach, signed. A 3-acre site with 45 touring pitches.

MABLETHORPE

Camping & Caravanning Club Site (TF499839)
Highfield, Church Ln LN12 2NU ☎ 01507 472374 (in season) & 01203 694995 Signposted
►►► **Family Park**
Open end Mar-end Sep Booking advisable bank hol & peak periods Last arrival 21.00hrs Last departure noon
Level, mainly grassy site off main road about 1m from sea. Take A1104 from Alford to Mablethorpe, turn R into Church Lane. Please see the advertisement on page 27 for details of Club Members' benefits. A 6-acre site with 105 touring pitches.
→
Credit Cards

Golden Sands Holiday Park (TF501861)
Quebec Rd LN12 1QJ ☎ 01507 477871 & 472671
Nearby town: Skegness
►►► **Family Park**
Open 22 Mar-Oct Booking advisable May/spring bank hol & Jul-Sep Last departure 10.00hrs
A clean and well-kept seaside holiday site. 1m W of town off A1031 Cleethorpes road. 1st floor entertainment rooms are only accessible via stairs (no lifts). A 23-acre site with 350 touring pitches and 1300 statics.
Mini bowling alley, snooker/pool, indoor fun palace.
→
Credit Cards

Kirkstead Holiday Park (TF509835)
North Rd, Trusthorpe LN12 2QD ☎ 01507 441483 (on A52) Signposted
►►► **Family Park** £6.50-£9.50 £6.50-£9.50 £4.50-£6.50
Open Mar-Nov Booking advisable bank hols & Jul-Aug Last arrival mdnt Last departure 15.00hrs
A pleasant family-run site with a newly-built quality toilet block. Situated 1m out of Mablethorpe towards Sutton-on-Sea, signed Kirkstead off Alford Rd. A 6-acre site with 30 touring pitches and 50 statics.
Snooker room, childrens room, evening bar meals.
→

MARKET RASEN

Racecourse Caravan Park (TF123883)
Legsby Rd LN8 3EA ☎ 01673 842307 & 843434
Signposted
Nearby town: Lincoln
►►► **Family Park**
Open 27 Mar-5 Oct Booking advisable Last arrival 22.00hrs Last departure 15.00hrs
Well-run, mainly level, grass site on racecourse 1m SE of town centre off A63 Louth road. A 3-acre site with 55 touring pitches.
Reduced rate for racing.
→
Credit Cards

Walesby Woodlands Caravan Park (TF117906)
Walesby Rd LN8 3UN ☎ 01673 843285
Signposted
►►► **Family Park**
Open Mar-Oct Booking advisable public hols Last arrival 22.00hrs Last departure 17.00hrs
A thoroughly well-planned, immaculate site. Out of Market Rasen on B1203 and turn L for .75m. A 3-acre site with 60 touring pitches.
Solarium.
→

OLD LEAKE

White Cat Park (TF415498)
Shaw Ln PE22 9LQ ☎ 01205 870121
Signposted
Nearby town: Boston
►►► **Family Park** ★ £5.25-£6.25 £5.25-£6.25 £5.25-£6.25
Open mid Mar-mid Nov Booking advisable bank hols Last arrival 22.00hrs Last departure 14.00hrs
An efficient and pleasant site in quiet rural surroundings just off A52, 7m NE of Boston. A 2.5-acre site with 40 touring pitches and 4 statics.
→

SUTTON ST JAMES

Foremans Bridge Caravan Park (TF409197)
PE12 0HU ☎ 01945 440346
Nearby town: Long Sutton
►►► **Family Park** ★ £5.50-£8 £5.50-£8
fr £5.50
Open Mar-Dec Booking advisable Last arrival 21.00hrs
A nicely-kept, trim site with good sanitary facilities. Take B1390 Long Sutton to Sutton St James rd, and site in 2m on L immediately after bridge. A 2.5-acre site with 40 touring pitches and 5 statics.

WOODHALL SPA

Bainland Country Park (TF215640)
Horncastle Rd LN10 6UX
☎ 01526 352903 & 353572 (1.5m from town, on B1191)
Signposted. Nearby town: Horncastle

£8.50-£25 £8.50-£25 £8.50-£20
Open all year Booking advisable all year Last arrival 20.00hrs Last departure 11.30hrs
More a country club than a purely touring park, this is one of the best equipped parks in the country with an impressive array of leisure facilities, combined with high standards of maintenance. Won the regional award for Central England in the 1996 AA Campsite of the Year competition. On B1191 about 2m E of town. A 12-acre site with 100 touring pitches and 10 statics.
Jacuzzi, solarium, sauna, par 3 golf, putting, boule.
See advertisement in Colour Section

Credit Cards

Camping & Caravanning Club Site (TF225633)
Wellsyke Ln, Kirkby-on-Bain LN10 6YU ☎ 01526 352911 (in season) & 01203 694995 Signposted
►►► **Family Park** ★ £8.70-£11.30 £8.70-£11.30
£8.70-£11.30
Open end Mar-early Nov Booking advisable bank hols & Jul-Aug Last arrival 21.00hrs Last departure noon
A pleasant site in silver birch wood and moorland. Take B1191 towards Horncastle. After 5m turn right towards Kirby-on-Bain. Signed. Please see the advertisement on page 27 for details of Club Members' benefits. A 6-acre site with 100 touring pitches.

Credit Cards

Many parks in this guide may exclude some categories of people from staying. Please check before you book, and see the important note on page 4.

LONDON

For the map, see Essex

E4 CHINGFORD

Lee Valley Campsite (TQ381970)
Sewardstone Rd E4 7RA ☎ 0181 529 5689 Signposted

►►►► **De-Luxe Park** ★ £10 £10 £10
Open Apr-Oct Booking advisable bank hols & Jul-Aug Last arrival 22.00hrs Last departure noon
Well-run useful North London site with excellent modern facilities and a peaceful atmosphere, with easy access to town. Overlooking King George's reservoir and close to Epping Forest. From M25 junct 26 to A112 and signed. A 12-acre site with 200 touring pitches.

Credit Cards

See advertisement on page 160

N9 EDMONTON

Lee Valley Leisure Centre Camping & Caravan (TQ360945)
Meridian Way N9 0AS
☎ 0181 803 6900 & 0181 345 6666 Signposted
Nearby town: Edmonton/Enfield
►►► **Family Park** ★ fr £7.10 fr £7.10 fr £5
Booking advisable Jul-Aug Last arrival 22.00hrs Last departure noon
A pleasant open site tucked away behind a large sporting complex with use of swimming pool, roller skating and golf driving range. Very good toilet facilities, and handy for London. 5m S of M25, signed from A10. A 4.5-acre site with 160 touring pitches.
Membership of adjacent sports complex.

Credit Cards

See advertisement on page 160

MERSEYSIDE

For the map of this county, see Shropshire

SOUTHPORT

Hurlston Hall County Caravan Park (SD398107)
Southport Rd L40 8HB ☎ 01704 841064
►►► **Family Park** ★ fr £8 fr £8
Open Etr-Oct Booking advisable bank hols

contd.

New touring park at side of existing static park in countryside about 10 mins drive from Southport. A peaceful tree-lined park with fishing and golf nearby. On A570, 3m from Ormskirk in Southport direction. A 5-acre site with 60 touring pitches and 68 statics.

Willowbank Holiday Home & Touring Park (SD305110)
Coastal Rd, Ainsdale PR8 3ST ☎ 01704 571566
►►► **Family Park**
Open Mar-Oct Booking advisable bank hols
Set in a wooded clearing on a nature reserve, this brand new site is just off the coastal road to Southport. Leave A56(T) at traffic lights onto coastal road to Southport, and site is 300 metres from traffic lights on left before railway bridge. A 6-acre site with 54 touring pitches and 52 statics.

AA members can call AA Hotel Booking Service on 0990 050505 to book at AA recognised hotels and B & Bs in the UK and Ireland, or through our Internet site: http://www.theaa.co.uk/hotels

NORFOLK

BARNEY

The Old Brick Kilns (TG007328)
Little Barney Ln, Barney NR21 0NL ☎ 01328 878305
Signposted
Nearby town: Fakenham

►►►► **De-Luxe Park** £8.50-£10.50 £8.50-£10.50 ▲ £8.50-£10.50
Open Mar-Oct (rs low season bar food/takeaway selected nights only) Booking advisable bank hols & Jul-Aug Last arrival 22.00hrs Last departure noon
A secluded and peaceful site with a small boating pool and mature trees. Excellent, well-planned toilet facilities. Approach from the A148 near Thursford towards Barney village and in .25m turn into no-through road. Site in .5m. A 6.5-acre site with 60 touring pitches.
Boules, outdoor draughts/chess, family games area.

Credit Cards

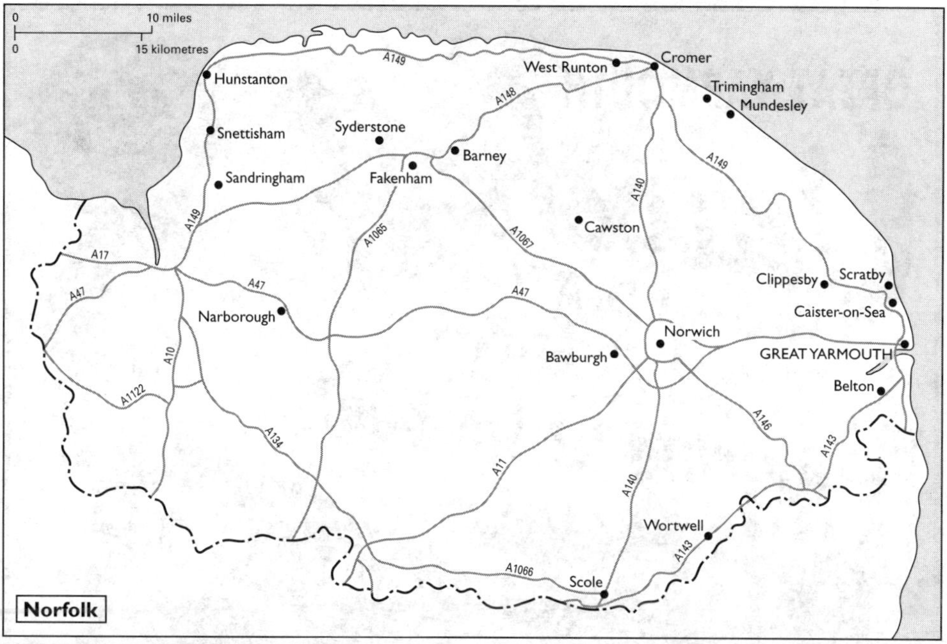

BAWBURGH

Caravan Club Site (TG150102)

Royal Norfolk Agricultural, Association Showground, Long Ln NR9 3LX ☎ 01603 742708

►►► **Family Park**

Open 26 Mar-11 Oct Booking advisable bank hols & mid Jul

A very pleasant tree-bordered site in the corner of the showground, at the end of a country lane. Take A1074 from Norwich ring rd to join A47, then leave at rndbt marked Bawburgh/Showground, and follow signs. A 5-acre site with 60 touring pitches.

Veg prep area.

→

BELTON

Rose Farm Touring & Camping Park (TG488033)

Stepshort NR31 9JS ☎ 01493 780896 Signposted

Nearby town: Great Yarmouth

►►► **Family Park** ★ £5-£6.50 £5-£6.50 ▲ £5-£6.50

Open all year (rs Dec & Jan repairs/decorating, please telephone) Booking advisable Aug Last arrival 22.00hrs

A very neat site with a good toilet block and tidy facilities. Follow signs to Belton off A143, turn right at the lane called Stepshort, and the site is first on right. A 6-acre site with 80 touring pitches.

→

Wild Duck Holiday Park (TG475028)

Howards Common NR31 9NE ☎ 01493 780268 Signposted

Nearby town: Great Yarmouth

►►► **Family Park** ▲

Open Mar-Oct Booking advisable Jun-Aug Last arrival 23.00hrs Last departure noon

Level grassy site in forest with small cleared areas for tourers and well laid out facilities. Signed from A143. A 60-acre site with 165 touring pitches and 240 statics.

Sauna, solarium, jacuzzi & fitness room.

→

Credit Cards

CAISTER-ON-SEA

Grasmere Caravan Park (TG521115)

9 Bultitude's Loke, Yarmouth Rd NR30 5DH

☎ 01493 720382 (from A149 at Stadium rdbt after .5m sharp left turn just past petrol station)

Signposted

Nearby town: Great Yarmouth

►►► **Family Park** £5.30-£7.50 £5.30-£7.50

Open Apr-Oct Booking advisable school & bank hols Last arrival 22.00hrs Last departure 11.00hrs

Mainly level grass and gravel site with mature trees. Set in meadowland in an urban area with access to A149. A 2-acre site with 46 touring pitches and 62 statics.

→

Credit Cards

Old Hall Leisure Park (TG521122)
High St NR30 5JL ☎ 01493 720400 (opposite church) Signposted
Nearby town: Great Yarmouth
►►► **Family Park** ★ £6-£10 £6-£10
Open Spring bank hol wk & 22 Jun-1 Sep (rs Apr-21 Jun pool closed, bar/rest limited opening) Booking advisable Spring bank hol & Jul-Aug Last arrival mdnt Last departure 10.00hrs
A small site at rear of hotel on main street (B1159) with a neat and attractive layout. Convenient for shops and beach. A 2-acre site with 35 touring pitches and 38 statics.

Credit Cards

CAWSTON

Haveringland Hall Caravan Park (TG153213)
NR10 4PN ☎ 01603 871302 Signposted
Nearby town: Alysham
► **Town & Country Pennant Park** ★ £7-£8.50 £7-£8.50 £6-£7.50
Open Mar-Oct Booking advisable public hol wks & Jul-Aug Last arrival 22.00hrs Last departure noon
A very pleasant site set in woodland and meadowland with direct access to lake. Level pitches in different area with interesting mature trees. 10m N of Norwich on Cawston road. A 120-acre site with 65 touring pitches and 80 statics.
14 acre fishing lake.

CLIPPESBY

Clippesby Holidays (TG423147)
NR29 3BJ ☎ 01493 369367 Signposted
Nearby town: Great Yarmouth
►►► **Family Park** ★ £8.50-£15 £8.50-£15 £8.50-£15
Open Etr wk, mid May-mid Sep (rs Mayday wknd some facilities may close) Booking advisable school hols Last arrival 17.30hrs Last departure 11.00hrs
A lovely country house estate with vans hidden among trees and a friendly welcome. From A1064 at Acle to B1152 and signed. A 30-acre site with 100 touring pitches and 22 statics.
Putting, bowls, adult bicycle hire & tea room.

Credit Cards

CROMER

Seacroft Camping Park (TG206424)
Runton Rd NR27 9NJ ☎ 01263 511722 Signposted
►►►► **De-Luxe Park** £7.50-£12 £7.50-£12 £7.50-£12

contd.

Open Mar-Oct Booking advisable school hols, 22-31 May & 4 Sep Last arrival 23.00hrs Last departure noon
A very good touring site, well laid out and landscaped. Toilets and showers tiled and spotless. 1m W of Cromer on A149 coast road. A 5-acre site with 120 touring pitches.
Baby change.

Credit Cards

Forest Park Caravan Site (TG233405)
Northrepps Rd NR27 OJR
01263 513290 Signposted
▶▶▶ **Family Park** £6.50-£9.50 £6.50-£9.50
Open Apr-Oct Booking advisable Etr, Spring bank hol & Jul-Aug Last arrival 22.00hrs Last departure 14.00hrs
Surrounded by forest, this gently sloping parkland offers a wide choice of pitches. Signed from A149 and B1159. An 85-acre site with 429 touring pitches and 372 statics.
BMX track.

Credit Cards

FAKENHAM

Caravan Club Site (TF926288)
Fakenham Racecourse NR21 7NY
01328 862388
Signposted
▶▶▶ **Family Park**
Open all year Booking advisable Etr & May-Aug Last departure noon
A level grassy site with mature trees, three-quarters of a mile SW of town off A1065 Swaffham road. Tourers move on race days to centre of course, and have free racing. An 11.5-acre site with 150 touring pitches.
TV aerial hook-ups & satellite channels.

GREAT YARMOUTH

See **Caister-on-Sea**

Vauxhall Holiday Park (TG520083)
4 Acle New Rd NR30 1TB 01493 857231
Signposted

★ £14-£20 £14-£20 £14-£20
Open Etr then mid May-Sep Booking advisable mid Jul-Aug Last arrival 21.00hrs Last departure 10.00hrs
A very large holiday complex with plenty of entertainment and access to beach, river, estuary, lake and main A47. A 16-acre site with 256 touring pitches and 446 statics.
Hairdressing & entertainment. Multi Sports Arena.

Credit Cards

HUNSTANTON

Searles of Hunstanton (TF671400)
South Beach PE36 5BB
01485 534211 & 532342 ext 100
Signposted

★ £8-£16 £8-£16 £7-£15
Open Etr-Nov (rs Mar-May & Oct-Nov certain facilities not open) Booking advisable bank hols & Jul-Aug Last arrival 21.00hrs Last departure 11.00hrs
A large seaside holiday complex with well-managed facilities, adjacent to sea and beach. On B1161, in South Hunstanton, off A149 King's Lynn road. An 18-acre site with 350 touring pitches and 450 statics.
Stables, entertainment programme & hire shop.

Credit Cards

KING'S LYNN

See **Narborough**

MUNDESLEY

Links Caravan Site (TG305365)
Links Rd NR11 8AE 01263 720665 Signposted
Nearby town: North Walsham
▶ **Town & Country Pennant Park**
Open Etr-1st wk Oct Booking advisable bank hols & peak season Last arrival 22.00hrs Last departure noon
A pleasant site on a south-facing slope with level pitches, offering distant rural views. From B1159 at Mundesley turn into Church Road. A 2-acre site with 32 touring pitches.

NARBOROUGH

Pentney Park (TF742141)
Gayton Rd, Pentney PE32 1HU 01760 337479
Signposted
Nearby town: Swaffham
▶▶▶ **Family Park**
Open all year (rs Nov-Feb outdoor swimming pool closed) Booking advisable bank hols Last arrival 22.30hrs Last departure 11.00hrs

The AA pennant classification has been revised for 1998. Please read the explanation of the scheme on page 10.

A well-run touring site set in woods and meadowland adjacent to A47 Swaffham-King's Lynn Road. A 16-acre site with 200 touring pitches.

Credit Cards

NORWICH

Camping & Caravanning Club Site (TG237063)
Martineau Ln NR1 2HX
☎ 01603 620060 (in season) & 01203 694995 (from A47 take A146 left to traffic lights, left & left again) Signposted
Town & Country Pennant Park ★ £8.70-£11.30 £8.70-£11.30 £8.70-£11.30
Open end Mar-end Sep Booking advisable bank hols & Jul-Aug Last arrival 21.00hrs Last departure noon
A small site on the outskirts of Norwich close to a river and screened by trees from the city. From A47 take A146 left to traffic lights, then left and left again. Please see the advertisement on page 27 for details of Club Members' benefits. A 2.5-acre site with 50 touring pitches.

Credit Cards

SANDRINGHAM

Camping & Caravanning Club Site (TF683274)
The Sandringham Estate, Double Lodges PE35 6EA
☎ 01485 542555 (in season) & 01203 694995 Signposted
Nearby town: King's Lynn
Family Park ★ £9.10-£12.10 £9.10-£12.10 £9.10-£12.10
Open end Feb-1 Dec Booking advisable bank hols & high season Last arrival 21.00hrs Last departure noon
A prestige site, very well landscaped with toilets and other buildings blending in with the scenery. Well signed off A149 Hunstanton/Kings Lyn rd and A148. Please see the advertisement on page 27 for details of Club Members' benefits. A 22-acre site with 250 touring pitches.

Credit Cards

SCOLE

Willows Camping & Caravan Park (TM146789)
Diss Rd IP21 4DH ☎ 01379 740271 Signposted
Nearby town: Diss
Family Park fr £7 fr £7 fr £7
Open May-Sep Booking advisable Spring bank hol & school hols Last arrival 23.00hrs Last departure noon
Level, peaceful site on the banks of the River Waveney, bordered by willow trees. From A140 take A1066 at rndbt opp Scole Village access. Site signed in 300 yds. A 4-acre site with 32 touring pitches.
Washing-up sinks.

SCRATBY

Scratby Hall Caravan Park (TG501155)
NR29 3PH ☎ 01493 730283 Signposted
Nearby town: Great Yarmouth
Family Park £4.50-£9.90 £4.50-£9.90 £4.50-£9.90
Open Spring bank hol-mid Sep (rs Etr-Spring bank hol & mid Sep-Oct reduced hours & shop closed) Booking advisable Spring bank hol wk & Jul-Aug Last arrival 10.00hrs Last departure noon
An immaculate grass site with very tidy toilet block and new children's play area, close to beach and the Norfolk Broads. Signed off B1159. A 5-acre site with 108 touring pitches.
Washing-up & food preparation room.

SNETTISHAM

Diglea Caravan & Camping Park (TF656336)
Beach Rd PE31 7RB ☎ 01485 541367 (turn left at sign Snettisham beach, site on left 1.5m from turning) Signposted
Nearby town: Hunstanton
Family Park ★ £5.50-£8.50 £5.50-£8.50 £5.50-£8.50
Open Apr-Oct Booking advisable bank hols & mid Jul-Aug Last arrival 22.30hrs Last departure noon
Undulating pasture land, close to the sea and in rural surroundings. Signed from A149. A 15-acre site with 200 touring pitches and 150 statics.

SYDERSTONE

The Garden Caravan Site (TF795355)
Bramer Hall ☎ 01485 578220
Family Park
Open 20 Mar-1 Nov
In the tranquil setting of a former walled garden beside a large farmhouse, with mature trees and shrubs, and surrounded by woodland, a brand new secluded site. Signed off B1454 between A148 and Dorking, 1m NW of Syderstone. 33 touring pitches.

TRIMINGHAM

Woodlands Caravan Park (TG274388)
NR11 8AL ☎ 01263 579208 Signposted
Nearby town: Cromer
Family Park ★ £6.50-£9 fr £5.50
Open Apr-Oct Booking advisable public hols & Jul-Aug Last arrival 23.00hrs Last departure noon
A pleasant woodland site close to the sea but well sheltered from winds. Pitches in open areas among the trees. 4m SE on coast road, B1159. A 10-acre site with 85 touring pitches and 179 statics.

Credit Cards

WEST RUNTON

Camping & Caravanning Club Site (TG189419)
Holgate Ln NR27 9NW ☎ 01263 837544 (in season) & 01203 694995 Signposted
Nearby town: Cromer
►►► **Family Park** ★ £9.10-£12.10 £9.10-£12.10 £9.10-£12.10
Open end Mar-early Nov Booking advisable bank hols & peak periods Last arrival 21.00hrs Last departure noon
A lovely, well-kept site with some gently sloping pitches on pleasantly undulating ground. Surrounded by woodland. Approach from A148 about 2m SW of Cromer, signposted into unclass road and reached only by a narrow gravel bridleway. Please see the advertisement on page 27 for details of Club Members' benefits. An 11.75-acre site with 225 touring pitches.

Credit Cards

WORTWELL

Little Lakeland Caravan Park (TM279849)
IP20 0EL ☎ 01986 788646 Signposted
Nearby town: Harleston
►►► **Family Park** ★ £6.70-£8.40 £6.70-£8.40
Open Mar-Oct (rs Mar-Etr restricted laundry facilities) Booking advisable bank hols & peak periods Last arrival 22.00hrs Last departure noon
A well-kept and pretty site built round a lake and with individual pitches in hedged enclosures. 2m NE of Harleston. A 4.5-acre site with 40 touring pitches and 16 statics.
Library & fishing on site.

Lone Pine Camping Site (TM274843)
Low Rd IP20 0HJ ☎ 01986 788596 & 01379 852423
Signposted Nearby town: Harleston
► **Town & Country Pennant Park** £4 £4
Open May-Sep Booking advisable bank hols
A sheltered grassy site with saplings and bushes set in downs and meadowland. Signed from village by post office. A 2-acre site with 27 touring pitches.

NORTHAMPTONSHIRE

For the map of this county, see Berkshire

THRAPSTON

Mill Marina (SP994781)
Midland Rd NN14 4JR ☎ 01832 732850
Signposted Nearby town: Kettering
► **Town & Country Pennant Park** ★ £8.80-£9.80 £7.80-£8.80 £6.80-£7.80
Open Apr-Dec (rs Jan-Mar) Booking advisable public hols & summer wknds Last arrival 21.00hrs Last departure 18.00hrs
Level riverside site with mature trees and bushes, with pleasure trips by boat from site. Take Thrapston exit from A14 or A605, signed. A 3-acre site with 45 touring pitches and 6 statics.
Slipway for boats & canoes;coarse fishing on site.

NORTHUMBERLAND

ALWINTON

Clennell Hall (NT928072)
Clennell NE65 7BG ☎ 01669 650341
Signposted Nearby town: Rothbury
►►► **Family Park** ★ £8.50-£11 £8.50-£11 £7
Open Mar-Jan (rs Feb by arrangement only) Booking advisable summer & bank hols Last arrival 23.00hrs Last departure 16.00hrs
A tranquil rural site on the fringe of the National Park NW of Rothbury. From B6341 take unclass rd signed Alwinton and caravan signs. A 14.5-acre site with 50 touring pitches and 18 statics.

BAMBURGH

Glororum Caravan Park (NU166334)
Glororum Farm NE69 7AW ☎ 01668 214457 Signposted
►►► **Family Park**
Open Apr-Oct Booking advisable school hols Last arrival 22.00hrs Last departure 10.00hrs
A well-run site with good facilities, pleasantly situated off B1341, 1m W of Bamburgh. The open countryside setting gives views of Bamburgh Castle and surrounding farmland. A 6-acre site with 100 touring pitches and 150 statics.

Waren Caravan Park (NU155343)
Waren Mill NE70 7EE ☎ 01668 214366 Signposted
►►► **Family Park**
Open Apr-Oct Booking advisable Spring bank hol & Jul-Aug Last arrival 22.00hrs Last departure noon
Attractive seaside site close to beach, surrounded by a slightly sloping grassy embankment affording shelter for caravans. Immaculate sanitary facilities. Situated 2m E of town on B1342. From A1 turn onto B1342 signed Bamburgh, and take unclassified road past Waren Mill, signed Budle. A 4-acre site with 105 touring pitches and 325 statics.
100 acres of private heathland.

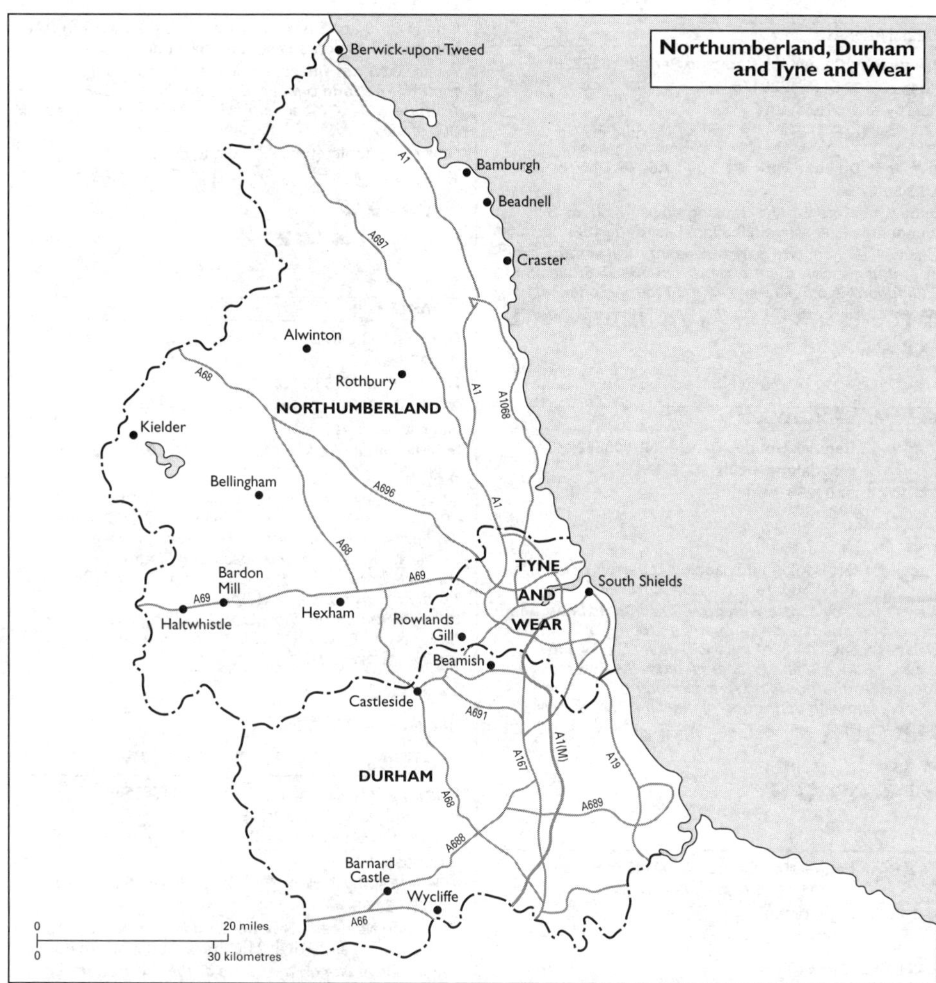

BARDON MILL

Ashcroft Farm (NY782645)
NE47 7JA ☎ 01434 344409
Nearby town: Hexham
Town & Country Pennant Park ★ fr £3.50
fr £3.50 £2.50-£3.50
Open Apr-Oct Booking advisable Last arrival 21.00hrs Last departure 13.00hrs
Level farm site adjacent to A69, between Haltwhistle and Hexham. Leave A69 at Bardon Mill, and site at end of village. Own sanitary facilities essential. A 2-acre site with 20 touring pitches.
Fishing.
→

BEADNELL

Camping & Caravanning Club Site (NU231297)
Anstead NE67 5BX
☎ 01665 720586 (in season) & 01203 694995
►►► **Family Park ★** £8.70-£11.30 £8.70-£11.30
Open end Mar-Sep Booking advisable bank hols & Jul-Aug Last arrival 21.00hrs Last departure noon
Level, grassy site set in coastal area with access to sea, beach and main road. From A1 follow B1340 signposted Seahouses-Bamburgh. Please see the advertisement on page 27 for details of Club Members' benefits. A 12-acre site with 150 touring pitches.

→

Credit Cards

BELLINGHAM

Brown Rigg Caravan & Camping Park (NY835826)
NE48 2JY ☎ 01434 220175
Nearby town: Hexham

►►►► **De-Luxe Park** £6.50-£7.50 £6.50-£7.50
£3.50-£7.50
Open wk before Etr-Oct Booking advisable bank & school hols Last arrival 20.30hrs Last departure noon
This well laid out site is in a pleasant rural setting, run by enthusiastic resident owners. On B6320 .5miles S of Bellingham. A 5.5-acre site with 60 touring pitches.

BERWICK-UPON-TWEED

Berwick Holiday Centre (NU000540)
Magdalene Fields TD15 1NE
☎ 01289 307113

Open Mar-Oct Booking advisable Last arrival 21.00hrs Last departure 10.00hrs
A large holiday centre with good touring facilities, and plenty of modern entertainment, shopping and sports facilities. Leave A1 N of Berwick, travel S on A1167 towards Berwick, and after crossing railway bridge turn left into Northumberland Ave, signed holiday centre. A 1.5-acre site with 35 touring pitches and 120 statics.

Haggerston Castle (NU041435)
Beal TD15 2PA ☎ 01289 381333
Signposted

★ £10-£20 £10-£20
Open Mar-Oct Booking advisable Last arrival 21.00hrs Last departure 10.00hrs
A large holiday centre with a very well equipped touring park, offering comprehensive holiday activities. On A1, 5.5m S of Berwick on Tweed, and signed. A 7-acre site with 156 touring pitches.

Credit Cards

Ord House Caravan Park (NT982515)
East Ord TD15 2NS
☎ 01289 305288 Signposted

►►►►► **Premier Park** ★ £7.25-£11.90
£7.25-£11.90 £7.25-£11.90
Open Mar-9 Jan Booking advisable bank hols & Jul-Aug Last arrival 23.00hrs Last departure noon
A very well-run site set in pleasant surroundings with mature trees and bushes. Situated on the A698, 1m from Berwick. A 6-acre site with 70 touring pitches and 200 statics.
Crazy golf, tabletennis,9 hole pitch/putt.

Credit Cards

CRASTER

Dunstan Hill Camping & Caravanning Club Site (NU236214)
Dunstan Hill NE66 3TQ
☎ 01665 576310 (in season) & 01203 694995
Nearby town: Alnwick
►►► **Family Park** ★ £9.10-£12.10 £9.10-£12.10
£9.10-£12.10
Open end Mar-early Nov Booking advisable Spring bank hol & Jul-Aug Last arrival 21.00hrs Last departure noon
An immaculately maintained site with pleasant landscaping close to the beach and historic town of Alnwick, but in a countryside setting. From B1340 at Embleton take unclass rd signed Craster. Please see the advertisement on page 27 for details of Club Members' benefits. A 12-acre site with 150 touring pitches.

Credit Cards

HALTWHISTLE

Camping & Caravanning Club Site (NY685621)
Burnfoot, Park Village NE49 OJP
☎ 01434 320106 (in season) & 01203 694995
Signposted
►►► **Family Park** ★ £5.60-£8.60 £5.60-£8.60
£5.60-£8.60
Open end Mar-early Nov Booking advisable bank hols & high season Last arrival 21.00hrs Last departure noon
An attractive site on the banks of the River South Tyne, amid mature trees, on the Bellister Castle Estate. Please see the advertisement on page 27 for details of Club Members' benefits. A 3-acre site with 60 touring pitches.

Credit Cards

HEXHAM

Caravan Club Site (NY919623)
Hexham Racecourse NE46 3NN ☎ 01434 606847
Signposted
►►► **Family Park**
Open Etr-1 Oct Booking advisable wknds & bank hols for electric hook-up Last arrival 20.00hrs Last departure noon
A part-level and part-sloping grassy site on racecourse overlooking Hexhamshire Moors. From Hexham take B6305 signed Allendale and Alston, turn left in 3m

signed racecourse. In 1.5m on right. A 4-acre site with 60 touring pitches.

Credit Cards

Causey Hill Caravan Park (NY925625)

Benson's Fell Farm NE46 2JN

☎ 01434 602834 & 604647

►►► **Family Park**

Open Apr-Oct Booking advisable public hols & Jul-Sep Last arrival 19.00hrs Last departure noon

A well-maintained site on very sloping ground with some level pitches. Attractively screened by trees. To avoid steep hill out of Hexham, follow B6305, signed Allendale, Alston, turn left in 3m onto unclass rd, and left again 300yds past race course. Site in 100yds. A 2-acre site with 30 touring pitches and 105 statics.

Off Licence.

KIELDER

Kielder Campsite (NY626938)

NE48 1EJ ☎ 01434 250291 Signposted

►►► **Family Park** ★ £7.50-£9 £7.50-£9

▲ £7.50-£9

Open Etr-Sep Booking advisable Whitsun & Jun-Aug Last arrival 23.00hrs Last departure 10.00hrs

Set in riverside fields with Kielder Water a few minutes' drive away. Proceed N from Kielder village towards the Scottish Border for approx 500yds, the site is on the right-hand side (E) of the road. A 10-acre site with 70 touring pitches.

Credit Cards

ROTHBURY

Coquetdale Caravan Park (NU055007)

Whitton NE65 7RU

☎ 01669 620549 (.5m SW on Newtown rd) Signposted

►►► **Family Park** ★ £8-£10 £8-£10 ▲ £7-£10

Open mid Mar/Etr-Oct Booking advisable bank hol wknds Last arrival anytime Last departure evening

Partly level and sloping grass site in hilly country adjacent to River Coquet, and overlooked by Simonside Hills and moorland; .5m SW of Rothbury on Newton road. A 2-acre site with 50 touring pitches and 180 statics.

Adventure playground, 5-a-side football posts.

AA members can call AA Hotel Booking Service on 0990 050505 to book at AA recognised hotels and B & Bs in the UK and Ireland, or through our Internet site: http://www.theaa.co.uk/hotels

NOTTINGHAMSHIRE

CLUMBER PARK

Camping & Caravanning Club Site (SK626748)

The Walled Garden S80 3BD ☎ 01909 482303 (in season) & 01203 694995 Signposted

Nearby town: Worksop

► **Town & Country Pennant Park** ★ £8.10-£10.30

▲ £8.10-£10.30

Open end Mar-early Nov Booking advisable bank hols & Jul-Aug Last arrival 21.00hrs Last departure noon

Pleasant and peaceful site, well-maintained and situated in the splendid wooded surroundings of Clumber Park. Members only caravans. Follow signs for chapel and site signed beside cricket field. Please see the advertisement on page 27 for details of Club Members' benefits. A 2.5-acre site with 56 touring pitches.

Credit Cards

NOTTINGHAM

See **Radcliffe on Trent**

RADCLIFFE ON TRENT

Thornton's Holt Camping Park (SK638377)

Stragglethorpe Rd, Stragglethorpe NG12 2JZ

☎ 0115 9332125 & 9334204 Signposted

Nearby town: Nottingham

contd.

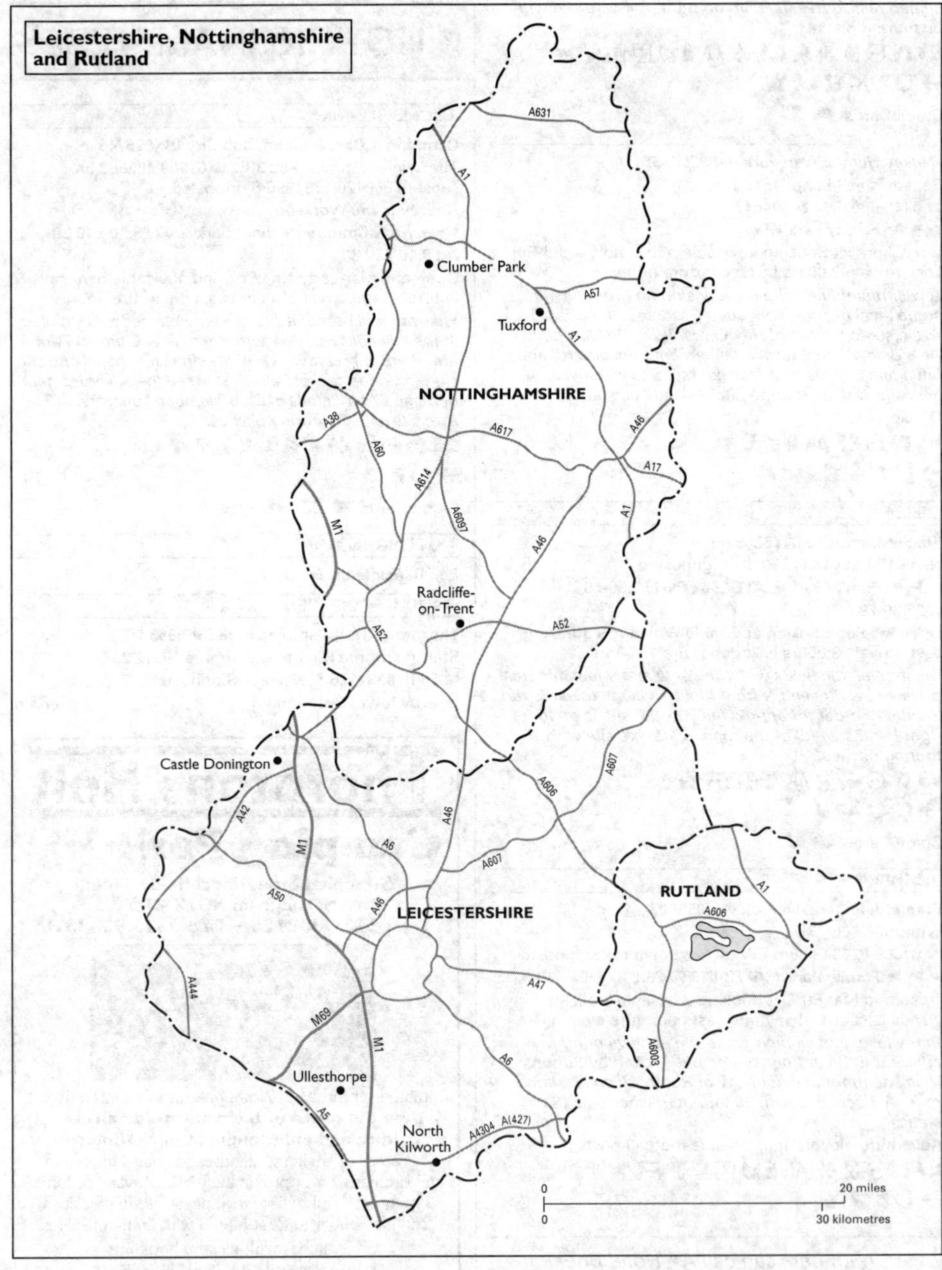
Leicestershire, Nottinghamshire and Rutland
A631
A1
Clumber Park
A57
Tuxford
A1
NOTTINGHAMSHIRE
A38
A60
A617
A46
A17
A614
A6097
M1
A1
A46
Radcliffe-on-Trent
A52
A52
Castle Donington
A607
A606
A42
M1
A46
A6
A607
RUTLAND
A1
A50
A46
LEICESTERSHIRE
A606
A444
A47
M69
M1
A6
A6003
Ullesthorpe
A5
A4304
A(427)
North Kilworth
0
20 miles
0
30 kilometres

►►► **Family Park** £7-£8 £7-£8 ▲ £7-£8
Open Apr-1 Nov (rs 2 Nov-Mar limited facilities) Booking advisable bank hols & wknds mid May-Oct Last arrival 21.00hrs Last departure 13.00hrs
A level grass site with young trees and bushes, set in meadowland .5m S of A52 and 2m N of A46. Nearby (2m) is the National Water Sports Centre. A 13-acre site with 84 touring pitches.
Washing-up facilities.

TUXFORD

Greenacres Touring Park (SK751719)
Lincoln Rd NG22 0JW ☎ 01777 870264 Signposted
Nearby town: Retford
►►► **Family Park** ★ £6.75 £6.75 ▲ £6.75
Open Mar-Oct Booking advisable public hols Last arrival 23.00hrs Last departure 18.00hrs
Level and slightly sloping grass site with trees, set in rural area outside Tuxford, .75m E of A1 on A6075 over railway bridge. A 4-acre site with 40 touring pitches and 14 statics.

Orchard Park Touring Caravan & Camping Park (SK754708)
Marnham Rd NG22 0PY ☎ 01777 870228 & 0402 433346 (1.25m SE of A1, off A6075 Lincoln rd) Signposted
Nearby town: Retford
►►► **Family Park** ★ £6.75 £6.75 ▲ £6.75
Open mid Mar-Oct Booking advisable bank hols & Jul-Aug Last arrival mdnt
A very pleasant developing site with newly-built toilet block. From Tuxford on A6075 .25m NE turn left to Marnham. Site signed on right in 800yards. A 7-acre site with 60 touring pitches.
Family shower room.

OXFORDSHIRE

For the map of this county, see Berkshire

BANBURY

Barnstones Caravan & Camping Site (SP455454)
Great Bourton OX17 1QU ☎ 01295 750289 Signposted
►►► **Family Park** £5 £5 ▲ £3.50
Open all year Booking advisable public hols
An excellent, well-run and beautifully laid-out site. Signposted from A423 (Coventry) Gt Bourton/Cropredy. A 3-acre site with 49 touring pitches.

Mollington Touring Caravan Park (SP443477)
The Yews, Mollington OX17 1AZ ☎ 01295 750731
Town & Country Pennant Park £5-£6 £5-£6 ▲ £4-£5
Open Mar-Nov Booking advisable banks hols Last arrival 22.00hrs
A new site on farm land at edge of the village, neat and well run. Leave M40 at junc 11 onto A422 signed Banbury, take A423 signed Southam, and site on left in 3.5m. A 2-acre site with 24 touring pitches.
Field play area.

BENSON

Benson Camping & Caravanning Park (SU613917)
OX10 6SJ ☎ 01491 838304 Signposted
Nearby town: Wallingford
Town & Country Pennant Park ▲
Open Apr-Oct Booking advisable bank hols & Jul-Aug Last arrival 19.00hrs Last departure noon
An attractive riverside site close to a busy road. Signed from A4074 in Benson. A 1-acre site with 26 touring pitches and 25 statics.

Credit Cards

BLETCHINGDON

Diamond Farm Caravan & Camping Park (SP513170)
Islip Rd OX5 3DR ☎ 01869 350909 Signposted
Nearby town: Oxford

►►►► **De-Luxe Park** £8-£10 £8-£10 ▲ £8-£10
Open all year (rs Oct-Mar shop, bar & swimming pool closed) Booking advisable bank hols & Jul-Sep Last arrival 22.00hrs Last departure noon
A well-run, quiet rural site in good level surroundings, and ideal for touring the Cotswolds. Situated alongside the B4027, 1m from the A43 and 7m N of Oxford in the heart of the Thames Valley. A 3-acre site with 37 touring pitches.
Cycle/jogging track, snooker table.

CASSINGTON

Cassington Mill Caravan Park (SP451099)
Eynsham Rd OX8 1DB ☎ 01865 881081 Signposted
Nearby town: Oxford
Town & Country Pennant Park ★ £7.50-£9 £7.50-£9 ▲ £7.50-£9
Open Apr-Oct Booking advisable bank hols & Jun-Aug Last arrival 21.00hrs Last departure noon
Secluded pretty site on the banks of the River Evenlode. First turn left 2.5m W of Oxford on A40 to Witney. A 4-acre site with 83 touring pitches and 50 statics.

Credit Cards

CHARLBURY

Cotswold View Caravan & Camping Site (SP365210)
Enstone Rd OX7 3JH ☎ 01608 810314 Signposted
Nearby town: Witney
►►► **Family Park** ★ £8-£10.50 £8-£10.50
£8-£10.50
Open Etr or Apr-Oct Booking advisable bank hols Last arrival 20.00hrs Last departure noon
A really first class Cotswold site, well-screened with attractive views. Signed from A44 on to B4022. A 7-acre site with 90 touring pitches.
Off-licence & cycle hire.

Credit Cards

CHIPPING NORTON

Camping & Caravanning Club Site (SP315244)
Chipping Norton Rd OX7 3PE
☎ 01608 641993 & 01203 694995 (1.5m S A361)
Signposted
►►► **Family Park** ★ £9.10-£12.10 £9.10-£12.10
£9.10-£12.10
Open Mar-Nov Booking advisable bank hols & Jul-Aug Last arrival 21.00hrs Last departure noon
A hilltop site surrounded by trees but close to a busy main road. Toilets very clean. Direct access off A361, but only from the road signed to Chadlington. Please see the advertisement on page 27 for details of Club Members' benefits. A 4-acre site with 76 touring pitches.

Credit Cards

HENLEY-ON-THAMES

Swiss Farm International Camping (SU759837)
Marlow Rd RG9 2HY ☎ 01491 573419 Signposted
►►► **Family Park**
Open Mar-Oct Booking advisable bank hols Last arrival 22.00hrs
Pleasantly screened rural site just outside Henley on A4155. A 6-acre site with 120 touring pitches and 6 statics.
Football pitch & fishing lake.

OXFORD

Oxford Camping International (SP518041)
426 Abingdon Rd OX1 4XN ☎ 01865 246551
Signposted
►►► **Family Park** fr £8 fr £8 fr £8
Open all year Booking advisable bank hols & Jul-Aug Last arrival 22.00hrs Last departure noon
A very busy town site with handy park-and-ride into Oxford. Situated on the south side of Oxford. Take A4144 to city centre from the ring road, site is .25m on left at rear of Texaco filling station. A 5-acre site with 129 touring pitches.

Credit Cards

STANDLAKE

Lincoln Farm Park (SP395028)
High St OX8 7RH ☎ 01865 300239 Signposted
Nearby town: Witney

►►►► **De-Luxe Park** ★ £10-£12 £10-£12
£10-£12
Open Mar-Oct Booking advisable bank hols, Jul-Aug & most wknds Last arrival 21.00hrs Last departure noon
An attractively landscaped park, in a quiet village setting on A415, with superb facilities and excellent maintenance. A 9-acre site with 87 touring pitches and 19 statics.
Indoor leisure centre, putting green.
See advertisement under Colour Section

Credit Cards

Hardwick Parks (SP388047)
Downs Rd OX8 7PZ ☎ 01865 300501 (4.5m S of Witney) Signposted
Nearby town: Witney
►►► **Family Park** ★ £7.25-£9.25 £7.25-£9.25 £7.25-£9.25
Open Apr-Oct Booking advisable bank hols Last arrival 21.00hrs Last departure 17.00hrs
A pleasant riverside site with views across the lake and its own water activities. Signed from A415 at Standlake. A 20-acre site with 250 touring pitches and 116 statics.
Fishing, windsurfing, boating, jet ski, water skiing.
Credit Cards

SHROPSHIRE

BRIDGNORTH

Stanmore Hall Touring Park (SO742923)
Stourbridge Rd WV15 6DT ☎ 01746 761761 (E on A458) Signposted
►►►► **De-Luxe Park** £10.40-£12.40 £10.40-£12.40 £8.80-£10.40
Open all year Booking advisable bank hols & Jul-Aug Last arrival 20.00hrs Last departure noon
A top class site in peaceful surroundings offering outstanding facilities. Situated on the A458 2m E of Bridgnorth in the grounds of Stanmore Hall and adj to the Midland Motor Museum. National winner of the AA's 1995 Campsite of the Year Award. A 12.5-acre site with 131 touring pitches.
Credit Cards

BROOME

Engine & Tender Inn (SO399812)
SY7 0NT ☎ 01588 660275
►**Town & Country Pennant Park**
Open all year Booking advisable bank hols Last arrival 11.00hrs Last departure 14.00hrs no cars by caravans no cars by tents
A pleasant country pub site with gently sloping ground, in a rural setting with a good set of facilities. W from Craven Arms on B4368, fork left to B4367, and site in village on right in 2m. A 2-acre site with 30 touring pitches and 2 statics.

ELLESMERE

See **Lyneal**

HAUGHTON

Camping & Caravanning Club Site (SJ546164)
Ebury Hill, Stelford TF6 6BU ☎ 01743 709334 (in season) & 01203 694995 Signposted
Nearby town: Shrewsbury
►**Town & Country Pennant Park** ★ £6.70-£8.30 £6.70-£8.30 £6.70-£8.30
Open end Mar-early Nov Booking advisable bank hols & high season Last arrival 21.00hrs Last departure noon
A wooded hill fort with a central lake overlooking the Shropshire countryside. Well-screened by very mature trees. Own sanitary facilities essential. 4m NE of Shrewsbury on B5062 Newport rd. Please see the advertisement on page 27 for details of Club Members' benefits. An 18-acre site with 160 touring pitches.
Fishing.
Credit Cards

HUGHLEY

Mill Farm Holiday Park (SO564979)
SY5 6NT ☎ 01746 785208 & 785255 Signposted
Nearby town: Much Wenlock
►**Town & Country Pennant Park**
Open Mar-Oct Booking advisable peak periods Last arrival 22.00hrs Last departure noon
A well-established farm site set in meadowland adjacent to river, with mature trees and bushes providing screening, situated below Wenlock Edge. A 7-acre site with 55 touring pitches and 75 statics.
Fishing & horse riding.

KINNERLEY

Cranberry Moss Camping & Caravan Park (SJ366211)
SY10 8DY ☎ 01743 741444 Signposted
Nearby town: Oswestry
►**Town & Country Pennant Park** ★ £5.50-£6.90 £5.50-£6.90 £1.60-£2.15
Open Apr-Oct Booking advisable bank hols & Aug Last departure noon
A very pleasant, quiet site with a variety of trees. NW of Shrewsbury off A5, take B4396 and site is 400yds on left. A 4-acre site with 60 touring pitches.

LYNEAL (NEAR ELLESMERE)

Fernwood Caravan Park (SJ445346)
SY12 0QF ☎ 01948 710221 Signposted
Nearby town: Ellesmere
►►►► **De-Luxe Park**
Open Mar-Nov Booking advisable bank hols Last arrival 21.00hrs Last departure 17.00hrs
A peaceful site set in wooded countryside, with screened, tree-lined touring area and fishing lake. 4m E of Ellesmere off B5063, signed on right. A 5-acre site with 60 touring pitches and 165 statics.

contd.

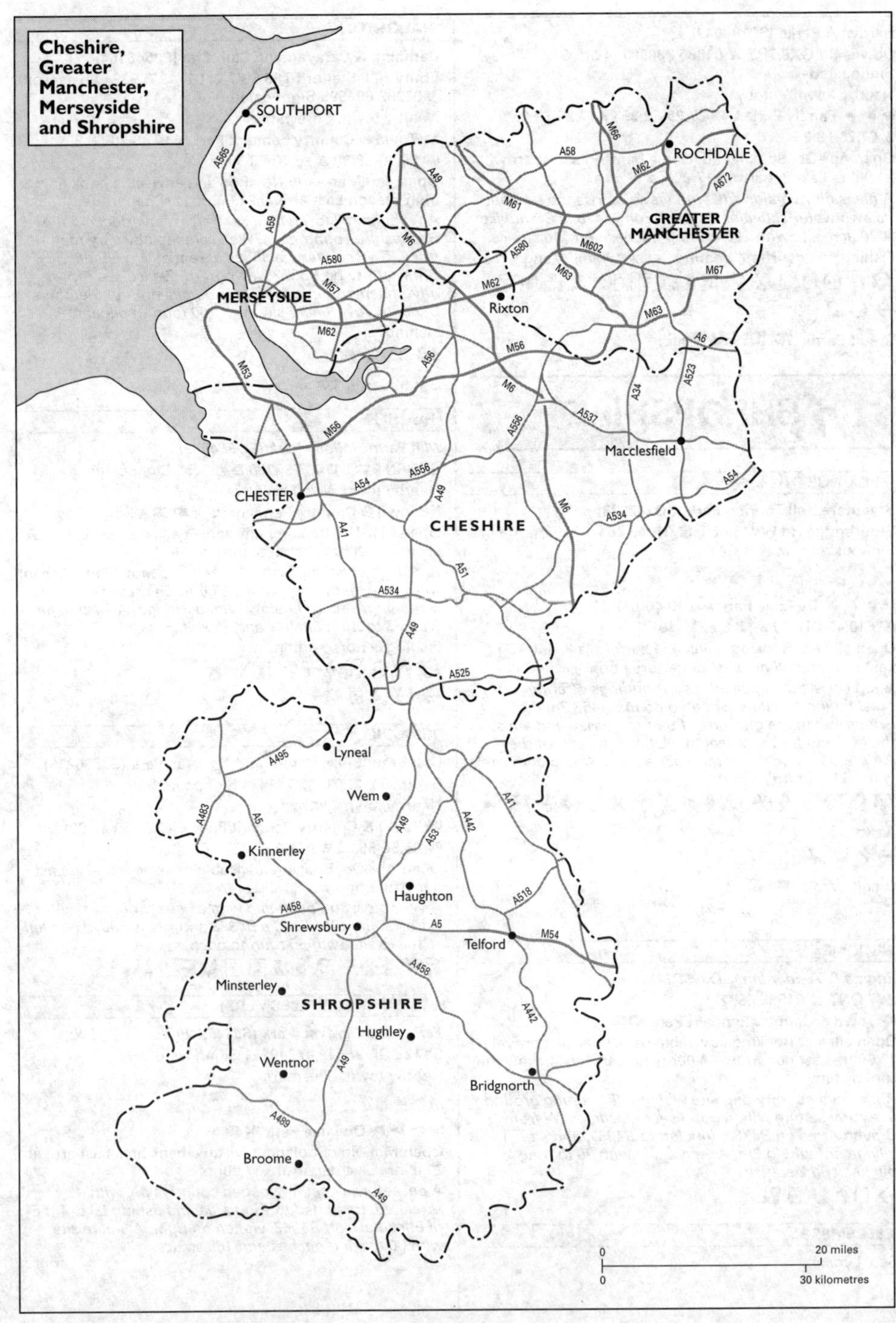

Cheshire, Greater Manchester, Merseyside and Shropshire
SOUTHPORT
ROCHDALE
GREATER MANCHESTER
MERSEYSIDE
Rixton
Macclesfield
CHESTER
CHESHIRE
Lyneal
Wem
Kinnerley
Haughton
Shrewsbury
Telford
Minsterley
SHROPSHIRE
Hughley
Wentnor
Bridgnorth
Broome
A565
A59
A580
M57
M62
M58
A49
M66
A58
M61
M6
M602
M63
M67
A6
A523
A34
M56
A56
M53
A537
A556
A54
A41
A534
A51
A525
A495
A483
A5
A53
A442
A518
A458
M54
A489
A672
0
20 miles
0
30 kilometres

Lake for coarse fishing on site.

MINSTERLEY

The Old School Caravan Park (SO322977)
Shelve SY5 0JQ ☎ 01588 650410 (5m SW on A488)
Signposted
Nearby town: Bishop's Castle
Town & Country Pennant Park ★ fr £5.50
fr £5.50 fr £5.50
Open Mar-Oct Booking advisable bank hols Last departure 10.30hrs
A well-designed site in a beautiful setting, 16miles S of Shrewsbury on A488. A 1-acre site with 12 touring pitches.
Dish washing with hot water.

SHREWSBURY

Beaconsfield Farm Caravan Park (SJ522189)
Battlefield SY4 4AA ☎ 01939 210370 & 210399 (A49, 1.5m N) Signposted
De-Luxe Park ★ £8-£10 £8-£10
Open all year Booking advisable bank hols & Aug Last arrival 19.00hrs
A newly-built family-run park on a working farm in open parkland, with a fishing lake. Take A49 at Hadnall, signed Astley, and site 2m N of Shrewsbury. An 8-acre site with 50 touring pitches.
Fly fishing, cycle hire.
See advertisement under Colour Section

TELFORD

Severn George Caravan Site (SJ705051)
Bridgnorth Rd TF7 4JB ☎ 01952 684789
Family Park
Open Mar-Nov
A very pleasant wooded site in the heart of Telford, well screened and immaculately maintained. From junc 4 of M54 take Queensway rd A464, then A442 signed Tweedale. From A5 take Shifnal rd A4169, then A442 to site. An 8-acre site with 79 touring pitches and 1 static.

WEM

Lower Lacon Caravan Park (SJ534304)
SY4 5RP ☎ 01939 232376 & 232856 (3m from A49 on B5065 toward Wem)
Signposted
Family Park ★ £9-£9.50 £9-£9.50
£9-£9.50
Open all year (rs Nov-Mar club wknds only, toilets closed if frost) Booking advisable public hols & Jul-Aug Last arrival 20.00hrs Last departure 19.00hrs
Level grass site set in meadowland with good sanitary facilities. 1.5m E of town centre on B5065. A 48-acre site with 270 touring pitches and 50 statics.
Pony rides & crazy golf.

Credit Cards

WENTNOR

The Green Caravan Park (S0380932)
SY9 5EF ☎ 01588 650605 & 650231
Signposted
Nearby town: Bishop's Castle
Family Park ★ fr £8 fr £8 fr £8
Open Etr-Oct Booking advisable bank hols Last arrival 21.00hrs Last departure 13.00hrs
A very pleasant spot with many recent improvments and more planned. Mostly level, grassy pitches. 1m NE of Bishops Castle to Lydham Heath on A489 turn rt, and site signed for 3m. A 15-acre site with 140 touring pitches and 20 statics.

Credit Cards

SOMERSET

BATH

Bath Marina & Caravan Park (ST719655)
Brassmill Ln BA1 3JT ☎ 01225 428778 & 424301
Signposted
De-Luxe Park ★ £10-£10.50 £10-£10.50
Open all year Booking advisable bank hols & Jun-Sep Last departure noon
A very pleasant site on the edge of Bath in park-like grounds among maturing trees and shrubs. From city head for suburb of Newbridge, and site is signed off A4, 1.5m W of Bath in Bristol/Wells direction. A 3-acre site with 88 touring pitches.

Credit Cards

Newton Mill Caravan and Camping Park (ST715649)
Newton Rd BA2 9JF ☎ 01225 333909 (3m NW off A4)
Signposted
De-Luxe Park ★ £10.50-£12.95
£9.50-£12.95 £8.50-£9.95
Open all year Booking advisable public hols & Jul-Aug

contd.

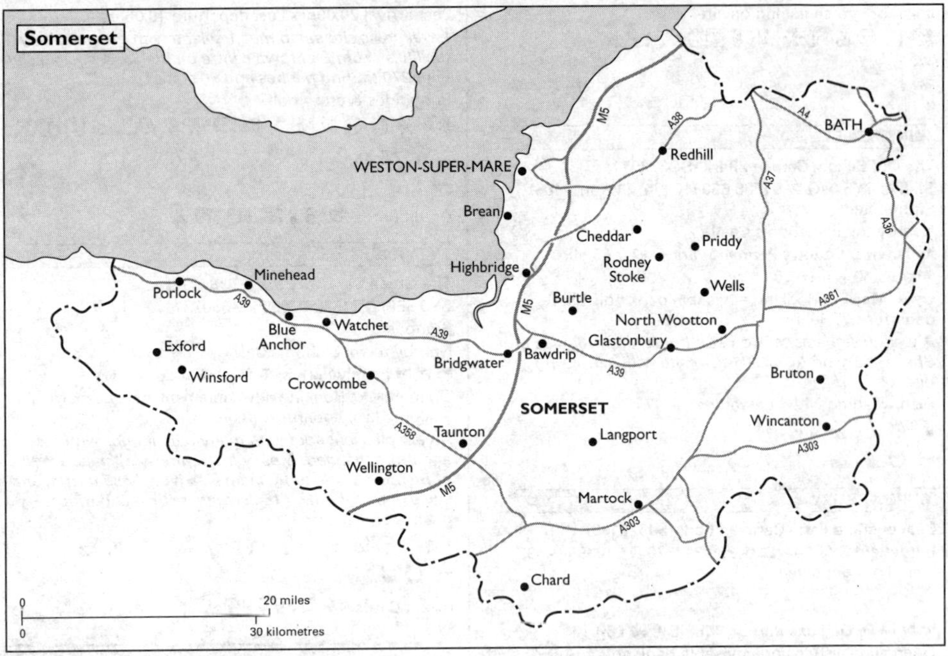

Somerset map showing: WESTON-SUPER-MARE, Redhill, BATH, Brean, Cheddar, Priddy, Highbridge, Rodney Stoke, Wells, Minehead, Burtle, North Wootton, Porlock, Blue Anchor, Watchet, Glastonbury, Bawdrip, Bruton, Exford, Bridgwater, SOMERSET, Crowcombe, Winsford, Taunton, Langport, Wincanton, Wellington, Martock, Chard

0 20 miles
0 30 kilometres

BATH MARINA & Caravan Park
NEWBRIDGE • BATH

BATH'S PREMIER PARK ON THE RIVER AVON

- This beautifully landscaped site overlooks the River Avon, only 1.5 miles from the attractions of the historic Roman spa city of Bath.
- Hard standing for 88 caravans.
- Electric points, flush toilets, showers, shaver points, laundry, children's playground, site shop, and tourist information. Dogs accepted on leash. Park & Ride bus.

 OPEN ALL YEAR ROUND

Telephone Bath (01225) 428778
or send for our brochure:
Bath Marina & Caravan Park, Brassmill Lane,
Bath, Avon BA1 3JT
Contact John and Gail Churchill

Last arrival 21.00hrs Last departure noon

Tranquil terraced site with excellent facilities by trout stream and partially bordered by woodland. Situated within easy reach of main routes. From Bath travel W on A4(T) to A39 rndbt, turn immed left and site on left in 1m. A 23-acre site with 180 touring pitches.

Satellite T.V hook ups.

Credit Cards

BAWDRIP

Fairways International Touring Caravan & Camp (ST349402)

Woolavington Corner, Bath Rd TA7 8PP ☎ 01278 685569 (3m NE of Bridgwater off B3141 jct A39) Signposted

Nearby town: Bridgwater

►►►► **De-Luxe Park** ★ £6-£8 £6-£8 £6-£8

Open Mar-15 Nov Booking advisable Spring bank hol & Jul-Aug Last departure noon

A well-planned new site offering good quality facilities. 100 yards off A39 on B3141, and 3.5m E of Bridgwater. A 5.5-acre site with 200 touring pitches.

Off-licence.

BLUE ANCHOR

Blue Anchor Park (ST025434)
TA24 6JT ☎ 01643 821360 Signposted
Nearby town: Minehead
►►► **Family Park** ★ £5.50-£13.50 £5.50-£13.50
Open Mar-Oct (rs Mar & Oct shop & swimming pool limited) Booking advisable bank hols & Jul-Aug Last arrival 22.00hrs Last departure 10.00hrs
Large coastal site, partly wooded on level ground overlooking bay with individual areas screened. .25m E of West Somerset Railway Station on B3191. A 29-acre site with 103 touring pitches and 300 statics.
Crazy golf.

Credit Cards

BREAN

Northam Farm Camping & Caravan Park (ST299556)
TA8 2SE ☎ 01278 751244 & 751222
►►► **Family Park**
Open Etr-Sep (rs Oct shop & takeaway closed) Booking advisable bank & school hols Last arrival 22.00hrs Last departure noon
An attractive site a short walk from the sea with game, coarse and sea fishing close by. Take road to Burnham, and site on left in 500yds. A 30-acre site with 299 touring pitches and 90 statics.
Pond fishing.

BRIDGWATER

Mill Farm Caravan & Camping Park (ST219410)
Fiddington TA5 1JQ ☎ 01278 732286
►►► **Family Park**
Established, mature site with helpful owners. From Bridgwater take A39 W, turn left at Cannington rndbt for 2m, and just past Apple Inn turn right towards Fiddington and follow camping signs. A 6-acre site with 125 touring pitches.

BRUTON

Batcombe Vale Caravan & Camping Park (ST681379)
Batcombe Vale BA4 6BW ☎ 01749 830246 (off B3081 between Evercreech & Bruton) Signposted
► **Town & Country Pennant Park** ★ £7-£8 £7-£8 £7-£8
Open Etr-Sep Booking advisable bank hols & Jul-Aug Last arrival 22.00hrs Last departure noon
A small, attractive and very quiet site in a secluded valley close to three lakes. Standards of maintenance remain high. Take Evercreech road from Bruton, signed. A 4-acre site with 30 touring pitches.
Wild landscaped garden in secluded valley of lakes

BURTLE

Ye Olde Burtle Inn (ST397434)
Catcott Rd TA7 8NG ☎ 01278 722269
Nearby town: Glastonbury
► **Town & Country Pennant Park**

contd.

Open all year Booking advisable Jul-Aug

Tenting only site in a cider apple orchard. Situated beside pub in centre of village. A 0.75-acre site with 30 touring pitches.

Skittke alley, pool, darts & cycle hire.

Credit Cards

CHARD

South Somerset Holiday Park (ST279098)

Howley TA20 3EA

☎ 01460 62221 & 66036 (3m W on A30)

►►►► **De-Luxe Park** ★ £5-£7 £5-£7 ▲ £5-£7

Open all year Booking advisable bank hols & High Season Last arrival 23.00hrs Last departure noon

An immaculate site with impressive facilities and levels of maintenance. 3m W of Chard on A30. A 7-acre site with 75 touring pitches and 42 statics.

Alpine Grove Touring Park (SY342071)

Forton TA20 4HD ☎ 01460 63479 Signposted

►►► **Family Park** ★ £6.50-£8 £6.50-£8 ▲ £6.50-£8

Open Etr-Sep Booking advisable bank hols & Jul-Aug Last arrival 23.00hrs

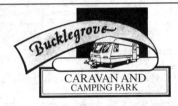

An attractive, quiet wooded site, close to Cricket St Thomas Park. Turn off A30 between Chard and Crewkerne towards Cricket St Thomas, follow signs from park, and site 2m on right. A 7.5-acre site with 40 touring pitches and 1 static.

CHEDDAR

Broadway House Holiday Caravan & Camping Park (ST448547)

Axbridge Rd BS27 3DB ☎ 01934 742610 Signposted

►►►► **De-Luxe Park** ★ £5-£12 £4-£9.50 ▲ £5-£12

Open end May-Sep (rs Mar-end May & Oct-Nov no bar & pool open, limited shop hours) Booking advisable bank hols & end Jul-Aug Last departure noon

A well-equipped family site on slopes of Mendips with exceptional adventure areas for children, jacuzzi and sun bed. Midway between Cheddar and Axbridge on A371. A 30-acre site with 200 touring pitches and 35 statics.

Sunbed, table tennis, crazy golf, full activity prog.

Credit Cards

Church Farm Caravan & Camping Park (ST460529)

Church St BS27 3RF ☎ 01934 743048 On entering village. Along A371 Post Marked Cross & Church the entrance is the first turning on the right. Signposted

Nearby town: Weston-Super-Mare

►►► **Family Park** ★ fr £6.50 fr £6.50 ▲ fr £6.50

Open Etr-Oct Booking advisable public hols Last arrival 22.00hrs Last departure noon

Spacious, flat, grassy site, well-screened at rear of farm and short walk from Cheddar. A 6-acre site with 44 touring pitches and 3 statics.

Hairdryers.

Froglands Farm Caravan & Camping Park (ST462529)

BS27 3RH ☎ 01934 742058 & 743304 Signposted

Nearby town: Wells

►►► **Family Park** ★ £6-£8 £5-£7 ▲ £5-£7

Open Etr or Apr-30 Oct Booking advisable Whitsun, Jul-Aug & school hols Last arrival 23.00hrs Last departure 13.00hrs

Farmland site on undulating ground with trees and shrubs, located on A371 Weston-Super-Mare to Wells road on SE outskirts of Cheddar. A 3-acre site with 68 touring pitches.

CROWCOMBE

Quantock Orchard Caravan Park (ST138357)
TA4 4AW ☎ 01984 618618 Signposted
Nearby town: Taunton
▶▶▶ **Family Park**
Open all year Booking advisable bank hols & Jul-Aug
Last arrival 10.00hrs Last departure noon
An attractive, quiet site at the foot of the Quantocks with good views, and set back from the A358. A 3.5-acre site with 65 touring pitches.
Barbecues provided, off-licence on site.

EXFORD

Westermill Farm (SS824398)
TA24 7NJ ☎ 01643 831238 & 831216 Signposted
Nearby town: Dulverton
Town & Country Pennant Park ★ fr £7 fr £7
Open Apr-Oct (rs Apr-23 May shop closed) Booking advisable Spring bank hol & Jul-Aug
An idyllic site for peace and quiet, in sheltered valley in the heart of Exmoor. Four waymarked walks over 500 acre working farm. Leave Exford on the Porlock road, after .25m fork left. Continue for 2.25m along valley past another campsite until 'Westermill' sign seen on tree, then fork left. Not suitable for caravans. A 6-acre site with 60 touring pitches.
Trout fishing on site. Information centre.

GLASTONBURY

Old Oaks Touring Park (ST521394)
Wick Farm, Wick BA6 8JS ☎ 01458 831437 (take A361 towards Shepton Mallet in 1.75m turn left at sign Wick 1, site on left in 1m) Signposted
▶▶▶ **Family Park** £7-£8.50 £7-£8.50 £7-£8.50
Open Mar-Oct Booking advisable bank hols & main season Last arrival 21.00hrs Last departure noon
An ideal family park on a working farm on the east side of Glastonbury Tor with panoramic views towards the Mendip Hills. Glastonbury's two famous 1,000 year old oaks - Gog and Magog - are on site, hence the name. From Glastonbury take the Shepton Mallet road. A 2.5-acre site with 40 touring pitches.
Fishing & off-licence on site.

Credit Cards

AA members can call AA Hotel Booking Service on 0990 050505 to book at AA recognised hotels and B & Bs in the UK and Ireland, or through our Internet site: http://www.theaa.co.uk/hotels

HIGHBRIDGE

Edithmead Leisure & Park Homes (ST337459)
TA9 4HE ☎ 01278 783475
Signposted
Nearby town: Burnham-on-Sea
►►► **Family Park**
Open 9 Feb-11 Jan Booking advisable bank hols & Jul-Sep Last arrival mdnt Last departure noon
Level, compact site adjacent to M5. From Highcliffe follow signs to M5 rndbt, and site on right. A 15-acre site with 250 touring pitches and 65 statics.
Amusement arcade.

New House Farm Caravan & Camping Park (ST338469)
Walrow TA9 4RA
☎ 01278 782218 & 783277
Signposted
Nearby town: Bridgwater
►►► **Family Park**
Open Mar-Oct Booking advisable Jul & Aug Last arrival 23.30hrs Last departure 18.30hrs
A very neat, quiet farm site with well-maintained facilities, sheltered by boundary hedging and trees. 3m from beaches. A 4-acre site with 30 touring pitches.

LANGPORT

Thorney Lakes Caravan Park (ST430237)
Thorney West Farm, Muchelney TA10 0DW
☎ 01458 250811
Town & Country Pennant Park ★ fr £6 fr £6 fr £6
Open Mar-Nov Booking advisable
A small basic but very attractive site. From Langport take Mucherley Rd, and site 3m on left. A 6-acre site with 16 touring pitches.
Coarse fishing on site.

MARTOCK

Southfork Caravan Park (ST448188)
Parrett Works TA12 6AE ☎ 01935 825661 Signposted
Nearby town: Yeovil
►►► **Family Park** ★ fr £7 fr £7 fr £7
Open all year Booking advisable bank hols & Jul-Aug Last arrival 23.00hrs Last departure noon
Well-kept and equipped level site, 1.5m from centre of Martock with good country views. An ideal touring centre. From South Petherton follow rd N for 2m. Site on left and signed. A 2-acre site with 30 touring pitches and 3 statics.
Caravan service/repair centre & accessories shop.

Credit Cards

MINEHEAD

Camping & Caravanning Club Site (SS958471)
Hill Rd, North Hill TA24 5SF ☎ 01643 704138 (in season) & 01203 694995 Signposted
►►► **Family Park** ★ £5.60-£8.60 £5.60-£8.60
Open end Mar-end Sep Booking advisable bank hols & Jul-Aug Last arrival 21.00hrs Last departure noon no cars by caravans
A secluded site offering glorious views of the Bristol Channel and Quantocks. The approach road is narrow with sharp bends. From town centre follow camping signs, and site on right at top of hill. Please see the advertisement on page 27 for details of Club Members' benefits. A 3.75-acre site with 60 touring pitches.

Credit Cards

Minehead & Exmoor Caravan Site (SS950457)
Minehead & Exmoor Caravan Park, Porlock Rd TA24 8SN ☎ 01643 703074 (1m W adj to A39) Signposted
►►► **Family Park** ★ £8 £8 £8
Open Mar-Oct Booking advisable bank hols & Jul-Aug Last arrival 23.00hrs Last departure noon
Small, terraced, grassy site near the town with many young trees and plants. Bordered by a stream on the edge of Exmoor. Adjacent to the A39. A 2.5-acre site with 50 touring pitches.

Credit Cards

NORTH WOOTTON

Greenacres Camping (ST553416)
Barrow Ln BA4 4HL ☎ 01749 890497 Signposted
Nearby town: Wells
Town & Country Pennant Park £8 £8
Open Apr-Oct Booking advisable school hols Last arrival 21.00hrs Last departure noon
An immaculately maintained site peacefully set within sight of Glastonbury Tor. Mainly family orientated with many thoughtful extra facilities provided. From North Wootton follow signs for 1.5m. A 4.5-acre site with 30 touring pitches.

PORLOCK

Burrowhayes Farm Caravan & Camping Site (SS897460)
West Luccombe TA24 8HU ☎ 01643 862463 (SE of Porlock .25m off A39)
Nearby town: Minehead
►►► **Family Park** ★ £5.50-£7.50 £5.50-£7.50 £5.50-£7.50
Open 15 Mar-Oct Booking advisable Etr, Spring bank hol & Jun-Sep Last departure noon
A delightful site on the edge of Exmoor, on slope to the river, and ideal for exploring surrounding area. From Porlock take A39 E, in .25m turn right, and site on right in 200yds. An 8-acre site with 140 touring pitches and 20 statics.
Pony-treking available.

Porlock Caravan Park (SS882469)
TA24 8NS ☎ 01643 862269 Signposted
►►► **Family Park** ★
Open 15 Mar-Oct Booking advisable Etr, Whitsun & Jul-Aug Last arrival 23.00hrs Last departure noon
A well-planned site, in valley with shrubs and trees, and an ideal touring centre for Exmoor. In village by West car park. A 3-acre site with 40 touring pitches and 56 statics.

PRIDDY

Mendip Heights Camping & Caravan Park (ST522519)
Townsend BA5 3BP ☎ 01749 870241 Signposted
Nearby town: Wells
►►► **Family Park** £6.40-£7 £6.40-£7 £6.40-£7
Open Mar-15 Nov Booking advisable bank & school hols Last arrival 22.30hrs
Quiet family site in high open-countryside overlooking the Mendip Hills and valleys, signposted from A39 at Green Ore. A 4.5-acre site with 90 touring pitches and 1 static.
Archery, canoeing, absailing, caving, table tennis.

REDHILL

Brook Lodge Camping & Caravan Park (ST486620)
Cowslip Green BS18 7RD ☎ 01934 862311 Signposted
Nearby town: Bristol
Town & Country Pennant Park ★ £8.50-£9 £8.50-£9 £8.50-£9
Open Mar-Oct (rs Nov-Feb) Booking advisable 22 May-4 Sep & bank hols Last arrival 23.50hrs Last departure noon
A pleasant, well-screened touring site, hidden from the A38 by hedging and trees. 1.5m S of Ripon on A38. A 3-acre site with 29 touring pitches.

RODNEY STOKE

Bucklegrove Caravan & Camping Park (ST487502)
Wells Rd BS27 3UZ ☎ 01749 870261 Signposted
Nearby town: Wells
►►►► **De-Luxe Park** ★ £5.50-£9.50 £5.50-£9.50 £5.50-£9.50
Open Mar-Oct Booking advisable bank hols & peak periods Last arrival 22.30hrs Last departure noon
A well-sheltered site on the southern slopes of the Mendip Hills providing superb views of Somerset. An ideal touring base off A371. A 5-acre site with 125 touring pitches and 35 statics.
See advertisement on page 178.
Credit Cards

TAUNTON

Ashe Farm Camping & Caravan Site (ST279229)
Thornfalcon TA3 5NW ☎ 01823 442567 Signposted
►►► **Family Park** £6-£7.50 £6-£7.50 fr £6
Open Apr-Oct Booking advisable Jul-Aug
Attractive site with clean facilities. Situated off A358, 4m SE of Taunton, 3.5m from junc 25 of M5. A 3-acre site with 30 touring pitches and 2 statics.

Holly Bush Park (ST220162)
Culmhead TA3 7EA
☎ 01823 421515 (5m S on B3170, turn right a crossroads signed Wellington, right at T jct, site 100yds on left) Signposted
►►► **Family Park** ★ £6-£7.50 £6-£7.50 £6-£7.50
Open all year Booking advisable bank hols & high season Last arrival 22.00hrs Last departure noon
A good basic site, ideal as overnight stop yet well positioned around attractive countryside with easy access to Wellington and Taunton. From Taunton take B3170 (Corfe), and at first crossrds in 5m turn right. Site on left past pub. A 2-acre site with 40 touring pitches.

WATCHET

Doniford Bay Holiday Park (ST095433)
TA23 OTJ ☎ 01984 632423
Nearby town: Minehead
►►► **Family Park**
Open Etr-end Oct Booking advisable Jul-Aug Last departure 10.00hrs
A level site with some hardstanding pitches for caravans and surfaced internal roadways. E of Watchet off A39 and overlooking the sea (Minehead Bay). A 5-acre site with 120 touring pitches.
Free evening entertainment, amusements, Go-Karts.

Credit Cards

WELLINGTON

Gamlins Farm Caravan Park (ST083195)
Gamlins Farm, Greenham TA21 OLZ
☎ 01823 672596 (4m W)
Signposted
►►► **Family Park**
Open Apr-Sep Booking advisable bank hols Last arrival 20.00hrs Last departure noon
A well-planned site in a secluded position with panoramic views. Situated off the A38 on the Greenham road. A 3-acre site with 25 touring pitches.

WELLS

Homestead Caravan & Camping Park (ST532474)
Wookey Hole BA5 1BW ☎ 01749 673022 Signposted
►►► **Family Park** ★ £8.60 £8 £8.80
Open Etr-Oct Booking advisable Last arrival 22.00hrs Last departure noon
Attractive small site by stream with mature trees. Set in hilly woods and meadowland with access to river and Wookey Hole. .5m NW off A371 Wells-Cheddar road. A 2-acre site with 50 touring pitches and 28 statics.
Childrens fishing.

WESTON-SUPER-MARE

Airport View Holiday Park (ST351611)
Moor Ln Worle ☎ 01934 622168
►►► **Family Park**
Open all year
A pleasant, well-cared for site with newly-built facilities. From A371 junc with A370 turn immediately east, and site signed. A 10-acre site with 135 touring pitches and 40 statics.

Country View Caravan Park (ST335647)
Sand Rd Sand Bay BS22 9UJ ☎ 01934 627595
Signposted
►►► **Family Park**
Open Mar-Oct Booking advisable bank hols & peak periods Last arrival 21.00hrs Last departure noon
A pleasant, flat, open site in a country area not far from the coast. Follow signs to Sand Bay, turn right into Sand Rd, and first caravan park on right. 3m N of town. An 8-acre site with 120 touring pitches and 65 statics.
See advertisement on page 177

Credit Cards

Purn International Holiday Park (ST332568)
Bridgwater Rd, Bleadon BS24 0AN ☎ 01934 812342
Signposted
►►► **Family Park**
Open Mar-7 Nov Booking advisable Last arrival mdnt Last departure 10.30hrs
A good flat site in a handy position for touring the Somerset coast. Take A370 from Weston-super-Mare towards Edithmead, and site on right by The Anchor Inn, about 1m from 1st rndbt. A 3.5-acre site with 168 touring pitches and 108 statics.
River with fishing.

The AA pennant classification has been revised for 1998. Please read the explanation of the scheme on page 10.

West End Farm Caravan & Camping Park (ST354600)
Locking BS24 8RH ☎ 01934 822529 (along A370, follow signs for Helicopter Museum, after museum turn right & follow site signs) Signposted
►►► **Family Park** £7.80-£8.80 £7.80-£8.80 £7.80-£8.80
Open all year Booking advisable peak periods Last arrival 22.00hrs Last departure noon
A flat, hedge-bordered site by helicopter museum with good clean facilities and landscaping. Good access to Weston-super-Mare and the Mendips. From Weston-super-Mare take A370 N to junc with A371, turn right then site in 1m on right. A 10-acre site with 75 touring pitches and 20 statics.

Weston Gateway Caravan Site (ST370621)
West Wick BS24 7TF ☎ 01934 510344 Signposted
►►► **Family Park**
Open all year (rs Nov-Mar chem wc disposal only, shop & club closed) Booking advisable Jul-Aug Last arrival mdnt Last departure 14.00hrs
A pleasant site set among trees and shrubs close to the A370 and junc 21 of M5. Plenty of entertainment but basic toilet block. A 15-acre site with 175 touring pitches.

WINCANTON

Wincanton Racecourse Caravan Club Site (ST708295)
BA9 8BJ ☎ 01963 34276 Signposted
Town & Country Pennant Park
Open Apr-Sep (rs Apr-5 May limited space/electric point on race day) Booking advisable bank hols Last arrival 20.00hrs Last departure noon
A well-kept level grassy site on Racecourse Downs one mile from the town centre on A303. Turn off main road at Hunters Lodge to A3081 from either direction. A 2-acre site with 50 touring pitches.
9 hole golf course.

Credit Cards

WINSFORD

Halse Farm Caravan & Camping Park (SS894344)
TA24 7JL ☎ 01643 851259 Signposted
Nearby town: Dulverton
►►► **Family Park**
Open all year Booking advisable Last arrival 22.00hrs Last departure noon
An Exmoor site overlooking a typical wooded valley with glorious views. Midway between Minehead and Tiverton. A 3-acre site with 44 touring pitches.

STAFFORDSHIRE

CANNOCK CHASE

Camping & Caravanning Club Site (SK039145)
Old Youth Hostel, Wandon WS15 1QW
☎ 01889 582166 & 01203 694995
Signposted
Town & Country Pennant Park ★ £8.70-£11.30 £8.70-£11.30 £8.70-£11.30
Open Mar-Nov Booking advisable bank hols & Jul-Aug Last arrival 21.00hrs Last departure noon
Very popular site in an excellent location in the heart of the Chase. A gently sloping site with timber-built facility blocks. From A460 take sign for Rawnsley/Hazleslade, then left in 400yds, and site .5m past golf club.Please see the advertisement on page 27 for details of Club Members' benefits. A 5-acre site with 60 touring pitches.

Credit Cards

CHEADLE

Quarry Walk Park (SK045405)
Coppice Ln, Croxden Common, Freehay ST10 1RQ
☎ 01538 723495
►►► **Family Park**
Open all year Booking advisable bank hols Last arrival 23.00hrs Last departure noon
A pleasant park in an old quarry, well-screened with mature trees and shrubs. Situated 1m from A522 Cheadle-Uttoxeter Rd at Freehay. A 14-acre site with 40 touring pitches.

LEEK

Camping & Caravanning Club Site (SK008599)
Blackshaw Grange, Blackshaw Moor ST13 8TL ☎ 01538 300285 & 01203 694995
►►► **Family Park** ★ £5.20-£7.80 £5.20-£7.80 £5.20-£7.80
Open 24 Mar-3 Nov Booking advisable Jan-Mar Last arrival 21.00hrs Last departure noon
A beautifully located club site, with well-screened pitches. 2m NE of Leek on A53 to Buxton; site at Blackshaw Moor and signed. A 6-acre site with 60 touring pitches.

Credit Cards

OAKAMOOR

Star Caravan & Camping Park (SK066456)
Cotton ST10 3BN ☎ 01538 702256 & 702219 (1.25m NE off B5417) Signposted
Nearby town: Leek
Town & Country Pennant Park ★ £6 £6 £6
Open Feb-Dec Booking advisable anytime Last arrival anytime Last departure 19.00hrs

contd.

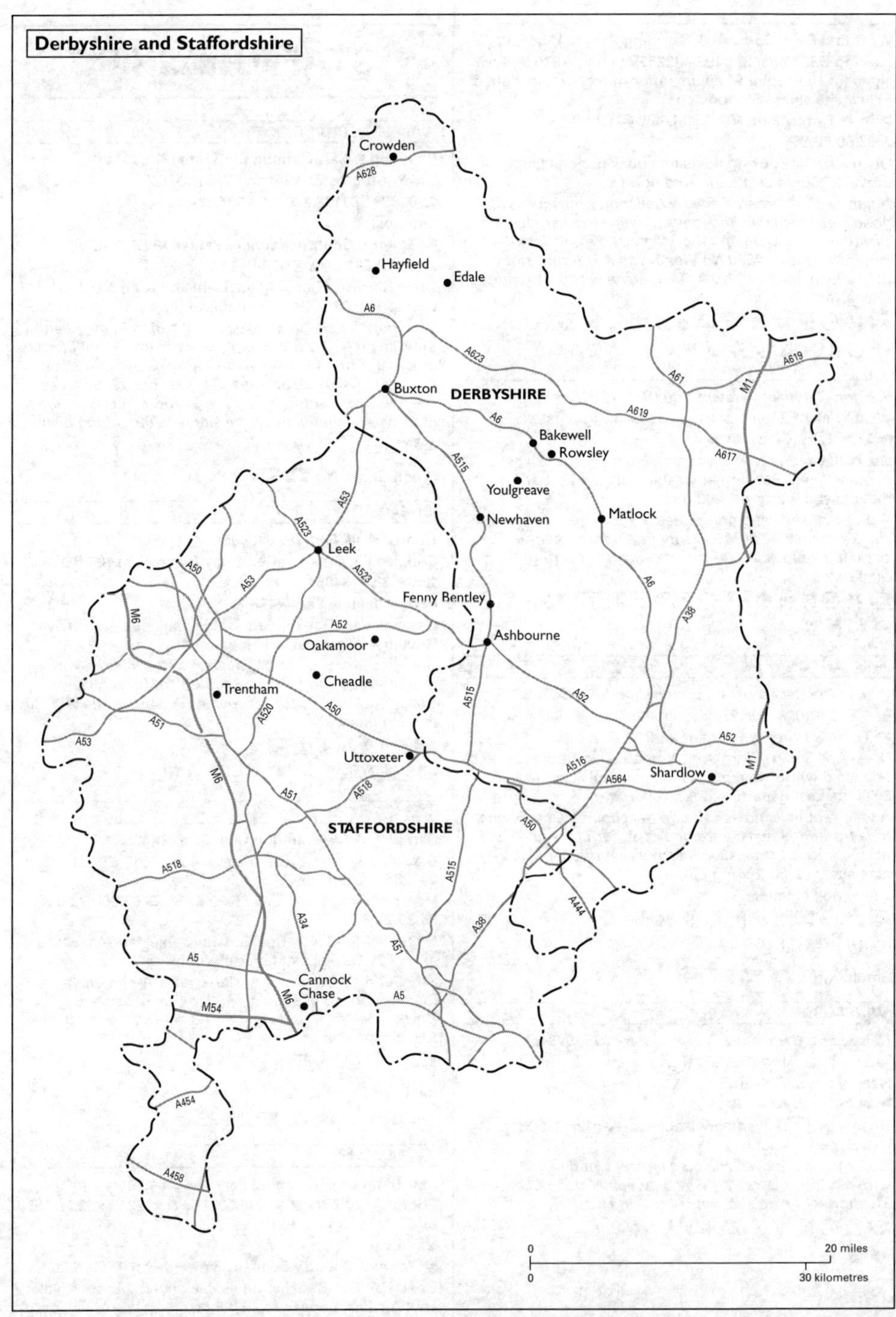
Derbyshire and Staffordshire
Crowden
A628
Hayfield
Edale
A6
A623
Buxton
DERBYSHIRE
A61
A619
M1
A619
A6
Bakewell
Rowsley
A617
A515
Youlgreave
A53
Newhaven
Matlock
A523
Leek
A50
A523
A53
Fenny Bentley
A6
A38
M6
A52
Oakamoor
Ashbourne
Cheadle
Trentham
A515
A52
A520
A50
A51
A53
A52
Uttoxeter
A516
A564
Shardlow
M1
M6
A518
A51
STAFFORDSHIRE
A50
A518
A515
A444
A34
A38
A51
A5
Cannock
Chase
M6
A5
M54
A454
A458
0
20 miles
0
30 kilometres

A pleasant, well screened site situated within one mile of Alton Towers. 1.25m N of Oakamoor off B5417. A 20-acre site with 120 touring pitches and 58 statics.

STOKE ON TRENT

See **Trentham**

TRENTHAM

Trentham Gardens Caravan & Leisure Park (SJ864409)
Trentham Gardens, Stone Rd ST4 8AX
☎ 01782 657519 & 657341 Signposted
Nearby town: Newcastle-under-Lyme
►►► **Family Park** ★ £5.50-£9 £5.50-£9 £5.50-£9
Open all year (rs Oct-Etr shop bar cafe closed) Booking advisable bank hols & during major events Last arrival 22.00hrs Last departure 18.00hrs
Wooded meadowland site by lakes. Access to A34 and exit 15 of M6. A 30-acre site with 250 touring pitches.
Shooting & fishing.

Credit Cards

UTTOXETER

Racecourse Site (SK099334)
Uttoxeter Racecourse ST14 8BD ☎ 01889 564172 & 562561 Signposted
►►► **Family Park**
Open Apr-Oct (rs Mar & Nov limited opening) Booking advisable bank hols & race meeting dates Last arrival 20.00hrs Last departure noon
Situated on SE edge of small market town, mainly level site in hilly country. Off B5017. A 3-acre site with 83 touring pitches.

Credit Cards

SUFFOLK

For the map, see Cambridgeshire

BUNGAY

Outney Meadow Caravan Park (TM333905)
Outney Meadow NR35 1HG
☎ 01986 892338 (signposted from rdbt at Jct of A143/A144) Signposted
►►► **Family Park** ★ £7-£10 £7-£10 £7-£10
Open Mar-Oct Booking advisable public hols Last arrival 22.00hrs Last departure 21.00hrs
A pleasant site with part river frontage and some watersports. Toilet facilities basic. W of village on A143, adjoining the roundabout. A 6-acre site with 45 touring pitches and 30 statics.
Fishing, rowing boat and canoe hire.

BUTLEY

Tangham Campsite (TM355485)
IP12 3NP ☎ 01394 450707 Signposted
Nearby town: Woodbridge
►►► **Family Park** ★ £7-£8.50 £7-£8.50 £7-£8.50
Open Etr/Apr-10 Jan Booking advisable bank hols Last arrival 22.00hrs Last departure noon
Good, quiet, level grass site, situated on the edge of a deep forest with attractive walks. From Woodbridge take B1084, after 5m turn right into forest. A 7-acre site with 90 touring pitches.
Washing-up sinks.

DUNWICH

Cliff House (TM475692)
Minsmere Rd IP17 3DQ
☎ 01728 648282 (from A12, follow sign to Dunwich Heath) Signposted
Nearby town: Southwold

►►►► **De-Luxe Park** ★ £8-£11 £8-£11 £8-£10
Open Etr or Apr-Oct Booking advisable all year Last arrival 21.00hrs Last departure 11.00hrs
A delightful park tucked away on the cliffs amidst woodland close to Minsmere Bird Reserve and centred around a large house and walled gardens. Central England regional winner of the Campsite of the Year Award for 1997/8. A 30-acre site with 95 touring pitches and 78 statics.
Campers wash room, pool, table tennis & darts.

Credit Cards

EAST BERGHOLT

Grange Country Park (TM098353)
The Grange CO7 6UX ☎ 01206 298567 & 298912 Signposted. Nearby town: Manningtree

►►►► **De-Luxe Park**
Open 31 Mar-Oct (rs Oct-Mar) Booking advisable for stays of 1 wk or more Last arrival 22.00hrs Last departure 18.00hrs
This level, grassy site is situated in hilly woodland with some moorland nearby. The park is sheltered by mature trees and bushes and provides first class sanitary facilities. 3m off A12 between Colchester and Ipswich. An 8-acre site with 120 touring pitches and 55 statics.
See advertisement under Colour Section

FELIXSTOWE

Peewit Caravan Park (TM290338)
Walton Av IP11 8HB ☎ 01394 284511 & 670217
Signposted
►►► **Family Park** ★ £6.50-£8.50 £6.50-£8.50
£6.50-£8.50
Open Apr or Etr-Oct (rs early & late season shop closed) Booking advisable school & bank hols Last arrival 21.00hrs Last departure 11.00hrs
A useful town site, not overlooked by houses. The site is neat and tidy, and the beach a few minutes away by car. Signed from A14 in Felixstowe. A 3-acre site with 65 touring pitches and 220 statics.
Bowling green, washing up sink.

GISLEHAM

Chestnut Farm Touring Park (TM510876)
NR33 8EE ☎ 01502 740227 Signposted
Nearby town: Lowestoft
► **Town & Country Pennant Park** ★ £5-£7.50
£5-£7.50 £5-£6.50
Open Apr-Oct Booking advisable bank hols Last arrival mdnt
A nice little farm site with old but well-maintained toilets in a peaceful setting. At southern roundabout of Kessingland bypass go west signposted Rushmere, Mutford and Gisleham. Take second turning on left. A 3-acre site with 20 touring pitches.
Fishing on site.

IPSWICH

Priory Park (TM198409)
IP10 0JT ☎ 01473 727393 & 726373 Signposted
►►► **Family Park** ★ £13 £13 £13
Open all year (rs Oct-Apr limited number of sites, club/pool closed) Booking advisable bank & school hols Last arrival 21.00hrs Last departure noon
Well-screened south-facing site with panoramic views overlooking Orwell. Convenient for Ipswich southern bypass. From bypass take Nacton exit then follow signs Ipswich/Airport for 300yds to site entrance. An 85-acre site with 110 touring pitches and 260 statics.
9 hole golf, small boat launching, table tennis.

Low House Touring Caravan Centre (TM227425)
Bucklesham Rd, Foxhall IP10 0AU
☎ 01473 659437 (4m E) Signposted
► **Town & Country Pennant Park** ★ £6.50-£8
£6.50-£8 £4.25-£6.50
Open all year Booking advisable anytime Last arrival anytime Last departure anytime
An appealing, secluded site with immaculate facilities and very caring owners. From A45 south ring road take slip road to A1156 signed East Ipswich. Turn right in 1m and right again in .5m. Site on left. Tents accepted only if room available. A 3.5-acre site with 30 touring pitches.
Temporary membership of sports centre opposite.

KESSINGLAND

Kessingland Beach Holiday Village (TM535852)
Beach Rd NR33 7RN ☎ 01502 740636 & 740879
Signposted
Nearby town: Lowestoft
►►►► **De-Luxe Park**
Open Mar-Nov Booking advisable Jun-Aug Last arrival 21.00hrs Last departure 14.00hrs
A large seaside holiday park with plenty of entertainment for all ages. A 65-acre site with 90 touring pitches and 209 statics.
Bowling green, sauna, amusements, mini ten-pin bowls.
Credit Cards

Camping & Caravanning Club Site (TM520860)
Suffolk Wildlife Park, Whites Ln NR33 7SL
☎ 01502 742040 (in season) & 01203 694995 (.5m S, off A12) Signposted
Nearby town: Lowestoft
►►► **Family Park** ★ £9.10-£12.10 £9.10-£12.10
£9.10-£12.10
Open end Mar-eraly Nov Booking advisable bank hols & Jul-Aug Last arrival 21.00hrs Last departure noon
An open site next to a wildlife park, with beaches close by. Very tidy and well maintained. Concessions to wildlife park. Please see the advertisement on page 27 for details of Club Members' benefits. A 6.5-acre site with 90 touring pitches.
Credit Cards

LEISTON

Cakes & Ale (TM432637)
Abbey Ln, Theberton IP16 4TE
☎ 01728 831655 & 01473 736650 Signposted
Nearby town: Aldeburgh
►►► **Family Park** ★ £8-£10 £8-£10 £8-£10
Open Apr-Oct (rs low season club, shop/reception open limited hours) Booking advisable public & school hols Last arrival 21.00hrs Last departure 16.00hrs
A large, well spread out site with many trees and bushes. Ideal centre for touring. From A12 at Saxmundham turn E onto B1119 for 3 miles. Then follow by-road over level crossing and signs to caravan park. A 5-acre site with 50 touring pitches and 200 statics.
Tennis, 5 acre recreation ground, golf.
Credit Cards

LOWESTOFT

See **Kessingland**

NEWMARKET

Camping & Caravanning Club Site (TL622625)
Rowley Mile Racecourse CB8 8JL
☎ 01638 663235 & 01203 694995 Signposted
Town & Country Pennant Park ★ £8.70-£11.30
£8.70-£11.30 £8.70-£11.30
Open May-Sep Booking advisable Last arrival 21.00hrs Last departure noon
A level grassy site on Newmarket Heath with panoramic country views. From centre of Newmarket follow signs for Horse Museum and Hospital. Site 1m W of town centre at top of hill and signed. Please see the advertisement on page 27 for details of Club Members' benefits. A 10-acre site with 90 touring pitches.
Recreation room.

Credit Cards

SAXMUNDHAM

Whitearch Touring Caravan Park (TM379610)
Main Rd, Benhall IP17 1NA ☎ 01728 604646 & 603773 Signposted
Town & Country Pennant Park ★ £8.50-£10
£8.50-£10 £8.50-£10
Open Apr-Oct Booking advisable bank hols
Attractive valley site with lake for coarse fishing and new, very clean toilet block. On the junction of A12 and B1121. A 14.5-acre site with 30 touring pitches.
Fishing lake

Marsh Farm Caravan Site (TM385608)
Sternfield IP171HW ☎ 01728 602168 (1.5m S) Signposted
Town & Country Pennant Park
Open all year Booking advisable Jun-Aug Last arrival 22.30hrs Last departure 22.30hrs
Very attractive venture site with adjoining lakes offering coarse fishing, and no sanitary facilities. Take Aldburgh rd from A12, at Snape crossroads turn left signed Sternfield, and pick up sign for farm. A 6-acre site with 30 touring pitches.

SHOTTISHAM

St Margaret's House (TM323447)
Hollesley Rd IP12 3HD
☎ 01394 411247 Signposted
Nearby town: Woodbridge
Town & Country Pennant Park ★ £5-£6.50
£5-£6.50 £5-£6.50
Open Apr or Etr-Oct Booking advisable bank hols & Jul-Aug Last arrival 22.00hrs Last departure noon
A pleasant little family run site in attractive village setting. Turn off B1083 at village and in .25m find site to SE of church. A 3-acre site with 30 touring pitches.
Milk, dairy products & newspapers to order.

WOODBRIDGE

Moon & Sixpence (TM263454)
Newbourn Rd, Waldringfield IP12 4PP
☎ 01473 736650 Signposted
Family Park ★ £10-£12 £10-£12
£10-£12
Open Apr-Oct (rs low season (Adults only) club/shop/reception open limited hours) Booking advisable school & bank hols Last arrival 21.00hrs Last departure noon
A splendid, well-planned site, with a lakeside sandy beach. Tourers are in a valley around the lake. Signed from A12 at Martlesham. A 5-acre site with 90 touring pitches and 175 statics.
2 acre lake with sandy beach.Woodland cycle trail.
See advertisement under Colour Section

Credit Cards

SURREY

For the map of this county, see Sussex, East

CHERTSEY

Camping & Caravanning Club Site (TQ052667)
Bridge Rd KT16 8JX
☎ 01932 562405 & 01203 694995 Signposted
Family Park ★ £9.10-£12.10 £9.10-£12.10
£9.10-£12.10
Open all year Booking advisable Jul-Aug & bank hols Last arrival 21.00hrs Last departure noon
A pretty riverside site with many trees and shrubs, and well-looked after grounds. Fishing and boating allowed on the River Thames. Please see the advertisement on page 27 for details of Club Members' benefits. A 12-acre site with 200 touring pitches.
Table tennis, pool, fishing.

Credit Cards

EAST HORSLEY

Camping & Caravanning Club Site (TQ083552)
Ockham Rd North KT24 6PE
☎ 01483 283273 & 01203 694995 (between A3 & A246, on B2039) Signposted
Family Park ★ £9.10-£12.10 £9.10-£12.10
£9.10-£12.10
Open end Mar-early Nov Booking advisable bank hols &

contd.

Jul-Aug Last arrival 21.00hrs Last departure noon
Beautiful lakeside site with plenty of trees and shrubs, and separate camping fields. Well-organised, friendly wardens. Situated between A3 and A246, on the B2039. Please see the advertisement on page 27 for details of Club Members' benefits. A 12-acre site with 135 touring pitches.
Table tennis, fishing, boating, dartboard.

Credit Cards

LINGFIELD

Long Acres Caravan & Camping Park (TQ368425)
Newchapel Rd RH7 6LE ☎ 01342 833205 & 884307
Signposted
Nearby town: East Grinstead
►►► Family Park
Open all year Booking advisable bank hols & for electric hook ups Last arrival 22.30hrs Last departure 13.00hrs
A pleasant ex-farm site, well-screened and well-maintained, with modern heated toilet facilities. Under Gatwick flight path. From A22 turn E into Newchapel Rd, signed. A 7-acre site with 60 touring pitches.
Quad bikes, free fishing, bike tracks & Go-Karts.

SUSSEX, EAST

BATTLE

Senlac Park Caravan & Camping Site (TQ722153)
Main Rd, Catsfield TN33 9DU ☎ 01424 773969 & 752590
Signposted
Nearby town: Hastings
▶ Town & Country Pennant Park
Open Mar-Oct Booking advisable bank hols Last arrival 21.00hrs Last departure noon
A pretty woodland site with many secluded bays, well landscaped and attractively laid out. From Battle take A271, then turn left on to B2204 signed Bexhill. A 5-acre site with 32 touring pitches.

Credit Cards

CROWBOROUGH

Camping & Caravanning Club Site (TQ520315)
Goldsmith Recreation Ground TN6 2TN
☎ 01892 664827 (in season) & 01203 694995 (just off A26) Signposted
►►► Family Park ★ £8.70-£11.30 £8.70-£11.30
£8.70-£11.30

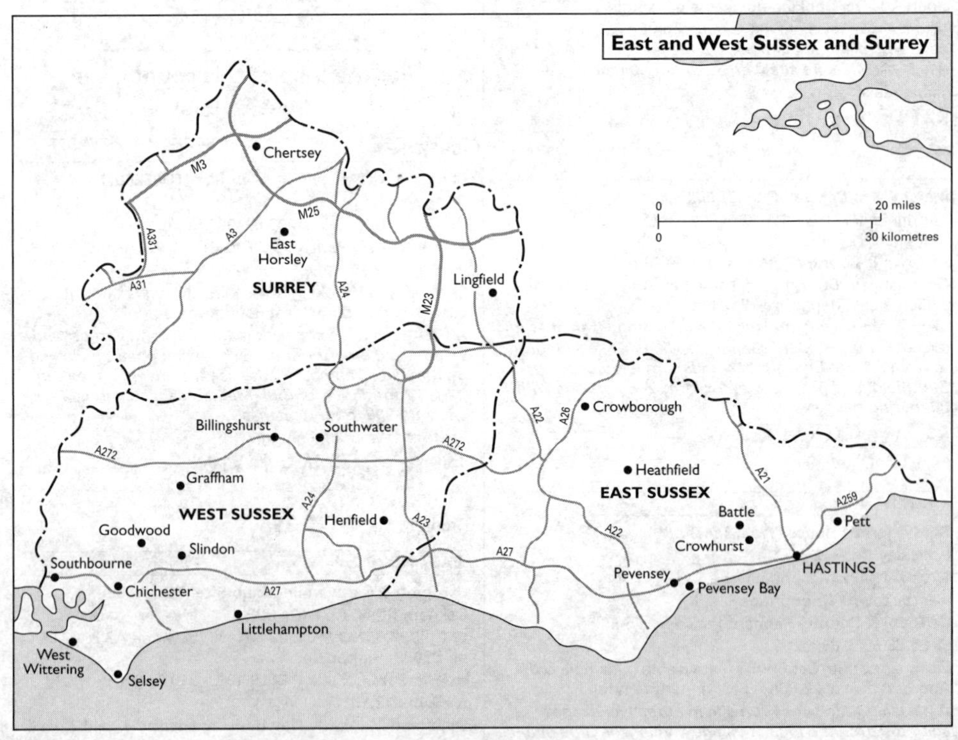

Open end Mar-Nov Booking advisable bank hols & peak periods Last arrival 21.00hrs Last departure noon
A spacious terraced site with stunning views of the surrounding countryside. Situated next to an excellent leisure centre, just off A26 (well signed) and 200yds from town centre. Please see the advertisement on page 27 for details of Club Members' benefits. A 13-acre site with 60 touring pitches.

Credit Cards

CROWHURST

Brakes Coppice Park (TQ765134)
Forewood Ln TN33 9AB ☎ 01424 830322 (off A2100) Signposted
Nearby town: Battle
►►► **Family Park** ★ £6-£7 £6-£7 ▲ £6-£7
Open Mar-Oct Booking advisable public hols & Jul-Aug Last arrival dusk Last departure noon
Secluded farm site in meadow surrounded by woodland with small stream and fishing lake. Off A2100. A 3-acre site with 30 touring pitches and 1 static.
Fishing.

HASTINGS & ST LEONARDS

Shearbarn Holiday Park (TQ842112)
TN35 5DX ☎ 01424 423583 & 716474 Signposted
►►► **Family Park** ▲
Open Mar-15 Jan (rs Mar-Etr, early May & mid Sep-15 Jan facilities may be closed or reduced) Booking advisable bank hols & Jun-Aug Last arrival 22.00hrs Last departure 10.00hrs
A large touring site with sea views. All entertainments are available at the static site nearby. A 16-acre site with 450 touring pitches and 250 statics.
Entertainment & amusements on site.

Credit Cards

HEATHFIELD

Greenview Caravan Park (TQ605223)
Broad Oak TN21 8RT ☎ 01435 863531 Signposted
►**Town & Country Pennant Park** ▲
Open Apr-Oct Booking advisable Jul-Aug Last arrival 22.00hrs Last departure 10.30hrs
Small, attractive site adjoining main A265 Broad Oak 1m E of Heathfield. A 3-acre site with 10 touring pitches and 51 statics.

PETT

Carters Farm (TQ887145)
Elm Ln TN35 4JD ☎ 01424 813206 & 812244 Signposted
Nearby town: Hastings
►**Town & Country Pennant Park** ★ £6-£8 £6-£8 ▲ £6-£7
Open Mar-Oct Last arrival 21.00hrs Last departure noon
A very secluded, long-established working farm site in partly sloping meadow. The sea is only 15 mins walk away. From A259 from Hastings turn right after Guestling, signed Pett. A 12-acre site with 100 touring pitches and 85 statics.

PEVENSEY

Camping & Caravanning Club Site (TQ682055)
Normans Bay BN24 6PP
☎ 01323 761190 (in season) & 01203 694995
Signposted
Nearby town: Eastbourne
►►► **Family Park** ▲
Open end Mar-early Nov Booking advisable bank hols & peak periods Last arrival 21.00hrs Last departure noon
A well-kept site with immaculate toilet block, right beside the sea. Pass through Elbourne, follow signs to Pevensey Bay, and take road signed Beachlands Only for 1m. Please see the advertisement on page 27 for details of Club Members' benefits. A 12-acre site with 200 touring pitches.

Credit Cards

PEVENSEY BAY

Bayview Caravan and Camping Park (TQ648028)
Old Martello Rd BN24 6DX
☎ 01323 768688
Signposted
Nearby town: Eastbourne
►►► **Family Park** £7.70-£8.35 £7.70-£8.35 ▲ £7.20-£7.70
Open Mar-Oct Booking advisable bank & school hols Last arrival 22.00hrs Last departure noon
A level and flat site two minutes' walk from the sea-shore located E of the town centre of the A259 in an area known as "The Crumbles". A 3.5-acre site with 49 touring pitches and 5 statics.

SUSSEX, WEST

For the map of this county, see Sussex, East

BILLINGSHURST

Limeburner's Camping (TQ073255)
Newbridge RH14 9JA ☎ 01403 782311 Signposted
Nearby town: Horsham
►**Town & Country Pennant Park** ★ £6.50 £6.50 ▲ £6.50
Open Apr-Oct Booking advisable bank hols & Jul-Aug Last arrival 22.00hrs Last departure 14.00hrs

contd.

Secluded rural site alongside the attractive 'Limeburner's Arms' public house. Located a short distance from the village of Billingshurst on the A272 Midhurst road and the River Arun. A 3-acre site with 42 touring pitches.

CHICHESTER

Southern Leisure Lakeside Village (SU875032)

Vinnetrow Rd PO20 6LB ☎ 01243 787715 Signposted

►►► **Family Park**

Open Etr-early Oct (rs Etr-24 May & Sep-early Oct swim pool closed, bar wknds only(ex BH)) Booking advisable bank hols & Jul-Aug Last arrival 18.00hrs Last departure 16.00hrs

A large touring site in secluded rural setting surrounded by several lakes. Level, grassy and well laid out with modern toilets and good leisure facilities. Signed from A27. A 50-acre site with 400 touring pitches.

Credit Cards

GOODWOOD

Caravan Club Site (SU885111)

Goodwood Racecourse PO18 0PX ☎ 01243 774486 Signposted

Nearby town: Chichester

Town & Country Pennant Park

Open Apr-Sep (rs during race meetings site is closed) Booking advisable public hols & Jul-Aug Last arrival 20.00hrs Last departure noon

A neat and tidy level grassy site on Goodwood Racecourse. Closed when race meetings are held. 5m N of Chichester. A 3-acre site with 70 touring pitches.

Credit Cards

GRAFFHAM

Camping & Caravanning Club Site (SU941187)

Great Bury GU28 0QJ ☎ 01798 867476 (in season) & 01203 694995 (5m S Petworth on unclass rd off A285) Signposted

Nearby town: Petworth

►►► **Family Park** ★ £8.70-£11.30 £8.70-£11.30 £8.70-£11.30

Open end Mar-early Nov Booking advisable bank hols & peak periods Last arrival 21.00hrs Last departure noon

A superb wooded site, with each pitch occupying its own private, well-screened area. From A285 towards Petworth turn first left after Duncton. Please see the advertisement on page 27 for details of Club Members' benefits. A 20-acre site with 90 touring pitches.

Credit Cards

HENFIELD

Harwoods Farm (TQ196153)
West End Ln BN5 9RF ☎ 01273 492820
Signposted
Nearby town: Brighton
**Town & Country Pennant Park** £4.50 £4.50
Open Etr-Oct Booking advisable bank hols Last arrival mdnt Last departure eves
A really unspoilt site down a rough, narrow lane in good walking area. A 1.75-acre site with 35 touring pitches.

LITTLEHAMPTON

White Rose Touring Park (TQ026041)
Mill Ln, Wick BN17 7PH
☎ 01903 716176 Signposted
►►► **Family Park**
Open 15 Mar-15 Jan Booking advisable bank hols & Jul-Aug Last departure noon
A well-maintained family run site providing level, well-drained ground surrounded by farmland. Located close to Arundel and Littlehampton which provide good local facilities. From A284 turn left into Mill Lane. Winner of the Best Campsite for South-East England 1996/7. A 7-acre site with 127 touring pitches and 14 statics.

Credit Cards

SELSEY

Warner Farm Touring Park (SZ845939)
Warner Ln, Selsey PO20 9EL
☎ 01243 604121 & 604499 (turn right onto School Lane & follow signs)
Signposted
Nearby town: Chichester

£6.50-£21 £6.50-£21 £6.50-£21
Open Mar-Oct Booking advisable 3 wks prior to arrival Last arrival 20.00hrs Last departure 10.00hrs
A new touring site adjoining three static sites under same ownership. A courtesy bus runs around the complex to entertainment and supermarkets. A 10-acre site with 200 touring pitches and 150 statics.

Credit Cards

SLINDON

Camping & Caravanning Club Site (SU958084)
Slindon Park BN18 0RG ☎ 01243 814387 (in season) & 01203 694995 Signposted
Nearby town: Chichester
Town & Country Pennant Park ★ £6.70-£8.30 £6.70-£8.30 £6.70-£8.30

contd.

Open end Mar-end Sep Booking advisable bank hols & peak periods Last arrival 21.00hrs Last departure noon
Beautiful former orchard, completely screened by NT trees and very quiet. Turn off A27 at Aldingbourne Nurseries, take second right into Britten's Lane signed Eartham, then take 2nd right for Slindon; and entrance is on right. Please see the advertisement on page 27 for details of Club Members' benefits. Own sanitary facilities essential. A 2-acre site with 46 touring pitches.

Credit Cards

SOUTHBOURNE

Camping & Caravanning Club Site (SU774056)
343 Main Rd PO10 8JH ☎ 01243 373202
Nearby town: Chichester
►►► **Family Park**
Open Feb-Nov Booking advisable bank hols, wknds & mid Jun-mid Sep Last arrival 22.00hrs Last departure 14.00hrs
Situated in open meadow and orchard, a very pleasant site with well looked after, clean facilities. Leave A27 at roundabout signed Bosham and Funtington, site 5m along A259. Please see the advertisement on page 27 for details of Club Members' benefits. A 2-acre site with 60 touring pitches.

→

Credit Cards

SOUTHWATER

Raylands Park (TQ170265)
Jackrells Ln RH13 7DH ☎ 01403 730218 & 731822 Signposted
Nearby town: Horsham
►►► **Family Park** ★ £8.50-£10 £8.50-£10 £6-£10
Open Mar-Oct Booking advisable bank hols & high season Last arrival 20.00hrs Last departure 14.00hrs
A very well run site in an excellent setting. Reasonably level ground, superb modern toilet blocks, a clubhouse and children's play area. Well maintained access roads. Signposted from the A24 in Southwater. A 6-acre site with 40 touring pitches and 60 statics.

→

WEST WITTERING

Wicks Farm Holiday Park (SZ796995)
Redlands Ln PO20 8QD ☎ 01243 513116 Signposted
Nearby town: Chichester
►►► **Family Park** ★ £8-£9.50 £8-£9.50
Open 14 Mar-Oct Booking advisable peak periods Last arrival 21.00hrs Last departure noon
A pleasant rural site, well-screened by trees with good walks nearby and 2m from coast. Signed from B2179. A 14-acre site with 40 touring pitches and 73 statics.
Bicycle hire.

→

Credit Cards

TYNE & WEAR

For the map of this county, see Northumberland

ROWLANDS GILL

Derwent Park Caravan Site (NZ168586)
NE39 1LG ☎ 01207 543383 Signposted
Nearby town: Newcastle
►►► **Family Park** £8.50-£9.50 £8.50-£9.50 £5.50-£9.50
Open Apr-Sep Booking advisable public hols & Jul-Aug Last arrival 22.30hrs Last departure noon
A very pleasant and well-maintained municipal site. Situated on edge of Rowlands Gill at junc of A694 and B6314. A 3-acre site with 47 touring pitches and 25 statics.
Fishing, crazy golf, giant draughts & chess, bowling.

→

Credit Cards

SOUTH SHIELDS

Lizard Lane Caravan & Camping Site (NZ399648)
Lizard Ln NE34 7AB ☎ 0191 454 4982 & 0191 455 7411 Signposted
►**Town & Country Pennant Park** ★ £6.50-£7.40 £6.50-£7.40 £6.50-£7.40
Open Mar-Oct Booking advisable for complete wks Jul-5 Sep Last arrival anytime Last departure 11.00hrs
Sloping, grass site near beach, 2m S of town centre on A183 Sunderland road. Well-kept and maintained. A 2-acre site with 45 touring pitches and 70 statics.

→

Credit Cards

Sandhaven Caravan & Camping Park (NZ376672)
Bents Park Rd NE33 2NL
☎ 0191 454 5594 & 0191 455 7411
Signposted
►**Town & Country Pennant Park** ★ £8.50-£9.60 £8.50-£9.60 £8.50-£9.60
Open Mar-Oct Booking advisable for complete wks Jul-5 Sep Last arrival anytime Last departure 11.00hrs
A spacious site adjoining the sea front, set in a well-screened and fenced area next to a public park. Situated on A183 .5 miles from the town centre with an entrance on Bents Park Road. A 3.5-acre site with 52 touring pitches and 46 statics.

→

Credit Cards

WARWICKSHIRE

For the map of this county, see Herefordshire

ASTON CANTLOW

Island Meadow Caravan Park (SP137596)
The Mill House B95 6JP
☎ 01789 488273 (.25 W)
Signposted
Nearby town: Stratford-upon-Avon

► ► ► ► **De-Luxe Park** ★ fr £8.50 fr £8.50
fr £6.50
Open Mar-Oct Booking advisable peak periods Last arrival 21.00hrs Last departure noon
A small well-kept site bordered by the River Alne and its mill stream. Mature willows line the banks. .25m W of Aston Cantlow on the road to Alcester. A 3-acre site with 24 touring pitches and 56 statics.
Free fishing for guests.

KINGSBURY

Camping & Caravanning Club Site (SP202968)
Kingsbury Water Park B76 0DY
☎ 01827 874101 (in season) & 01203 694995
(off unclass rd joining A4097 & A4091)
Nearby town: Sutton Coldfield
► ► ► **Family Park** ★ £6.60-£9.50 £6.60-£9.50
£6.60-£9.50
Open end Mar-early Nov Booking advisable bank hols & Jul-Aug Last arrival 21.00hrs Last departure noon
A former gravel pit, now reclaimed and landscaped, the site is part of a level complex of lakes, canals, woods and marshland with good access roads. 2m SW on A5 take A4097 for 1m. Please see the advertisement on page 27 for details of Club Members' benefits. An 18-acre site with 120 touring pitches.

Credit Cards

Tame View Caravan Site (SP209979)
Cliff B78 2DR ☎ 01827 873853 (1m N A51)
Signposted
Nearby town: Tamworth
► **Town & Country Pennant Park** £2-£2.25 £2-£2.25
£2-£2.25
Open all year Booking advisable 1 month in advance Last arrival 23.00hrs Last departure 23.00hrs
Enclosed level small meadow on high bank overlooking River Tame, with no sanitary facilities. 400 yards off A51 Tamworth to Kingsbury road, 1m N of Kingsbury opposite restaurant. No through road sign. A 5-acre site with 55 touring pitches.
Fishing.

WOLVEY

Wolvey Villa Farm Caravan & Camping Site (SP428869)
LE10 3HF ☎ 01455 220493 & 220630
Signposted
Nearby town: Hinckley
► ► ► **Family Park** £5.30-£5.50 £5.30-£5.50
£5.20-£5.40
Open all year Booking advisable Spring bank hol-mid Aug Last arrival 23.15hrs Last departure noon
Level, grass site with mature trees and bushes set in meadowland. About 1m S of Wolvey. Ideally located to explore the Midlands area. From M6 junc 2, take B4056 (signed Ansty) to Wolvey for 3m. A 7-acre site with 110 touring pitches.
Fishing, putting green, off licence.

WIGHT, ISLE OF

For the map , see Hampshire

BEMBRIDGE

See **Whitecliff Bay**

FRESHWATER

Heathfield Farm Camping (SZ335879)
Heathfield Rd PO40 9SH ☎ 01983 752480
► ► ► **Family Park**
Open all year
Pleasant, well maintained small park on the edge of Freshwater, with views across the Solent. A 4-acre site with 50 touring pitches.

NEWBRIDGE

Orchards Holiday Caravan Park (SZ411881)
PO41 0TS ☎ 01983 531331 Signposted
Nearby town: Yarmouth

► ► ► ► ► **Premier Park** ★ £6.85-£9.95
£6.85-£9.95 £6.85-£9.95
Open 20 Mar-Oct (rs Etr-Apr & late Sep-Oct outdoor pool late-May-early Sep) Booking advisable Etr, Spring bank hol & late Jun-Aug Last arrival 23.00hrs Last departure 11.00hrs
An excellent, well-managed site set in downs and meadowland adjacent to B3401 and near the sea. Signed left at Horse and Groom pub on A3054. An 8-acre site with 175 touring pitches and 60 statics.

contd.

Coarse fishing, petanque.
See advertisement under Colour Section

Credit Cards

NEWCHURCH

Southland Camping Park (SZ557847)
PO36 0LZ ☎ 01983 865385 Signposted
Nearby town: Sandown

▶▶▶▶ **De-Luxe Park** £6.60-£8.80 £6.60-£8.80
▲ £6.60-£8.80
Open Etr-Sep Booking advisable Jul-Aug Last arrival 22.00hrs Last departure 11.00hrs
Beautifully maintained site, peacefully located on the outskirts of the village in the Arreton Valley off A3056. A 7-acre site with 100 touring pitches.
12 volt transformers available.
See advertisement under SANDOWN

Credit Cards

PONDWELL

Pondwell Camp Site (SZ622911)
PO34 5AQ ☎ 01983 612330 Signposted
▶▶▶ **Family Park** ▲
Open May-26 Sep Booking advisable Aug Last arrival 23.00hrs Last departure 11.00hrs
A secluded site in quiet rural surroundings close to the sea, slightly sloping with some level areas, and modern toilet facilities. Signed from Ryde on B3330. A 9-acre site with 250 touring pitches.

Credit Cards

SANDOWN

Adgestone Camping Park (SZ590855)
Lower Adgestone Rd PO36 OHL
☎ 01983 403432 & 403989 (2m NW)
Signposted

▶▶▶▶▶ **Premier Park** ★ £7-£9.90 £7-£9.90
▲ £7-£9.90
Open Etr-Sep (rs Off peak limited opening of takeaway) Booking advisable high season Last arrival dusk Last departure 11.00hrs
A well-managed site in a quiet location not far from the town. The slightly sloping pitches are surrounded by flower beds and trees. 2m NW of Sandown. Winner of the Best Campsite of the Year Award for South-East England. A 15.5-acre site with 200 touring pitches.
River fishing, football pitch, petanque, volleyball.
See advertisement under Colour Section

Credit Cards

Cheverton Farm Camping Park (SZ570834)
Newport Rd, Apse Heath PO36 9PJ
☎ 01983 866414 (take A3056 from Newport)
Signposted
Nearby town: Shanklin

▶▶▶▶ **De-Luxe Park** ★ £5-£6.50 £5-£6.50
▲ £5-£6.50
Open Mar-Oct Booking advisable school hols Last arrival 21.00hrs Last departure noon
A terraced site with good quality facilities, bordering on open farmland. Off A3056 Newport Rd. A 5-acre site with 60 touring pitches.

Credit Cards

SHANKLIN

Landguard Camping Park (SZ577825)
Landguard Manor Rd PO37 7PH ☎ 01983 867028
Signposted

►►►► **De-Luxe Park** ★ £6-£10 £6-£10 £6-£10

Open May-Sep Booking advisable school hols Last arrival 22.00hrs Last departure noon

Part of a holiday complex, the touring area is secluded and surrounded by trees, in a rural setting. A 6-acre site with 150 touring pitches.

Horse riding.

Credit Cards

WHITECLIFF BAY

Whitecliff Bay Holiday Park (SZ637862)
Hillway PO35 5PL ☎ 01983 872671
Signposted

►►►► **De-Luxe Park** ★ £5.80-£8 £5.80-£8 £5.80-£8

Open May-Oct (rs Mar-Apr limited entertainments) Booking advisable Jul-Aug

A large seaside complex on two sites, with tourers and tents on one and tourers and statics on the other. Toilets of a very high standard. Many entertainments and easy access to beach. A 19-acre site with 450 touring pitches and 227 statics.

Leisure centre with fun pool, spa bath & sauna.

See advertisement under BEMBRIDGE

Credit Cards

WROXALL

Appuldurcombe Gardens Caravan & Camping Park (SZ546804)
Appuldurcombe Rd PO38 3EP ☎ 01983 852597
Signposted

►►► **Family Park**

Open Spring bank hol-Aug bank hol (rs Mar-Spring bank hol & Aug bank hol-Oct pool & bar closed, shop restricted hrs) Booking advisable Jul-Aug Last arrival 23.00hrs Last departure noon

An attractive secluded site with a small stream running through it. Situated a few miles from Ventnor. A 12-acre site with 110 touring pitches and 42 statics.

Crazy golf & putting.

See advertisement on page 196.

YARMOUTH

See **Newbridge**

WILTSHIRE

CALNE

Blackland Lakes Holiday & Leisure Centre (ST973687)
Stockley Ln SN11 0NQ ☎ 01249 813672 Signposted

►►►► **De-Luxe Park**
Open all year (rs Nov-mid Mar bookings only) Booking advisable all year Last arrival 23.00hrs Last departure noon
A level, well-kept site in a rural area surrounded by Colstowe, and N and W Downs. Good outdoor facilities on site. From Calne take A4(T) E for 1.5m, turn right at camp sign, and site on left in 1m. A 17-acre site with 180 touring pitches.
Nature trail, wildfowl sanctuary, fishing facilities

DEVIZES

Bell Caravan Park (SU054580)
Andover Rd, Lydeway SN10 3PS ☎ 01380 840230

►►► **Family Park** £6.75-£8.25 £6.75-£8.25 £6.75-£8.25
Open Etr or Apr-Sep Booking advisable bank hols & Jul-Aug
An attractive base for touring the area, with all level pitches. 3m S of Devizes on A342. A 3-acre site with 30 touring pitches.

Credit Cards

Lakeside (ST092626)
Rowde SN10 2LX ☎ 01380 722767 Signposted
►►► **Family Park**
Open Apr-Oct Booking advisable bank hols & Jun-Aug Last arrival 22.00hrs Last departure noon
Pleasant level site on lakeside with attractive trees and shrubs set in countryside. From Devizes take A342 Calne rd N, take right fork at A342/A361, and site on right in 1m. A 4-acre site with 55 touring pitches.
Fishing.

LACOCK

Piccadilly Caravan Site (ST913683)
Folly Ln West SN15 2LP ☎ 01249 730260
Signposted
Nearby town: Chippenham
►►► **Family Park** £7-£8.50 £7-£8.50 £7-£8.50

contd.

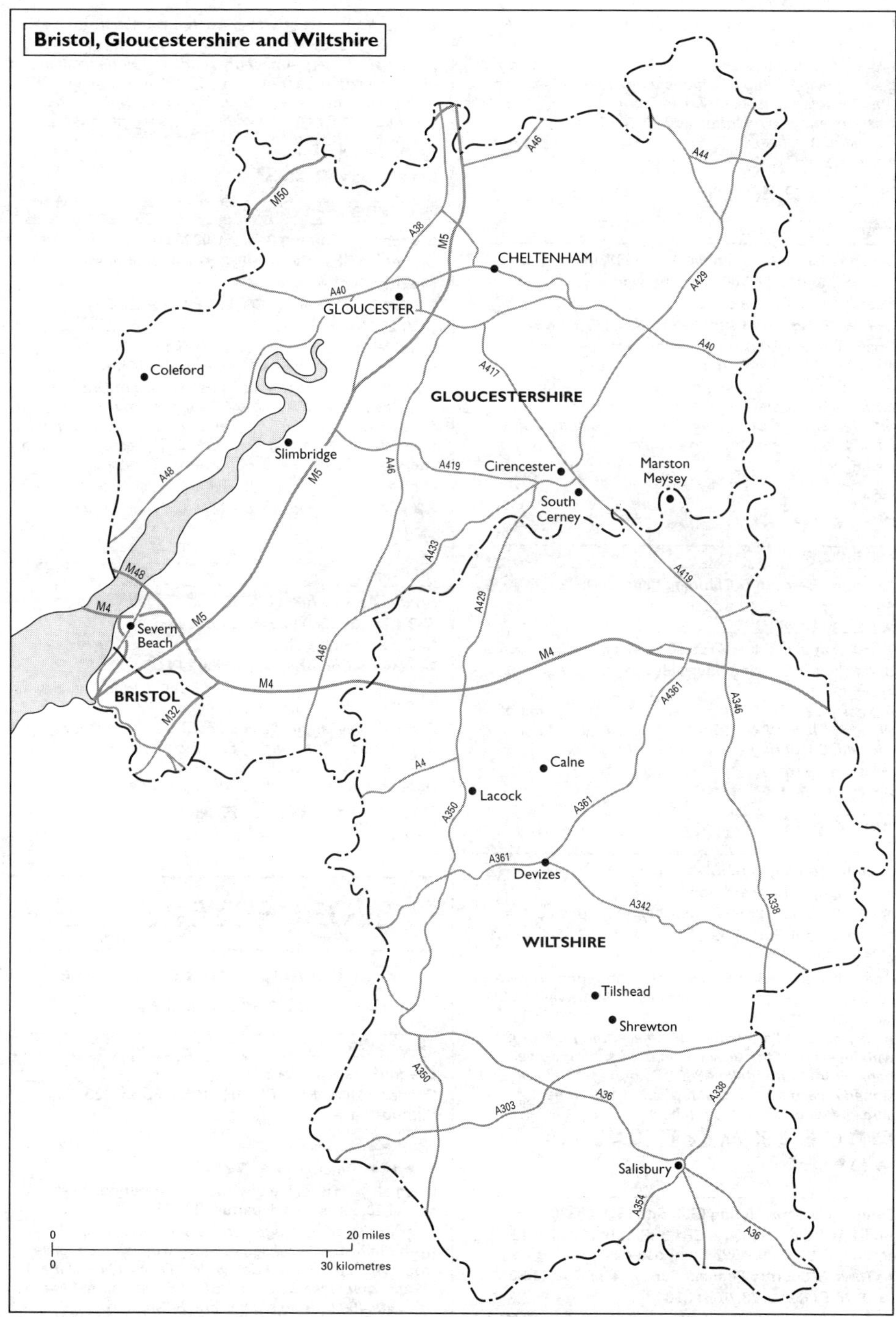
Bristol, Gloucestershire and Wiltshire
CHELTENHAM
GLOUCESTER
Coleford
GLOUCESTERSHIRE
Slimbridge
Cirencester
Marston
Meysey
South
Cerney
Severn
Beach
BRISTOL
Calne
Lacock
Devizes
WILTSHIRE
Tilshead
Shrewton
Salisbury
M50
A38
M5
A46
A44
A429
A40
A417
A48
A419
M48
M4
A433
A346
A4361
M32
A4
A350
A361
A342
A338
A36
A303
A354
0
20 miles
0
30 kilometres

Open Apr-Oct Booking advisable school & bank hols Last departure noon

A good family site, well-established and overlooking Lacock village. 4m S of Chippenham. From Melksham on A350 towards Lacock for 3m, turn left at sign marked Gastard, and site on left in 200yds. A 2.5-acre site with 41 touring pitches.

MARSTON MEYSEY

Second Chance Caravan Park (SU140960)

SN6 6SZ ☎ 01285 810675 Signposted

Nearby town: Cricklade

►Town & Country Pennant Park £6 £6 £6

Open Mar-Nov Booking advisable peak periods Last arrival 21.30hrs Last departure 13.30hrs

A quiet and beautiful site with good toilet facilities, attractively situated near the source of the Thames. Situated 3m E of Cricklade off A419. A 1.75-acre site with 22 touring pitches and 4 statics.

Fishing on site, canoeing.

SALISBURY

Alderbury Caravan & Camping Park (SU197259)

Southampton Rd, Whaddon SP5 3HB

☎ 01722 710125

► ► ► **Family Park** ★ £6.50-£8 £6.50-£8 fr £6.50

Open all year Booking advisable anytime Last arrival 23.00hrs

A pleasant and friendly new site, set in the village of Whaddon just off A36, 3m from Salisbury. A 1.5-acre site with 39 touring pitches and 1 static.

Washing-up room.

Coombe Touring Park (SU099282)

Race Plain, Netherhampton SP2 8PN

☎ 01722 328451 (2m SW off A3094) Signposted

► ► ► **Family Park** ★ £5-£7.50 £5-£7.50 £5-£7.50

Open all year (rs Sep-Etr gas only, shop) Booking advisable bank hols (by letter only) Last arrival 21.00hrs Last departure noon

A very neat and attractive site adjacent to racecourse with views over the downs and outstanding flower beds. From Wilton take A3094 S, then first right on bend signed racecourse. Site at top of hill and signed. A 3-acre site with 50 touring pitches.

Camping & Caravanning Club Site (SU140320)

Hudsons Field, Castle Rd SP1 3RR ☎ 01722 320713 (in season) & 01203 694995 Signposted

►Town & Country Pennant Park ★ £8.70-£11.30 £8.70-£11.30 £8.70-£11.30

Open end Mar-end Sep Booking advisable bank hols & peak periods Last arrival 21.00hrs Last departure noon

A well-kept site with friendly and helpful wardens. Take A345 Salisbury to Amesbury road, and Hudson's Field is close to Old Sarum Fort, 1m on L. Please see the advertisement on page 27 for details of Club Members' benefits. A 4.5-acre site with 100 touring pitches.

Credit Cards

SHREWTON

Stonehenge Touring Park (SU061456)

Orcheston SP3 4SH ☎ 01980 620304 Signposted

Nearby town: Amesbury

► ► ► **Family Park** ★ £6.25-£9 £6.25-£9 £6.25-£9

Open all year Booking advisable bank hols & Jul-Aug Last arrival 21.00hrs Last departure 11.00hrs

A quiet site adjacent to the small village of Orcheston near the centre of Salisbury Plain and 4m from Stonehenge. Site maturing and popular. From Shrewton take A360 N, then first right fork to Orcheston and follow site signs. A 2-acre site with 30 touring pitches and 6 statics.

TILSHEAD

Brades Acre (SU035477)

SP3 4RX ☎ 01980 620402 Signposted

Nearby town: Salisbury

►Town & Country Pennant Park

Open all year Booking advisable public hols Last arrival 21.00hrs Last departure 11.00hrs

A small, pleasantly situated country site set among trees and shrubs in the heart of Salisbury Plain. From Tilshead turn S on A360 to end of village, and site on right. A 2-acre site with 25 touring pitches.

WORCESTERSHIRE

For the map of this county, see Herefordshire

BROADWAY

Leedon's Park (SP080384)

Childswickham Rd WR12 7HB ☎ 01386 852423 Signposted

► ► ► ► **De-Luxe Park**

Open all year Booking advisable peak periods Last arrival 20.00hrs Last departure 11.00hrs

A large site on the edge of the Vale of Evesham, 1m from the historical village of Broadway; an ideal base from which to tour the Cotswolds. From A44 Evesham-Oxford road, take B4632 6m SE of Evesham. A 16-acre site with 450 touring pitches and 86 statics.

See advertisement under GLOUCESTER, page 140

Credit Cards

EVESHAM

Weir Meadow Holiday & Touring Park (SP047443)
Lower Leys WR11 5AB ☎ 01386 442417 Signposted
►►► **Family Park** ★ £6.85-£8.75 £6.85-£8.75
Open Etr or Apr-Oct Booking advisable bank hols Last arrival dusk Last departure noon
Although in the centre of town the site has a peaceful riverside setting. Turn off Port Street by Workmen's Bridge in Evesham, A44. A 10-acre site with 100 touring pitches and 120 statics.
Slipway, boating, fishing and sailing.

HANLEY SWAN

Camping & Caravanning Club Site (SO812436)
WR8 0EE ☎ 01684 310280 & 01203 694995 Signposted
Nearby town: Great Malvern
►►► **Family Park** ★ £5.60-£8.60 £5.60-£8.60
▲ £5.60-£8.60
Open mid Mar-mid Nov Booking advisable Jan-Mar Last arrival 21.00hrs Last departure noon
Well-established wooded park, ideally located for exploring the Malvern Hills and Worcester. From A38 take B4424 travelling S or B4211 N towards Hanley Swan, and site signed. A 12-acre site with 200 touring pitches.

Credit Cards

HONEYBOURNE

Ranch Caravan Park (SP113444)
WR11 5QG ☎ 01386 830744 (go through village crossroads towards Bideford, entrance 400m on left side) Signposted
Nearby town: Evesham

►►►► **De-Luxe Park** ★ £6-£11 £6-£11
Open Mar-Nov (rs Mar-May & Sep-Nov swimming pool closed, shorter club hours) Booking advisable school hols Last arrival 20.00hrs Last departure noon
A clean, well-run site with trees and bushes, set in farmland in the Vale of Evesham 2m from B4035. A 12-acre site with 100 touring pitches and 180 statics.
See advertisement under EVESHAM

Credit Cards

MALVERN

Riverside Caravan Park (SO833463)
Little Clevelode WR13 6PE ☎ 01684 310475 (on B4424)
Signposted
►►► Family Park ★ fr £6 fr £6 fr £6
Open Mar-Dec (rs Nov, Dec & Mar water supply depends on weather) Booking advisable bank hols & end Jun-Aug Last arrival 21.00hrs Last departure noon
An open field site with some sloping pitches and a large play area. From A449 signed on to B4424. A 10-acre site with 70 touring pitches and 130 statics.
Slipway for boats, fishing on river.

ROMSLEY

Camping & Caravanning Club Site (SO955795)
Fieldhouse Ln B62 0NH ☎ 01562 710015 (in season) & 01203 694995
Nearby town: Halesowen
►►► Family Park
Open end Mar-early Nov Booking advisable bank hols & peak periods Last arrival 21.00hrs Last departure noon
A very pretty, well tended park surrounded by wooded hills. Turn off B4551 at Sun Inn, then take 5th turn left, and the park is 300 yds on. Please see the advertisement on page 27 for details of Club Members' benefits. A 6.5-acre site with 130 touring pitches.

Credit Cards

WOLVERLEY

Camping & Caravanning Club Site (SO833792)
Brown Westhead Park DY10 3PX
☎ 01562 850909 & 01203 694995
Signposted
Nearby town: Kidderminster
►►► Family Park ★ £8.70-£11.30 £8.70-£11.30 £8.70-£11.30
Open end Mar-early Nov Booking advisable bank hols & Jul-Aug Last arrival 21.00hrs Last departure noon
Very pleasant grassy site on edge of the village, with good access to nearby motorways. At junction of A449 and B4189 take road signed Wolverley, and site .25m on right. Please see the advertisement on page 27 for details of Club Members' benefits. A 12-acre site with 120 touring pitches.
Table tennis, darts.

Credit Cards

AA members can call AA Hotel Booking Service on 0990 050505 to book at AA recognised hotels and B & Bs in the UK and Ireland, or through our Internet site: http://www.theaa.co.uk/hotels

YORKSHIRE, EAST RIDING OF

For the map of this county, see Lincolnshire

BRANDESBURTON

Dacre Lakeside Park (TA118468)
YO25 8SA ☎ 01964 543704 & 542372
Signposted
Nearby town: Hornsea
►►► Family Park ★ £6.50-£7 £6.50-£7 £6.50-£7
Open Mar-Oct Booking advisable bank hols Last arrival 21.00hrs Last departure noon
A pleasant, level grassy site beside a lake with good adjacent sports facilities. Off the A165 bypass, midway between Beverley and Hornsea. A 4-acre site with 90 touring pitches.
Windsurfing, fishing, tennis, squash & bowling green.

BRIDLINGTON

FANGFOSS

Fangfoss Old Station Caravan Park (SE747527)
Old Station House YO4 5QB ☎ 01759 380491
Signposted
Nearby town: York
►►► **Family Park** £7-£7.50 £7-£7.50 £5.50-£7.50
Open Mar-Oct Booking advisable bank hols Last arrival 22.30hrs Last departure noon
A well-maintained site in a pleasant rural area. The track and sidings of the old railway station are grassed over and provide excellent hardstanding with a level landscaped field adjacent. Take A166 to Stamford Bridge where site clearly signed. A 4.5-acre site with 45 touring pitches.

Credit Cards

HULL

See **Sproatley**

RUDSTON

Thorpe Hall Caravan & Camping Site (TA108677)
Thorpe Hall YO25 0JE ☎ 01262 420393 & 420574 (on B1253) Signposted
Nearby town: Bridlington
►►► **Family Park** ★ £5.20-£9.30 £5.20-£9.30 £4.20-£8.40
Open Mar-Oct Booking advisable bank hols & peak periods Last arrival 22.00hrs Last departure noon
A very attractive and well-ordered site in the walled garden of a large estate on edge of village. 5m from Bridlington on B1253. A 4.5-acre site with 90 touring pitches.
Covered outside washing up sinks with hot water.

SKIPSEA

Far Grange Park (TA181530)
Windhook, Hornsea Rd YO25 8SY
☎ 01262 468248 & 468293
Signposted. Nearby town: Hornsea

★ £9-£13 £9-£13 £9-£13
Open Mar-Oct Booking advisable bank & school hols
Last arrival 21.00hrs Last departure 11.00hrs
A well-developed holiday site with pleasing public buildings and well-laid out grounds of shrubs, hedges and trees. Adjacent to a private sandy beach on a fairly quiet part of the coast. On B1242, 2m S of village on seaward side next to golf course. A 30-acre site with 170 touring pitches and 500 statics.
Fishing, snooker, gym, sauna, solarium.

Credit Cards

See advertisement on page 202.

Low Skirlington Caravan Park (TA188528)
YO25 8SY ☎ 01262 468213 & 468466 (on B1242) Signposted
Nearby town: Bridlington
►►► **Family Park** ★ £8.50-£9 £8.50-£9 ▲ £8.50-£9
Open Mar-Oct Booking advisable Jul-Aug
Part-level, part-sloping, grass site with young trees and bushes, set in meadowland adjacent to sea and beach 3m N of Hornsea on B1242. A 24-acre site with 285 touring pitches and 450 statics.
Sauna, sunbed, jacuzzi & bowls.
See advertisement under BRIDLINGTON

Credit Cards

SPROATLEY

Burton Constable Caravan Park (TA186357)
Old Lodges HU11 4LN ☎ 01964 562508 Signposted
Nearby town: Kingston-upon-Hull
►►► **Family Park** ▲
Open Mar-Oct Booking advisable bank hols Last arrival 23.00hrs Last departure dusk
A beautiful site close to boating and fishing lakes in the grounds of Burton Constable Hall. Off A165 to B1328 to Sproatley, signed. A 20-acre site with 109 touring pitches and 66 statics.

STAMFORD BRIDGE

Weir Caravan Park (SE713557)
YO4 1AN ☎ 01759 371377 (A166 Bridlington rd) Signposted
►►► **Family Park** ★ £7.75-£9.75 £7.75-£9.75 ▲ £7.75-£9.75
Open Mar-Oct Booking advisable bank hols & Jul-Aug Last arrival 21.30hrs Last departure noon
Slightly sloping grass site near urban area and River Derwent. 50yds off A166 on entering village from York. An 8-acre site with 50 touring pitches and 125 statics.
Fishing & boating on site. Sauna & Solarium.

YORKSHIRE, NORTH

See also Yorkshire, South, Yorkshire, West, Yorkshire, East Riding

ACASTER MALBIS

Chestnut Farm Caravan Park (SE589456)
YO2 1UQ ☎ 01904 704676 Signposted
Nearby town: York
►►► **Family Park** ★ fr £10 fr £10 ▲ fr £7.50
Open Apr-Oct Booking advisable public hols & Jul-Aug Last arrival 23.00hrs Last departure noon
Level, grassy site with assorted trees and shrubs, adjacent to river. Leave A64 at Copmanthorpe, turning S signed Acaster Malbis. Site on unclass rd in 2m. A 5-acre site with 25 touring pitches and 56 statics.

Moor End Farm (SE589457)
YO2 1UQ ☎ 01904 706727 Signposted
Nearby town: York
▷ **Town & Country Pennant Park** fr £8 fr £7 ▲ fr £8
Open Etr or Apr-Oct Booking advisable bank hols & end Jul-early Aug Last arrival 22.00hrs Last departure 14.00hrs
Level, grassy site with hedges, well-drained and maintained. Set in meadowland adjacent to road. Leave A64 at Copmanthorpe, turning S signed Acaster Malbis. Site on unclass rd in 2m. A 1-acre site with 10 touring pitches and 5 statics.
Dishwashing sink & fridge/freezer.

ALLERSTON

Vale of Pickering Caravan Park (SE879808)
Carr House Farm YO18 7PQ ☎ 01723 859280 Signposted
►►►► **De-Luxe Park** ★ £6-£9 £6-£9 ▲ £6-£9
Open Apr-Oct (rs Mar) Booking advisable anytime Last departure noon
A well-maintained modern site with good facilities set in

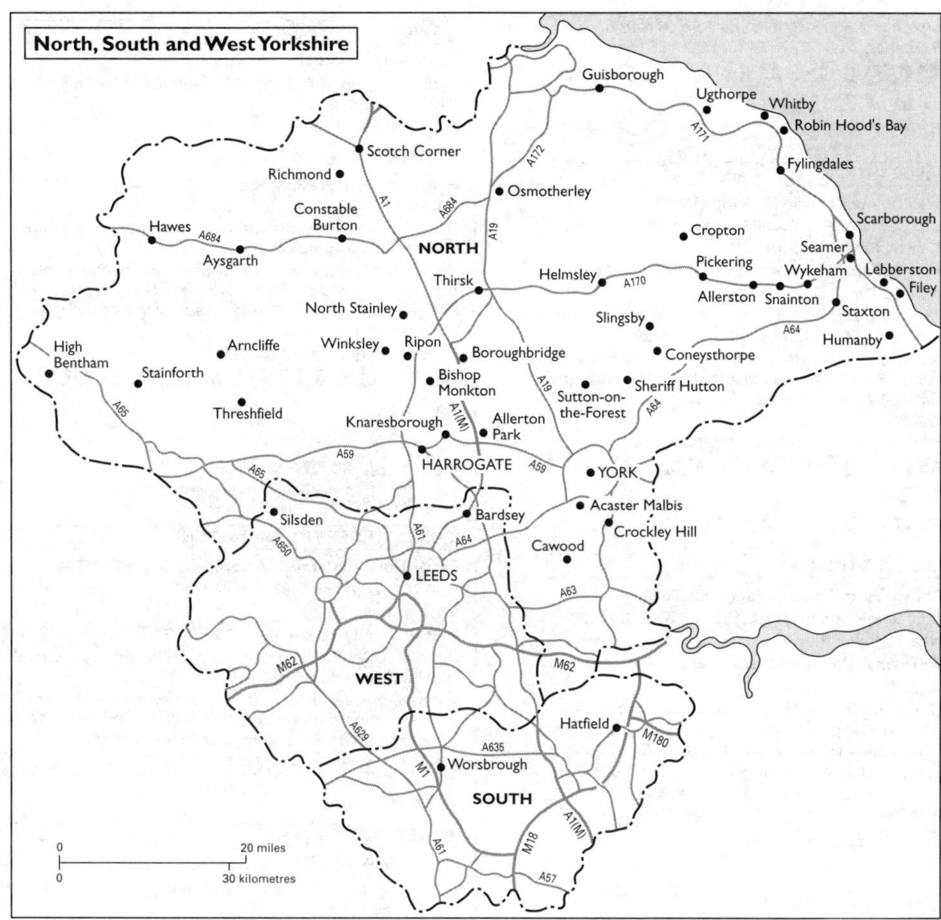

rolling countryside, and convenient for North Yorkshire Moors and wolds. On the B1415, 1.75m off the main Pickering to Scarborough road. An 8-acre site with 120 touring pitches and 1 static.

ALLERTON PARK

Allerton Park Caravan Site (SE417576)
Allerton Mauleverer HG5 0SE
☎ 01423 330569 (0.25m E of A1 off the A59)
Signposted
Nearby town: Knaresborough

► ► ► ► De-Luxe Park ★ £7.75-£9.75 £7.75-£9.75 ▲ £7.75-£9.75
Open Feb-3 Jan (rs Feb & Nov-Dec) Booking advisable bank hols Last arrival 21.00hrs Last departure 17.00hrs

An immaculately maintained site set in parkland surrounded by mature trees, and offering peace and quiet. Off A59, 400yards E of junc with A1(M). A 12-acre site with 45 touring pitches and 80 statics.

ARNCLIFFE

Hawkswick Cote Caravan Park (SD947703)
BD23 5PX ☎ 01756 770226
Nearby town: Skipton

► ► ► ► De-Luxe Park ▲
Open Mar-14 Nov Booking advisable bank hols & Jul-Aug Last arrival 22.00hrs Last departure noon
A spacious site in the Dales, with mature landscaping and views of the surrounding fells. From B6160 1m N of Kilnsey, take unclassified road signed Arncliffe, and site

contd.

on left in 1.5m. A 3-acre site with 50 touring pitches and 90 statics.

AYSGARTH

Westholme Caravan Park (SE016882)
DL8 3SP ☎ 01969 663268 Signposted
Nearby town: Leyburn
►►► **Family Park** ★ £6.50-£9 £6.50-£9 £6.50-£9
Open Mar-Oct Booking advisable bank hols & Jul-Aug Last arrival 23.00hrs Last departure noon
A beckside site with level grassy pitches in various paddocks set into the hillside. 1m E of Aysgarth on A684. A 4-acre site with 70 touring pitches and 44 statics.
Library, quiet room & fishing free on site.

BISHOP MONKTON

Church Farm Caravan Park (SE286658)
Knaresborough Rd HG3 3QQ ☎ 01765 677405
Nearby town: Ripon
► **Town & Country Pennant Park** ★ fr £4 fr £4 fr £4
Open Apr-Oct Booking advisable peak periods
Mainly level tree-lined field, adjacent to farm in picturesque village. From A61, 3.5m S of Ripon, take unclass rd signed Bishop Monkton. At crossrds in 1m turn right signed Knaresborough, and site on right in 500 metres. A 5-acre site with 30 touring pitches.

BOROUGHBRIDGE

Camping & Caravanning Club Site (SE384662)
Bar Ln, Roecliffe YO5 9LS
☎ 01423 322683 (in season) & 01203 694995
Signposted
►►► **Family Park** ★ £8.70-£11.30 £8.70-£11.30 £8.70-£11.30
Open all year Booking advisable bank hols & Jul & Aug Last arrival 21.00hrs Last departure noon
A quiet, riverside site with boating and riding available. Close to the dales and the market town of Boroughbridge. Follow sign for Roecliffe. Please see the advertisement on page 27 for details of Club Members' benefits. A 6-acre site with 82 touring pitches.
Credit Cards

The AA pennant classification has been revised for 1998. Please read the explanation of the scheme on page 10.

CAWOOD

Cawood Holiday Park (SE563385)
Ryther Rd YO8 0TT ☎ 01757 268450 (0.5m NW on B1233) Signposted
Nearby town: York
►►►► **De-Luxe Park** £8.50-£10.50 £8.50-£10.50 £8.50-£10.50
Open Mar-Jan Booking advisable bank hols & Jul-Aug Last arrival 23.00hrs Last departure noon
A continually improving site with a very high level of maintenance and excellent toilet facilities. 0.5 miles NW of Cawood on B1223. An 8-acre site with 60 touring pitches and 10 statics.
Coarse fishing, childrens boating.
Credit Cards

CONEYSTHORPE (NEAR MALTON)

Castle Howard Caravan & Camping Site (SE705710)
YO6 7DD ☎ 01653 648366 & 648316 Signposted
Nearby town: Malton
►►► **Family Park** ★ fr £7 fr £7 fr £3.50
Open Mar-Oct Booking advisable public hols Last arrival 19.00hrs Last departure 14.00hrs
Tranquil grassy site adjacent to lake on Castle Howard Estate. A superb touring centre. Well signed from A64. A 13-acre site with 70 touring pitches and 122 statics.

CONSTABLE BURTON

Constable Burton Hall Caravan Park (SE158907)
DL8 5LJ ☎ 01677 450428 Signposted
Nearby town: Leyburn
►►► **Family Park**
Open Apr-Oct Booking advisable public hols Last arrival 22.00hrs Last departure noon
A part-level, part-sloping site within parkland of Constable Burton Hall in farmland at entrance to Wensleydale. Located off A684 but screened behind old deer park wall. A 10-acre site with 120 touring pitches.

CROCKEY HILL

Swallow Hall Caravan Park (SE657463)
YO1 4SG ☎ 01904 448219 (E off A19)
Nearby town: York
► **Town & Country Pennant Park** ★ £7.50-£11 £7.50-£11 £7.50-£11
Open Mar-Oct Booking advisable Etr & Spring bank hol Last arrival 22.00hrs
A quiet site on meadowland at the edge of a forest within easy reach of the centre of York. From A19 at Crockey Hill turn E onto unclass rd, and site 2m on left.

A 5-acre site with 30 touring pitches.
Golf driving range & 18 hole course.

CROPTON

Spiers House Campsite (SE756918)
YO18 8ES ☎ 01751 417591 (1m N on Rosedale rd) Signposted
Nearby town: Pickering
►►► **Family Park** ★ £6-£7 £6-£7 ▲ £6-£7
Open Etr-2 Oct Booking advisable bank & school hols Last arrival 21.00hrs Last departure 16.00hrs
Beautiful forest site in a clearing with good facilities and peaceful surroundings. Walks are marked by Forestry Commission. Approach by signs from A170, and 1m N of Cropton on Rosedale Rd turn right into forest at signpost A 15-acre site with 150 touring pitches.

FILEY

Flower of May Holiday Park (TA085835)
Lebberston Cliff YO11 3NU
☎ 01723 584311 (Lebberston 2.5m NW off A165) Signposted
Nearby town: Scarborough
★ £6.50-£10.50 £6.50-£10.50 ▲ £6.50-£10.50
Open Etr-Oct (rs early & late season) Booking advisable Spring bank hol wk & Jul-Aug Last arrival 22.00hrs Last departure noon
A delightful family site with level grassy pitches, excellent facilities and direct access to the beach. Signed off A165 on Scarborough side of Filey. Winner of the 1995 Campsite of the Year Award for the North of England. A 13-acre site with 270 touring pitches and 179 statics.
Squash, gymnasium, bowling & 9-hole golf.

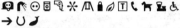

Crows Nest Caravan Park (TA086834)
Gristhorpe YO14 9PS ☎ 01723 582206
►►►► **De-Luxe Park** ★ £7-£13 £7-£13
Open Mar-Oct Booking advisable
A beautifully situated park on the coast between Scarborough and Filey, family owned and run to a high standard. On the seaward side of A165, signed off rndbt. A 2-acre site with 49 touring pitches and 217 statics.

Filey Brigg Touring Caravan & Country Park (TA115812)
North Cliff YO14 0XX ☎ 01723 513852 Signposted
►►► **Family Park** ▲
Open Etr-Oct Booking advisable bank hols & Jul-Aug Last arrival 21.00hrs Last departure noon
Level grassy park with some mature trees, near sea and beach, and located within a country park. Signed via unclassified road from A1039 on N of Filey. A 9-acre site with 128 touring pitches.
Credit Cards

Muston Grange Caravan Park (TA113797)
Muston Rd YO14 0HU ☎ 01723 512167 & 01947 810415 winter
►►► **Family Park** ★ £5-£7.25 £5-£7.25
Open Etr/Apr-20 Oct Booking advisable bank hols & Jul-Aug Last arrival 22.00hrs Last departure noon
A large touring park with views over the Yorkshire Wolds, with a footpath to Filey town and beach. Situated on A1039 near its junction with A165 on Bridlington side of Filey. A 10-acre site with 220 touring pitches.

FYLINGDALES ('FLASK' INN)

Grouse Hill Caravan Park (NZ928002)
Flask Bungalow Farm YO22 4QH ☎ 01947 880543 Signposted
Nearby town: Whitby
►►► **Family Park** £6-£8 £6-£8 ▲ £6-£8
Open Spring bank hol-Sep (rs Etr-May shop & reception restricted) Booking advisable public hols Last arrival 22.00hrs Last departure noon
Set in the midst of spectacular scenery in North Yorkshire Moors National Park adjacent to A171 Whitby-Scarborough road. A 14-acre site with 175 touring pitches.

GRASSINGTON

See **Threshfield**

GUISBOROUGH

Tockett's Mill Caravan Park (NZ626182)
Skelton Rd TS14 6QA ☎ 01287 610182 Signposted
►►► **Family Park** £7.50-£9.50 £7.50-£9.50
Open Mar-Oct Booking advisable bank hols & high season Last arrival 21.00hrs Last departure noon
Situated in a private wooded valley alongside a stream, the site is centred around a preserved watermill. 1.5m W of Guisborough on A173. A 7-acre site with 30 touring pitches and 75 statics.

HARROGATE

High Moor Farm Park (SE242560)
Skipton Rd HG3 2LT ☎ 01423 563637 & 564955 (4m W on A59) Signposted

►►►► **De-Luxe Park** ★ £9 £9 ▲ £9
Open Apr-Oct Booking advisable public hols Last arrival 23.30hrs Last departure 15.00hrs
An excellent site with first class facilities, set beside a small wood and surrounded by thorn hedges. On the A59, Harrogate-Skipton road. A 15-acre site with 320 touring pitches and 180 statics.
Course fishing, 9 hole golf course.

Ripley Caravan Park (SE289610)
Knaresborough Rd HG3 3AU ☎ 01423 770050 Signposted
Nearby town: Harrogate

►►►► **De-Luxe Park** ★ £6.25-£7.25 £6.25-£7.25 ▲ £6.25-£7.25
Open Etr-Oct Booking advisable bank hols Last arrival 21.00hrs Last departure noon
A well-run rural site with easy access on B6165 .75m S of Ripley. An 18-acre site with 100 touring pitches.
Nursery playroom, sauna, sunbed, tennis net, football.

Rudding Holiday Park (SE333531)
Follifoot HG3 1JH ☎ 01423 870439 (3m S) Signposted

►►►► **De-Luxe Park** ★ £8.60-£19.80 £8.60-£19.80 ▲ £6-£11.60
Open 22 Mar-3 Nov (rs 1-21 Mar no hot water no shop) Booking advisable bank hols Last arrival 22.30hrs Last departure 18.00hrs
A spacious site set in mature parkland and walled gardens, situated 3m SE of Harrogate signed off A661. From A1 take A59 to A658, turn S signed Bradford, and in 4.5m turn right and signed. A 55-acre site with 141 touring pitches and 95 statics.
Golf course, driving range & cycle hire.

Credit Cards

Shaws Trailer Park (SE325557)
Knaresborough Rd HG2 7NE ☎ 01423 884432 & 883622 (on A59 opposite Hospital) Signposted
►►► **Family Park** ★ fr £7.50 fr £6.50 ▲ fr £7

Open all year Booking advisable public hols Last arrival 21.00hrs Last departure noon

A level, grassy site with mature trees. On A59 Harrogate-Knaresborough road. An 11-acre site with 43 touring pitches and 146 statics.

HAWES

Bainbridge Ings Caravan & Camping Site (SD879895)

DL8 3NU ☎ 01969 667354 (approaching Hawes from Bainbridge on A684, turn left at signpost marked Gayle, 300yds on left) Signposted

Town & Country Pennant Park ★ £6-£7.50 £5.50-£7 £5.50-£7

Open Apr-Oct Booking advisable school hols Last arrival 22.00hrs Last departure 14.00hrs

A family run site in open countryside, close to Hawes in the heart of Upper Wensleydale. Leave A684 on unclass rd signed Gayle. Site 440yds on left. A 5-acre site with 55 touring pitches and 14 statics.

HELMSLEY

Golden Square Touring Caravan Park (SE604797)

Oswaldkirk YO6 5YQ ☎ 01439 788269 (2.5m S B1257 between Sproxton & Oswaldkirk)

Signposted

►►►► De-Luxe Park

Open Mar-Oct Booking advisable bank hols Last arrival 23.30hrs Last departure noon

All-round excellent site with manicured grounds and first class toilets. Set in a quiet rural situation with lovely views over the N Yorks Moors. Off A170 on unclass road leading to B1257 near Ampleforth. An 8-acre site with 129 touring pitches.

Microwave oven.

Foxholme Caravan Park (SE658828)

Harome YO6 5JG ☎ 01439 770416 & 771241 (follow A170from Helmsley in direction of Scarborough, turn right signposted Harome) Signposted

►►► Family Park £6.50-£7 £6.50-£7 £6.50-£7

Open Etr-Oct Booking advisable bank & school hols Last arrival 23.00hrs Last departure noon

A quiet site with mostly individual pitches divided by mature trees. Set in superb wooded countryside 1m S of Beadlam on unclass road. A 6-acre site with 60 touring pitches.

See advertisement on page 208

Wrens of Ryedale Caravan Site (SE656840)
Gale Ln, Nawton YO6 5SD ☎ 01439 771260 Signposted
Nearby town: Kirkbymoorside
►►► **Family Park** ★ £5.50-£8 £5.50-£8
£5.50-£8
Open Apr-16 Oct Booking advisable bank hols Last arrival 22.00hrs Last departure noon
A level, grassy site with mature trees and bushes, and open views, .5m S of Beadlam village off A170. A 2.5-acre site with 30 touring pitches.
Bike & caravan hire.

HIGH BENTHAM

Riverside Caravan Park (SD665688)
Wenning Av LA2 7HS ☎ 01524 261272 & 262163 Signposted
►►► **Family Park** ★ fr £7.80 fr £7.80 fr £5
Open Mar-Oct Booking advisable bank hols Last arrival 20.00hrs Last departure 13.00hrs
This site is set on the banks of the River Wenning, in delightful countryside and screened by trees. Off B6480, and signed from town centre. A 12-acre site with 30 touring pitches and 170 statics.
Free fishing.

HUNMANBY

Orchard Farm Holiday Village (TA105779)
Stonegate YO14 0PU ☎ 01723 891582 Signposted
Nearby town: Scarborough

►►►► **De-Luxe Park** ★ £5.50-£10 £5.50-£10
£5-£10
Open Etr-Oct (rs Nov-Mar no bar or pool facilities) Booking advisable bank hols & peak season Last arrival 23.00hrs Last departure 11.30hrs
A level grassy site with pitches around lake and model railway, close to Hunmanby village, with coarse fishing on site. Signed from A1039. A 14-acre site with 91 touring pitches and 6 statics.
Veg prep area, boating lake, fishing.

Credit Cards

KNARESBOROUGH

Scotton Holiday Park (SE327587)
New Rd, Scotton HG5 9HH
☎ 01423 864413 Signposted
►►► **Family Park** ★ £6.50-£7.50 £6.25-£7.50
£5.20-£6.50
Open Mar-7 Jan Booking advisable bank hols Last arrival 09.30hrs Last departure 13.00hrs
A very pleasant grassy park on the edge of the village and close to River Widd. From Knaresborough on B6165 towards Pateley Bridge, turn right immediately inside Scotton boundary. An 8.5-acre site with 65 touring pitches and 41 statics.

Credit Cards

Kingfisher Caravan Park (SE343603)
Low Moor Ln, Farnham HG5 9DQ ☎ 01423 869411
►►► **Family Park** ★ £6-£7 £6-£7 £5-£6
Open mid Mar/Etr-Oct Booking advisable bank hols & 15 Jul-1 Sep Last arrival 23.00hrs Last departure 16.00hrs
A large grassy site with open spaces set in wooded area in rural countryside. From Knaresborough take A6055, after 1m turn L towards Farnham, and L again in village, signed Scotton. Site 1m on L. A 4-acre site with 35 touring pitches and 30 statics.

LEBBERSTON

Lebberston Touring Caravan Park (TA082823)
Beckfield Green Ln YO11 3PF ☎ 01723 585723 & 582254 Signposted
►►► **Family Park** ★ fr £6 fr £6
Open beg May-Sep Booking advisable bank hols Last arrival 22.00hrs Last departure noon

A part-level and part-sloping grass site with saplings and bushes. Off A165 Filey-Scarborough road. A 7.5-acre site with 125 touring pitches.
Washing up sinks.
See advertisement under SCARBOROUGH

NORTH STAINLEY

Sleningford Water Mill Caravan Camping Park (SE280783)
HG4 3HQ ☎ 01765 635201 (5m NW of Ripon on A6108) Signposted
Nearby town: Ripon
►►► **Family Park** ★ £7-£10.50 £7-£10.50 ▲ £7-£10.50
Open Etr & Apr-Oct Booking advisable bank hols & school holidays Last arrival 22.00hrs Last departure 12.30hrs
Level, grassy site with mature trees set in woods and meadowland adjacent to River Ure and A6108, 4m N of Ripon. A 14-acre site with 80 touring pitches.
Off-licence, canoe access, fly fishing.

OSMOTHERLEY

Cote Ghyll Caravan Park (SE461983)
DL6 3AH ☎ 01609 883425 (off A19 at junction A684, at village cross turn left up hill) Signposted
Nearby town: Northallerton
►►► **Family Park** ★ fr £6 fr £5.50 ▲ fr £5.25
Open Apr-Oct Booking advisable bank hols & Jul-Aug Last arrival 21.00hrs Last departure noon
Quiet, peaceful site in pleasant valley on edge of moors, close to village. From junction of A1/A684 take unclass rd signed Osmotherley. In village turn left at T junc, and site on right in 0.5 miles. A 4-acre site with 77 touring pitches and 17 statics.

PICKERING

Upper Carr Touring Park (SE804816)
Upper Carr Ln, Malton Rd YO18 7JP ☎ 01751 473115
►►► **Family Park** ▲
Open Mar-Oct
Attractive and well-maintained rural touring park set amongst mature trees and hedges, with adjacent 9-hole golf course. A 4-acre site with 80 touring pitches.
Off-licence.

Wayside Caravan Park (SE764859)
Wrelton YO18 8PG ☎ 01751 472608 Signposted
►►► **Family Park** ★ fr £7.50 fr £7 ▲ fr £7
Open Etr-early Oct Booking advisable Etr, Spring bank hol & Jul-Aug Last arrival 23.00hrs Last departure noon
A level, grassy, well-maintained site divided up by mature hedges into small areas off the A170 at Wrelton village. A 5-acre site with 75 touring pitches and 80 statics.

RICHMOND

Brompton-on-Swale Caravan & Camping Park (NZ199002)
Brompton-on-Swale DL10 7EZ
☎ 01748 824629 (1.5m SE B6271 towards Brompton-on Swale) Signposted
Nearby town: Darlington
►►►► **De-Luxe Park** ★ £6.90-£10.40 £6.90-£10.40 ▲ £5-£9.65
Open Etr or Mar-Oct Booking advisable school & bank hols Last arrival 22.00hrs Last departure 14.00hrs
A riverside site on former meadowland with mature trees and other natural features. Very well-equipped and maintained, adjacent to main road on the banks of the River Swale. Take B1263 off A1 signed Richmond, and site 1m on left. A 7-acre site with 150 touring pitches and 22 statics.
Fishing & canoeing on site.

Swale View Caravan Site (NZ134013)
Reeth Rd DL10 4SF ☎ 01748 823106 Signposted
►►► **Family Park** ★ fr £4.90 fr £4.90 ▲ fr £4.90
Open Mar-Oct Booking advisable bank hols & summer hols Last arrival 21.00hrs Last departure noon
A level, grassy site shaded by trees, lying on the banks of the River Swale in picturesque country. From Richmond take B6270 signed Reeth for 2.5m. A 4-acre site with 60 touring pitches and 100 statics.

RIPON

Riverside Meadows Country Caravan Park (SE317726)
Ure Bank Top HG4 1JD ☎ 01765 602964 & 607764 Signposted
►►► **Family Park** ★ £8.50-£9.50 £7.50-£8.50 ▲ £5-£8.50
Open May-Oct (rs Mar-Apr bar open wknds only) Booking advisable bank hols & high season Last departure noon
This pleasant and well-maintained site stands on high ground overlooking the River Ure, 1 mile from town centre. There is no access to the river from the site. Leave A1 at junc with A61 signed Ripon, at bypass rndbt turn right onto unclass rd, then 2nd left at 2nd rndbt. A 28-acre site with 200 touring pitches and 200 statics.

ROBIN HOOD'S BAY

Middlewood Farm Holiday Park (NZ945045)
Middlewood Ln YO22 4UF ☎ 01947 880414
Nearby town: Whitby
►►► **Family Park** ★ £6.50-£8.50 £6.50-£7.50
£5-£8.50
Open Etr-Oct Booking advisable Last arrival 22.00hrs Last departure noon
A peaceful family park on a working farm, close to Robin Hood's Bay in a picturesque fishing village. Leave A171 towards Robin Hood's Bay, into Fylingthorpe village, and turn into Middlewood Lane to park. A 4.5-acre site with 140 touring pitches and 30 statics.

SCARBOROUGH

Cayton Village Caravan Park (TA057837)
Mill Ln, Cayton YO11 3NN ☎ 01723 583171 & 01904 624630 (in winter) Signposted
►►► **Family Park**
Open Etr/Apr-1 Oct Booking advisable bank hols Last arrival 20.00hrs Last departure noon
A pleasant, landscaped site in an attractive rural area. Situated off A165 Scarborough to Filey Rd, adjoining Cayton Village. An 11-acre site with 200 touring pitches.

Jacobs Mount Caravan Park (TA021868)
Jacobs Mount, Stepney Rd YO12 5NL
☎ 01723 361178 (2m in W on A170 Thirsk Road) Signposted
►►► **Family Park** ★ £5.75-£8.50 £5.75-£8.50
£5.75-£8.50
Open Mar-Oct (rs Mar-May & Oct limited hours at shop/bar) Booking advisable bank hols & late Jun-early Sep Last arrival 21.00hrs Last departure noon
A gently sloping site situated in attractive countryside 2m from the coast, with direct access from A170. A 2.5-acre site with 56 touring pitches and 44 statics.
Dish wash & food preparation area.

Scalby Close Park (TA018925)
Burniston Rd YO13 0DA ☎ 01723 365908
Signposted
►►► **Family Park** £4-£8.50 £4-£8.50
£4-£8.50
Open Mar-Oct Booking advisable bank hols & high season Last arrival 22.00hrs Last departure noon
A small family-run site situated 2m N of Scarborough on the A165. A 3-acre site with 42 touring pitches and 5 statics.

Credit Cards

Scalby Manor Caravan & Camping Park (TA025911)
Field Ln, Burnston Rd YO11 2EP ☎ 01723 366212
Signposted
►►► **Family Park**
Open Etr-Oct Booking advisable bank hols Jul & Aug Last arrival 21.00hrs Last departure noon
Slightly undulating, grassy site in rural surroundings. On the A165, 2m N of town centre. A 22-acre site with 300 touring pitches.
Off-licence.

Credit Cards

SCOTCH CORNER

Scotch Corner Caravan Park (NZ210054)
DL10 6NS ☎ 01748 822530 & 826272 (winter)
Signposted Nearby town: Richmond
►►► **Family Park**
Open Etr-mid Oct Booking advisable public hols & Jul-Aug Last arrival 22.30hrs Last departure noon
A well-maintained site with excellent facilities. Off A6108, approach from Scotch Corner is towards Richmond for approx 200yds then make U-turn, crossing central reservation and proceed approx 160yds back towards Scotch Corner for site entrance. A 7-acre site with 96 touring pitches.

Credit Cards

SEAMER

Arosa Caravan & Camping Park (TA011830)
YO12 4QB ☎ 01723 862166
►►► **Family Park**
Open Mar-4 Jan
A very well laid out site with screening from mature trees, approx 4m from Scarborough. From junc with unclass rd and A64 S of Seamer, travel N into village. Site 250yards along Ratten Road. A 3.5-acre site with 92 touring pitches.

SHERIFF HUTTON

Camping & Caravanning Club Site (SE638652)
Bracken Hill YO6 1QG
☎ 01347 878660 (in season) & 01203 694995
Signposted
Nearby town: York
►►► **Family Park** ★ £8.70-£11.30 £8.70-£11.30 £8.70-£11.30
Open end Mar-early Nov Booking advisable bank hols & peak periods Last arrival 21.00hrs Last departure noon
The site is within easy reach of York in a quiet rural setting. From A1237 (York northern ring road) take unclass rd signed Strensall and Sheriff Hutton, through Strensall turn left on unclass rd signed Sheriff Hutton and site 2m on right. Please see the advertisement on page 27 for details of Club Members' benefits. A 10-acre site with 90 touring pitches.

Credit Cards

SLINGSBY

Camping & Caravanning Club Site (SE699755)
Railway St YO6 7AA ☎ 01653 628335 (in season) & 01203 694995 Signposted
►►► **Family Park** ★ £8.10-£10.30 £8.10-£10.30 £8.10-£10.30
Open end Mar-early Nov Booking advisable bank hols & peak periods Last arrival 21.00hrs Last departure noon
A part-grassy, part-hardstanding site near village centre, signed from B1257. Please see the advertisement on page 27 for details of Club Members' benefits. A 3-acre site with 60 touring pitches.

Credit Cards

Robin Hood Caravan & Camping Park (SE701748)
Green Dyke Ln YO6 7AU ☎ 01653 628391 Signposted
Nearby town: Malton
►►► **Family Park** ★ £6-£7 £6-£7 £5-£6
Open Mar-Oct Booking advisable bank hols & 15 Jul-1 Sep Last arrival 22.00hrs Last departure 16.00hrs
A pleasant, well-maintained grassy site, well-situated for touring Yorks Dales. Situated on B1257. A 2-acre site with 39 touring pitches and 7 statics.
Caravan hire, washing up area. Off-license.

SNAINTON

Jasmine Caravan Park (SE928813)
Cross Ln YO13 9BE ☎ 01723 859240 Signposted
Nearby town: Scarborough
►►► **Family Park** ★ £6-£8.50 £6-£8.50 £6-£8.50
Open Mar-Dec Booking advisable 3 wks in advance for bank hols Last arrival 22.00hrs Last departure noon
A well-screened rural site on edge of the village, 1m off A170 Pickering-Scarborough road; turn off opposite school into Barker Lane. A 5-acre site with 90 touring pitches and 10 statics.

STAINFORTH

Knight Stainforth Hall Caravan & Campsite (SD816672)
BD24 0DP ☎ 01729 822200 Signposted
Nearby town: Settle
►►► **Family Park** fr £7.75 fr £7.75 fr £7.75
Open May-Oct Booking advisable bank hols & Jul-Aug Last arrival 22.00hrs Last departure noon
A very well-maintained site located near a river in the Yorkshire Dales National Park. Approach only possible from B6479 at Giggleswick. A 6-acre site with 100 touring pitches and 60 statics.
Fishing on site.

Credit Cards

STAXTON

Spring Willows Touring Caravan Park (TA026794)
Main Rd, Staxton Roundabout YO12 4SB
☎ 01723 891505 (jct A64/A1039) Signposted
Nearby town: Scarborough
►►►► **De-Luxe Park** ★ £6.50-£15 £6.50-£15 £6.50-£15
Open Mar-Dec (rs Mar & Oct-Dec bar, pool & take-away restricted) Booking advisable bank hols, Etr, Jul & Aug Last arrival 18.00hrs Last departure 11.00hrs
A sheltered grassy site in a former sandpit, with level pitches divided by shrubs and bushes, and offering a wide variety of amenities. 6m from Scar at junct of A64 and A1039. A 10-acre site with 184 touring pitches.
Washing-up facilities, sauna, solarium, coffee lounge

SUTTON-ON-THE-FOREST

Goosewood Caravan Park (SE595636)
YO6 1ET ☎ 01347 810829 (From A1237 outer York ring rd, take B1363 signed Helmsley North, pass Haxby/Wigginton jct & take next right) Signposted
Nearby town: York
►►►► **De-Luxe Park** ★ £7.50-£9 £7.50-£9
Open 22 Mar-Oct Booking advisable bank hols Last arrival 20.00hrs Last departure noon
An immaculately maintained site with its own lake and seasonal fishing, set in attractive woodland within the Vale of York. From A1237 (York northern ring road) take B1363, in 1.5m take unclass rd signed Farlington, and turn right in .25m. Take right turn in .5m, and site on right. A 12-acre site with 75 touring pitches.
Fishing lake.

THIRSK

Sowerby Caravan Park (SE437801)
Sowerby YO7 3AG ☎ 01845 522753 (0.5m S off A168) Signposted
►►► **Family Park** £6.25-£6.75 £6.25-£6.75 £6.25-£6.75
Open Mar-Oct Booking advisable bank hols Last arrival 22.00hrs
A level grassy site, 1m from town on the Sowerby Road, with a tree-lined river bank. From junc A168/A19 S of Thirsk, follow A19 for 1m, turn right on unclass rd signed Sowerby. Site on left in 1m. A 1-acre site with 25 touring pitches and 85 statics.

THRESHFIELD

Wood Nook Caravan Park (SD974641)
Skirethorns BD23 5NU ☎ 01756 752412 Signposted
Nearby town: Grassington

►►►► **De-Luxe Park** ★ £7-£9.50 £7-£9.50 £7-£8.50
Open Mar-Oct Booking advisable bank hols & peak periods Last arrival 22.00hrs Last departure noon
Gently sloping site in a rural setting, completely hidden by natural features of surrounding hills and woodland. Site on unclass rd 1m NW of Threshfield, W of B6160. A 2-acre site with 48 touring pitches and 10 statics.
See advertisement under GRASSINGTON

Credit Cards

UGTHORPE

Burnt House Holiday Park (NZ784112)
YO21 2BG ☎ 01947 840448 Signposted
Nearby town: Whitby
►►► **Family Park**
Open Mar-Oct Booking advisable bank hols & Jul-Aug Last arrival 21.00hrs
Level grass site with trees and bushes set in moorland. 4.5m from sea and beach and 9m W of Whitby off A171 Teeside road. A 7.5-acre site with 99 touring pitches and 41 statics.

WHITBY

Northcliffe Holiday Park (NZ930076)
YO22 4LL ☎ 01947 880477 (3.5m S, off A171) Signposted

►►►► **De-Luxe Park** £6-£10 £6-£10 £6-£10
Open Etr or end Mar-Oct Booking advisable school & bank hols & Jul-Aug Last arrival 21.00hrs Last departure 11.00hrs
A lovely little site in a peaceful position on the outskirts of Whitby, with clifftop views and country walks. Situated 3.5m S off A171. A 2-acre site with 30 touring pitches and 171 statics.
off-licence.

Credit Cards

Rigg Farm Caravan Park (NZ915061)
Stainsacre YO22 4LP ☎ 01947 880430 (3.5m S on unclass off A171 at High Hawsker) Signposted
►►► **Family Park**
Open Mar-Oct Booking advisable bank hols & Jul-Aug Last arrival 21.00hrs Last departure 13.00hrs
A neat rural site with good views in peaceful surroundings. Site is off B1416 on unclass road. From A171 Scarborough rd turn L onto B1416 signed Ruswarp. In 3.25m turn R onto unclass road signed Sneatonthorpe-Hawsker-Stainsacre. In 1.25m turn L signed Hawsker-Robin Hoods Bay-Scarborough, site in .5m. A 2-acre site with 14 touring pitches and 15 statics.

York House Caravan Park (NZ926071)
YO22 4LW ☎ 01947 880354 (3.5m S, off A171) Signposted
►►► **Family Park** ★ £6.50-£7.50 £6.50-£7.50 £6.50-£7.50
Open Mar-Oct Booking advisable Spring bank hol & mid Jul-Aug Last arrival 23.00hrs Last departure noon
A very well-kept site in an undulating position located south of Whitby, ideal for touring coast or moors. Just off A171 at Hawsker and signed. A 3-acre site with 59 touring pitches and 41 statics.
Open area for games.

WINKSLEY

Woodhouse Farm Caravan & Camping Park (SE241715)
HG4 3PG ☎ 01765 658309 Signposted
Nearby town: Ripon
►►► **Family Park** £7-£11 £7-£11 £6.50-£7.50
Open Mar-Oct Booking advisable bank hols & mid Jul-Aug Last arrival 22.30hrs Last departure noon
An attractive rural site on a former working farm, with existing hedges used to screen pitches, and meadowland and mature woods surrounds. Friendly, knowledgable owners. Situated 6m W of Ripon off B6265 Pateley Bridge road, 2.5m from Fountains Abbey. A 16-acre site with 140 touring pitches and 62 statics.
Barbecue hire, coarse fishing lake.
See advertisement under RIPON

Credit Cards

WYKEHAM

St Helens Caravan Park (SE967836)
St Helens in the Park YO13 9QD ☎ 01723 862771 Signposted
Nearby town: Scarborough

►►►► **De-Luxe Park** ★ £6.80-£8.80 £6.80-£8.80 £6.80-£8.80
Open Mar-Oct (rs Nov-Jan shop/laundry/main showerbathblock closed) Booking advisable bank hols & Jul-Aug Last arrival 22.00hrs Last departure 17.00hrs
Set on the edge of the North York Moors National Park this delightfully landscaped site was winner of the 1994 Best Campsite of the Year Award. The park is extremely well-maintained and thoughtfully laid out with

strategically placed, top quality facilities. Situated on A170 in village 150yds on L past Downe Arms Hotel towards Scarborough. A 25-acre site with 250 touring pitches.
Caravan storage.
See advertisement under SCARBOROUGH

Credit Cards

YORK

Rawcliffe Manor Caravan Site (SE583553)
Manor Lane, Shipton Rd YO3 6TZ ☎ 01904 624422 Signposted

►►►► **De-Luxe Park** ★ £7.50-£11 ▲ £4.20-£11
Open all year Booking advisable all times Last arrival 20.00hrs Last departure noon
A level site divided into hedged paddocks, with immaculate landscaping incorporating rose trees throughout. A 4.5-acre site with 120 touring pitches.
Petanque pitches & satellite TV.

Credit Cards

YORKSHIRE, SOUTH

For the map of this county, see Yorkshire, North

DONCASTER

See **Hatfield**

HATFIELD

Hatfield Waterpark (SE670098)
DN7 6EQ ☎ 01302 841572 & 737343 Signposted
Nearby town: Doncaster
► **Town & Country Pennant Park** ★ fr £6.20 fr £6.20 ▲ £3.30-£6.20
Open Apr-Oct Booking advisable bank hols Last arrival 19.00hrs Last departure noon
A clean, well-run site with fishing and good supervised marina facilities, including windsurfing, sailing and canooing equipment for hire. Signed from Hatfield off A18. A 10-acre site with 75 touring pitches.
Canoeing, rowing, sailing, windsurfing & fishing.

SHEFFIELD

See **Worsbrough**

WORSBROUGH

Greensprings Touring Park (SE330020)
Rockley Abbey Farm, Rockley Ln S75 3DS ☎ 01226 288298 Signposted
Nearby town: Barnsley
►►► **Family Park** ★ fr £6 fr £6 ▲ fr £6
Open Apr-Oct Booking advisable when hook up is required Last arrival 21.00hrs Last departure noon
Part-level, part-sloping, grass site with young trees and bushes, set in woods and meadowland with access to river. From exit 36 off M1 turn along A61 to Barnsley, then signposted. A 4-acre site with 65 touring pitches.
Cycle hire.

YORKSHIRE, WEST

For the map of this county, see Yorkshire, North

BARDSEY

Glenfield Caravan Park (SE351421)
Blackmoor Ln LS17 9DZ ☎ 01937 574657 Signposted
Nearby town: Leeds
►►► **Family Park** ★ fr £6.50 fr £6.50
Open all year Booking advisable
A rural site in a hedge-lined meadow with level pitches. From A58 at Bardsey turn into Church Lane, continue into Brickmoor Lane, and site on right in 0.5m. A 4-acre site with 30 touring pitches and 1 static.

Moor Lodge Park (SE352423)
Blackmoor Ln LS17 9DZ ☎ 01937 572424 Signposted
Nearby town: Leeds
► **Town & Country Pennant Park** fr £6.50 fr £6.50
Open all year Booking advisable all Times
A neat, well-kept site in a peaceful and pleasant rural location convenient to surrounding areas of interest. From the Bracken Fox public house on the A58 Wetherby-Leeds rd, turn into Syke Lane, then right into Blackmore Lane. Site signed on right. A 7-acre site with 12 touring pitches and 60 statics.

LEEDS

Roundhay Park Site (SE339376)
Roundhay Park, Elmete Ln, off Wetherby Rd LS8 2LG
☎ 0113 2652354 (in season) & 2661850 Signposted
Town & Country Pennant Park ★ £8-£8.40
£8-£8.40 ▲ £4
Open Mar-26 Nov Booking advisable Spring bank hol & Jul-Aug Last arrival 21.00hrs Last departure noon
On a south-facing hillside, adjacent to Roundhay Park, 3.5m from city centre. A very well-maintained site. An 8-acre site with 60 touring pitches.

SILSDEN

Dales Bank Holiday Park (SE036483)
Low Ln BD20 9JH ☎ 01535 653321 & 656523 (1m NW on unclass rd) Signposted
Town & Country Pennant Park ▲
Open Apr-Oct (rs Mar) Booking advisable public hols Last arrival 22.00hrs Last departure 16.00hrs
A pleasant farm site with very good facilities in open countryside of typical Dales scenery. From A6034 in town centre turn N, take left then right turns into Bradley Rd, and after 1m turn right. Site in 500yds. A 3-acre site with 40 touring pitches and 12 statics.

Credit Cards

CHANNEL ISLANDS

There is no map of the Channel Islands

GUERNSEY

CATEL (CASTEL)

Fauxquets Valley Farm
CC GY5 7QA ☎ 01481 55460 Signposted
Nearby town: St Peter Port
►►► **Family Park** ▲ £8.40-£9.80
Open May-mid Sep (rs Apr no pool or farmhouse kitchen use) Booking advisable last 2 wks Jul-1st 3 wks Aug
Beautiful, quiet farm site in a hidden valley yet close to the sea. Friendly, helpful owners who understand campers' needs. 3m W of St Peter Port, near German Underground Hospital. A 3-acre site with 90 touring pitches.

Credit Cards

VALE

La Bailloterie Camping
GY3 5HA ☎ 01481 43636 Signposted
Nearby town: St Sampsons
►►► **Family Park** ▲ £7-£8.80
Open 15 May-15 Sep Booking advisable Jul-Aug Last arrival 23.00hrs
Pretty little site with one large touring field and a few small, well-screened paddocks, on a working freesia farm. 3m N of St Peter Port, take Vale Road to Crossways and turn right into Rue du Braye. Site 1st left at sign. An 8-acre site with 100 touring pitches.
Volleyball net & boules pitch.

JERSEY

ST BRELADE

Rose Farm
Route Des Genets JE3 8DE ☎ 01534 41231 Signposted
Nearby town: St Aubin

►►►► **De-Luxe Park** ▲
Open May-Sep Booking advisable as early as possible
An attractive site set in a valley close to St Aubins, with friendly owners and secluded pitches. Facilities are of a very good standard. Located 1m W of St Aubin's village on A13; at junc with A57 turn right into Rose Farm Lane. A 5-acre site with 150 touring pitches.
See advertisement in Colour Section

ST MARTIN

Beuvelande Camp Site
Beuvelande JE3 6EG ☎ 01534 853575 & 852223

►►►► **De-Luxe Park** ▲
Open May-Sep
An old established site with refurbished facilities, in peaceful countryside close to St Martin. Take A6 from St Helier to St Martin, and follow signs. A 6-acre site with 150 touring pitches.

Rozel Camping Park
Summerville Farm JE3 6AX ☎ 01534 856797 & 851656
Nearby town: St Helier

►►►► **De-Luxe Park** ★ ▲
Open May-mid Sep (rs May & Sep snack bar closed)

Booking advisable Jul-Aug Last departure noon
An attractive and well-maintained secluded holiday site offering excellent amenities in a lovely farm location. From St Helier follow Bagatelle Road (A6) or St Saviour's Road (A7) then B38. Last arrival and departure time as soon as possible after car ferry docks. A 4-acre site with 70 touring pitches and 20 statics.

→

Credit Cards

ISLE OF MAN

For map, see Cumbria

KIRK MICHAEL

Glen Wyllin Campsite (SC302901)
IM6 1AL ☎ 01624 878231 & 878836
Nearby town: Peel
►►► **Family Park** ★ fr £6 fr £6
Open mid May-mid Sep Booking advisable end May-mid Jun
Caravans are not allowed on the Island. This tree-lined glen is divided by a tarmac road leading down to the beach. Just off A3 TT course at Kirk Michael, clearly signed on edge of village. A 9-acre site with 70 touring pitches.

→

LAXEY

Laxey Commissioners Campsite (SC438841)
Quarry Rd, (off Minorca Hill) ☎ 01624 861241 & 861816 Signposted
Town & Country Pennant Park ★ fr £6 fr £6
Open Apr-Sep Booking advisable Apr-May Last arrival anytime
Level grassy site in hilly country with access to sea, beach and hills. Excellent facilities for tenters, including camper's kitchen. A 2-acre site with 50 touring pitches.

→

PEEL

Peel Camping Park (SC252839)
Derby Rd IM5 1RG ☎ 01624 842341 & 843667 (on A20) Signposted
Town & Country Pennant Park ★ fr £7 fr £7
Open mid May-mid Sep Booking advisable 1st week in Jun
A pleasant grass site on the edge of town surrounded by hedges. On A20 .25m from Peel, past Clothmaker's School. A 4-acre site with 120 touring pitches.

→

SCOTLAND

The directory which follows has been divided into three geographical regions. Counties have not been shown against individual locations as recent legislation has created a number of smaller counties which will be unfamiliar to the visitor. The postal authorities have confirmed that it is no longer necessary to include a county name in addresses, provided a post code is shown. All locations appear on the regional maps in their appropriate counties.

HIGHLANDS & ISLANDS

This region includes the counties of Aberdeen City, Aberdeenshire, Highland, Moray, Orkney, Shetland and Western Isles which reflect the recent national changes.

ABERDEEN

Hazlehead Caravan Park & Campsite (NJ893057)
Groats Rd AB1 8BL ☎ 01224 647647 & 321268 (Apr-Sep) Signposted
Town & Country Pennant Park ★
Open Apr-Sep Booking advisable Jun-Aug Last arrival 20.00hrs Last departure noon
A wooded, landscaped site close to park of the same name, on western outskirts of city off A944. From outer ring road A92 take A944 signed Alford, in 1m turn left into Groats Rd (signed camping), and site on right in 400 metres. A 6-acre site with 165 touring pitches.

→

ABERLOUR

Aberlour Gardens Caravan Park (NJ282434)
AB38 9LD ☎ 01340 871586 Signposted

►►►► **De-Luxe Park**
Open Apr-Oct Booking advisable bank hols & Jul-Aug
A quiet walled garden park with very clean modern facilities. Signed off A95 halfway between Aberlour and Craigellachie. A 3.5-acre site with 30 touring pitches and 26 statics.

→

ABOYNE

Aboyne Loch Caravan Park (NO538998)
AB34 5BR ☎ 013398 86244 & 01330 811351 (1m E of Aboyne off A93) Signposted

►►►► **De-Luxe Park**
Open 31 Mar-Oct Booking advisable Jul-Aug Last arrival 20.00hrs Last departure 11.00hrs
Attractively-sited caravan park set amidst woodland

contd.

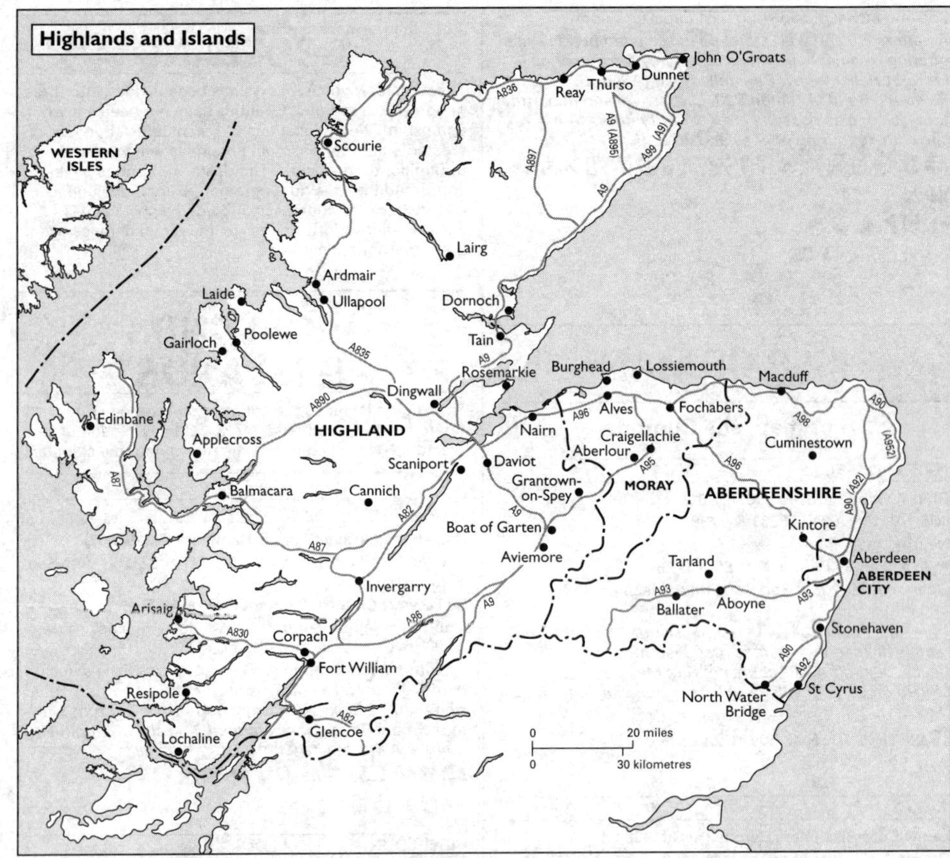

beside Aboyne Loch in scenic Deeside. On A93, 1m E of Aboyne. A 4-acre site with 55 touring pitches and 40 statics.

Coarse fishing.

ALVES

North Alves Caravan Park (NJ122633)

IV30 3XD ☎ 01343 85223 Signposted

►►► **Family Park**

Open Apr-Oct Booking advisable peak periods Last arrival 23.00hrs Last departure noon

A quiet rural site in attractive rolling countryside within 3m of a good beach. From A96 take unclass rd signed Alves. A 10-acre site with 45 touring pitches and 12 statics.

APPLECROSS

Applecross Campsite (NG714443)

IV54 8ND ☎ 01520 744268 & 744284 Signposted

Nearby town: Dingwall

►►► **Family Park**

Open Etr-Oct (rs Apr, May, Sep & Oct only 1 toilet block open) Last arrival 22.00hrs

A quiet site in a lovely remote area close to mountains, moorland and beach. Caravans should approach via Shieldaig. On unclass rd off A896, 300yds from village. A 6-acre site with 60 touring pitches and 4 statics.

Bakery.

Credit Cards

The AA pennant classification has been revised for 1998. Please read the explanation of the scheme on page 10.

ARDMAIR

Ardmair Point Caravan Park (NH108983)
IV26 2TN ☎ 01854 612054 Signposted
Nearby town: Ullapool

►►►► **De-Luxe Park** ★ £7-£9 £7-£9 ▲ £7-£9
Open May-Sep Booking advisable Jul-Aug Last arrival 22.00hrs Last departure noon
An excellent touring site on small peninsula 3.5m N of Ullapool on A835, with superb views of surrounding mountains and sea lochs. A 4-acre site with 45 touring pitches.
Boats, fishing, canoes, windsurfers for hire.

Credit Cards

ARISAIG

Gorten Sands Caravan Site (NM640879)
Gorten Farm PH39 4NS ☎ 01687 450283 Signposted
Nearby town: Mallaig
►►► **Family Park** fr £8.50 fr £7 ▲ fr £7
Open Etr-Sep Booking advisable Jul-Aug Last arrival 23.00hrs Last departure 13.00hrs
A well-run site with mainly modern facilities. 2m NW of Arisaig on A830, turn left at sign "Back of Keppoch" and follow to end of road. A 6-acre site with 42 touring pitches and 3 statics.

Portnadoran Caravan Site (NM651892)
Bunacaimbe PH39 4NT ☎ 01687 450267 (2m N on A830) Signposted
Nearby town: Mallaig
►►► **Family Park** ★ £5-£8 £5-£8 ▲ £5-£7
Open Apr-Oct Booking advisable Jul-Aug Last arrival 23.00hrs Last departure noon
Small, level, grassy site situated close to sandy beach overlooking the Islands of Eigg, Rhum and Skye. Very welcoming. Signed .25m off A380, 1.5m N of Arisaig. A 2-acre site with 55 touring pitches and 9 statics.

AVIEMORE

Dalraddy Holiday Park (NH859083)
PH22 1QB ☎ 01479 810330 (3.5m S on B9152) Signposted
►►► **Family Park** ★ £6.50-£8 £6.50-£8 ▲ £3-£5.95
Open all year (rs Nov open 10am-4pm) Booking advisable Jul-Aug Last arrival 19.00hrs Last departure noon
A secluded site off the A9, 3.5m S of Aviemore, set amidst heather and young birch trees, with mountain views. A 25-acre site with 30 touring pitches and 94 statics.

Credit Cards

Glenmore Forest Camping & Caravan Park (NH975097)
Glenmore PH22 1QU ☎ 01479 861271 (at town turn right onto B970) Signposted
►►► **Family Park** ★ £7-£8.10 £7-£8.10 £7-£8.10
Open Dec-Oct Booking advisable New year, Etr & Jul-Aug Last arrival 20.00hrs Last departure noon
An attractive forest site with grassy areas, landscaped with mature trees, and close to the eastern end of Loch Morlich at the head of Glenmore. There are sandy beaches close by. Signed off B970 on Cairngorms rd. A 17-acre site with 220 touring pitches.
Credit Cards

Rothiemurchus Camping & Caravan Park (NH916108)
Coylumbridge PH22 1QU ☎ 01479 810120 (1.5m E on A951) Signposted
►►► **Family Park** ★ £8-£11.50 £8-£11.50 £6-£8
Open all year Booking advisable Jul-Aug Last arrival 22.00hrs Last departure 11.00hrs no cars by tents
A secluded site in tree-studded undulating ground off approach road to the Cairngorm Mountains. An attractive natural site offering good facilities. A 4-acre site with 39 touring pitches and 50 statics.

BALLATER

Anderson Road Caravan Site (NO371955)
Anderson Rd AB3 5QW ☎ 013397 55727 (in season) & 01569 762001 Signposted
►►►► **De-Luxe Park**
Open Apr-mid Oct Booking advisable anytime Last arrival 20.00hrs Last departure 10.00hrs
This well-equipped site is in a beautiful setting bordered by the River Dee with wooded hills behind. From A93 turn W into Victoria Rd, and left into Braiche Rd. Near town centre. A 5-acre site with 66 touring pitches and 93 statics.

BALMACARA

Reraig Caravan Site (NG815272)
IV40 8DH ☎ 01599 566215 Signposted
Nearby town: Kyle
►►► **Family Park** £6.80 £6.80 £6.80
Open mid Apr-Sep Last arrival 22.00hrs Last departure noon
Set on level, grassy ground surrounded by trees, the site looks south towards Loch Alsh and Skye. Very nicely organised with a high standard of maintenance. On A87 at rear of Balmacara Hotel. A 2-acre site with 45 touring pitches.
Hard standings available & dish washing sinks.
Credit Cards

Balmacara Woodland Campsite (NG802279)
IV40 8DN ☎ 01599 566374 Signposted
Nearby town: Kyle of Lochalsh
► **Town & Country Pennant Park** ★ £4-£5 £4-£5 £4-£5
Open Etr-Sep Last arrival 22.00hrs Last departure noon
An attractive and sheltered wooded site situated 3.5m E of Kyle of Lochalsh, off the A87 (signposted Balmacara Square). A 7-acre site with 58 touring pitches.
Forest walks & orienteering.

BOAT OF GARTEN

Campgrounds of Scotland (NH939191)
PH24 3BN ☎ 01479 831652
Signposted
Nearby town: Aviemore
►►► **Family Park**
Open all year Booking advisable 26 Dec-2 Jan & 25 Jul-7 Aug Last arrival 22.00hrs Last departure 11.00hrs
Level, grass site with young trees and bushes set in mountainous woodland in the village itself, near the River Spey and Loch Garten, off A95. A 3.5-acre site with 37 touring pitches and 60 statics.

BURGHEAD

Red Craig Hotel Caravan & Camping Park (NJ124689)
Mason Haugh IV30 2XX ☎ 01343 835663
Signposted
Nearby town: Elgin
►►► **Family Park**
Open Apr-Oct Booking advisable Jul & Aug Last arrival 22.30hrs Last departure noon
A slightly sloping site with level pitches, overlooking the Moray Forth. On outskirts of Burghead at junc of B9012 and B9040. A 3-acre site with 30 touring pitches and 8 statics.
Credit Cards

CANNICH

Cannich Caravan and Camping Park (NH345317)
IV4 7LN ☎ 01456 415364 & 415263
Signposted
Nearby town: Inverness
►►► **Family Park**
Open Mar-Nov Booking advisable Jul & Aug Last arrival 23.00hrs Last departure noon
A well-run site with plenty of potential, situated on A831 200 yards SE of Cannich Bridge. A 12-acre site with 140 touring pitches and 9 statics.
Mountain bike hire & fishing.

CORPACH

Linnhe Caravan & Chalet Park (NN074771)
PH33 7NL ☎ 01397 772376 (on A830, 1m W of village, 5m from Fort William) Signposted
Nearby town: Fort William

►►►► **De-Luxe Park** ★ £9.50-£12 £9.50-£12 £6-£7.50
Open Etr-Oct (rs 15 Dec-Etr shop & main toilet block closed) Booking advisable school hols & peak periods Last arrival 21.00hrs Last departure 11.00hrs no cars by tents
An excellently maintained site in a beautiful setting. Situated 1m W of Corpach on A830 on shores of Loch Eil with Ben Nevis to E and mountains to Sunart to W. A 5.5-acre site with 73 touring pitches and 100 statics.
Launching slipway, private beach, free fishing.
See advertisement under FORT WILLIAM

Credit Cards

CRAIGELLACHIE

Camping & Caravanning Club Site (NJ257449)
Elchies AB38 9SD
☎ 01340 810414 (in season) & 01203 694995 (travel N on A941, site 2.5m on left)
Signposted
►►► **Family Park**
Open all year Booking advisable bank hols & Jul-Aug Last arrival 21.00hrs Last departure noon
A rural site with views across meadowland towards Speyside, and the usual high Club standards. From Craigellachie travel N on A941, turn left onto B9102 (signed Archiestown), and site is 2.5m on left. Please see the advertisement on page 27 for details of Club Members' benefits. A 6-acre site with 75 touring pitches.

Credit Cards

CUMINESTOWN

East Balthangie Caravan Park (NJ841516)
East Balthangie AB53 7XY ☎ 01888 544261
Nearby town: Turriff
▻**Town & Country Pennant Park** ★ £6-£7.50 £6-£7.50 £5
Open Mar-Oct Booking advisable Jul & Aug Last arrival 22.00hrs Last departure noon
A small farm site with level pitches, sheltered by trees to N and with extensive views to the S. A remote rural setting. From N leave A98 to head S on A9027 to New Byth, then unclass rd signed New Deer to junc with farm rd in 2.25m. A 2-acre site with 12 touring pitches and 7 statics.

DAVIOT

Auchnahillin Caravan Park (NH742386)
IV1 2XQ ☎ 01463 772286 (A9 to Daviot off onto B9154 1.5m) Signposted
Nearby town: Inverness
►►► **Family Park** ★ £7-£9 £7-£9 £3.50-£8
Open Etr-Oct Booking advisable Jun-Aug Last arrival 22.00hrs Last departure noon
Level grassy site with clean and spacious facilities, surrounded by hills and forest. Situated 7m SE of Inverness on B9154 off A9; follow Daviot East signs. A 10-acre site with 65 touring pitches and 35 statics.

DINGWALL

Camping & Caravanning Club Site (NH555588)
Jubilee Park IV15 9QZ ☎ 01349 862236 (in season) & 01203 694995 Signposted

►►►► **De-Luxe Park** ★ £9.10-£12.10 £9.10-£12.10 £9.10-£12.10
Open end Mar-early Nov Booking advisable bank hols & Jul-Aug Last arrival 21.00hrs Last departure noon
An attractive site with well-equipped facilities and a high standard of maintenance, close to the town centre. Cross bridge at Dingwall rlwy stn then turn L past football ground. Please see the advertisement on page 27 for details of Club Members' benefits. A 6-acre site with 80 touring pitches.

Credit Cards

DORNOCH

Grannie's Heilan Hame Holiday Park (NH818924)
Embo IV25 3QD ☎ 01862 810383 & 810753 (A949 to Dornoch, turn left in square & follow signs for Embo) Signposted
Nearby town: Inverness
►►► **Family Park** ★ £7-£15 £7-£15 £7-£13
Open all year Booking advisable Jun-Aug Last arrival 23.30hrs Last departure 14.00hrs
An ideal Highland touring centre set on the beach. Signed off unclass rd at Embo. A 60-acre site with 300 touring pitches and 121 statics.
Spa bath, sauna, solarium & mini ten-pin bowling.

Credit Cards

DUNNET

Dunnet Bay Caravan Club Site (ND219703)
KW14 8XD ☎ 01847 821319 & 01955 607772 Signposted
Nearby town: Thurso
►►► **Family Park**
Open mid Apr-mid Sep Booking advisable Jul-Aug & for

contd.

electric hook-ups Last arrival 20.00hrs Last departure noon

This is a mainly level grassy site with gravel driveways, set alongside 3 miles of white-shell sands. Access is directly onto A836 approx 8m E of Thurso, immediately W of the village of Dunnet. A 5-acre site with 45 touring pitches.

Credit Cards

FOCHABERS

Burnside Caravan Site (NJ350580)

Keith Rd IV32 7PF ☎ 01343 820511 & 820362 Signposted

Nearby town: Elgin

►►► **Family Park** ★ £7.50-£9 £7.50-£9 ▲ £5-£9

Open Apr-Oct Booking advisable Jul-Aug Last departure noon

Attractive site in tree-lined sheltered valley with footpath to the village. .5m E of town off the A96. A 5-acre site with 110 touring pitches and 60 statics.

FORT WILLIAM

Glen Nevis Caravan & Camping Park (NN124722)

Glen Nevis PH33 6SX ☎ 01397 702191 & 706181 Signposted

►►►► **De-Luxe Park** ★ £7.40-£10.50 £7.10-£10.20 ▲ £7.10-£10.20

Open 15 Mar-Oct (rs Mar & mid-end Oct limited shop & restaurant facilities) Booking advisable Jul-Aug Last arrival 22.00hrs Last departure noon

A tasteful site with well-screened enclosures, at the foot of Ben Nevis, in the midst of some of the Highlands' most spectacular scenery. 2m off A82 on Glen Nevis rd. A 30-acre site with 380 touring pitches and 30 statics.

Licensed club/bar adjacent to site.

Credit Cards

GAIRLOCH

Gairloch Caravan & Camping Park (NG798773)

Strath IV21 2BT ☎ 01505 614343 & 01445 712373 Signposted

►►► **Family Park** ★ £8-£9 £7-£8 ▲ £6-£8

Open Apr-15 Oct Booking advisable bank hols & Jul-Aug Last arrival 21.30hrs Last departure noon

A clean, well-maintained site on flat coastal grassland close to Loch Gairloch, signed off A832. A 6-acre site with 70 touring pitches and 3 statics.

Adjacent cafe, restaurant, activity centre & bar.

Credit Cards

Sands Holiday Centre (NG758784)
IV21 2DL ☎ 01445 712152 (take B8021 to Melvaig for 4m) Signposted
►►► **Family Park** ★ £8.50 £8.50 £8.50
Open 20 May-10 Sep (rs Apr-19 May & 11 Sep-mid Oct no shop or laundry some toilets closed) Booking advisable Jul-Aug Last arrival 22.00hrs Last departure noon
Part-level site close to sandy beach with a panoramic outlook towards Skye. 3m W of Gairloch on B8021. A 51-acre site with 360 touring pitches and 20 statics.
Boat slipway.

→

Credit Cards

GLENCOE

Invercoe Caravan Site (NN098594)
PA39 4HP ☎ 01855 811210 Signposted
Nearby town: Fort William

►►►► **De-Luxe Park** £9-£12 £9-£12 £8-£12
Open Etr-mid Oct Booking advisable Jul-Aug for electric hook ups Last departure noon
Level, grass site set on the shore of Loch Lever with excellent mountain views. Located on the Kinlochleven road on the edge of Glencoe village, signed .25m N of A82 on B863.. A 5-acre site with 60 touring pitches and 5 statics.

Glencoe Campsite (NN111578)
Carnoch PA39 4LA ☎ 01855 811397 & 811278 (out of season) (1m E on A82) Signposted
Nearby town: Fort William
►►► **Family Park** ★ £6-£8 £6-£8 £3-£8
Open Etr/Apr-Oct Booking advisable Jul-Aug Last arrival 22.00hrs Last departure 17.00hrs
Part-level, part-sloping, grass, gravel and sand site with young trees and bushes in mountainous woodland. Direct access to river and main A82 road. A 40-acre site with 150 touring pitches.

GRANTOWN-ON-SPEY

Grantown on Spey Caravan Park (NJ028283)
Seafield Avenue, PH26 3JQ ☎ 01479 872474 (from town turn N at Bank of Scotland Park, straight ahead from .25m) Signposted
►►► **Family Park** ★ £6-£9.25 £6-£9.25 £5-£9.25
Open Etr-Sep Booking advisable Etr, May day, Whitsun & Jul-Aug Last arrival 22.00hrs
Attractive site with mature trees and bushes near river, and set amidst hills, mountains, moors and woodland. Good standards and personal attention. Signed .5m off main street in town. A 15-acre site with 100 touring pitches and 45 statics.
Picnic tables, football pitch. Free dishwashing.

Credit Cards

INVERGARRY

Faichemard Farm (NH288016)
PH35 4HG ☎ 01809 501314 Signposted
►►► **Family Park**
Open Apr-Oct
Attractive park with clean, well-maintained facilities and spacious pitches. Situated 1m W of Invergarry off A87. A 10-acre site with 40 touring pitches.

Faichem Park (NH285023)
Ardgarry Farm, Faichem PH35 4HG ☎ 01809 501226
Nearby town: Fort Augustus
►►► **Family Park** £6.50-£7 £6.50-£7 £6.50-£7
Open 15 Apr-15 Oct Booking advisable Jul-Aug Last arrival 22.00hrs Last departure noon
Small, quiet touring site with good, clean facilities and panoramic views. Meticulously maintained. The site is located just off the A87 about 1m W of Invergarry, signed Faichem. A 2-acre site with 30 touring pitches.

JOHN O'GROATS

John O'Groats Caravan Site (ND382733)
KW1 4YS ☎ 01955 611329 Signposted
Nearby town: Wick
►►► **Family Park** ★ £7-£8 £7-£8 £7-£8
Open Apr-Oct Booking advisable Last arrival 22.00hrs Last departure noon
Good clean and attractive site in open position above the seashore and looking out towards the Orkney Islands, at the end of A9. Passenger ferry nearby. A 4-acre site with 90 touring pitches.

KINTORE

Hillhead Caravan Park (NJ777163)
AB51 OYX ☎ 01467 632809 Signposted
Nearby town: Inverurie
►►► **Family Park** £5.95-£7.50 £5.95-£7.50 £5.95-£7.50
Open 31 Mar-Oct Booking advisable at all times Last arrival 22.00hrs Last departure 13.00hrs
An attractive, peaceful site in the R Don Valley, about 1m from the village and A96. Follow B994 (signed Kemnay), turn right in 0.5m onto unclass rd (signed Kintore). A 1.5-acre site with 24 touring pitches and 5 statics.
Caravan repair service & caravan storage, shop.

Credit Cards

LAIDE

Gruinard Bay Caravan Park (NG906908)
Laide IV22 2ND
☎ 01445 731225 (from A835 Signposted
Nearby town: Aultbea
►►► **Family Park** fr £8 fr £8 fr £8
Open Apr-Oct Booking advisable Jul-Aug Last arrival 22.00hrs Last departure noon
Campers receive a warm welcome at this spotless, lovingly managed site on the outskirts of Laide. On A832, 300yds N of village. A 3.25-acre site with 43 touring pitches and 14 statics.
Dishwashing sinks/free hot water. Laundry service.

LAIRG

Dunroamin Caravan Park (NC585062)
Main St IV27 4AR ☎ 01549 402447
Signposted
►►► **Family Park**
Open Apr-Oct Booking advisable anytime Last arrival 23.00hrs Last departure noon
A small, attractive and well laid out site on A839 in village. A 4-acre site with 50 touring pitches and 10 statics.
Credit Cards

Woodend Caravan & Camping Site (NC551127)
Achnairn IV27 4DN ☎ 01549 402248 (A836 turn left onto A838 then 1st right signposted) Signposted
►►► **Family Park** ★ £5.50-£6.50 £5.50-£6.50 £5.50-£6.50
Open Apr-Sep Booking advisable Last arrival 23.00hrs
A clean, fresh site set in hilly moors and woodland with access to sea, beach, river and Loch Shin. 4m N of Lairg off A838, signed at Achnairn. A 4-acre site with 60 touring pitches and 5 statics.

LOCHALINE

Fiunary Camping & Caravanning Park (NM614467)
Morvern PA34 5XX ☎ 01967 421225 Signposted
Nearby town: Fort William
►►► **Family Park**
Open May-Oct (rs Apr hot water & showers not available) Booking advisable Last arrival 22.00hrs Last departure noon
A small, carefully maintained site with beautiful lochside views, quiet and secluded and in an area of great interest to naturalists. Signed 5m W of Lochaline and ferry on Loch Shore at Fiunary. A 3-acre site with 25 touring pitches and 2 statics.

LOSSIEMOUTH

Silver Sands Leisure Park (NJ205710)
Covesea, West Beach IV31 6SP
☎ 01343 813262 (2m W B9040) Signposted
►►►► **De-Luxe Park** £7.25-£10.75 £7.25-£10.75 £7.25-£10.75
Open Jun-Sep (rs Apr, May & Oct shops & entertainment restricted) Booking advisable Jul-Aug Last arrival 23.00hrs Last departure noon
A holiday park with entertainment for all during the peak season. From Lossiemouth follow B9040 to site. A 7-acre site with 140 touring pitches and 180 statics.
Childrens entertainment.
Credit Cards

MACDUFF

Wester Bonnyton Farm Site (NJ741638)
Gamrie AB45 3EP ☎ 01261 832470
► **Town & Country Pennant Park**
Open Mar-Oct Booking advisable
A farm site in a screened meadow, with level touring pitches enjoying views across Moray Firth. From A98 1m S of Macduff join B9031, signed Rosehearty, and site on right in 1.25m. A 1-acre site with 10 touring pitches and 18 statics.

NAIRN

Nairn Lochloy Holiday Park (NH895574)
East Beach IV12 4PH ☎ 01667 453764 Signposted
►►► **Family Park** ★ £7-£15 £7-£15 £7-£13
Open Mar-Oct Booking advisable Jun-Aug Last arrival 22.00hrs Last departure 14.00hrs
A level site bordered by the beach, the River Nairn and golf course. Signed off A96 in Nairn close to town centre. An 18.25-acre site with 100 touring pitches and 230 statics.
Discount on adjacent golf course.

Credit Cards

Delnies Woods Caravan Park (NH852552)
Delnies Wood IV12 5NX ☎ 01667 455281 Signposted
►►► **Family Park**
Open Etr-Oct Booking advisable end Jun-early Aug Last arrival 22.00hrs Last departure noon
An attractive site amongst pine trees. Situated about 3m W of Nairn on the A96. A 7-acre site with 50 touring pitches and 16 statics.

Credit Cards

Spindrift Caravan & Camping Site (NH863537)
Little Kildrummie IV12 5QU
☎ 01667 453992 (take B9090 S for 1.5m, turn right at sharp left hand bend signposted Kildrummie, site 400yds on left)
►►► **Family Park** ★ £5.50-£8.50 £5.50-£8.50 £5.50-£8.50
Open Apr-Oct Booking advisable Jul-Aug Last arrival 22.00hrs Last departure noon
An informal site in attractive setting with good facilities and first class maintenance. Signed off B9090, 2m S of Nairn. A 3-acre site with 40 touring pitches.
Fishing permits available from reception.

NORTH WATER BRIDGE

Dovecot Caravan Park (NO648663)
AB30 1QL ☎ 01674 840630 Signposted
►►► **Family Park** ★ £6.75-£7.75 £6.75-£7.75 £5.50-£6.50
Open Apr-Oct Booking advisable Jul & Aug for hook up Last arrival 20.00hrs Last departure noon
A level grassy site in a country area close to the A90, with mature trees screening one side and the R North Esk on the other. A handy overnight stop in a good touring area. Leave A90 at North Water Bridge on unclassified road signed Edzell/RAF Edzell, and site on left in 0.25m. A 6-acre site with 25 touring pitches and 44 statics.

POOLEWE

Camping & Caravanning Club Site (NG862812)
Inverewe Gardens IV22 2LF
☎ 01445 781249 (in season) & 01203 694995 (on A832, .25m N) Signposted
►►► **Family Park** ★ £8.70-£11.30 £8.70-£11.30 £8.70-£11.30
Open end Mar-early Nov Booking advisable bank hols & Jul-Aug Last arrival 21.00hrs Last departure noon
A well-run site located in Loch Ewe Bay, not far from Inverewe Gardens. On A832, .25m N of Poolewe village. Please see the advertisement on page 27 for details of Club Members' benefits. A 3-acre site with 55 touring pitches.

Credit Cards

REAY

Dunvegan Euro Campsite (NC960644)
KW14 7RQ ☎ 01847 81405 Signposted
► **Town & Country Pennant Park**
Open May-Oct Booking advisable at anytime Last arrival 22.00hrs Last departure noon
A lovingly maintained site with immaculate facilities. The site is adjacent to the A836 in the centre of the village. A 1-acre site with 20 touring pitches.

RESIPOLE (LOCH SUNART)

Resipole Farm (NM725639)
PH36 4HX ☎ 01967 431235 Signposted
Nearby town: Ardnamurchan

►►►► **De-Luxe Park** £9-£10 £9-£10 £9-£10
Open Apr-Sep (rs Oct shop closed) Booking advisable bank hols Last arrival 22.00hrs Last departure 11.00hrs
A well-managed site in beautiful surroundings, with deer frequently sighted. On A861 5m W of Strontian and 2m E of Salen. An 8-acre site with 45 touring pitches and 15 statics.
Private slipway, 9 hole golf.

Credit Cards

ROSEMARKIE

Camping & Caravanning Club Site (NH739569)
IV10 8UW
☎ 01381 621117 (in season) & 01203 694995 Signposted
Nearby town: Fortrose
►►► **Family Park** ★ £8.10-£10.30 £8.10-£10.30 £8.10-£10.30
Open end Mar-early Sep Booking advisable bank hols & Jul-Aug Last arrival 21.00hrs Last departure noon
A very clean and well-maintained site. At Rosemarkie turn right onto Promenade, and site is in 100 yards, or

contd.

turn right at Fortrose police station and follow signs. Please see the advertisement on page 27 for details of Club Members' benefits. A 4-acre site with 60 touring pitches.

Credit Cards

ST CYRUS

East Bowstrips Caravan Park (NO745654)
DD10 0DE ☎ 01674 850328 Signposted
Nearby town: Montrose

►►►► **De-Luxe Park** £6.50-£7.50 £6.50-£7.50 £5.50-£7.50
Open Etr or Apr-Oct Booking advisable Jun-Aug Last arrival 22.00hrs Last departure noon
A quiet, rural site close to seaside village, with thoughtfully modernised facilities and a particular welcome for the disabled. From A92 travelling N turn left after post office and hotel, follow unclass road, then take first L and second R. A 2-acre site with 30 touring pitches and 18 statics.

SCANIPORT

Scaniport Caravan & Camping Park (NH628398)
IV1 2DL ☎ 01463 751351
Nearby town: Inverness
► **Town & Country Pennant Park**
Open Etr-Sep Last arrival 23.45hrs Last departure 20.00hrs
A simple, pleasant site with some trees, set in hills, woods and moorland near canal. On B862 Inverness-Foyers road about 5m S of Inverness. Entrance to site is opposite shop at Scaniport. A 2-acre site with 30 touring pitches.
Dish washing sinks.

SCOURIE

Scourie Caravan & Camping Park (NC153446)
Harbour Rd IV27 4TG ☎ 01971 502060 & 502061 Signposted
►►► **Family Park**
Open Etr-Sep Last arrival 22.00hrs Last departure noon
An attractive and well-equipped site adjacent to beach and sea in centre of village off the Ullapool-Durness road A894. A 4-acre site with 60 touring pitches.

The AA pennant classification has been revised for 1998. Please read the explanation of the scheme on page 10.

SKYE, ISLE OF

EDINBANE

Loch Greshornish Caravan Site (NG343524)
Borve, Arnisort IV51 9PS ☎ 01470 582230 Signposted
Nearby town: Portree
►►► **Family Park** ★ £6-£7.50 £6-£7.50 £6-£7.50
Open Apr-Oct Booking advisable Jul-Aug Last arrival 22.00hrs Last departure noon
A pleasant, open site, mostly level and with a high standard of maintenance. Situated by the loch-shore at Edinbane, approx 12m from Portree on the A850 Dunvegan road. A 5-acre site with 130 touring pitches.

STONEHAVEN

Queen Elizabeth Caravan Site (NO875866)
AB3 2RD ☎ 01569 764041(in season) & 762001 Signposted
►►► **Family Park**
Open Apr-mid Oct Booking advisable anytime Last arrival 20.00hrs Last departure 10.00hrs
A gently sloping grass site offering a good range of recreational facilities, situated between a main road and seafront adjoining a public park. Situated at junc of A90 and B979. A 4.5-acre site with 35 touring pitches and 76 statics.
Site adjacent to Leisure Centre & outdoor pool.

TAIN

Meikle Ferry Caravan & Camping Park (NH748844)
IV19 1JX ☎ 01862 892292 2 miles north of Tain on A9. At roundabout take A836. In 200 yds turn right for park. Signposted
►►► **Family Park** ★ £7-£8.50 £7-£8.50 £4.50-£6
Open all year Booking advisable Jul-Aug Last arrival 22.00hrs Last departure noon
A pleasant family site with meticulously maintained facilities, on A9 N of Tain, at S end of Dornoch Firth Bridge. A 2-acre site with 30 touring pitches and 15 statics.
Restaurant adjacent to site.

TARLAND

Drummie Hill Caravan Park (NJ474045)
AB34 4UP ☎ 013398 81388 & 81264 Signposted
Nearby town: Aboyne
►►► **Family Park**
Open Apr-mid Oct Booking advisable Jul-Aug Last arrival 23.00hrs Last departure noon
A level, sheltered site screened by mature trees. Enter Tarland on B9119, bear left before bridge and continue for 600yds. Site is on left. A 4-acre site with 45 touring pitches and 80 statics.

THURSO

Thurso Caravan & Camping Site (ND111688)

Smith Ter, Scrabster Rd KW14 7JY ☎ 01847 894545 & 01955 607772 Signposted

Town & Country Pennant Park

Open May-Sep Booking advisable 14 days in advance Last arrival 22.00hrs Last departure noon

Exposed grassy site, set high above the coast on the W side of town with panoramic views out to sea. Signed on A882 on W edge of Thurso. A 4.5-acre site with 117 touring pitches and 10 statics.

ULLAPOOL

Broomfield Holiday Park (NH123939)

West Shore St IV26 2UR ☎ 01854 612020 & 612664 Signposted

► ► ► Family Park

Open Apr-Oct

A level grass site by the shore of Loch Broom close to the harbour and town centre. A 10-acre site with 140 touring pitches.

The AA pennant classification has been revised for 1998. Please read the explanation of the scheme on page 10.

CENTRAL SCOTLAND

This region includes the counties of Angus, Argyll & Bute, City of Edinburgh, Clackmannanshire, Dundee City, East Lothian, Falkirk, Fife, Inverclyde, Midlothian, Perthshire & Kinross, Stirling and West Lothian which reflect the recent national changes.

ABERFELDY

Aberfeldy Caravan Park (NN858495)

Dunkeld Rd PH15 2AQ ☎ 01887 820662

► ► ► Family Park ★ fr £8.90 fr £8.90 fr £7

Open late Mar-late Oct Booking advisable Jul-mid Sep Last arrival 20.00hrs Last departure noon

A very well-run and well-maintained site, with good facilities and some landscaping, at the eastern end of the town and lying between main road and banks of the River Tay. Good views from site of surrounding hills. Off A827 on E edge of town. A 4-acre site with 103 touring pitches and 30 statics.

Credit Cards

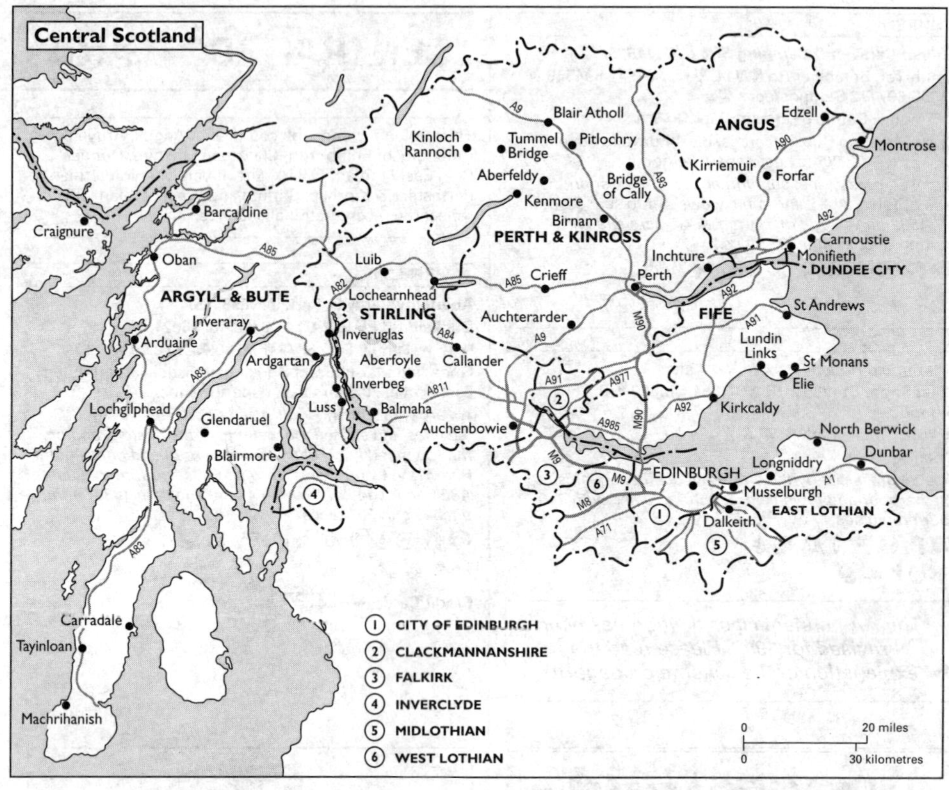

ABERFOYLE

Trossachs Holiday Park (NS544976)

FK8 3SA ☎ 01877 382614 (access on E side of A81 1m S of junc A821) Signposted

Nearby town: Stirling

▶ ▶ ▶ ▶ **De-Luxe Park** £8.50-£10.50 £8.50-£10.50 ▲ £8.50-£10.50

Open Mar-Oct Booking advisable anytime Last arrival 21.00hrs Last departure noon

An imaginatively designed terraced site offering a high degree of quality all round, with fine views across Flanders Moss. Sited off A81, 3m S of Aberfoyle. A 40-acre site with 45 touring pitches and 38 statics.

Cycle hire.

Credit Cards

Cobleland Campsite (NS531989)

FK8 3UX ☎ 01877 382392 (access on E side of A81 1m S of junc A821) Signposted

▶ ▶ ▶ **Family Park** ★ £7.90 £7.90 ▲ £7.90

Open Etr-29 Oct Booking advisable bank hols & May-Aug Last arrival 20.00hrs Last departure noon

Set within the Queen Elizabeth Forest Park, this grass and tree-studded site offers seclusion, views, forest walks and free fishing on the River Forth which borders the camping area. Signed on unclass road off A81 approx 1.5 miles S of Aberfoyle. An 8-acre site with 100 touring pitches.

Fishing & swimming in river.

Credit Cards

ARDGARTAN

Ardgartan Campsite (NN275030)

G83 7AL ☎ 01301 702293 & 0131 314 6100 Signposted

Nearby town: Helensburgh

▶ ▶ ▶ **Family Park** ★ £7 £7 ▲ £7

Open Etr-29 Sep Booking advisable Jul-Aug Last arrival 22.30hrs Last departure noon

Situated on a small promontory alongside Loch Long with access to shingle beach; a grassy site on two levels. Direct access from A83 beside Loch ong at Ardgartan before road turns to climb. A 17-acre site with 160 touring pitches.

Slip-way for launching small boats.

Credit Cards

ARDUAINE

Arduaine Caravan & Camping Park (NM800101)
PA34 4XA ☎ 01852 200331 Signposted
Nearby town: Kilmelford
Town & Country Pennant Park
Open Mar-Oct Booking advisable Spring bank hol & Jul-Aug Last arrival 22.00hrs Last departure noon
Gently sloping grass site pleasantly situated by the seashore beside a small jetty with views of Shuna, Scarba, Jura and Luing. Access is from the A816. A 5-acre site with 40 touring pitches.
Free dinghy launching into sea.

AUCHENBOWIE

Auchenbowie Caravan & Camping Site (NS795880)
FK7 8HE ☎ 01324 822141
Nearby town: Stirling
►►► **Family Park** £7 £7 £5.50-£7
Open Apr-Oct Booking advisable mid Jul-mid Aug Last departure noon
A mainly level, grassy site in quiet rural location .5m S of junction 9 of M9. Turn right off A872 for half a mile, signposted. A 3.5-acre site with 60 touring pitches and 7 statics.
Paddling pool.
See advertisement under STIRLING

Credit Cards

AUCHTERARDER

Auchterarder Caravan Park (NN964138)
Nether Coul PH3 1ET
☎ 01764 663119 (1m E off B8062)
Signposted
Nearby town: Perth
►►► **Family Park** £8 £8 £6-£8
Open all year Booking advisable Jul-Aug Last arrival 22.00hrs Last departure noon
A small, level touring site, well-run and well-maintained. From N turn right off A9 on A823 to Auchterarder, after 2 miles turn left onto B8062 signed Dunning. Turn left after 100m into site. A 4-acre site with 23 touring pitches.
Private fishing.

BALMAHA

Camping & Caravnning Club Site (NN407927)
Milarrochy Bay G63 0AL ☎ 01360 870236
Signposted
►►► **Family Park**
Open mid Mar-beg Nov Booking advisable
Situated on the quieter side of Loch Lomond next to the 75,000 acre Queen Elizabeth Forest. Leave A811 at S end of loch by the B837 to Balmaha, through village for 1.5m. A 7-acre site with 140 touring pitches.

Cashel Caravan & Camping Site (NS396939)
G63 0AW ☎ 01360 870234 (on B837)
Nearby town: Drymen
►►► **Family Park** ★ £7.90 £7.90 £7.90
Open Etr-30 Oct Booking advisable public hols & Jul-Aug Last arrival 20.00hrs Last departure noon
An attractive and well-wooded site, lying on the eastern shores of Loch Lomond within the Queen Elizabeth Forest Park, offering seclusion to campers and splendid views over the loch. Caravanners should beware of a steep hill at a quick right hand turn when leaving Balmaha. Situated 3m beyond Balmaha village on A837 Drymen-Rowardennan road. A 12-acre site with 100 touring pitches.
Boating on Loch Lomond.

Credit Cards

BARCALDINE

Camping & Caravanning Club Site (NM966420)
PA37 1SG
☎ 01631 720348 (in season) & 01203 694995
Signposted
Nearby town: Oban

►►►► **De-Luxe Park** ★ £8.70-£11.30
£8.70-£11.30 ▲ £8.70-£11.30
Open end Mar-early Nov Booking advisable bank hols & Jul-Aug Last arrival 21.00hrs Last departure noon
A sheltered site within the grounds of a former walled garden, bordered by Barcaldine Forest, close to Loch Creran, situated 10m N of Oban off A828. Please see the advertisement on page 27 for details of Club Members' benefits. A 4-acre site with 75 touring pitches.

Credit Cards

BIRNAM

Erigmore House Holiday Park (NO036416)
PH8 9XX ☎ 01350 727236 Signposted
Nearby town: Perth

►►►► **De-Luxe Park**
Open Mar-Oct Booking advisable all times Last arrival 23.30hrs Last departure noon
A predominantly touring site in the grounds of 18th-century Erigmore House which has a wide variety of unusual trees including Japanese maple and cherry. Site well-secluded from the main road and a considerable degree of privacy can be found. Situated on B898. An 18-acre site with 24 touring pitches and 183 statics.
Sauna, solarium & spa bath.

Credit Cards

BLAIR ATHOLL

River Tilt Caravan Park (NN875653)
PH18 5TE ☎ 01796 481467 Signposted

►►►► **De-Luxe Park** ▲
Open mid Mar-Nov Booking advisable Jul-Aug Last arrival 21.00hrs Last departure 11.00hrs
Level, grass site with trees and bushes set in hilly woodland country on the banks of the River Tilt, next to golf course. 7m N of Pitlochry on A9, take B8079 to Blair Atholl, and site at rear of Tilt Hotel.. A 2-acre site with 37 touring pitches and 92 statics.
Multi-gym, sauna & solarium.

Credit Cards

See advertisement under PITLOCHRY

Blair Castle Caravan Park (NN874656)
PH18 5SR ☎ 01796 481263 Signposted
Nearby town: Pitlochry

►►►► **De-Luxe Park** £8-£9.50 £8-£9.50
▲ £6.50-£9
Open Apr-late Oct (rs Apr-Jun & Sep-mid Oct restaurant) Booking advisable bank hols & Jul-Aug Last arrival 21.30hrs Last departure noon
Attractive site set in impressive seclusion within the Atholl estate, surrounded by mature woodland and the R Tilt. From A9 junc with B8079 At Aldclune, travel NE to Blair Atholl, and site on right after crosing bridge in village. A 32-acre site with 283 touring pitches and 112 statics.

Credit Cards

BLAIRMORE

Gairletter Caravan Park (NS193845)
PA23 8TP ☎ 01369 810208 & 810220
Nearby town: Dunoon
►►► **Family Park**
A quiet lochside site, family run and long established, with a new toilet block and recreation facilities. From Dunoon take A885 to Ardbeg, then A880 to Blairmore. Site at water's edge on right in .5m. A 1.5-acre site with 12 touring pitches and 28 statics.
Pool table

BOTHWELL

BRIDGE OF CALLY

Corriefodly Holiday Park (NO134513)
PH10 7JG ☎ 01250 886236 Signposted
Nearby town: Blairgowrie
►►►► **De-Luxe Park** ★ £7.50-£9 £7.50-£9 £5-£7
Open early Dec-early Nov Booking advisable bank hols & Jul-Aug Last arrival 22.00hrs Last departure noon
A secluded riverbank site in a wooded area 150 yards N of Bridge of Cally on A924. A 17.5-acre site with 38 touring pitches and 72 statics.
Bowling green & fishing on site.

CALLANDER

Callander Holiday Park (NN615073)
Invertrossachs Rd FK17 8HW ☎ 01877 330265
Signposted
►►►► **De-Luxe Park** £11 £11
Open 15 Mar-Oct Booking advisable Jun-Aug Last arrival 22.00hrs Last departure noon
An attractive terraced park with glorious views over the surrounding countryside. From A84 in centre of Callander take A81 Glasgow road over bridge, then turn right in 200 yards towards Invertrossachs road, and site in .5 mile. A 10-acre site with 28 touring pitches and 110 statics.
Fishing on site.

Gart Caravan Park (NN643070)
The Gart FK17 8LE ☎ 01877 330002
Signposted
►►►► **De-Luxe Park** £11-£11.50 £11-£11.50
Open Etr or Apr-15 Oct Booking advisable Last arrival 22.00hrs Last departure noon
A well-screened site bordered by trees and shrubs and with helpful owners. 1m E of Callander on A84. A 25-acre site with 122 touring pitches and 66 statics.
contd.

Fishing on site.

Credit Cards

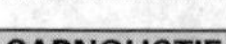

CARNOUSTIE

Woodlands Caravan Park (NO560350)
Newton Rd DD7 6HR ☎ 01241 854430 & 853246 Signposted
►►► **Family Park**
Open late Mar-early Oct Booking advisable Jul-mid Aug Last arrival 21.00hrs Last departure noon
An excellent, well-maintained site with good facilities. Set in a quiet area of town, well-signed from A930. A 5.5-acre site with 108 touring pitches and 4 statics.

CARRADALE

Carradale Bay Caravan Site (NR815385)
PA28 6QG ☎ 01583 431665 Signposted
Nearby town: Campbeltown
►►► **Family Park** £7.50-£12.80 £7.50-£12.80 £7.50-£12.80
Open Etr-Sep Booking advisable bank hols & Jul-Aug Last arrival 22.00hrs Last departure noon
A beautiful, natural site on the sea's edge with superb views over Kilbrannan Sound to Isle of Arran. Approach from north is via Tarbert, leaving by A83 Campbeltown road; within 5m turn onto B8001, then B842 Carradale road. This is a single-track road with passing places. In Carradale take road to the pier, site is in .5m. An 8-acre site with 75 touring pitches and 3 statics.
Canoe use.

CRIEFF

Crieff Holiday Village (NN857225)
Turret Bank PH7 4JN
☎ 01764 653513 Signposted
►►► **Family Park** ★ £8-£9 £8-£9 £7.50-£8
Open all year Booking advisable Jul-Aug Last arrival mdnt
A level site by the riverside, Im W of Crieff on A85. A 3-acre site with 40 touring pitches and 40 statics.

Credit Cards

DALKEITH

Fordel (NT359668)
Lauder Rd EH22 2PH
☎ 0131 663 3046 & 0131 660 3921 Signposted
►►► **Family Park** ★ £8.50-£12.50 £8.50-£12.50 £7-£8
Open Apr-Sep Booking advisable Jul-Aug Last departure noon
A small, tree lined, grassy site on A68 1.5m S of Dalkeith. A 3-acre site with 35 touring pitches.

Credit Cards

DUNBAR

Thurston Manor Holiday Home Park (NT712745)
Innerwick EH42 1SA ☎ 01368 840643 (.5m from A1) Signposted
►►►► **De-Luxe Park** ★ £10-£14.50 £10-£14.50 £7-£14.50
Open Mar-Oct Booking advisable Etr, bank hols & high season Last arrival 9.00hrs Last departure noon
A developing site with good facilities and level pitches. From A1, 6m N of Cockburnspath, take unclass rd signed Innerwick, in .5m turn R, and site in .5m on R. A 250-acre site with 100 touring pitches and 200 statics.
Private lake, pony treking, fitness room, sauna.

Credit Cards

Camping & Caravanning Club Site (NT723773)
Barns Ness EH42 1QP ☎ 01368 863536 (in season) & 01203 694995 (4m E) Signposted
► **Town & Country Pennant Park** ★ £8.10-£10.30 £8.10-£10.30 £8.10-£10.30
Open end Mar-early Nov Booking advisable bank hols & high season Last arrival 21.00hrs Last departure noon
A grassy, landscaped site close to the foreshore and lighthouse on a coastline noted for its natural and geological history. 4m E of Dunbar, approached off A1. Please see the advertisement on page 27 for details of Club Members' benefits. A 10-acre site with 80 touring pitches.

Credit Cards

DUNKELD

See **Birnam**

DUNOON

See **Blairmore**

EDINBURGH

Mortonhall Caravan Park (NT265680)
38 Mortonhall Gate EH16 6TJ ☎ 0131 664 1533 Signposted
►►►► **De-Luxe Park**
Open 28 Mar-Oct Booking advisable Jul-Aug Last arrival 22.00hrs Last departure noon
Located on the S side of Edinburgh within 20 minutes' car ride of the city centre, this site is part of a 200-acre

estate surrounding the 18th-century Mortonhall mansion designed by Robert Adam. A large site with high standards. Take the new city bypass to junction with A702 and follow signs to Mortonhall. A 22-acre site with 250 touring pitches and 18 statics.

EDZELL

Glenesk Caravan Park (NO602717)

DD9 7YP ☎ 01356 648565 & 648523 (1m NW off B966) Signposted

Nearby town: Brechin

▶▶▶ **Family Park** £6.50-£9 £6.50-£9 ▲ £5-£6

Open Apr-Oct Booking advisable public hols & mid Jun-Aug Last arrival 22.00hrs Last departure 16.00hrs

A carefully improved and maintained woodland site surrounding a small fishing lake. Situated on unclass road to Glen Esk, 1m N of the B966. An 8-acre site with 45 touring pitches and 10 statics.

ELIE

Shell Bay Caravan Park (NO465005)

KY9 1HB ☎ 01333 330283 Signposted

Nearby town: Leven

▶▶▶ **Family Park** £9-£11 £9-£11 ▲ £7.50-£9.50

contd.

Open 21 Mar-Oct Booking advisable Jul-Aug Last arrival 20.00hrs Last departure noon

Large, mainly static holiday site utilizing natural coastal area of a secluded bay. 1.5m NW of Elie off A917, signed off unclass road, with direct access to beach. A 5-acre site with 120 touring pitches and 250 statics.

Credit Cards

FORFAR

Lochside Caravan Park (NO450505)

Forfar Loch Country Park DD8 1BT ☎ 01307 464201 & 468917 Signposted

►►►► **De-Luxe Park**

Open late Mar-early Oct Booking advisable mid Jun-Aug Last arrival 21.00hrs Last departure noon

A pleasant, well laid out site close to the loch and leisure centre. Well-signed off ring road (A94). A 4.75-acre site with 74 touring pitches.

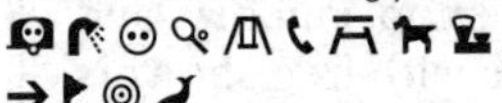

See advertisement on page 233.

GLENDARUEL

Glendaruel Caravan Park (NR005865)

PA22 3AB ☎ 01369 820267 Signposted

►►► **Family Park** ★ £8-£9.50 £8-£9.50 £7.50-£9.50

Open Apr-Oct Booking advisable Spring bank hol & mid Jul-Aug Last arrival 22.00hrs Last departure noon

Attractive, grassy, level site in 23 acres of wooded parkland in a valley surrounded by mountains. Situated off A886, with many rare species of trees on site. A 3-acre site with 40 touring pitches and 30 statics.

Bicycles for hire, fishing sea trout & salmon.

Credit Cards

INCHTURE

Inchmartine Caravan Park & Nurseries (NO263277)

Dundee Rd PH14 9QQ ☎ 01821 670212 & 686251 Signposted

Nearby town: Perth

► **Town & Country Pennant Park** £8 £8

Open Mar-Oct Last arrival 20.00hrs Last departure noon

A quiet site with excellent toilet facilities, adjacent to A85 Perth-Dundee road. An 8-acre site with 45 touring pitches.

The AA pennant classification has been revised for 1998. Please read the explanation of the scheme on page 10.

INVERARAY

Argyll Caravan Park (NN075055)

PA32 8XT ☎ 01499 302285 Signposted

►►►► **De-Luxe Park** ★ £8-£9.50 £8-£9.50 £6.50-£8.20

Open Apr-Oct Last arrival anytime Last departure noon

A mainly grassy site with some hardstandings on the shores of Loch Fyne, with ample on-site facilities. 2.5m S of Inveraray on A83. A 6-acre site with 140 touring pitches and 240 statics.

Mini football pitch.

Credit Cards

INVERBEG

Inverbeg Holiday Park (NS348983)

G83 8PD ☎ 01436 860267 & 0131 654 0142 Signposted

Nearby town: Luss

►►► **Family Park**

Open Mar-Oct Booking advisable Spring bank hol, Jul-Aug & hol wknds Last arrival 23.00hrs Last departure noon

A well-maintained site on a small promontory alongside Loch Lomond with direct access to shingle beach and a small marina. Signed with access off A82, 4m N of Luss. Very fast section of road and great care should be taken. A 4-acre site with 35 touring pitches and 120 statics.

Sailing & fishing.

INVERUGLAS

Loch Lomond Holiday Park (NN320092)

G83 7DW ☎ 01301 704224 Signposted

Nearby town: Helensburgh

►►►► **De-Luxe Park** ★ £7-£12.50 £7-£12.50

Open Mar-Oct (rs Dec-Jan main amenity building restricted hours) Booking advisable May-Aug Last arrival 21.00hrs Last departure 11.45hrs

A lovely setting on the shores of Loch Lomond with views of forests and mountains, and boat hire available. Situated on A 82 between Tarbet and Ardlui. A 6-acre site with 18 touring pitches and 72 statics.

Satellite TV, pool tables, boat hire.

Credit Cards

KENMORE

Kenmore Caravan & Camping Park (NN772458)
PH15 2HN ☎ 01887 830226 Signposted
Nearby town: Aberfeldy

▶▶▶▶ **De-Luxe Park** ★ £8-£9 £7-£8
▲ £7-£8
Open 25 Mar-Oct Booking advisable mid Jul-mid Aug Last arrival 22.00hrs Last departure 14.00hrs
A pleasant riverside site with an air of spaciousness and a very good licensed bar/restaurant. On A827 opposite Loch Tay 8.5 miles W of Aberfeldy. A 12-acre site with 160 touring pitches and 60 statics.
Cycle hire, 9 hole golf, games & TV room.

Credit Cards

KINLOCH RANNOCH

Kilvrecht Campsite (NN623567)
PH17 ☎ 01350 727284
▷ **Town & Country Pennant Park** ★ fr £5 fr £5
▲ fr £3
Open 26 Mar-25 Oct
A basic site in a large clearing in the forest, about .75 mile from Loch Rannoch shore, with no hot water.

Approach along unclass road along loch shore with Forestry Commission signs. A 17-acre site with 60 touring pitches.

KIRKCALDY

Dunnikier Caravan Park (NT283940)
Dunnikier Way KY1 3ND ☎ 01592 267563 & 266701 Signposted
▶▶▶ **Family Park** ★ £8-£10 £8-£10 ▲ £5.50-£8
Open Mar-Jan Booking advisable peak periods Last arrival 19.00hrs Last departure noon
A level site set in mature parkland adjacent to the B981 but screened by trees. An 8-acre site with 60 touring pitches.

KIRRIEMUIR

Drumshademuir Caravan Park (NO381509)
Roundyhill DD8 1QT ☎ 01575 573284 Signposted
Nearby town: Forfar

▶▶▶▶ **De-Luxe Park** £8.25-£9 £8.25-£9 ▲ £6.50
Open mid Mar-end Oct Booking advisable public hols & Jun-Aug Last arrival 23.00hrs Last departure 18.00hrs
Part-sloping grass site in valley overlooking farmland, 2.5m S of Kirriemuir on A928. A 7.5-acre site with 80 touring pitches and 34 statics.
Bar food & putting.

LOCHEARNHEAD

Balquhidder Braes Caravan Park (NN581218)
Balquhidder Station FK19 8NX ☎ 01567 830293 Signposted
Nearby town: Callander
▷ **Town & Country Pennant Park** ★ £7-£9 fr £7
▲ £6-£8
Open Mar-Oct Booking advisable bank hols & Jul-Aug Last arrival 22.00hrs Last departure 11.30hrs
A level grass site with some trees for shelter, a good base for hill walking and water sports. 10m N of Callander on A84, 1m before Lochearnhead. A 4-acre site with 50 touring pitches and 10 statics.
Dish washing room.

LOCHGILPHEAD

Lochgilphead Caravan Site (NR859881)
PA31 8NX ☎ 01546 602003 Signposted
▶▶▶ **Family Park** ★ £7.50-£8.50 £7.50-£8.50
▲ £7.50-£8.50
Open Apr-Oct Booking advisable Jul-Aug

contd.

Mainly level, grassy site close to the shore of Loch Gilp, an inlet of Loch Fyne. Situated beside the A83 and convenient to the town centre facilities. Fishing and sailing available on the Loch. A 7-acre site with 70 touring pitches and 30 statics.

Mountain bike hire.

Credit Cards

LONGNIDDRY

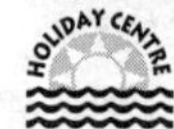

Seton Sands Holiday Village (NT420759)

EH32 0QF ☎ 01875 813333

Nearby town: Port Seton

★ £4-£10 £4-£10

Open Mar-Oct Booking advisable Last arrival 23.00hrs Last departure noon

A large, mainly static park, with reasonable touring facilities on a grassy paddock near the road. Take A1 to Tranent slip road, then B6371 to Cockenzie, and right onto B1348. Park 1m on left. A 1.75-acre site with 60 touring pitches and 120 statics.

Credit Cards

LUIB

Glendochart Caravan Park (NN477278)

FK20 8QT ☎ 01567 820637

Signposted

Nearby town: Stirling

►►► **Family Park**

Open Etr-Oct (rs Mar-Etr no showers) Booking advisable Jul & Aug Last arrival 22.00hrs Last departure noon

A small, well-maintained site with imaginative landscaping. Set on hillside in Glendochart with glorious mountain and hill-country views, 5m E of Crianlarich on the A85. A 7-acre site with 45 touring pitches and 40 statics.

LUNDIN LINKS

Woodland Gardens Caravan & Camping Site (NO418031)

Blindwell Rd KY8 5QG ☎ 01333 360319 (turn off A915 at E end of town, signposted on A915) Signposted

Nearby town: Leven

►►► **Family Park** £6.60 £6.60 £6.60

Open Mar-Oct Booking advisable Jul-Aug Last arrival 22.00hrs Last departure noon

A secluded and sheltered site off the A917 coast road at Largo. Approach along narrow, well signed road. A 1-acre site with 20 touring pitches and 5 statics.

LUSS

Camping & Caravanning Club Site (NS360936)

G83 8NT ☎ 01436 860658 (in season) & 01203 694995 (.25m N on A82) Signposted

Nearby town: Dumbarton

► **Town & Country Pennant Park** ★ £9.10-£12.10

Open end Mar-early Nov Booking advisable bank hols & Jul-Aug Last arrival 21.00hrs Last departure noon

Lovely grass tenting site on W shore of Loch Lomond. Motorvans and caravans of Club members only permitted. .25m N of Luss village on A82 Glasgow-Fort William road. Please see the advertisement on page 27 for details of Club Members' benefits. A 10-acre site with 90 touring pitches.

Credit Cards

MACHRIHANISH

Camping & Caravanning Club Site (NR647208)

East Trodigal PA28 6PT ☎ 01586 810366 (in season) & 01203 694995

Nearby town: Campbeltown

►►► **Family Park** ★ £8.10-£10.30 £8.10-£10.30 £8.10-£10.30

Open end Mar-Sep Booking advisable bank hols & high season Last arrival 21.00hrs Last departure noon

A very open site with superb sea views, situated adjacent to the golf course. On B843 .75m before village. Please see the advertisement on page 27 for details of Club Members' benefits. A 10-acre site with 96 touring pitches.

Credit Cards

MONIFIETH

Riverview Caravan Park (NO502322)

Milton Mill DD5 4NZ ☎ 01241 853246 Signposted

Nearby town: Dundee

►►► **Family Park**

Open Apr-Oct Booking advisable Jul-Aug Last arrival 22.00hrs Last departure 12.30hrs

A seafront site in a quiet location with direct access to the beach, and close to town centre and amenities. Signs from A930 when approaching from north. No signs on south approach but follow signs for Barry Links. An 8-acre site with 165 touring pitches and 2 statics.

MONTROSE

South Links Caravan Park (NO725575)

Traill Dr DD10 8EJ ☎ 01674 72026 & 72105 Signposted

►►► **Family Park**

Open late Mar-early Oct Booking advisable mid Jun-Aug Last arrival 21.00hrs Last departure noon

A well-maintained site with good facilities, partly overlooked by a processing plant. From A92 follow signs for golf course. A 10.75-acre site with 172 touring pitches.

MOTHERWELL

Strathclyde Country Park Caravan Site (NS717585)
366 Hamilton Rd ML1 3ED ☎ 01698 266155 Signposted
Nearby town: Hamilton
►►► **Family Park** ★ £7.75 £7.75 ▲ £3.50-£6.65
Open Apr-Oct Booking advisable Jun-Aug Last arrival 10.30hrs Last departure noon
A level grass site situated in a country park amidst woodland and meadowland with lots of attractions. Direct access to park from junc 5 of M74. 250 touring pitches.
See advertisement under BOTHWELL

MULL, ISLE OF

CRAIGNURE

Shieling Holidays (NM724369)
PA65 6AY ☎ 01680 812496 Signposted
Nearby town: Tobermory
►►► **Family Park** ★ £9-£10.50 £9-£10.50 ▲ £9-£10.50
Open Apr-Oct Booking advisable Spring bank hol & Jul-Aug Last arrival 22.00hrs Last departure noon
A lovely site on the water's edge with spectacular views. Less than 1m from ferry landing. A 7-acre site with 30 touring pitches and 12 statics.
Adventure playground, boat hire.

Credit Cards

MUSSELBURGH

Drum Mohr Caravan Park (NT373734)
Levenhall EH21 8JS ☎ 0131 665 6867 (1.5m E between B1361 & B1348) Signposted
►►►► **De-Luxe Park** £8-£9 £8-£9 ▲ £8-£9
Open Mar-Oct Booking advisable Jul-Aug Last arrival 22.00hrs Last departure noon
This attractive park is set 2 miles east of Musselburgh between the A198 and B1348. A 9-acre site with 120 touring pitches.
See advertisement under Preliminary Section

NORTH BERWICK

Tantallon Caravan Park (NT570850)
Lime Grove E39 5NJ ☎ 01620 893348 Signposted
►►► **Family Park** ▲
Open Mar-Oct Booking advisable Jul-Aug Last arrival 20.00hrs Last departure noon
Level grass site in meadowland in urban area with direct access to sea and beach. Located off A198 Dunbar road. A 10-acre site with 250 touring pitches and 60 statics.

OBAN

Oban Divers Caravan Park (NM841277)
Glenshellach Rd PA34 4QJ ☎ 01631 562755 Signposted
►►►► **De-Luxe Park** ★ £6-£8 £6-£8 ▲ £5-£8
Open 15 Mar-Nov Booking advisable Etr, Whit & Jul-Aug
A well-maintained site amidst mountain scenery with a stream running through. The site specialises in facilities for divers. S out of Oban on the one-way system signed for ferry. Before ferry turn go left for Glenshellach, signed in .5m. A 4-acre site with 50 touring pitches.

PERTH

Cleeve Caravan Park (NO097227)
Glasgow Rd PH2 0PH ☎ 01738 639521 & 475211
►►►► **De-Luxe Park** ★ fr £8.90 ▲ fr £8.90
Open late Mar-late Oct Booking advisable Jul-mid Sep Last arrival 21.00hrs Last departure noon
Mature woodland surrounds this park, which offers pitches on terraced levels or in a walled garden. All facilities immaculately maintained. Adjacent to the A93 Perth to Glasgow road, 2m W of Perth. A 5.5-acre site with 100 touring pitches.
contd.

Free use of microwave.

Credit Cards

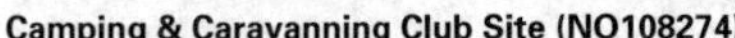

Camping & Caravanning Club Site (NO108274)
Scone Racecourse, Scone PH2 6BB ☎ 01738 552323 (in season) & 01203 694995 (adjacent to racecourse off A93) Signposted

►►► **Family Park** ★ £9.10-£12.10 £9.10-£12.10 £9.10-£12.10

Open end Mar-early Nov Booking advisable bank hols & peak periods Last arrival 21.00hrs Last departure noon

A sheltered site in wooded area adjacent to the racecourse off A93, 1m N of Perth. Please see the advertisement on page 27 for details of Club Members' benefits. A 12-acre site with 150 touring pitches and 20 statics.

Recreation room.table tennis.

Credit Cards

PITLOCHRY

Faskally Caravan Park (NN916603)
PH16 5LA ☎ 01796 472007 Signposted

►►►► **De-Luxe Park**

Open 15 Mar-Oct Booking advisable Jul-Aug Last arrival 23.00hrs

A secluded riverbank site in sloping meadowland surrounded by trees. 1.5 miles N of Pitlochry on B8019. A 23-acre site with 255 touring pitches and 65 statics.

Steam room, spa, sauna & mini golf.

Credit Cards

Milton of Fonab Caravan Site (NN945573)
PH16 5NA ☎ 01796 472882 (.5m S) Signposted

►►►► **De-Luxe Park** £9-£9.50 £9-£9.50 £9-£9.50

Open Apr-Oct Booking advisable Jul-Aug Last arrival 21.00hrs Last departure 13.00hrs

Level, grass site with mature trees on banks of River Tummel, .5m S of town off A924. A 12-acre site with 154 touring pitches and 36 statics.

Mountain bike hire, free trout fishing.

ST ANDREWS

Craigtoun Meadows Holiday Park (NO482150)
Mount Melville KY16 8PQ ☎ 01334 475959 Signposted

►►►►► **Premier Park** ★ £11.75-£12.75
£11.75-£12.75 ▲ £9.50-£12.75
Open Mar-Oct Booking advisable bank hols & Jun-Aug Last arrival 21.00hrs Last departure 13.00hrs
An attractive site set unobtrusively in mature woodlands with large pitches in hedged paddocks, 2m from sea and sandy beaches. 2m from St Andrews on the Craigtoun road. A 10-acre site with 98 touring pitches and 143 statics.
Adult mini-gymnasium.

Credit Cards

Kinkell Braes Caravan Site (NO522156)
KY16 8PX ☎ 01334 474250
►►► **Family Park**
Open 21 Mar-Oct Booking advisable Jun-Aug Last departure noon
A mainly static site with touring area giving views across St Andrews and the Eden estuary. On A917 1m S of St Andrews. A 4-acre site with 100 touring pitches and 392 statics.

Credit Cards

ST MONANS

St Monans Caravan Park (NO529019)
KY10 2DN ☎ 01333 730778 & 310185 Signposted
Nearby town: St Andrews
► **Town & Country Pennant Park** ▲
Open 21 Mar-Oct Booking advisable Jul-Aug Last arrival 22.00hrs Last departure noon
Mainly static site on fringe of coastal village adjacent to main road and public park. On A917, 100yds E of St Monans. A 1-acre site with 18 touring pitches and 112 statics.

STIRLING

See **Auchenbowie**

TARBERT

See **Tayinloan**

TAYINLOAN

Point Sands Holiday Park (NR698484)
Point Sands PA29 6XG ☎ 01583 441263 Signposted
►►► **Family Park** £9-£12 £8-£12 ▲ £6-£10
Open Apr-Oct Booking advisable Jul-Aug Last arrival 23.00hrs Last departure 21.00hrs

contd.

Attractive level site by lovely safe sandy beach on western shore of Kintyre peninsula, with superb views of Gigha, Islay and Jura.
direct access from A83 at Tayinloan. A 15-acre site with 60 touring pitches and 70 statics.

→

Credit Cards 

TUMMEL BRIDGE

Tummel Valley Holiday Park (NN764592)
PH16 5SA ☎ 01882 634221 Signposted
Nearby town: Pitlochry

►►►► **De-Luxe Park** ★ £9-£15 £9-£15 £7-£13
Open Mar-Oct Booking advisable Jun-Aug Last arrival 23.00hrs Last departure 14.00hrs
Well-developed site amongst mature forest in this attractive valley. From A9 N of Pitlochry turn W on B8019. A 55-acre site with 50 touring pitches and 130 statics.
Bicycle hire, crazy golf, fishing rod hire.

→

Credit Cards

SOUTHERN LOWLANDS & BORDERS

This region includes the counties of City of Glasgow, Dumfries & Galloway, East Ayrshire, East Dunbartonshire, East Renfrewshire, North Ayrshire, North Lanarkshire, Renfrewshire, Scottish Borders, South Ayrshire, South Lanarkshire, West Dumbartonshire which reflect the recent national changes.

ANNAN

Galabank Caravan Park (NY192676)
North St DG12 5BQ ☎ 01461 203311 ext 67257
Signposted
►**Town & Country Pennant Park**
Open Etr-Sep
A tidy, well-maintained grassy little site close to the centre of town but with pleasant rural views, and skirted by River Annan. Follow B721 into town centre, turn rt at traffic lights into Lady St and site 500yds on left. A 1-acre site with 30 touring pitches.

→

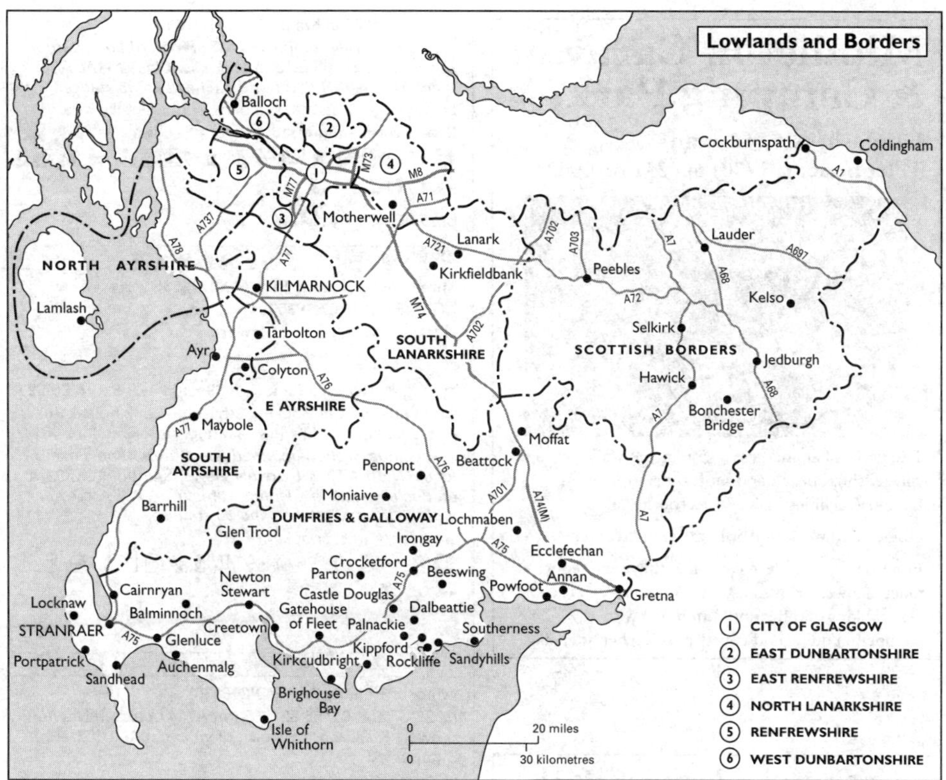

ARRAN, ISLE OF

LAMLASH

Middleton Caravan & Camping Park (NS027301)
KA27 8NN ☎ 01770 600251 & 600255
Signposted
▶▶▶ **Family Park** ★ fr £7.50 fr £7 fr £6.50
Open late Apr-mid Oct Booking advisable Jul-Aug (for static caravans only) Last arrival 21.30hrs Last departure noon no cars by caravans
A grassy site sheltered by hills and mature trees, with lovely views. Close to sea and village amenities in a very pleasant location. A 3.5-acre site with 70 touring pitches and 60 statics.
See advertisement on page 242

AUCHENMALG

Cock Inn Caravan Park (NX238518)
DG8 0JT ☎ 01581 500227 Signposted
Nearby town: Stranraer
▶▶▶ **Family Park** £7-£11.50 £7-£11.50 £6-£8.50
Open Mar-Oct Booking advisable bank hols & Jul-Aug Last arrival 22.00hrs Last departure 11.00hrs
A grassy site in meadowland, close to sea, beach and main (A747 Glenluce-Port William) road. Overlooks Luce Bay. A 2-acre site with 40 touring pitches and 80 statics.
See advertisement on page 241

AYR

Heads of Ayr Leisure Park (NS300184)
Dunure Rd KA7 4LD ☎ 01292 442269 Signposted
▶▶▶ **Family Park** ★ £8-£10.50 £7-£9 £7-£10.50
Open Mar-Nov Booking advisable bank hols & Jul-Aug Last arrival 23.30hrs Last departure 15.00hrs
A small family-run site with attractive, well-screened pitches, .5m from beach overlooking Firth of Clyde. On R of A719 Ayr to Dunure road, 5m S of Ayr. An 8-acre site with 36 touring pitches and 126 statics.

BALLOCH

Tullichewan Caravan Park (NS383816)
Old Luss Rd G83 8QP ☎ 01389 759475 Signposted
▶▶▶ **Family Park** ★ £8-£11.50 £8-£11.50 £8-£11.50
Open all year Booking advisable bank hols & Jul-Aug

contd.

Last arrival 22.00hrs Last departure noon
A popular, well-equipped site at S end of Loch Lomond, surrounded by woodland and hills. Close to the A82. A 9-acre site with 120 touring pitches and 35 statics.
Leisure suite - sauna, spa bath, sunbeds.Bike hire.
See advertisement under Colour Section

Credit Cards

BALMINNOCH

Three Lochs Holiday Park (NX272655)
DG8 OEP ☎ 01671 830304
Nearby town: Newton Stewart

►►►► **De-Luxe Park** ★ £9-£10 £9-£10 ▲ £6-£9
Open Etr-mid Oct Booking advisable bank hols & Jul-Aug Last arrival 22.00hrs Last departure 11.00hrs
A spacious, well-maintained site in moorland close to lochs, N off A75, with lovely views. Signed off B7027 on an unclass road in Glenluce direction. . A 15-acre site with 45 touring pitches and 90 statics.
Games room & snooker.

BARRHILL

Windsor Holiday Park (NX216835)
KA26 OPZ ☎ 01465 821355 (on A714 between Newton Stewart & Girvan, 1m north of village of Barrhill) Signposted
Nearby town: Girvan
►►► **Family Park** ★ £7.50-£8.50 £7.50-£8.50 ▲ £7-£7.50
Open all year (rs Nov-Feb open wknds only) Booking advisable Jun-Aug Last arrival 22.00hrs Last departure 16.00hrs
A small site in a rural location, well-screened from A714 by small, mature trees. 1m NW of village. A 6-acre site with 30 touring pitches and 26 statics.

Credit Cards

BEATTOCK

Beattock House Hotel Caravan Park (NT079027)
DG10 9QB ☎ 01683 300403 & 300402 Signposted
Nearby town: Moffat
► **Town & Country Pennant Park** ★ fr £7 fr £7 ▲ fr £6
Open Mar-Oct (rs winter parking limited) Booking advisable
Pleasant, well-maintained level touring site set amongst trees in the grounds of a country house, adjacent to A74. A 2-acre site with 35 touring pitches.
Fishing.

BEESWING

Beeswing Caravan Park (NX885485)
Kirkgunzeon DG2 8JL ☎ 01387 760242 (off A711)
Nearby town: Dumfries
►►► **Family Park** ★ £5.80-£6.80 £5.80-£6.80
£5.80-£6.80
Open Mar-Oct Booking advisable
A delightful park in open countryside, with lovely rural views in a peaceful setting. Midway between Dumfries and Dalbeattie on A711, 0.5m S of Beeswing. A 6-acre site with 25 touring pitches and 3 statics.

BONCHESTER BRIDGE

Bonchester Bridge Caravan Park (NT586123)
Fernbank TD9 8JN ☎ 01450 860676
Nearby town: Edinburgh
►►► **Family Park** ★ fr £5 fr £5 fr £4
Open Apr-Oct Booking advisable Jul-Aug Last arrival 22.00hrs Last departure noon
Neat little country village site close to Bure Water, on A6088 N of village centre.. A 3-acre site with 25 touring pitches.

BRIGHOUSE BAY

Brighouse Bay Holiday Park (NX628453)
DG6 4TS ☎ 01557 870267 Signposted
Nearby town: Kirkcudbright

►►►►► **Premier Park**
Open all year Booking advisable Etr, Spring bank hol & Jul-Aug Last arrival 21.30hrs Last departure 11.30hrs
This grassy site enjoys a marvellous coastal setting adjacent to the beach and with superb sea views. Pitches have been imaginatively sculpted into the meadowland with stone walls and hedges blending in with the site's mature trees. These features together with the large range of leisure activities available make this an excellent holiday centre. Turn left off B727 4 miles S of Kircudbright at signpost to Brighouse Bay on unclass rd. Winner of the 1997/8 Campsite of the Year Award, and Best Campsite for Scotland. A 30-acre site with 190 touring pitches and 120 statics.
Mini golf, riding, fishing, watersports,9 hole golf.
See advertisement under Colour Section

CAIRNRYAN

Cairnryan Caravan & Chalet Park (NX075673)
DG9 8QX ☎ 01581 200231 Signposted
Nearby town: Stranraer
►►► **Family Park** ★ fr £8 fr £8 fr £5
Open Etr/Mar-Oct (rs Apr-21 May restricted pub hours) Booking advisable Jul-Aug Last arrival 23.00hrs Last departure noon
Mainly static site immediately opposite ferry terminal for N Ireland (Larne). Ideal stopover site with good views of Loch Ryan. A 7.5-acre site with 15 touring pitches and 83 statics.
Snooker & pool tables.

CASTLE DOUGLAS

Lochside Caravan & Camping Site (NX766618)
Lochside Park DG7 1EZ
☎ 01556 502949 & 01556 502521 (off A75)
Signposted
►►► **Family Park** ★ £7.10-£8.70 £7.10-£8.70
£7.10-£8.70
Open Etr-mid Oct Last departure noon
Municipal touring site incorporating park with recreational facilities, on southern edge of town in attractive setting adjacent to Carlingwark Loch. Situated off B736 Auchencairn road. A 5.5-acre site with 161 touring pitches.
Putting, rowing boats (wknds & high season)

COCKBURNSPATH

Chesterfield Caravan Site (NT772701)
Neuk Farm TD13 5YH
☎ 01368 830459 Signposted
Nearby town: Dunbar
►►► **Family Park** ★ fr £6 fr £6 fr £6
Open Apr-Sep Booking advisable Jul-Aug Last arrival 21.00hrs Last departure noon
Secluded grass site set in Border country, screened by gorse-covered hills. Situated approx .5m from the village and within 3m of the sea. From A1 take unclass rd signed Cockburnspath, and site is .5m along unclass rd 200yds S of village. A 5-acre site with 33 touring pitches and 40 statics.

COLDINGHAM

Scoutscroft Holiday Centre (NT906662)
St Abbs Rd TD14 5NB ☎ 018907 71338
►►► **Family Park** ★ £8-£11 £8-£11 £4.50-£8
Open Mar-Oct Booking advisable bank hols & Jul-Aug Last arrival mdnt Last departure noon
A large grassy site on edge of village. 0.75m from the sea. From A1 take B6438 signed Coldingham and St Abbs, and site on edge of Coldingham village. A 6-acre site with 70 touring pitches and 120 statics.
Sub Aqua Centre.

Credit Cards

COYLTON

Sundrum Castle Holiday Park (NS405208)
KA6 6JM ☎ 01292 570057 Signposted
Nearby town: Ayr

►►►► **De-Luxe Park**
Open Mar-Oct Booking advisable all times Last arrival 23.30hrs Last departure 14.00hrs no cars by tents
A large family holiday centre, with plenty of on-site entertainment, just a 10 min drive from the centre of Ayr. Set off the A70. A 30-acre site with 52 touring pitches and 250 statics.
Amusement arcade.

Credit Cards

CREETOWN

Castle Cary Holiday Park (NX475576)
DG8 7DQ ☎ 01671 820264 Signposted

►►►►► **Premier Park**
Open all year (rs Oct-Mar reception/shop, no heated outdoor pool) Booking advisable Bank hols & Jul-Aug Last arrival anytime Last departure noon
This attractive site in the grounds of Cassencarie House is sheltered by woodlands, and faces south towards Wigtown Bay. The park is in a secluded location with beautiful landscaping and excellent facilities. Winner of the 1996 Campsite of the Year Award for Scotland. A 6-acre site with 50 touring pitches and 26 statics.
Mountain bike hire, crazy golf, snooker & fishing.
See advertisement under Colour Section

Creetown Caravan Park (NX474586)
Silver St DG8 7HU
☎ 01671 820377 (turn down between EllangowanHotel & clock tower) Signposted
►►► **Family Park** ★ £8.50-£10.20 £8.50-£10.20 £7-£10.20
Open Mar-Oct Booking advisable Jul & Aug Last arrival 22.30hrs Last departure 14.00hrs
Neat and well-maintained park set in village centre with views across the estuary. Off A75 into village of Creetown, turn between clock tower and hotel, then turn left along Silver Street. A 2-acre site with 15 touring pitches and 50 statics.

The AA pennant classification has been revised for 1998. Please read the explanation of the scheme on page 10.

CROCKETFORD

Park of Brandedleys (NX830725)
DG2 8RG ☎ 01556 690250 Signposted
Nearby town: Dumfries

►►►►► **Premier Park** ★ £9-£13 £9-£13 £9-£13
Open Etr-Oct (rs Mar-Etr some facilities restricted) Booking advisable public hols & Jul-Aug Last arrival 22.00hrs Last departure noon
A well-maintained site in an elevated position off the A75, with fine views of Auchenreoch Loch and beyond. Excellent on-site amenities. A 9-acre site with 80 touring pitches and 27 statics.
Putting, badminton court & outdoor draughts.
See advertisement under Colour Section

Credit Cards

DALBEATTIE

Islecroft Caravan & Camping Site (NX837615)
Colliston Park, Mill St DG5 4HE
☎ 01556 610012 & 01556 502521 Signposted
► **Town & Country Pennant Park** ★ £5.55-£6.60 £5.55-£6.60 £5.55-£6.60
Open Etr-Sep Last departure noon
A neat site in two sections tucked away to rear of town, close to local park. Access is via Mill Street. A 3.5-acre site with 74 touring pitches.

ECCLEFECHAN

Hoddom Castle Caravan Park (NY154729)
Hoddom DG11 1AS ☎ 01576 300251 Signposted
Nearby town: Lockerbie

►►►►► **Premier Park** £6.50-£11 £6.50-£11 £5.50-£11
Open Etr or Apr-Oct (rs early season cafeteria closed) Booking advisable bank hols & Jul-Aug Last arrival 21.00hrs Last departure 15.30hrs
A beautiful site within the grounds of Hoddom Castle, with amenities housed in the keep and outhouses. 2m SW of Hoddom Bridge which carries B725 over River Annan. Winner of the Best Campsite for Scotland Award 1996/7. A 12-acre site with 170 touring pitches and 29 statics.
Nature trails, visitor centre & 9 hole golf course.
See advertisement under LOCKERBIE

Credit Cards

Cressfield Caravan Park (NY196744)
DG11 3DR ☎ 01576 300702 Signposted
Nearby town: Lockerbie

►►►► **De-Luxe Park** ★ £6.30-£7.50 £6.30-£7.50 £5-£7.50
Open all year Booking advisable Last arrival 23.00hrs Last departure 13.00hrs
An open, spacious park with views to the hills, ideal as a stopover or for touring the area. Take loop service road from A74(M) to Ecclefechan, and site is at S end of town. A 12-acre site with 65 touring pitches and 48 statics.
Sports enclosure, golf nets, petanque, giant chess.

GATEHOUSE OF FLEET

Auchenlarie Holiday Farm (NX536522)
DG7 2EX ☎ 01557 840251 (4m W on main A75)

►►►► **De-Luxe Park** ★ £6-£10 £6-£10 £6-£10
Open Mar-Oct Booking advisable all year
A well-organised family park with good facilities, set on cliffs overlooking Wigtown Bay towards the Isle of Whithorn, and with its own sandy beach. Direct access off A75, 5m W of Gatehouse-of-Fleet. A 5-acre site with 35 touring pitches and 202 statics.

Credit Cards

Anwoth Caravan Site (NX595563)
DG7 2JU ☎ 01557 814333 & 840251 Signposted
►►► **Family Park** ★ £5-£9 £5-£9
Open Mar-Oct Booking advisable Jul-Aug Last arrival 22.00hrs Last departure noon
A sheltered touring site close to the town centre, signed from town centre, on right towards Stranraer direction. A 2-acre site with 28 touring pitches and 38 statics.

Credit Cards

Mossyard Caravan & Camping Park (NX546518)
DG7 2ET ☎ 01557 840226 (4m W of town)
►►► **Family Park** ★ £6-£7 £6-£7 £5-£7
Open Etr/Apr-Oct Booking advisable
A grassy park with its own beach, located on a working farm, and offering an air of peace and tranquility. Located 0.75m off A75 on private tarmaced farm road, 4.5m W of Gatehouse-of-Fleet. A 6.5-acre site with 35 touring pitches and 15 statics.

GLENLUCE

Glenluce Caravan & Camping Park (NX201576)
DG8 0QR ☎ 01581 300412 Signposted
Nearby town: Stranraer
►►► **Family Park** ★ £7.50-£9 £7.50-£9 £5.50-£8
Open Mar-Oct Booking advisable Jul-Aug Last arrival 22.00hrs Last departure noon
A neat, well-maintained site situated beside a small river close to the village centre. Off A75 Stranraer road. Concealed entrance at telephone kiosk in centre of main street. A 5-acre site with 30 touring pitches and 30 statics.

Whitecairn Farm Caravan Park (NX225599)
DG8 0NZ ☎ 01581 300267 Signposted
Nearby town: Stranraer
►►► **Family Park** £7.50-£8.50 £7.50-£8.50 £7.50-£8.50
Open Mar-Oct Booking advisable all times Last arrival 22.00hrs Last departure 11.00hrs
A well-maintained farmland site, in open countryside with extensive views. 1.5m N of Glenluce village on Glenluce-Glassnock Bridge Rd. A 3-acre site with 10 touring pitches and 40 statics.

GLEN TROOL

Caldons Campsite (NX400790)
DG8 6SU ☎ 01671 402420
►►► **Family Park** ★ £6.50 £6.50 £6.50
Open Etr-Sep Booking advisable Etr, Spring bank hol & Jul-Aug
Secluded Forestry Commission site amidst fine hill, loch and woodland scenery in Galloway Forest Park. 13m N of Newton Stewart. A 25-acre site with 160 touring pitches.

Credit Cards

Glen Trool Holiday Park (NX400790)
DG8 6RN ☎ 01671 840280 Signposted
Nearby town: Newton Stewart
►►► **Family Park** £8-£9 £8-£9 £8-£9
Open Mar-Oct Booking advisable Jul-Aug Last arrival 21.00hrs Last departure noon
A small compact site close to the village of Glen Trool and bordered by the Galloway National Park. 9m N of Newton Stewart. A 1-acre site with 14 touring pitches and 26 statics.
Trout pond for fly fishing, bikes for hire.

Credit Cards

GRETNA

Braids Caravan Park (NY313674)
Annan Rd DG16 5DQ ☎ 01461 337409 Signposted
Nearby town: Annan
►►► **Family Park** ★ £6.75 £6.75 £6-£8
Open all year Booking advisable Jul-Sep Last arrival 24.00hrs Last departure noon
A well-maintained grassy site in centre of the village just inside Scotland. Situated on B721 .5m from village on right, towards Annan. A 4-acre site with 70 touring pitches and 8 statics.

HAWICK

Riverside Caravan Park (NT537169)
TD9 8SY ☎ 01450 373785 Signposted
►►► **Family Park**
Open Apr-10 Sep (rs 11 Sep-Nov) Booking advisable May bank hol & Jul-Aug Last arrival 20.30hrs Last departure noon
A pleasant grassy site situated on banks of River Teviot. Near A698 Hawick-Kelso road 2.5m E of Hawick. A 2-acre site with 25 touring pitches and 54 statics.
Fishing.

IRONGRAY

Barnsoul Farm (NX876778)
DG2 9SQ ☎ 01387 730249
► **Town & Country Pennant Park**
Open Apr-Oct Booking advisable Jul & Aug
A scenic farm site set in 250 acres of woodland, parkland and ponds. Leave A75 between Dumfries and Crocketford at brown site sign onto unclass rd signed Shawhead at T-junc. Turn right and immed left signed Dunscore, and site 1m on left. A 4-acre site with 50 touring pitches and 6 statics.

ISLE OF WHITHORN

Burrowhead Holiday Village (NX450345)
DG8 8JB ☎ 01988 500252
►►► **Family Park**
Open Mar-Oct Booking advisable
Large holiday park in 100 acres on coast of Solway Firth, about 2m from old-fashioned harbour at Isle of Whithorn. Leave A75 at Newton Stewart on A714, take A746 to Whithorn, then road to Isle of Whithorn. A 100-acre site with 100 touring pitches and 400 statics.

JEDBURGH

Camping & Caravanning Club Site (NT658219)
Elliot Park, Edinburgh Rd TD8 6EF ☎ 01835 863393 (in season) & 01203 694995 Signposted
►►► **Family Park** ★ £8.10-£10.30 £8.10-£10.30 £8.10-£10.30
Open end Mar-early Nov Booking advisable bank hols & Jul-Aug Last arrival 21.00hrs Last departure noon
A touring site on northern edge of town, nestling at foot of cliffs close to Jed Water. From S on A68 bypass town, take 1st right over bailey bridge. From N A68, 1st left past "Welcome" sign, following signs. Please see the advertisement on page 27 for details of Club Members' benefits. A 3-acre site with 60 touring pitches.
Credit Cards

Jedwater Caravan Park (NT665160)
TD8 6QS ☎ 01835 840219 (4.5m S of Jedburgh off A68 on unclass rd) Signposted
►►► **Family Park**
Open Etr-Oct Booking advisable high season Last arrival mdnt Last departure noon
A quiet riverside site 4.5m S of Jedburgh, close to A68 but unaffected by traffic noise. Ideal for touring Borders and Northumberland. A 10-acre site with 30 touring pitches and 60 statics.
Pitch/putt, bike hire, trampoline, football field.

KELSO

Springwood Caravan Park (NT720334)
TD5 8LS ☎ 01573 224596 (1m S on A699)
Signposted
►►►► **De-Luxe Park** ★ £8-£9 £8-£9 £8-£9
Open end Mar-mid Oct Booking advisable bank hols & Jul-Aug Last arrival 23.00hrs
A very well-maintained site with a pleasant atmosphere. Set in a secluded position close to the tree-lined River Teviot about 1m W of town. On A699 (signed Newton St Boswells). A 4-acre site with 50 touring pitches and 260 statics.
Credit Cards

KILMARNOCK

Cunningham Head Estate Caravan Park (NS370418)
Cunningham Head, Irvine KA3 2PE ☎ 01294 850238 Signposted
► **Town & Country Pennant Park**
Open Apr-Sep (rs Apr-Jun & Sep bar & games room open wknds only) Booking advisable Jul-Aug Last arrival 22.00hrs Last departure noon
A rural site in the grounds of a farmland estate, 3.5m NE of Irvine on B769. From Irvine take A736 Glasgow road, at Stanecastle roundabout turn E on to B769 Stewarton road. Park is 3m on left. A 7-acre site with 120 touring pitches and 70 statics.

KIPPFORD

Kippford Caravan Park (NX844564)
Kippford Caravan Park DG5 4LF ☎ 01556 620636 Signposted
Nearby town: Dalbeattie
►►► **Family Park** £9-£11 £9-£11 ▲ £6-£11
Open Mar-Oct Booking advisable Last arrival 21.00hrs Last departure 11.00hrs
Part-level, part-sloping grass site surrounded by trees and bushes, set in hilly country adjacent to Urr Water estuary and stony beach. On A710. An 18-acre site with 45 touring pitches and 119 statics.
Childrens adventure playground.

KIRKCUDBRIGHT

Seaward Caravan Park (NX662494)
Dhoon Bay DG6 4TJ ☎ 01557 870267 & 331079 (2m SW off B727 Borgue Road) Signposted
►►►► **De-Luxe Park** ▲
Open Mar-Oct (rs Mar-mid May & mid Sep-Oct swimming pool closed) Booking advisable Spring bank hols & Jul-Aug Last arrival 21.30hrs Last departure 11.30hrs
This very attractive elevated site has outstanding views over the Dee estuary. Facilities are well organised and neatly kept. On B727 from Kirkcudbright towards Borgue. An 8-acre site with 26 touring pitches and 30 statics.
TV aerial hook-up, mini golf. Dishwashing.

Silvercraigs Caravan & Camping Site (NX686508)
Silvercraigs Rd DG6 4BT ☎ 01557 330123 & 01556 502521 Signposted
► **Town & Country Pennant Park** ★ £6.60-£8.15 £6.60-£8.15 ▲ £6.60-£8.15
Open Etr-mid Oct Last departure noon
A well-maintained municipal site overlooking town and harbour, just a short stroll to the town centre. A 6-acre site with 50 touring pitches.

KIRKFIELDBANK

Clyde Valley Caravan Park (NS868441)
ML11 9TS ☎ 01555 663951 Signposted
► **Town & Country Pennant Park** ▲
Open Apr-Oct Booking advisable anytime Last arrival 23.00hrs Last departure noon
Level, grass site with trees and bushes set in hilly country with access to river. From Glasgow on A72, cross river bridge at Kirkfieldbank and site is on left. From Lanark on A72, turn right at bottom of very steep hill before going over bridge. A 5-acre site with 50 touring pitches and 115 statics.

LANARK

Newhouse Caravan & Camping Park (NS926456)
Ravenstruther ML11 8NP ☎ 01555 870228 Signposted
►►► **Family Park** ▲
Open mid Mar-mid Oct Booking advisable Jul-Aug Last arrival 22.00hrs Last departure noon
Pleasant level grass and gravel site, with young trees and bushes, situated on A70 Ayr-Edinburgh road, 3m E of Lanark. A 5-acre site with 45 touring pitches and 3 statics.
Caravan storage compound.

LAUDER

Thirlestane Castle Caravan & Camping Site (NT536473)
Thirlestane Castle TD2 6RU ☎ 01578 722254 0976 231032 Signposted
►►► **Family Park** fr £7 fr £7 ▲ fr £7
Open Etr-Oct Booking advisable Jul-Aug
Mainly level grass site set in the grounds of the impressive Thirlestane Castle. Set off the A697, S of the village. A 5-acre site with 60 touring pitches.

LOCHMABEN

Halleaths Caravan Site (NY098818)
DG11 1NA ☎ 01387 810630 Signposted
Nearby town: Lockerbie
►►► **Family Park** ▲
Open Mar-Nov Booking advisable bank hols & Jul-Aug Last arrival 22.00hrs Last departure noon
Level, grassy site in a sheltered position with a wood on one side and a high hedge on the other. From Lockerbie on A74(M) take A709 to Lochmaben - .5m on right after crossing River Annan. An 8-acre site with 70 touring pitches and 12 statics.
Fishing (charged).

Kirkloch Brae Caravan Site (NY082825)
☎ 01461 203311 Signposted
► **Town & Country Pennant Park** ▲
Open Etr-Oct
A grassy lochside site with superb views and well-maintained facilities. Signed from centre of town. A 1.5-acre site with 30 touring pitches.

LOCHNAW

Drumlochart Caravan Park (NW997634)
DG9 0RN ☎ 01776 870232 Signposted
Nearby town: Stanraer

►►►► **De-Luxe Park**
Open Mar-Oct Booking advisable bank hols & Jul-Aug Last arrival 22.00hrs Last departure noon
A peaceful rural site in hilly woodland, adjacent to Loch Ryan and Luce Bay, offering coarse fishing. 5m NW of Stranraer on B7043. A 9-acre site with 30 touring pitches and 96 statics.
Fly-fishing on stocked trout loch.

LOCKERBIE

See **Ecclefechan**

MAYBOLE

The Ranch (NS286102)
Culzean Rd KA19 8DU ☎ 01655 882446
Nearby town: Ayr

►►►► **De-Luxe Park** ★ £9-£11 £9-£11
Open Mar-Oct & wknds in winter Booking advisable bank hols & Jul-Sep Last arrival 20.00hrs Last departure noon
A small well run touring site with good views and many on site amenities. Situated on the L of B7023, 1m S of Maybole towards Culzean. A 9-acre site with 40 touring pitches and 68 statics.
Mini gym, sauna & sunbed.

Camping & Caravanning Club Site (NS247103)
Culzean Castle KA19 8JK ☎ 01655 760627 (in season) & 01203 694995 (on A719) Signposted

►►►► **De-Luxe Park** ★ £8.70-£11.30 £8.70-£11.30 £8.70-£11.30
Open end Mar-early Nov Booking advisable bank hols & Jul-Aug Last arrival 21.00hrs Last departure noon
A mainly level, grassy site situated at the entrance to the castle and country park, surrounded by trees on three sides and with lovely views over Culzean Bay. Signed at entrance to Culzean Castle on A719. Please see the advertisement on page 27 for details of Club Members' benefits. A 6-acre site with 90 touring pitches.

Credit Cards

MOFFAT

Camping & Caravanning Club Site (NT085050)
Hammerlands Farm DG10 9QL ☎ 01683 220436 (in season) & 01203 694995 Signposted
►►► **Family Park** ★ £9.10-£12.10 £9.10-£12.10 £9.10-£12.10
Open end Mar-early Nov Booking advisable Spring bank hol & peak periods Last arrival 21.00hrs Last departure noon
Well-maintained level grass touring site. Leave A74 onto A701 to Moffat centre, take A708 and site is signed. Please see the advertisement on page 27 for details of Club Members' benefits. A 14-acre site with 200 touring pitches.

Credit Cards

MONIAIVE

Woodlea Hotel (NX767895)
DG3 4EN ☎ 01848 200209
Nearby town: Dumfries
► **Town & Country Pennant Park** ★ £6-£12 £6-£12
Open Apr-Oct Booking advisable anytime Last arrival 23.00hrs Last departure noon
A small site in hotel grounds with bays amongst shrubs and trees. It lies 1.5m W of Moniaive on A702. A 1-acre site with 8 touring pitches.
Badminton, bowls, croquet, putting, sauna & solarium.

NEWTON STEWART

Creebridge Caravan Park (NX415656)
Minnigaff DG8 6AJ ☎ 01671 402324 & 402432 Signposted
▶▶▶ **Family Park** ★ fr £7.70 fr £7.30 fr £6.60
Open Apr-Oct (rs Mar only one toilet block open) Booking advisable Jul-Aug Last arrival 20.00hrs Last departure noon
A level urban site a short walk from the amenities of town. .25m E of Newton Stewart at Minnigaff on the bypass, signed off A75. A 4.5-acre site with 36 touring pitches and 50 statics.
Security street lighting.

Talnotry Campsite (NX492719)
Queens Way, New Galloway Rd DG8 7BL ☎ 01671 402420 & 402170 (7m NE off A712) Signposted
▶**Town & Country Pennant Park** ★ fr £5 fr £5 fr £5
Open Apr-Sep Booking advisable Etr
An attractive open grassy site set amidst the superb scenery of Galloway Forest Park close to A712 and the picturesque Queens Way. A 15-acre site with 60 touring pitches.
Credit Cards

PALNACKIE

Barlochan Caravan Park (NX819572)
DG7 1PF ☎ 01556 600256 & 01557 870267 Signposted
Nearby town: Dalbeattie
▶▶▶ **Family Park**
Open Apr-Oct (rs Apr-mid May & mid Sep-end Oct swimming pool) Booking advisable Spring bank hol & Jul-Aug Last arrival 21.30hrs Last departure 11.30hrs
An attractive terraced site in a sheltered position but with fine, open views. On A711. A 9-acre site with 20 touring pitches and 40 statics.
Fishing, pitch & putt. Dishwashing facilities.

PARTON

Loch Ken Holiday Park (NX687702)
DG7 3NE ☎ 01644 470282 (on A713) Signposted
Nearby town: Castle Douglas
▶▶▶ **Family Park** £7-£9.50 £7-£9.50 £6-£8.50
Open mid Mar-mid Nov (rs Mar/Apr (ex Etr) & late Sep-Nov restricted shop hours) Booking advisable Etr, Spring bank hol & Jun-Aug Last arrival 20.00hrs Last departure noon
An attractive touring site on eastern shores of Loch Ken, with superb views. Off A713. A 7-acre site with 52 touring pitches and 33 statics.
Bike, boat & canoe hire, fishing on loch.

PEEBLES

Crossburn Caravan Park (NT248417)
The Glades, 95 Edinburgh Rd EH45 8ED ☎ 01721 720501 (.5m N on A703) Signposted
▶▶▶ **Family Park** ★ fr £9 fr £8.50 fr £8
Open Apr-Oct Booking advisable Jul-Aug Last arrival 23.00hrs Last departure 14.00hrs
A level site in a peaceful and relatively quiet location, despite the proximity of the main road which partly borders the site, as does the Eddleston Water. Facilities maintained to a high standard. A 6-acre site with 35 touring pitches and 95 statics.
9 hole putting course & mountain bikes for hire.
Credit Cards

Rosetta Caravan & Camping Park (NT245415)
Rosetta Rd EH45 8PG ☎ 01721 720770 Signposted
▶▶▶ **Family Park** ★ £8.75-£9.25 £8.75-£9.25 £6.50-£7.50
Open Apr-Oct Booking advisable public & bank hols Last arrival 23.00hrs Last departure 15.00hrs
A pleasant parkland site set in hilly woodland country. From N signed from A703, 1m S of Redscarhead, 2m N of Peebles. A 25-acre site with 160 touring pitches and 29 statics.
Bowling & putting greens.

PENPONT

Penpont Caravan and Camping Park (NX852947)
DG3 4BH ☎ 01848 330470 Signposted
▶**Town & Country Pennant Park** ★ £6.80 £5.70-£6.80 £6-£7.60
Open Etr or Apr-Oct Booking advisable Jul-Aug Last arrival 23.00hrs Last departure 14.00hrs
Peaceful, grassy, slightly sloping site in a rural area, excellently situated for touring. From Thornhill on the A702, site on left 0.5 miles before Penpont village. A 1.5-acre site with 20 touring pitches and 20 statics.

PORTPATRICK

Galloway Point Holiday Park (NX005537)
Portree Farm DG9 9AA ☎ 01776 810561 Signposted
Nearby town: Stranraer
▶▶▶ **Family Park** £8-£11 £8-£11 £7-£11
Open Etr-Oct Booking advisable Mar, & May-Oct Last arrival 23.00hrs Last departure 14.00hrs
Strung out along gorse-clad downland, the holiday park looks out on the North Channel 1m S of town. An 18-acre site with 100 touring pitches and 60 statics.

Sunnymeade Caravan Park (NX005540)
DG9 8LN ☎ 01776 810293
Nearby town: Stranraer
Town & Country Pennant Park ★ £7-£8.50
£7-£8.50 fr £7
Open mid Mar-Oct Booking advisable
A mainly static park with mostly grass touring pitches, and views of the coast and Irish Sea. Approach on A77, then 1st unclassified road on left after entering village. First caravan park on left at top of hill. A 2-acre site with 15 touring pitches and 75 statics.

POWFOOT

Queensberry Bay Caravan Park (NY135653)
DG12 5PU ☎ 01461 700205 Signposted
Nearby town: Annan
Family Park
Open Etr-Oct Booking advisable Jul-Aug Last arrival 20.00hrs Last departure noon
A flat, mainly grassy site in a quiet location on the shores of the Solway Firth with views across the estuary to Cumbrian hills. Follow sign to Powfoot off B724 and drive through village past golf club on single track road on shore edge to site in .75m. A 5-acre site with 100 touring pitches and 60 statics.
See advertisement under ANNAN, page 240

ROCKCLIFFE

Castle Point Caravan Park (NX851539)
DG5 4QL ☎ 01556 630248 Signposted
Nearby town: Dalbeattie
Family Park £7.50-£9.50 £7.50-£9.50
£7.50-£9.50
Open Etr-Sep (rs Mar-Etr & 1-30 Oct limited supervision) Booking advisable Whit wk & Jul-Aug Last arrival 23.00hrs Last departure 11.00hrs
A level, grassy site with superb views across the estuary and surrounding hilly countryside. Leave A710 onto unclass rd to Rockcliffe, site signed on left before descent into village. A 3-acre site with 29 touring pitches and 8 statics.

SANDHEAD

Sands of Luce Caravan Park (NX103510)
D69 9JR ☎ 01776 830456 Signposted
Nearby town: Stranraer

De-Luxe Park £6.50-£8 £6-£7.50
£6.50-£8
Open mid Mar-Oct Booking advisable Jul-Aug Last arrival 22.00hrs Last departure noon
A friendly site on a beautiful sandy beach, with lovely views across Luce Bay. Facilities are well-maintained and clean. Turn left off A75 onto B7084 2m from Glenluce, signed Sandhead and Drunmore, and site signed on left in 5m. A 5-acre site with 36 touring pitches and 34 statics.
Boat launching, dishwashing sinks.

SANDYHILLS

Sandyhills Bay Leisure Park (NX892552)
DG5 4NY ☎ 01557 870267 & 01387 780257 (7m from Dalbeattie, 6.5m from Kirkbean) Signposted
Nearby town: Dalbeattie
Family Park
Open Apr-Oct Booking advisable Spring bank hol & Jun-Aug Last arrival 21.30hrs Last departure 11.30hrs
A flat, grassy site adjacent and with access to south-facing Sandyhills Bay and beach, sheltered by woods and hills with superb views. Site on A710 coast road. A 6-acre site with 26 touring pitches and 34 statics.
Dishwashing facilities.

SELKIRK

Victoria Park Caravan & Camping Park (NT465287)
Victoria Park, Buccleuch Rd TD7 5DN ☎ 01750 20897 Signposted
Town & Country Pennant Park ★ £6-£7 £6-£7
£6-£7
Open Apr-Oct (rs 10-18 Jun site closed) Booking advisable Jul-Aug Last arrival 21.00hrs Last departure 14.00hrs
A consistently well-maintained site with good basic facilities forming part of public park and swimming pool complex close to River Ettrick. From A707/A708 N of town, cross river bridge, take first left then left again. A 3-acre site with 60 touring pitches.
Mini gymnasium, sauna, sunbed.

SOUTHERNESS

Southerness Holiday Village (NX976545)
DG2 8AZ ☎ 01387 880256 & 880281 Signposted
Nearby town: Dumfries

De-Luxe Park ★
Open Mar-Oct Booking advisable Last departure 16.00hrs
A large family campsite with plenty of on-site entertainment situated close to sandy beach. Near centre of Southerness. An 8-acre site with 200 touring pitches and 350 statics.
Amusement centre, disco, videos.

Credit Cards

STRANRAER

Aird Donald Caravan Park (NX075605)
London Rd DG9 8RN ☎ 01776 702025 Signposted

►►►► **De-Luxe Park** ★ £8.20-£8.50 £8.20-£8.50 £3.70-£7.90
Open all year Booking advisable Last departure 16.00hrs
A spacious touring site, mainly grass but with tarmac hard-standing area. On the fringe of town screened by mature shrubs and trees. Ideal stopover en route to N.I. ferry ports. A 12-acre site with 100 touring pitches.

TARBOLTON

Middlemuir Park (NS439263)
KA5 5NR ☎ 01292 541647 Signposted
Nearby town: Ayr
►►► **Family Park**
Open all year Booking advisable bank hols & Jul-Aug Last arrival 18.00hrs Last departure noon
A rural site in the partly-walled garden where Montgomerie House used to stand. Set in rolling farmland off the B743 Ayr-Mauchline road. A 17-acre site with 25 touring pitches and 45 statics.

WALES

The directory which follows has been divided into three geographical regions. Counties have not been shown against individual locations as recent legislation has created a number of smaller counties which will be unfamiliar to the visitor. The postal authorities have confirmed that it is no longer necessary to include a county name in addresses, provided a post code is shown. All locations appear on the regional maps in their appropriate counties.

NORTH WALES

This region includes the counties of Conwy, Denbighshire, Flintshire, Gwynedd, Isle of Anglesey and Wrexham which reflect the recent national changes.

ABERGELE

See **Betws-Yn-Rhos**

ABERSOCH

Bryn Cethin Bach Caravan Park (SH304290)
Lon Garmon LL53 7UL ☎ 01758 712719 & 712751
Nearby town: Pwllheli

►►►► **De-Luxe Park** ★ £8-£10 £8-£10
Open Apr-Oct (rs Mar-May shop closed) Booking advisable Spring bank hol & Jul-Aug Last arrival 18.00hrs Last departure noon
A well-run family site within .5m of sandy beaches, the harbour and all the facilities of Abersoch. Offering lovely views and a first class toilet block. A 2-acre site with 15 touring pitches and 53 statics.
Lake & fishing.

Seaview (SH305262)
Sarn Bach LL53 7ET ☎ 01758 712052 & 713256 Signposted
Nearby town: Pwllheli
► **Town & Country Pennant Park** ★ £7.50-£9 £7.50-£9 £4-£6
Open Mar-Oct Booking advisable from March Last arrival 23.00hrs Last departure noon
Gently sloping family site in quiet elevated position near to Abersoch, on the Lleyn Peninsula. Very sharp turn opposite the telephone kiosk in Sarn Bach for site 200yds on right. A 4-acre site with 97 touring pitches.

ANGLESEY, ISLE OF

AMLWCH

Point Lynas Caravan Park (SH474930)
Llaneilan LL68 9LT ☎ 01407 831130 & 01248 852423
► **Town & Country Pennant Park** ★ £6-£8 £6-£8 £5-£8
Open Mar-Oct Booking advisable bank hols Last arrival 22.00hrs Last departure noon
This first-class site is near a sheltered rocky cove, safe for swimming. 1 mile N of Penysarn on A5025; turn right at garage on to unclass rd to Llaneilian. Site on left just before beach. A 2-acre site with 6 touring pitches and 44 statics.
Childrens sandpit & climbing bars.

BRYNSIENCYN

Fron Caravan & Camping Site (SH472669)
LL61 6TX ☎ 01248 430310 Signposted
Nearby town: Bangor
►►► **Family Park** ★ £7.50-£10 £7.50-£10 £7.50-£9
Open Etr-Sep Booking advisable Spring bank hol & Jul-Aug Last arrival 23.00hrs Last departure noon
Quiet family site in pleasant rural area, ideally situated for touring Anglesey and North Wales. Off A4080 Llanfair PG-Newborough road, 1m W of Brynsiencyn. A 5.5-acre site with 60 touring pitches.

The AA pennant classification has been revised for 1998. Please read the explanation of the scheme on page 10.

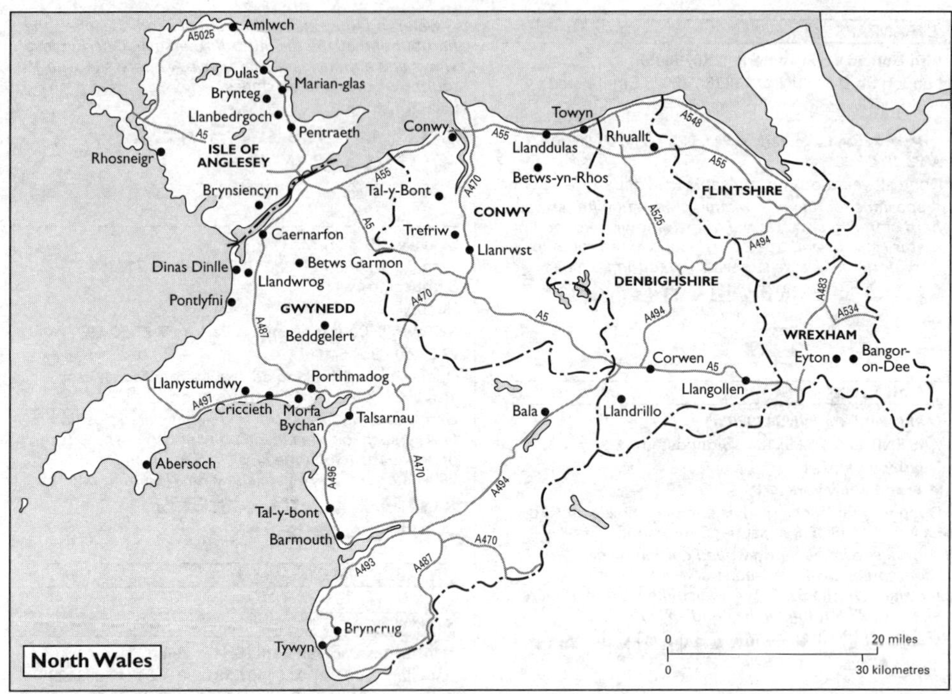

BRYNTEG

Nant Newydd Caravan Park (SH485814)

LL78 8JH ☎ 01248 852842 & 852266 Signposted
Nearby town: Bangor

►►►► De-Luxe Park ★ £7-£11 £7-£11 ▲ £7-£11

Open Mar-Oct (rs May & Sep pool restricted) Booking advisable Jul-Aug Last arrival mdnt Last departure 17.00hrs

Gently sloping grass site with mature trees and bushes set in meadowland adjacent to main road, 1m from Brynteg on B5110 towards Llangefni. A 4-acre site with 30 touring pitches and 83 statics.

Satalite TV & licensed shop.

See advertisement under BENLLECH BAY, page 255

Ysgubor Fadog Caravan & Camping Site (SH497820)

Ysgubor Fadog LL78 8QA ☎ 01248 852681 Signposted
Nearby town: Bangor

►Town & Country Pennant Park ★ £4.50 £4.50 ▲ £3-£4.50

Open Etr-Sep Booking advisable Whitsun & school hols Last arrival 20.00hrs Last departure 18.00hrs

A peaceful and remote site reached along a narrow lane where care is needed. From Benllech take B5108, and after sports field take 3rd on left. A 2-acre site with 15 touring pitches and 1 static.

DULAS

Tyddyn Isaf Caravan Park (SH486873)

Lligwy Bay LL70 9PQ ☎ 01248 410203 (.5m off A5025 between Benllech & Amlwch) Signposted
Nearby town: Benllech

►►►► De-Luxe Park ★ £7-£12 £7-£12 ▲ £7-£9

Open Mar-Oct (rs Mar-Etr & Oct clubhouse limited, shut from mid Sept) Booking advisable May bank hol & Jun-Aug Last arrival 22.00hrs Last departure 11.00hrs

A lovely site located on gently rising ground adjacent to sandy beach affording magnificent views. A 6-acre site with 60 touring pitches and 50 statics.

LLANBEDRGOCH

Ty Newydd Caravan Park & Country Club (SH508813)
LL76 8TZ ☎ 01248 450677 Signposted
Nearby town: Benlech
►►► **Family Park** ★ £6-£14 £6-£14 ▲ £6-£14
Open Whit-mid Sep (rs Mar-Whit & mid Sep-Oct club/shop wknds only outdoor pool closed) Booking advisable Etr, Whit & Jul-Aug Last arrival 23.30hrs Last departure 10.00hrs
A low density site with many facilities including a health centre. Site N of village on unclass rd between A5025 and B5108. A 4-acre site with 40 touring pitches and 60 statics.
Health centre.
See advertisement under BENLLECH BAY

MARIANGLAS

Home Farm Caravan Park (SH498850)
LL73 8PH ☎ 01248 410614

►►►► **De-Luxe Park** ★ £6.50-£8.50 £6.50-£8.50 ▲ £5-£8.50
Open Apr-Oct Booking advisable bank hols Last arrival 21.00hrs Last departure noon
A first class site with friendly, helpful owners. On A5025, 2m N of Benllech, with park entrance 300 metres beyond church. Winner of the Best Campsite for Wales Award 1996/7. A 6-acre site with 61 touring pitches and 72 statics.
Indoor adventure playground.
See advertisement under Colour Section

Credit Cards

PENTRAETH

Rhos Caravan Park (SH517794)
LL75 8DZ ☎ 01248 450214 (.75m N on A5025)
Signposted. Nearby town: Benllech
►►► **Family Park** £6-£10 £6-£8 ▲ £5.50-£7.50
Open Etr-Oct (rs Mar shop & showers restricted) Booking advisable Spring bank hol & Jul-Aug Last arrival 22.00hrs Last departure noon
Site on level, grassy ground off main road to Amlwch. On left side of A5025, 1m N of Pentraeth. A 15-acre site with 98 touring pitches and 60 statics.

RHOSNEIGR

Bodfan Farm (SH324737)
LL64 5XA ☎ 01407 810563
Nearby town: Holyhead
► **Town & Country Pennant Park** ▲
Open Etr-Oct Booking advisable Apr-Sep Last arrival 23.00hrs Last departure 23.00hrs
A farm site on gentle sloping ground with sea and country views. Within walking distance of sea. Follow school sign on way out of Rhosneigr. A 15-acre site with 60 touring pitches.

BALA

Camping & Caravanning Club Site (SH962391)
Crynierth Caravan Park, Cefn-Ddwysarn LL23 7IN
☎ 01678 530324 (in season) & 01203 694995 (3.25m NE off A494) Signposted
►►► **Family Park** ★ £8.70-£11.30 £8.70-£11.30 ▲ £8.70-£11.30
Open end Mar-end Oct Booking advisable bank hols & peak periods Last arrival 21.00hrs Last departure noon
A quiet pleasant site with interesting views and high class facilities. Situated just off A494 4m E of Bala. Please see the advertisement on page 27 for details of Club Members' benefits. A 4-acre site with 50 touring pitches.

Credit Cards

Pen Y Bont Touring & Camping Park (SH932350)
Llangynog Rd LL23 7PH ☎ 01678 520549 & 0589 987499 (from A494 in Bala take B4391, site .75m along on right) Signposted
►►► **Family Park** ★ £7.95-£8.95 £7.45-£8.45 ▲ £6.95-£7.95

contd.

Open Apr-Oct Booking advisable all year Last arrival 24.30hrs Last departure 13.00hrs

Part-level, part-sloping, grass and gravel site with trees and bushes set in mountainous woodland country, adjacent to river Dee and Bala Lake. .5m from Bala on side of B4391. A 7-acre site with 85 touring pitches.

Dish washing & vegetable preparation area.

Pen-y-Garth Camping & Caravan Park (SH940349)

Rhos-y-Gwaliau LL23 7ES ☎ 01678 520485 & 0850 773642 Signposted

►►► **Family Park** ★ £6.95-£8.25 £6.95-£8.25 £6.95-£8.25

Open Mar-Oct Booking advisable bank hols & Jul-Aug Last arrival 22.00hrs Last departure noon

A level site with well-laid out pitches for tourers, amidst attractive scenery. From Bala take B4391 and in 1m follow unclass rd signed YH/Lake Vyrnwy. Site on right at top of hill. A 20-acre site with 63 touring pitches and 54 statics.

Table tennis,10acres recreation, dish washing room

BANGOR-ON-DEE

Camping & Caravanning Club Site (SJ385448)

The Racecourse LL13 0DA ☎ 01978 781009 (in season) & 01203 694995 Signposted

►►► **Family Park** ★ £8.10-£10.30 £8.10-£10.30 £8.10-£10.30

Open end Mar-Nov Booking advisable bank hols & peak periods Last arrival 21.00hrs Last departure noon

A mainly level, grassy site within the racecourse which lies in a bend of the River Dee. Please see the advertisement on page 27 for details of Club Members' benefits. A 6-acre site with 100 touring pitches.

Credit Cards

BARMOUTH

Hendre Mynach Caravan Park (SH605170)

Llanaber Rd LL42 1YR ☎ 01341 280586 Signposted

►►►► **De-Luxe Park** ★ £6-£10 £6-£9 £6-£8

Open Mar-Nov (rs Mar-Etr & Oct-Nov (ex half term) no shop) Booking advisable bank hols & Jul-Aug Last arrival 23.00hrs Last departure noon

A lovely site with immaculate facilities, situated off the A496 on the northern outskirts of Barmouth and near to railway, with almost direct access to promenade and beach. A 10-acre site with 205 touring pitches.

TV & satellite hook ups.

BEDDGELERT

Beddgelert Forest Campsite (SH578491)

LL55 4UU ☎ 01766 890288 (2m N on A4085) Signposted

►►► **Family Park** ★ £7-£8 £7-£8 £7-£8

Open all year Booking advisable 31 Mar-Sep Last arrival 14.00hrs Last departure 20.00hrs

Well-run and very popular site amidst trees and bushes. Set in mountainous woodland country near to river and main road. Site in 1m N of Beddgelert on A4085. A 25-acre site with 280 touring pitches.

Credit Cards

BENLLECH BAY

See **Brynteg & Llanbedrgoch** under **Anglesey, Isle of**

BETWS GARMON

Bryn Gloch Caravan & Camping Park (SH534574)

LL54 7YY ☎ 01286 650216 Signposted

Nearby town: Caernarfon

►►►► **De-Luxe Park** ★ £7-£8 £7-£8 £7-£8

Open all year Booking advisable school & bank hols Last arrival 23.00hrs Last departure 17.00hrs

An excellent family-run site with new and improved toilets, and some level pitches in beautiful surroundings. Site on A4085 between Beddgelert and Caernarfon. A 12-acre site with 92 touring pitches and 14 statics.

Family bathroom & mother & baby room.

See advertisement on page 256.

Credit Cards

BETWS-YN-RHOS

Hunters Hamlet Caravan Park (SH928736)
Sirior Goch Farm LL22 8PL
☎ 01745 832237 & 0421 552106
Nearby town: Abergele
▶▶▶ **Family Park** ★ £8-£10 £7-£10

Open 21 Mar-Oct Booking advisable bank hols & Jul-Aug Last arrival 22.00hrs Last departure noon

A delightful little site next to the owners' Georgian farmhouse. An excellent purpose-built toilet block with good quality fittings and furniture. From A55 into Abergele take A548, turn right in 3m onto B5381, and site in .5m on left. A 1.5-acre site with 23 touring pitches.

Stabling for horses.

Credit Cards

BRYNCRUG

Woodlands Holiday Park (SH618035)
LL36 9UH ☎ 01654 710471 (2m NE) Signposted
Nearby town: Tywyn
►►► **Family Park**
Open Etr & Apr-Oct Booking advisable Jul-Aug Last arrival 22.00hrs Last departure 11.00hrs
A tarmac site at the end of a large holiday complex, partly surrounded by trees. 2m from Tywyn on B4405 road to Tal-y-Llyn. A 2-acre site with 20 touring pitches and 122 statics.
Entertainment in high season.
See advertisement on page 255
Credit Cards

CAERNARFON

Bryn Teg Holiday Park (SH524636)
Llanrug LL55 4RF ☎ 01286 871374 & 01492 532197 (3m E A4086)
►►►► **De-Luxe Park**
Open Etr-14 Jan (rs mid Oct-Etr pool, bar & shop closed) Booking advisable bank hols & peak season Last arrival 20.00hrs Last departure noon
A large site set in undulating countryside, with mostly level pitches. Signed off A4086 near Llanrug, behind Bryn Bras Castle. A 10-acre site with 168 touring pitches and 287 statics.
12 acre lake with coarse & trout fishing.
Credit Cards

Cadnant Valley Caravan Park (SH487628)
Cadnant Valley Park, Llanberis Rd LL55 2DF ☎ 01286 673196 Signposted
►►► **Family Park** £6.50-£8 £6.50-£8 ▲ £6-£7.50
Open 15 Mar-Oct Booking advisable bank hols & Jul-Aug Last arrival 22.00hrs Last departure noon
Situated close to the main Caernarfon-Llanberis road and conveniently near the town. Level, terraced pitches in a secluded, landscaped, wooded valley with some near a stream. On the outskirts of Caernarfon on B4086 to llanberis. A 4.5-acre site with 69 touring pitches.
Outdoor table tennis.

Glan Gwna Holiday Park (SH502622)
Caeathro LL55 2SG ☎ 01286 673456
►►► **Family Park** ★ £7-£12 ▲ £7-£12
Open Etr-Oct (rs mid Apr-May & mid Sep-Oct some facilities are closed) Booking advisable bank hols Last arrival 23.00hrs Last departure noon
Beautifully situated on a bend in the River Afon, and part of a large holiday complex with excellent facilities.

Take A4085 signed Beddgelert, 1m from Caernarfon. A 7-acre site with 100 touring pitches and 130 statics.
Horse riding & fishing.

Ty'n yr Onnen Mountain Farm Caravan & Camping (SH534588)
Waunfawr LL55 4AX ☎ 01286 650281 Signposted
►►► **Family Park** ★ £7-£8 £6-£7 ▲ £6-£7
Open Spring bank hol-Oct (rs Etr & Mayday bank hol open if weather premitting) Booking advisable Spring bank hol & Jul-Aug Last arrival 21.00hrs Last departure 10.00hrs
A gently sloping site on a 200-acre sheep farm, set in magnificent surroundings with mountain views. At Waunfawr on A4085, turn down unclass rd opposite church, and signed. A 4-acre site with 20 touring pitches and 4 statics.
Fishing.

Riverside Camping (SH505630)
Caer Glyddyn, Pont Rug LL55 2BB ☎ 01286 672524 & 678781 eves (2m E on A4086) Signposted
► **Town & Country Pennant Park** £7-£8 £6.50-£7 ▲ £3-£7
Open Etr-end Oct Booking advisable Jul-Aug Last arrival anytime Last departure 20.00hrs
Level, grassy site bordered by a salmon river, 2m E of Caernarfon on A4086. Entrance to site at Seiont Nurseries and Garden Centre. A 4.5-acre site with 55 touring pitches.
River swimming.

CONWY

Conwy Touring Park (SH779757)
LL32 8UX ☎ 01492 592856 (1.5m S on B5106) Signposted
►►► **Family Park** ★ £4.85-£9.95 £4.85-£9.95 ▲ £4-£9.95
Open Etr-Oct Booking advisable public hols & Jul-Aug Last arrival 21.00hrs Last departure noon
An excellent site, with informally sited pitches set high up above the Conway Valley, and a good range of facilities. A 70-acre site with 319 touring pitches.
Indoor playground monitored by staff.
Credit Cards

CORWEN

Glan Ceirw Caravan Park (SJ067454)
Ty Nant LL21 0RF ☎ 01490 420346
►►► **Family Park** ▲
Open Mar-Oct
A small riverside site in a rural location, 300yds off A5. On unclass loop rd off A5 between Corwen and Betws-y-

contd.

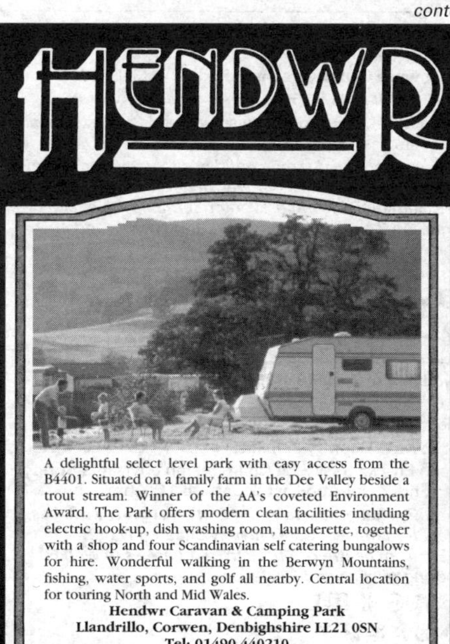

Coed, 1.5m from Cerrigydruidion. A 1.5-acre site with 15 touring pitches and 29 statics.

Llawr-Betws Farm Caravan Park (SJ016424)
LL21 0HD ☎ 01490 460224 Signposted
Nearby town: Bala
Town & Country Pennant Park £6-£8 £6-£7 £4-£5
Open Mar-Oct Booking advisable bank hols & Jul-Aug Last arrival 23.00hrs Last departure noon
Mainly level site with grass and mature trees, 3m W of Corwen off A494 Bala road. A 5-acre site with 65 touring pitches and 72 statics.
Fishing.

CRICCIETH

Llwyn-Bugeilydd Farm (SH498398)
LL52 0PN ☎ 01766 522235 Signposted
Town & Country Pennant Park ★ £6.50-£8 £5-£8 £5-£6.50
Open Etr or Apr-Oct Booking advisable Etr, Whit & Jul-Aug Last arrival anytime Last departure 11.00hrs
A beautiful little site, well-maintained and in excellent condition, with sea and mountain views. Situated 1m N of Criccieth on B4411, and first site on right. A 6-acre site with 45 touring pitches.

Tyddyn Cethin Farm (SH492404)
LL52 0NF ☎ 01766 522149
Town & Country Pennant Park ★ £7-£9.50 £7-£9.50 £5-£6.50
Open Mar-Oct Booking advisable Feb-Mar Last arrival 22.00hrs Last departure noon
A very good quiet family holiday site with enthusiastic proprietors, on banks of River Dwyfor. Travel N from Criccieth on B4411 and Tyddyn Cethin is 4th site on right. An 8-acre site with 60 touring pitches and 40 statics.
Fishing on site.

Tyddyn Morthwyl (SH488402)
LL52 0NF ☎ 01766 522115 (1.25m N on B4411)
Signposted
Town & Country Pennant Park ★ £5 £5 £5
Open Etr-Oct (rs Mar & Oct) Booking advisable Spring bank hol & Jul-Aug Last departure 14.00hrs
A quiet, sheltered site with good level grassy pitches, ideal for families. Conveniently situated N of B4411, 1.5m from centre of Criccieth. A 10-acre site with 60 touring pitches and 22 statics.

DINAS DINLLE

Dinlle Caravan Park (SH443568)
LL54 5TW ☎ 01286 830324 (2m W of Dinas Dinlle coast)
Signposted
►►► Family Park
Open May-Aug (rs Mar-Apr & Sep-Nov club shop restricted hours) Booking advisable Spring bank hol & Jul-Aug Last arrival 23.00hrs Last departure noon
A very accessible, well-kept grassy level site, adjacent to sandy beach, with good views to Snowdonia. Turn right off A499 at sign for Caernarfon Airport An 11-acre site with 200 touring pitches and 138 statics.
See advertisement under CAERNARFON, page 256

Credit Cards

EYTON

Plassey Touring Caravan & Leisure Park (SJ353452)
The Plassey LL13 0SP ☎ 01978 780277
Signposted
Nearby town: Wrexham
►►► Family Park £10-£12 £10-£12 £10-£12
Open Mar-Oct Booking advisable bank hols & school hols Last arrival 20.00hrs Last departure 20.00hrs
A mainly level grassy site with trees and meadowland, off the B5426. A 10-acre site with 120 touring pitches and 40 statics.
Sauna, sunbed, badminton, table tennis,9 hole golf.

Credit Cards

LLANDDULAS

Bron Y Wendon Caravan Park (SH904786)
Wern Rd LL22 8HG
☎ 01492 512903 (A55 heading west, turn at sign for Llanddulas (A547) then sharp right, continue for 200 yds under A55 bridge, park on left)
Signposted
Nearby town: Colwyn Bay

►►►► De-Luxe Park £8-£9 £8-£9
Open 21 Mar-30 Oct Booking advisable bank hols Last arrival anytime Last departure 11.00hrs
A good quality site with sea views from every pitch and excellent purpose-built ablution block. Tightly sandwiched between main railway line and new N Wales coast highway (A55). Leave this road at the Llanddulas interchange (A547). An 8-acre site with 130 touring pitches.

Credit Cards

LLANDRILLO

Hendwr Caravan Park (SJ035386)
LL21 0SN ☎ 01490 440210 Signposted
Nearby town: Corwen
►►► **Family Park** ★ fr £7 fr £7 fr £7
Open Apr-Oct (rs Nov-Mar no toilet facilities during this period) Booking advisable bank & school hols Last arrival 22.00hrs Last departure 16.00hrs
Level grass site with mature trees near river, hills, woods and moorland. SW of Corwen on A5, left onto B4401 for 4m. A 4-acre site with 40 touring pitches and 80 statics.
Wet weather camping facilities.
See advertisement under CORWEN, page 257

LLANDWROG

White Tower Caravan Park (SH453582)
LL54 5UH ☎ 01286 830649 & 0836 676609 Signposted
Nearby town: Caernarfon

►►►► **De-Luxe Park** ★ £5-£8.75 £5-£8.75 £5-£8.75
(rs Mar-mid May & Sep-Oct swimming pool & bar wknds only) Booking advisable bank hols & Jul-Aug Last arrival 23.00hrs Last departure noon
A level, well-maintained site with lovely Snowdonia views, 1.5m from village along Tai'r Eglwys Road. From Caernarfon take A487 signed Porthmadog, cross over rndbt, then take 1st right and site on right in 3 miles. A 3-acre site with 52 touring pitches and 53 statics.

LLANGOLLEN

Ty-Ucha Caravan Park (SJ232415)
Maesmawr Rd LL20 7PP ☎ 01978 860677 Signposted
►►► **Family Park** fr £7 fr £6
Open Etr-Oct (rs Mar toilet block closed) Booking advisable public hols Last arrival 22.00hrs Last departure 14.00hrs
A very well-run site in beautiful surroundings conveniently placed close to A5, 1m E of Llangollen. Ideal for country and mountain walking, with small stream on its southern boundary. A 4-acre site with 40 touring pitches.

LLANRUG

See **Caernarfon**

LLANRWST

Bodnant Caravan Site (SH805609)
Nebo Rd LL26 0SD ☎ 01492 640248 (S, turn off A470 opp Birmingham garage for B5427 signed Nebo, site 300yds on right) Signposted
►►► **Family Park** £7-£8 £7-£8 £7-£8
Open Mar-end Oct Booking advisable Etr, May Day, Spring bank hol & Jul-Aug Last arrival 22.00hrs Last departure 11.00hrs
Small, well-maintained, level touring site, S of village off A470. Twelve times winner of 'Wales in Bloom' competition for best kept touring caravan site in Wales. A 5-acre site with 40 touring pitches and 2 statics.
Two outside dishwashing sinks.

Maenan Abbey Caravan Park (SH790656)
LL26 0UL ☎ 01492 660630 Signposted
►►► **Family Park** ★ £4.50-£8.50 £4.50-£8.50
Open Mar-Oct Booking advisable peak periods Last arrival 22.30hrs Last departure noon
An excellent site, level, grassy and well-screened, in the beautiful Conwy Valley. Site on A470 2m N of Llanrwst. A 3-acre site with 26 touring pitches and 72 statics.

LLANYSTUMDWY

Camping & Caravanning Club Site (SH469384)
Tyddyn Sianel LL52 0LS ☎ 01766 522855 (in season) & 01203 694995 Signposted
Nearby town: Criccieth
►►► **Family Park** ★ £9.10-£12.10 £9.10-£12.10 £9.10-£12.10
Open end Mar-early Nov Booking advisable bank hols & peak periods Last arrival 21.00hrs Last departure noon
Well-maintained, attractive grassy site alongside the A497 with a good range of facilities. Please see the advertisement on page 27 for details of Club Members' benefits. A 4-acre site with 70 touring pitches.
Playfield

Credit Cards

MORFA BYCHAN

Gwyndy Caravan Park (SH543371)
Black Rock Sands LL49 9YB ☎ 01766 512047 Signposted
Nearby town: Porthmadog
►►► **Family Park** ★ £6.20-£8.20 £6.20-£8.20 £6.20-£8.20
Open Mar-Oct Booking advisable bank hols & Jul-Aug Last departure 11.00hrs
A quiet family site a minute's walk to the beach at Black Rock Sands. A 5-acre site with 15 touring pitches and 44 statics.

PONTLLYFNI

St Ives Touring Caravan Park (SH432524)
Lon-Y-Wig LL54 5EG ☎ 01286 660347

►►►► **De-Luxe Park** ★ £6-£8 £6-£8 £6-£8
Open Mar-Oct Booking advisable all times Last arrival

contd.

21.00hrs Last departure noon
An immaculate little site with good facilities, within easy walking distance of beach. Off A499 along lane towards beach from village centre. A 1-acre site with 20 touring pitches.

Llyn-y-Gele Farm & Caravan Park (SH432523)
LL54 5EL ☎ 01286 660283 & 660289 Signposted
Nearby town: Caernarfon
Town & Country Pennant Park
Open Etr-Sep Booking advisable Jul-Aug Last arrival 22.00hrs Last departure 13.00hrs
Quiet farm site within 5-7 minutes' walking distance of the beach in the centre of the village. Centrally situated for touring the Lleyn Peninsula, Anglesey and Snowdonia, off A499. A 4-acre site with 6 touring pitches and 24 statics.

PONT-RUG

See **Caernarfon**

PORTHMADOG

Tyddyn Llwyn Caravan Park & Camping Site (SH561384)
Black Rock Rd LL49 9UR ☎ 01766 512205 & 514196
Family Park ★ £8-£12 £8-£12 £8-£12
Open Mar-Oct Booking advisable school hols Last arrival 23.00hrs Last departure noon
Set in an amphitheatre of wooded hills, with both level and slightly sloping pitches in beautiful countryside. Turn S (signed Black Rock Sands) in centre of Porthmadog, and site entrance in 0.5m. A 14-acre site with 150 touring pitches and 53 statics.
See advertisement under Colour Section

RHUALLT

Penisar Mynydd Caravan Park (SJ093770)
Caerwys Rd LL17 0TY ☎ 01745 582227 (2m NE) Signposted
Nearby town: Dyserth
Town & Country Pennant Park fr £6
Open Etr or Apr-Oct Booking advisable bank hols
A beautifully situated site, close to seaside resort of Rhyl. 2m NE of Penisar. From Chester take A55 westerly beyond Prestatyn exit, and take second right turn in 2 miles. From Llandudno take first left at top of Rhuallt Hill. A 2-acre site with 30 touring pitches.

Have you completed and returned the prize draw card inside the front cover of this guide? If not, do so today for the chance of a weekend break.

TALSARNAU

Barcdy Touring Caravan & Camping Park (SH623368)
LL47 6YG ☎ 01766 770736 Signposted
Nearby town: Harlech
De-Luxe Park ★ £7-£8.50 £7-£8.50 £7-£8.50
Open Spring bank hol-mid Sep (rs Etr-Spring bank hol & mid Sep-Oct only two fields open, food shop closed) Booking advisable from Feb
A quiet picturesque site on the southern edge of the Vale of Ffestiniog near Dwryd estuary. Very well-run and maintained. On A496 N of Talsarnau. A 12-acre site with 68 touring pitches and 30 statics.
Dishwashing sinks hot water charged.

Credit Cards

TAL-Y-BONT

Benar Beach Camping & Touring Park (SH573226)
LL43 2AR ☎ 01341 247571 & 247001
Nearby town: Barmouth
Town & Country Pennant Park ★ £5-£10 £5-£10 £4-£6
Open Mar-3 Oct Booking advisable peak periods
Friendly family site 1 mile from A496 halfway between Harlech and Barmouth. Adjacent to sandy beach with view of mountains. A 5-acre site with 40 touring pitches.
Satellite & TV hook-ups.

TAL-Y-BONT (NEAR CONWY)

Tynterfyn Touring Caravan Park (SH768692)
LL32 8YX ☎ 01492 660525 (5m S of Conwy on B5106, rd sign Tal-y-Bont, 1st on left)
Nearby town: Conwy
Town & Country Pennant Park fr £4.80 fr £4.80 fr £3.50
Open Mar-Oct Booking advisable bank hols & Jul-Aug Last arrival 22.00hrs Last departure noon
Small, family site on level ground situated in the lovely Conwy Valley. On the B5106, .25m N of village. A 2-acre site with 15 touring pitches.

TOWYN (NEAR ABERGELE)

Ty Mawr Holiday Park (SH965792)
Towyn Rd LL22 9HG ☎ 01745 832079 (on A548, .25m W of town)
Nearby town: Rhyl
Family Park
Open Etr-Oct (rs Apr (excluding Etr)) Booking advisable at all times Last departure 10.00hrs
A well laid out coastal site with very good leisure facilities, on the A548 .25m west of Towyn village. An

18-acre site with 348 touring pitches and 352 statics.
Free evening entertainment, sauna, solarium.

Credit Cards

TREFRIW

Plas Meirion Caravan Park (SH783630)
Gower Rd LL27 ORZ ☎ 01492 640247
Nearby town: Betws-y-Coed
Town & Country Pennant Park ★ £6-£8.50 £6-£8.50
Open Etr-Oct Booking advisable school hols Last arrival 22.00hrs Last departure 10.30hrs
A level site with mature trees set in the Conwy Valley. Off B5106. A 2-acre site with 5 touring pitches and 26 statics.

TYWYN

See **Bryncrug**

Ynysymaengwyn Caravan Park (SH601021)
LL36 9RY ☎ 01654 710684
Town & Country Pennant Park ★ £5-£7.50
£4-£6.50
Open Etr or Apr-Oct Booking advisable Jul-Aug Last arrival 23.00hrs Last departure noon
This site is ideally situated with the full amenities of the seaside on one hand and beautiful countryside and hills on the other. On right of A493 almost halfway between Bryncrug and Tywyn. A 4-acre site with 80 touring pitches and 115 statics.

MID WALES

This region includes the counties of Ceredigion, Carmarthenshire, Pembrokeshire and Powys which reflect the national changes.

ABERAERON

Aeron Coast Caravan Park (SN462633)
North Rd SA46 0JF ☎ 01545 570349 (on A487)
Family Park £7-£10 £6.50-£9.50 £6.50-£9.50
Open Etr or Apr-Oct Booking advisable bank & school hols Last arrival 20.00hrs Last departure noon
A large site sloping gently towards the sea, run by enthusiastic owners. On A487 at entrance to Aberaeron from the N, turn right near petrol stn. An 8-acre site with 50 touring pitches and 150 statics.
Disco & indoor leisure rooms.

ABERYSTWYTH

Ocean View Caravan Park (SN592842)
North Beach, Clarach Bay SY23 3DT ☎ 01970 828425 & 623361 (off A487, N)
Family Park £7-£9
Open Apr-Oct Booking advisable bank hols Last arrival 22.00hrs Last departure noon
A neat and tidy site on gently sloping ground in a sheltered valley with views to the sea. Follow unclass rd signed Clarach from S end of Bow St on A487. A 2-acre site with 24 touring pitches and 50 statics.

BETTWS EVAN

Pilbach Caravan Park (SN306476)
SA44 5RT ☎ 01239 851434 Signposted
Nearby town: Aberporth
Family Park ★ £7.50-£9.85 £7.50-£9.85
£7.50-£9.85
Open Spring bank hol-Sep (rs Mar-Spring bank hol & Oct swimming pool closed) Booking advisable Spring bank hol & Jul-Aug Last arrival 22.00hrs Last departure 10.30hrs
An exceptionally well-run small site set in secluded countryside. 3m N of Newcastle Emlyn and 7m E of Cardigan. A 3-acre site with 65 touring pitches and 70 statics.

Credit Cards

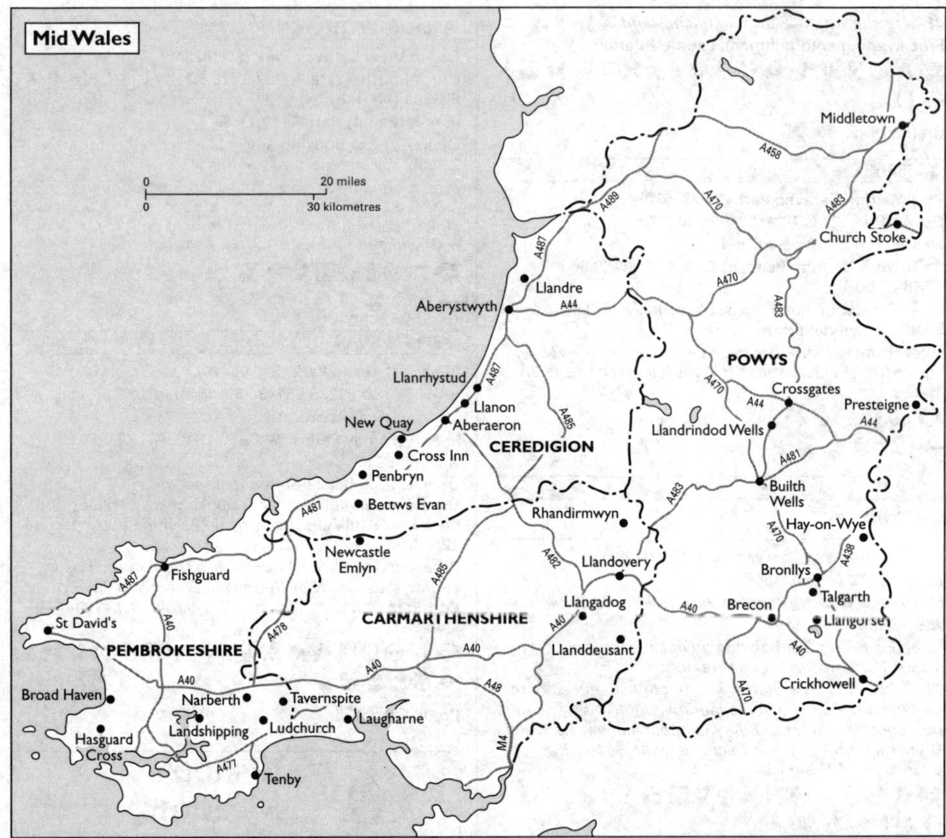

BRECON

Brynich Caravan Park (SJ071279)

Brynich LD3 7SH ☎ 01874 623325 (1m E ON a470 near Jct wih A40) Signposted

►►►► **De-Luxe Park** ★ £7.50-£8.50 £7.50-£8.50 ▲ £7.50-£8.50

Open Etr-Oct Booking advisable bank & school hols

Very attractive and well-appointed site offering commanding views of the Brecon Beacons. Ideal as a touring base or for longer stays. Adjacent to the A470, 1m E of Brecon. A 20-acre site with 130 touring pitches.

Adventure playground, off-licence, dish washing.

See advertisement under Colour Section

Bishops Meadow Caravan Park (SO060300)

Bishops Meadow, Hay Rd LD3 9SW ☎ 01874 622051 & 622392 (on B4602) Signposted

►►► **Family Park** ★ fr £8 fr £8 ▲ £5-£8

Open Etr-Oct Booking advisable bank hols

Part of a large leisure complex with a wide range of facilities. On B4062 between Brecon and Hay-on-Wye. A 3.5-acre site with 82 touring pitches.

See advertisement on page 261

Credit Cards

BROAD HAVEN

Creampots Touring Caravan & Camping Park (SM882131)

Havenway SA62 3TU ☎ 01437 781776 (5m W of Haverfordwest, turn left off B4341 towards Milford Haven, 2nd park on right) Signposted

Nearby town: Haverfordwest

► **Town & Country Pennant Park** £5.40-£7.50 £4.90-£7 ▲ £3.90-£6

Open Etr or Mar-Oct Booking advisable mid Jul-Aug

Last arrival 23.00hrs Last departure noon

Large, well-maintained fields with a good toilet block. Turn L off B4341 Haverfordwest-Broad Haven road at

Broadway, and Creampots is second park 500 yards on R. A 5-acre site with 72 touring pitches and 1 static.
Milk, eggs & papers daily.

South Cockett Caravan & Camping Park (SM879135)
SA62 3TU ☎ 01437 781296 & 781760 (1.5m E off B4341) Signposted
Nearby town: Broadhaven
Town & Country Pennant Park ★ £5.20-£6.95 £4.70-£6.45 £4.20-£5.50
Open Etr-Oct Booking advisable Jul-Aug Last arrival 13.00hrs
Small farm-style campsite rurally located and offering high standards of modern toilet facilities. Conveniently positioned close to the coastline and is a good touring base. A 6-acre site with 70 touring pitches and 1 static.

BRONLLYS

Anchorage Caravan Park (SO142351)
LD3 0LD ☎ 01874 711246 & 711230 Signposted
Nearby town: Brecon
Family Park fr £7 fr £7 fr £7
Open all year (rs Nov-Mar TV room closed) Booking advisable bank hols Last arrival 23.00hrs Last departure 18.00hrs
A well-maintained site. Touring pitches are on grassy slopes and level ground with good mountain views of the Brecon Beacons National Park. 8m NE of Brecon, on A438. An 8-acre site with 110 touring pitches and 101 statics.
Baby bath room.

BUILTH WELLS

Fforest Fields Caravan & Camping Park (SO100535)
Hundred House LD1 5RT ☎ 01982 570406 & 570220 (from town follow to 'New Radnor' on A481, 4m signed entrance on right) Signposted
Family Park £7.50 £6.50 £3-£6.50
Open Etr & Apr-Oct Booking advisable bank hols & Jul-Aug Last arrival 23.00hrs Last departure 18.00hrs
A sheltered site in a hidden valley, with wonderful views. On A481, 5 miles E of Builth Wells. A 7-acre site with 40 touring pitches.

Llewelyn Leisure Park (SO003514)
Cilmery LD2 3NU ☎ 01982 552838 & 01831 101052 (2m W on A483) Signposted
Family Park
Open Etr-Oct (rs Nov-Etr toilet/shower facilities in house) Booking advisable Jul-Aug Last arrival 22.00hrs Last departure 11.00hrs
A small site with great potential situated 2m W of Builth Wells, on S of A483 in Cilmery Village. A 0.75-acre site with 25 touring pitches and 26 statics.
Free library service.

Credit Cards

CHURCH STOKE

Daisy Bank Caravan Park (SO303929)
SY15 6EB ☎ 01588 620471 (on A489 between Lydham & Churchstoke) Signposted
Nearby town: Bishops Castle
De-Luxe Park ★ £5.50 £5.50
Open Feb-Nov Booking advisable bank hols Last arrival 21.00hrs Last departure 19.00hrs
A brand new site, well-landscaped with quality facilities. Marvellous views and welcoming owners. From A49 at Craven Arms take A489 to Churchstoke. Turn off 1.5m after Bishops Castle. A 4-acre site with 40 touring pitches.

Bacheldre Watermill Touring & Camping Park (SO243928)
Bacheldre Watermill SY15 6TE ☎ 01588 620489 (2.5m W off A489 Churchstoke / Newtown) Signposted
Nearby town: Montgomery
Town & Country Pennant Park £6 £6 £6
Open Etr-Oct Booking advisable bank hols
Secluded little site in the grounds of a working water mill. On A489, 2.5m W of Church Stoke. A 2-acre site with 25 touring pitches.

CRICKHOWELL

Riverside Caravan & Camping Park (SO215184)
New Rd NP8 1AY ☎ 01873 810397 Signposted
Family Park
Open Mar-Oct Booking advisable for stays over 1 wk Last arrival 23.00hrs
A clean and well-maintained site, adjacent to the River Usk, in lovely tranquil surroundings. The site does not take children. On A4077, and well signed from A40. A 3.5-acre site with 35 touring pitches and 20 statics.

CROSSGATES

Greenway Manor (SO081651)
LD1 6RF ☎ 01597 851230
Family Park
Open May-Oct
A small secluded site in the wooded and lawned grounds of a newly-refurbished hotel. Immediately off A44, 0.5m W of Crossgates. A 2-acre site with 13 touring pitches.

contd.

The Park Motel (SO081651)
Rhayader Rd LD1 6RF ☎ 01597 851201
Nearby town: Llandrindod Wells
Town & Country Pennant Park ★ £6.75-£7.50 £6.75-£7.50 £6.75-£7.50
Open Mar-Oct Booking advisable bank hols Last arrival 22.30hrs Last departure noon
This quiet rural site, set in beautiful countryside, has flat pitches and is well-sheltered by trees. It is an ideal touring centre, situated off A44. A 1-acre site with 10 touring pitches and 15 statics.

CROSS INN

Camping & Caravanning Club Site (SN383566)
Llwynhelyg SA44 6LW ☎ 01545 560029 (in season) & 01203 694995 Signposted
Nearby town: Cardigan
Family Park ★ £8.70-£11.30 £8.70-£11.30 £8.70-£11.30
Open end Mar-early Nov Booking advisable bank hols & peak periods Last arrival 21.00hrs Last departure noon
An excellent, attractive touring site in an elevated rural position. Winner of the 1995 Campsite of the Year Award for Wales. From A487 at Synod take A486, signed New Quay, then left in centre of Cross Inn village with site in 1mile. Please see the advertisement on page 27 for details of Club Members' benefits. A 13.5-acre site with 90 touring pitches.

Credit Cards

FISHGUARD

Fishguard Bay Caravan & Camping Park (SM984383)
Dinas Cross SA42 OYD ☎ 01348 811415 (2m E off A487) Signposted
Family Park ★ £7.75-£9.75 £7.75-£9.75 £6.75-£8.75
Open Mar-9 Jan Booking advisable Jul-Aug Last departure noon
Well-run part level and sloping grass site with bushes near the sea. 1m N of A487. A 3-acre site with 50 touring pitches and 50 statics.
View point.

Credit Cards

Gwaun Vale Touring Park (SM977356)
Llanychaer SA65 9TA ☎ 01348 874698 (1.5m SE on B4313) Signposted
Family Park ★ £5.50-£6.50 £5.50-£6.50 £5.50-£6.50
Open Mar-9 Jan Booking advisable Jul-Aug
A beautiful and immaculate site run by an enthusiastic owner. 1.5m from Fishguard on the B4313 Llanychaer/Gwaun Valley road. A 1.75-acre site with 30 touring pitches.
Free loan of Boules, video films, guide books.

HASGUARD CROSS

Hasguard Cross Caravan Park (SM850108)
SA62 3SL ☎ 01437 781443 Signposted
Nearby town: Haverfordwest
Family Park ★ £5.50-£7.50 £5.50-£7.50
Open all year Booking advisable Spring bank hol & Jun-Aug Last arrival 23.00hrs Last departure 11.00hrs
A very clean, efficient and well-run site in Pembrokeshire National Park with views of surrounding hills. 1.5m from sea and beach at Little Haven. Approach to B4327 from Haverfordwest to Dale, after 7m turn right at crossroads and site is first entrance on right. A 3-acre site with 25 touring pitches and 35 statics.

HAY-ON-WYE

Hollybush Inn (SO205406)
HR3 5PS ☎ 01497 847371 (Off B4350) Signposted
Town & Country Pennant Park ★ fr £6 fr £6 £5-£7
Open Good Fri-Oct Booking advisable bank hols Last arrival 23.00hrs Last departure 13.00hrs
A neat little site adjacent to a small inn and close to the R Wye. 2m from Hay-on-Wye off B4350. A 3-acre site with 22 touring pitches and 5 statics.
Canoe launch.

LANDSHIPPING

New Park Farm (SN026111)
SA67 8BG ☎ 01834 891284
Nearby town: Narberth
Town & Country Pennant Park
Open May Day wknd-Oct Booking advisable peak periods Last arrival 20.00hrs Last departure noon
A nice, quiet site on a smallholding with basic but adequate facilities. 7m W of Narberth, along unclass rd off A4075. A 2-acre site with 5 touring pitches and 30 statics.

LAUGHARNE

Ants Hill Caravan Park (SN299118)
SA33 4QN ☎ 01994 427293 Signposted
Nearby town: Carmarthen
Family Park
Open Etr-Oct Booking advisable Jul-Aug & public hols Last arrival 23.00hrs Last departure 10.30hrs
A small, well-run touring site on sloping grass, located near the village, on the Taff estuary. Care should be taken on descent into Laugharne on A4066 as site entrance is on minor road to left. A 4-acre site with 60 touring pitches and 60 statics.

LITTLE HAVEN

See **Hasguards Cross**

LLANDDEUSANT

Cross Inn & Black Mountain Caravan Park (SN773259)
SA19 9YG ☎ 01550 740621 Signposted
Nearby town: Llandeilo
Town & Country Pennant Park ★ fr £6 fr £6 £4-£6
Open all year Booking advisable bank hols Last departure 10.30hrs
A very pleasant small site in a secluded position. Take unclassified road south out of Trecastle, pass Castle Hotel and continue for approx seven miles. A 5-acre site with 40 touring pitches and 20 statics.

LLANDOVERY

Erwlon Caravan & Camping Park (SN776343)
Brecon Rd SA20 0RD ☎ 01550 720332 Signposted
Nearby town: Carmarthen
► ► ► **Family Park** ★ £5 £5 £5
Open all year Booking advisable bank hols Last arrival anytime Last departure noon
Long established family-run site set beside a brook in the Brecon Beacons foothills. On the A40, 1 mile E of Llandovery. An 8-acre site with 40 touring pitches.

LLANDRE

Riverside Park (SN634878)
Lon Glanfred SY24 5BY ☎ 01970 820070 Signposted
Nearby town: Borth
► ► ► **Family Park**
Open Mar-Oct Booking advisable bank & school hols Last arrival 23.30hrs Last departure noon
A quiet site with good quality facilities and easy access to the seaside. Set amongst well-wooded hills and bounded by a stream. On A487, 4m north of Aberystwyth, take B4353 and turn right at second turning. A 4-acre site with 24 touring pitches and 76 statics.
River fishing on site.

LLANDRINDOD WELLS

Disserth Caravan & Camping Park (SO035583)
Disserth, Howey LD1 6NL ☎ 01597 860277 Signposted
► ► ► **Family Park** ★ £6.50-£7.85 £6.50-£7.85 £6.50-£7.85
Open Mar-Oct Booking advisable early as possible Last arrival 22.00hrs Last departure noon
A peaceful site nestling in a beautiful valley on the banks of R Ithon, a tributary of the R Wye. Take A470 from Aberystwyth towards Builth Wells, turn left at Newbridge on Wye, and right towards Disserth. A 2.5-acre site with 25 touring pitches and 21 statics.
Private trout fishing.

Credit Cards

Dalmore Camping & Caravanning Park (SO045568)
Howey LD1 5RG ☎ 01597 822483 (Howey 3m S A483)
Town & Country Pennant Park ★ £5.50-£6.50 £5.50-£6.50 £5.50-£6.50
Open Mar-Oct Booking advisable Jun-Aug Last arrival 22.00hrs Last departure noon
A clean, tidy site on A483 but screened from road and traffic noise by hedgerow. Wonderful views. 1.5m S of village. A 2-acre site with 20 touring pitches and 20 statics.

LLANGADOG

Abermarlais Caravan Park (SN695298)
SA19 9NG ☎ 01550 777868 & 777797 (on A40 6m W of Llandovery) Signposted
Nearby town: Llandovery
► ► ► **Family Park** ★ fr £7 fr £7 fr £7
Open Apr-Oct (rs Nov, Dec & Mar 1 wc, water point no hot water if frosty) Booking advisable bank hols & 15 Jul-Aug Last arrival 23.00hrs Last departure noon
An attractive, well-run site with a welcoming atmosphere. Part-level, part-sloping grass in a wooded valley on edge of Brecon Beacons National Park. It is by the River Marlais and off A40 Llandeilo-Llandovery road. A 17-acre site with 88 touring pitches.

contd.

Volleyball, badminton court & softball tennis net.

LLANGORSE

Lakeside Caravan Park (SO128272)
LD3 7TR ☎ 01874 658226
Nearby town: Brecon
►►► **Family Park**
Open Jun-Sep (rs Apr, May & Oct swimming pool clubhouse & restaurant) Booking advisable peak periods Last arrival 21.30hrs Last departure noon
A much improved site with an enthusiastic warden, located next to Llangorse Lake. An ideal centre for water sports enthusiasts. A 2-acre site with 40 touring pitches and 72 statics.
Boat hire & launching, windsurfing, fishing.

Credit Cards

LLANON

Woodlands Caravan Park (SN511668)
SY23 5LX ☎ 01974 202342 & 202454 Signposted
Nearby town: Aberaeron
►►► **Family Park** ★ £7.50-£8.50 £7.50-£8.50
£5.50-£7.50
Open Apr-Oct (rs Mar toilet block closed) Booking advisable school hols Last arrival 21.30hrs Last departure noon
A level grass site surrounded by mature trees and shrubs near woods and meadowland, adjacent to a stoney beach. 11m from Aberstwyth on A487. A 4-acre site with 80 touring pitches and 60 statics.

LLANRHYSTUD

Pengarreg Caravan Park (SN539697)
SY23 5DJ ☎ 01974 202247 Signposted
► **Town & Country Pennant Park**
Open Mar-Oct Booking advisable Last arrival mdnt Last departure 10.00hrs
A gently sloping site fronted by a pebble beach, with cliff walks and boat launching facilities. On A487 W of Llanrhystud at S end of village. A 7-acre site with 50 touring pitches and 155 statics.
Slipway to beach for sailing.

LUDCHURCH

Woodland Vale Caravan Park (SN140113)
SA67 8JE ☎ 01834 831319
►►► **Family Park**
Open Mar-Oct Booking advisable bank hols & Jul-Aug Last arrival 21.00hrs Last departure 14.00hrs
Site with informally sited pitches set between areas of water created in an old quarry. N of Ludchurch on unclass rd, the continuation S of B4314. A 1.5-acre site with 30 touring pitches and 80 statics.

MIDDLETOWN

Bank Farm Caravan Park (SJ293123)
SY21 8EJ ☎ 01938 570526 & 570260 Signposted
Nearby town: Welshpool
► **Town & Country Pennant Park** ★ £6.50-£7.50
£6.50-£7.50 fr £5
Open May-Oct Booking advisable bank hols Last arrival 20.00hrs
A grass site with two different areas - one gently sloping and the other mainly level. Immediate access to hills, mountains and woodland. On A458 W of Middletown. A 2-acre site with 20 touring pitches and 33 statics.
Trout pool.

NARBERTH

Noble Court Caravan & Camping Park (SN111158)
Redstone Rd SA67 7ES ☎ 01834 861191 (.5m off A40 on B4313) Signposted
Nearby town: Tenby

►►►► **De-Luxe Park** ★ £6-£13.50 £6-£13.50
£6-£13.50
Open Mar-Oct (rs early & late season swimming pool closed) Booking advisable Jul-Aug Last arrival 22.00hrs Last departure noon
Mostly sloping site with good views and a high standard of service. On B4313 between Narberth & A40. A 14-acre site with 92 touring pitches and 60 statics.
30 Acres of adjoining land for walks & picnics.

Credit Cards

NEWCASTLE EMLYN

Afon Teifi Caravan & Camping Park (SN338405)
Pentrecagal SA38 9HT ☎ 01559 370532 (2m E A484)

►►►► **De-Luxe Park**
Open Apr-Oct (rs Nov-Mar when facilities limited, no toilet block) Booking advisable peak periods Last arrival 23.00hrs
Very attractive and well-managed site in secluded valley. Signed off A484, 2m E of Newcastle Emlyn. A 6-acre site with 110 touring pitches and 3 statics.
15 acres of woodland, fields & walks.

Cenarth Falls Holiday Park (SN265421)
Cenarth SA38 9JS ☎ 01239 710345 (just off A484 on outskirts of Cenarth) Signposted
Nearby town: Cardigan

►►►► **De-Luxe Park** £7.75-£12.75 £7.75-£12.75 £7.75-£12.75
Open Mar-9 Jan (rs Mar-mid May & mid Sep-9 Jan swim pool closed, clubhouse wknds only) Booking advisable bank hols & Jul-Aug Last arrival 20.00hrs Last departure noon
A rapidly developing, former static site, very well run with excellent facilities. Signed immed off A484, .5m W of Cenarth. Winner of the Best Campsite of the Year Award for Wales, 1997/8. A 2-acre site with 30 touring pitches and 89 statics.
Clubhouse, pool table & video machines.

Credit Cards

NEW QUAY

Cei Bach Country Club (SN409597)
Parc-y-Brwcs, Cei Bach SA45 9SL
☎ 01545 580237 (off A487 onto B4342 signed to Cei Bach) Signposted
Nearby town: Aberaeron

►►►► **De-Luxe Park** £6-£12 £6-£12 £6-£12
Open Good Fri-last Sun in Sep Booking advisable Etr, Spring bank hol & school hols Last arrival 22.00hrs Last departure 11.00hrs
A very good site in a beautiful situation overlooking Cardigan Bay with views of the distant cliffs. An attractive setting with thoughtful landscaping the owners the Wynne family have a welcoming attitude. Winner of the 1996 Campsite of the Year Award for Wales. Turn off A487 onto B4342 road to New Quay, then follow signs for Cei Bach. A 3-acre site with 60 touring pitches.

Credit Cards

PENBRYN

Talywerydd Touring Caravan & Camping Park (SN297507)
SA44 6QY ☎ 01239 810322 Signposted
Nearby town: Cardigan

►►►► **De-Luxe Park** £6-£10 £6-£10 £6-£10
Open Mar-Oct Booking advisable Jul-Aug Last arrival 22.00hrs Last departure 11.00hrs
Small family site with seaviews from every pitch, off A487. Take 2nd turn off A487 signed Penbryn, and site 500yds on left. A 4-acre site with 40 touring pitches.
Crazy golf, 9 hole pitch & putt, microwave available

PRESTEIGNE

Rock Bridge Park (SO294654)
LD8 2NF ☎ 01547 560300 Signposted
►►► **Family Park**
Open Apr-Sep Booking advisable public & school hols Last arrival 21.30hrs Last departure noon
Part-level, part-sloping grass site with trees and bushes, set in meadowland with access to River Lugg. 1m W of Presteigne off B4356. A 3-acre site with 35 touring pitches and 30 statics.

RHANDIRMWYN

Camping & Caravanning Club Site (SN779435)
SA20 0NT ☎ 01550 760257 (in season) & 01203 694995 Signposted
Nearby town: Llandovery

►►►► **De-Luxe Park** ★ £9.10-£12.10 £9.10-£12.10 £9.10-£12.10
Open end Mar-early Nov Booking advisable bank hols & peak periods Last arrival 21.00hrs Last departure noon

contd.

Set on the banks of the Afon Tywi near the Towy Forest and the Llyn Brianne reservoir, this first class site has superb views on all sides. Take A40 through Llandovery, turn right immediately after crossing river at sharp left-hand bend, signed Rhandirmwyn. At T junction turn right recrossing river, and then left. In approx 6m at Royal Oak Inn site signed on left. Please see the advertisement on page 27 for details of Club Members' benefits. An 11-acre site with 90 touring pitches.

Credit Cards

ST DAVID'S

Caerfai Bay Caravan & Tent Park (SM759244)
SA62 6QT ☎ 01437 720274 Signposted
►►► **Family Park** £6-£10 £4.50-£6 ▲ £4.50-£6
Open Etr-Oct Booking advisable school hols Last arrival 21.00hrs Last departure 11.00hrs
Grassy site with bushes set in meadowlands, with magnificent coastal scenery overlooking St Brides Bay - bathing beach 300yds from park entrance. Off A487, end of unclass road to Caerfai Bay. A 7-acre site with 82 touring pitches and 33 statics.

Hendre Eynon Camping & Caravan Site (SM773280)
SA62 6DB ☎ 01437 720474 Signposted
►►► **Family Park** ★ £5-£8.50 £4-£8 ▲ £4-£8.50
Open May-Sep (rs 27 Mar-Apr one toilet block & showers only) Booking advisable school hols Last arrival 21.00hrs Last departure noon
A country site on a working farm with a modern toilet block. 2m NE of St Davids on unclassified road. A 7-acre site with 48 touring pitches and 2 statics.

Camping & Caravanning Club Site (SM805305)
Dwr Cwmdig, Berea SA62 6DW ☎ 01348 831376 (in season) & 01203 694995 Signposted
Town & Country Pennant Park ★ £8.10-£10.30 £8.10-£10.30 ▲ £8.10-£10.30
Open end Mar-end Sep Booking advisable bank hols & peak periods Last arrival 21.00hrs Last departure noon
Immaculately kept small grassy site in open country near the Pembrokeshire Coastal Path. Situated at the junction of two unclass roads 1.5m W of Croesgoch on the A487 St David's-Fishguard road. Please see the advertisement on page 27 for details of Club Members' benefits. A 4-acre site with 40 touring pitches.

Credit Cards

The AA pennant classification has been revised for 1998. Please read the explanation of the scheme on page 10.

Tretio Caravan & Camping Park (SM787292)
SA62 6DE ☎ 01437 720270 & 781359 Signposted
Nearby town: Haverfordwest
Town & Country Pennant Park £5-£7 £4.50-£6.50 ▲ £4.50-£6.50
Open 14 Mar-14 Oct Booking advisable bank hols & mid Jul-Aug Last arrival 23.00hrs Last departure 17.00hrs
A gently sloping touring site with well-converted facilities. On minor rd linking St David's with Croesgoch, 4m from St David's. A 4.5-acre site with 40 touring pitches and 10 statics.

TALGARTH

Riverside International (SO148346)
Bronllys LD3 0HL ☎ 01874 711320 & 712064 (on A479 opposite Bronllys Castle) Signposted
Nearby town: Brecon
►►► **Family Park** ★ £8-£9 £8-£9 ▲ £8-£9
Open Etr-Oct Booking advisable bank hols & Jul-Aug Last arrival 22.00hrs Last departure 16.00hrs
Well-appointed touring site with pitches available on riverside. Elevated position with magnificent views of the Black Mountains. Off A479. A 9-acre site with 80 touring pitches.
Leisure facilities, sauna, jacuzzi, sunbed & gym.

TAVERNSPITE

Pantglas Farm Caravan Park (SN175122)
SA34 0NS ☎ 01834 831618 Signposted
Nearby town: Whitland
►►► **Family Park** £5-£6.50 £5-£6.50 ▲ £5-£6.50
Open Etr-15 Oct Booking advisable Spring bank hol & Jul-Aug Last arrival 23.00hrs Last departure 11.00hrs
A quiet, family-run site in a rural setting, with a welcoming attitude towards children. On B4328 between Ludchurch and Tavernspite; at village pump take middle turning, and site signed on right. A 7-acre site with 75 touring pitches.
Year round caravan weekly storage £2.

TENBY

Kiln Park Holiday Centre (SN119002)
Marsh Rd SA70 7RB
☎ 01834 844121 & 0345 433433
★ £5-£12 £5-£12 ▲ £3-£6.50
Open Mar-Oct (rs Mar-mid May & Oct) Booking advisable all times Etr-Sep Last arrival 21.00hrs Last departure 10.00hrs no cars by caravans
A large, commercial, touring, camping and static holiday site, situated on level ground on the town's outskirts. A short walk through dunes leads to the sandy south-facing beach. On A4139. A 103-acre site with 240 touring pitches and 620 statics.
Entertainment complex.

Credit Cards

Rowston Holiday Park (SN133024)
New Hedges SA70 8TL ☎ 01834 842178 & 814090
Signposted
►►►► **De-Luxe Park** ★ £10-£16 £10-£16
▲ £8-£16
Open Apr-mid Oct (rs Oct-Jan 10 no site shop & laundry) Booking advisable May & Jul-Aug Last arrival 21.00hrs Last departure 10.00hrs
A really top class site in all ways, commanding views over woodland and Carmarthon Bay. A 10-acre site with 100 touring pitches and 136 statics.
Dishwashing sinks under canopy.

Trefalun (SN093027)
Devonshire Dr, St Florence SA70 8RH ☎ 01646 651514 Signposted

►►►► **De-Luxe Park** ★ £6-£10 £6-£10 £5-£7
Open Etr-Oct Booking advisable bank hols & Jul-Aug Last arrival 20.00hrs Last departure noon

A well-maintained level grass site with bushes and trees W of St Florence 3m off B4318. A 7-acre site with 35 touring pitches and 10 statics.

Credit Cards

Well Park Caravan & Camping Site (SN128028)
SA70 8TL ☎ 01834 842179 Signposted

►►►► **De-Luxe Park** ★ £5-£10 £5-£10 £5-£8.50
Open Apr-Oct (rs Apr-mid May & mid Sep-Oct shop closed) Booking advisable Spring bank hol & Jul-Aug Last arrival 22.00hrs Last departure 11.00hrs

An excellent, well-run site with trees and bushes. 1.5m N of Tenby off A478 New Hedges by-pass. A 7-acre site with 100 touring pitches and 42 statics.
Off-licence in shop.

Wood Park Caravans (SN128025)
New Hedges SA70 8TL ☎ 01834 843414 Signposted

►►►► **De-Luxe Park** ★ £5-£10 £5-£10 £4-£8
Open Spring bank hol-Sep (rs Etr-Spring bank hol & Sep-Oct bar shop & launderette may not open) Booking advisable Spring bank hol & Jul-Aug Last arrival 22.00hrs Last departure 10.00hrs

A well-run, slightly sloping, part-level grass site with trees and bushes. 1.5m N of Tenby off A478 New Hedges by-pass. A 3-acre site with 60 touring pitches and 90 statics.
Outside dish/clothes washing area.

AA members can call AA Hotel Booking Service on 0990 050505 to book at AA recognised hotels and B & Bs in the UK and Ireland, or through our Internet site: http://www.theaa.co.uk/hotels

SOUTH WALES

This region includes the counties of Blaenau Gwent, Bridgend, Caerphilly, Cardiff, Merthyr Tydfil, Monmouthshire, Neath Port Talbot, Newport, Rhondda Cynon Taff, Swansea, Torfaen and Vale of Glamorgan which reflect the recent national changes.

CARDIFF

Pontcanna Caravan Park (ST171773)
Pontcanna Fields, off Sophia Close, Riverside CF1 9JJ
☎ 01222 398362 & 471612

►►►► **De-Luxe Park** ★ £11.25-£13.75
£11.25-£13.75
Open Mar-Oct Booking advisable Last arrival telephone Last departure noon
An excellent site with good amenities, and very close to centre of Cardiff. Take A48 turn off M4 through Cardiff, turn left at lights at Llandaff, and follow signs to Sophia Gardens and the Welsh Institute of Sport. A 2-acre site with 43 touring pitches.

CHEPSTOW

St Pierre Camping & Caravan Site (ST509901)
Portskewett ☎ 01291 425114
►►► **Family Park**
Open Mar-Oct
Well-established site with immaculately kept facilities and a peaceful atmosphere, overlooking the Severn Estuary. From Chepstow take A48 towards Newport, turn left at first rndbt, then immed left. A 4-acre site with 50 touring pitches.
Boule, croquet.

DINGESTOW

Bridge Caravan Park & Camping Site (SO459104)
Bridge Farm NP5 4DY ☎ 01600 740241 Signposted
Nearby town: Monmouth
►►► **Family Park**
Open Etr-Oct Booking advisable bank hols Last arrival 22.00hrs Last departure 16.00hrs
An excellent site in a quiet village setting, signposted from Raglan and located off the A449, South Wales-Midlands road. A 4-acre site with 94 touring pitches.
Fishing.

LLANTWIT MAJOR

Acorn Camping & Caravan Site (SS973678)
Ham Ln South CF61 1RP ☎ 01446 794024 & 0589 421112 Signposted
Nearby town: Cardiff
►►► **Family Park** ★ £5.50-£6.50 £5.50-£6.50
£5.50-£6.50
Open Etr or 1st Feb - 8th Dec Booking advisable bank hols & Aug Last arrival 23.00hrs Last departure noon
A quiet country site on meadowland, with individual

contd.

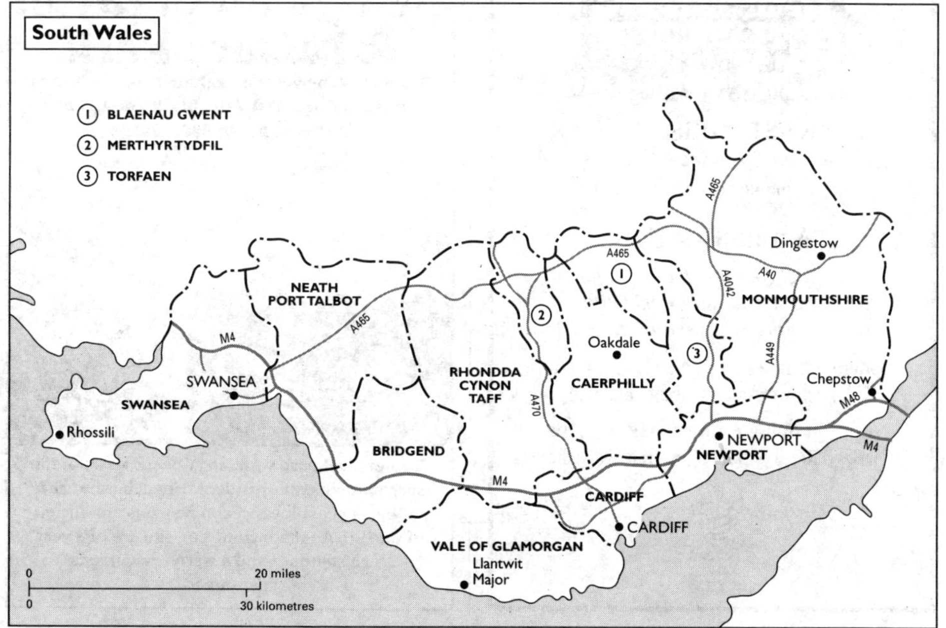

pitches marked out by hedges and shrubs. From Llantwit Major follow B4265 south. Approach site through Ham Manor residential park. A 4.5-acre site with 90 touring pitches and 15 statics.

Llandow Touring Caravan Park (SS956713)
Marcross CF7 7PB ☎ 01446 794527 & 792462 (2m NW) Signposted
Nearby town: Cowbridge
►►► **Family Park** ★ £5.50-£7.50 £5.50-£7.50 ▲ £5-£7.50
Open Feb-Nov Booking advisable bank hols & end Jun Last arrival 10.00hrs Last departure noon
A large level touring park with a new purpose-built toilet block, within easy reach of Glamorgan's Heritage Coast, and a short distance from Cardiff and Porthcawl. Signed off B4270. A 6-acre site with 100 touring pitches.
Caravan Storage

NEWPORT

Tredegar House & Park (ST285855)
NP1 9YW ☎ 01633 816650 & 815880 (2.5m west A48 close to M4 junc 28) Signposted
►►► **Family Park** ★ £7 £7 ▲ £5-£7
Open Etr-Oct Booking advisable public hols & Jul-Aug Last arrival 21.00hrs Last departure noon
Set in peaceful corner of a country park, sheltered by mature trees and shrubs, the touring park offers a full range of excellent facilities. Signed off M4, junction 28. A 4-acre site with 55 touring pitches.
House tours, craft workshop, carriage rides, boating.

Credit Cards

OAKDALE

Penyfan Caravan & Leisure Park (SO189012)
Manmoel Rd NP2 0HY ☎ 01495 226636 (off B4251) Signposted
Nearby town: Blackwood
►►► **Family Park** ★ fr £7 fr £7 ▲ fr £7
Open all year Booking advisable bank hols
A constantly improving site with good facilities for the whole family, including a licensed bar with bar meals. From junc 28 on M4 follow A467 to Crumlin, turn left on to B4251, and follow signs towards site. A 4-acre site with 75 touring pitches and 9 statics.

Credit Cards

RHOSSILI

Pitton Cross Caravan & Camping Park (SS434877)
SA3 1PH ☎ 01792 390593 & 390593 (2m W of Scurlage on B4247)
Nearby town: Swansea
►►► **Family Park** ★ £8-£10 £8-£9 ▲ £7.50-£10

Open Etr-Oct (rs Apr-early May & Sep-Oct some facilities may be closed) Booking advisable Spring bank hol & Jul-Aug Last arrival 21.00hrs Last departure noon

Constantly improving farm site within walking distance of the coast, with enthusiastic proprietors. On B4247, 1 mile inland from Rhossili. A 6-acre site with 100 touring pitches.

Motor caravan service bay, pets corner.

Credit Cards

SWANSEA

Riverside Caravan Park (SS679991)

Ynys Forgan Farm, Morriston SA6 6QL ☎ 01792 775587 (1m NE of A48/A4067 unclass 1m M4 junc 45) Signposted

►►► **Family Park** ★ £9-£11 £9-£11 £5-£11

Open all year (rs winter months pool) Booking advisable bank hols & main school hols Last arrival mdnt Last departure noon

A large site close to the M4, an ideal base for touring Mumbles, Gower beaches and Brecon National Park. Signed directly off junc 45 of M4. A 70-acre site with 120 touring pitches.

Fishing on site by arrangement.

Credit Cards

NORTHERN IRELAND

CO ANTRIM

BALLYCASTLE

Silver Cliffs Holiday Village

21 Clare Rd BT54 6DB ☎ 012657 62550 (0.25m W off A2) Signposted

►►► **Family Park**

Open 17 Mar-Oct Booking advisable 11-25 Jul & 22-25 Aug Last arrival 20.00hrs Last departure 17.00hrs

A typical large seaside site with a swimming pool and bar. Close to the beach and River Glenshesk, .25m W of Ballycastle off B15. A 2-acre site with 50 touring pitches and 250 statics.

Sun beds, sauna, & snooker.

Credit Cards

CUSHENDALL

Cushendall Caravan Camp

62 Coast Rd BT44 0QW

☎ 012667 71699 Signposted

► **Town & Country Pennant Park**

Open mid Mar-mid Oct Booking advisable peak periods Last arrival 23.00hrs Last departure 14.00hrs

A pleasant site next to the beach and sailing club on the A2, 1m S of town. A 1-acre site with 14 touring pitches and 55 statics.

CUSHENDUN

Cushendun Caravan Park

14 Glendun Rd BT44 0PX

☎ 01266 761254 Signposted

► **Town & Country Pennant Park** ★ fr £7.90 fr £7.90 fr £7.90

Open Etr-Sep Booking advisable Jul-Aug Last arrival 22.00hrs Last departure 12.30hrs

A small touring site with mostly level pitches next to larger static site. From A2 take B52 for 1m, clearly signed. A 0.5-acre site with 15 touring pitches and 50 statics.

LARNE

Curran Caravan Park

131 Curran Rd ☎ 01574 260088 Signposted

►►► **Family Park**

Open Apr-Sep Booking advisable main season

contd.

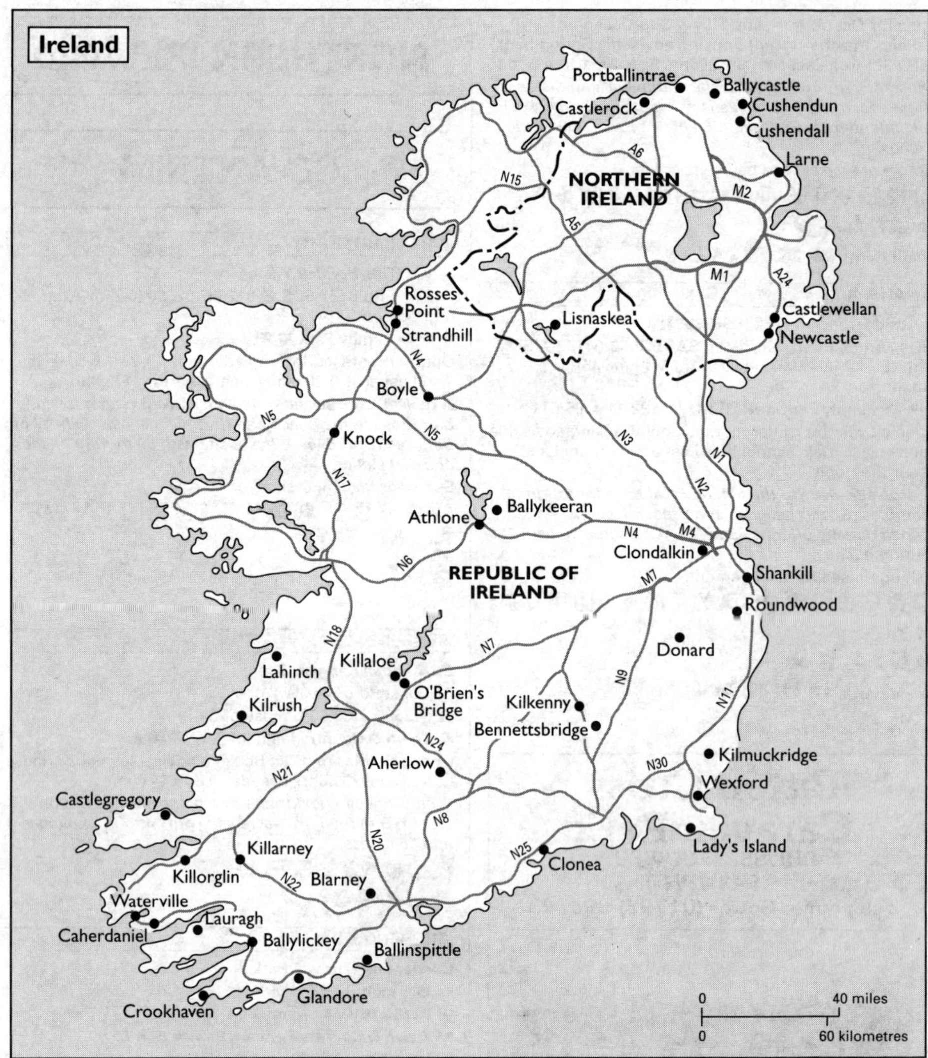

Please note that caravan and camping parks are listed county by county and under alphabetical order of place name within each county. Northern Irealnd counties are listed first, followed by those in the Republic. Place names are highlighted on the location map, but no map references are given against the directory entries.

Prices given in the Republic of Ireland entries are in Irish Punts (IR£) Please consult yur bank for the current exchange rate

A tidy and very clean council site ideal for the ferry. Site on A2 .25m from ferry, and clearly signed. A 3-acre site with 40 touring pitches.
Bowling & putting greens.

PORTBALLINTRAE

PortBallintrae Caravan Park
Ballaghmore Av BT57 8RX ☎ 012657 31478 Signposted
Nearby town: Bushmills
Town & Country Pennant Park ★ £10-£11 £10-£11 £3-£11
Open Apr-Sep Booking advisable Etr & Jul-Aug Last arrival 20.30hrs Last departure 14.00hrs
Very tidy site, popular for Giants Causeway. In Portballintrae village clearly signed from A2, .25m from Bushmills Distillery. A 12-acre site with 53 touring pitches and 150 statics.

CO DOWN

CASTLEWELLAN

Castlewellan Forest Park
Dept of Agriculture, Forest Service BT31 9BH
☎ 013967 78664 Signposted
►►► **Family Park** ★ £9.50-£11 £9.50-£11 £9.50-£11
Open all year Booking advisable wknds & Jul-Aug Last arrival 22.00hrs Last departure 15.00hrs
Attractive forest park site, situated down a long drive with views of the castle. Site broken up into smaller areas by mature trees and shrubs. Off A25 in Castlewellan; turn right at Upper Square and turn into Forest Park, clearly signed. A 5-acre site with 90 touring pitches.
Lake, arboretum, fishing on site. First aid.

NEWCASTLE

Tollymore Forest Park
☎ 01396 722428 Signposted
►►► **Family Park**
Open 15 Mar-15 Nov (rs 16 Nov-14 Mar) Booking advisable Jul & Aug & wknds Apr-Sep Last arrival 21.00hrs Last departure 17.00hrs
Popular site with family field and large tent area. From A2 at Newcastle take B180, and site clearly signed on right. A 7.5-acre site with 100 touring pitches.

CO FERMANAGH

LISNASKEA

Lisnaskea Caravan Park
BT92 0NZ ☎ 01365 721040 Signposted
Nearby town: Enniskillen
Town & Country Pennant Park ★ £9-£10 £9-£10 £5.50-£6.50
Open Apr-Sep Booking advisable Jul-Aug Last arrival 21.00hrs Last departure noon
From A34 turn onto B514 for Lisnaskea, and site signed .5m before town. A 4-acre site with 43 touring pitches.

CO LONDONDERRY

CASTLEROCK

Castlerock Holiday Park
24 Sea Rd ☎ 01265 848381 Signposted
►►► **Family Park**
Open Etr-Oct Booking advisable Jul-Aug Last arrival 21.00hrs Last departure noon
A mainly static site at the seaside with a tidy touring area, 2 minutes from the beach. From A2 to Castlerock, turn right before the rlwy stn into site; signed. A 2-acre site with 40 touring pitches and 210 statics.

REPUBLIC OF IRELAND

CO CLARE

KILLALOE

Lough Derg Caravan and Camping Park
☎ 061 376329 Signposted

►►►►► **Premier Park**
Open 29 Apr-Sep Last arrival 21.00hrs Last departure noon
A 4.5-acre site with 57 touring pitches and 15 statics.
Boats for hire, boat slipway, fishing.

KILRUSH

Aylevarroo Caravan and Camping Park
☎ 065 51102 (off N67) Signposted
►►► **Family Park**
Open 24 May-13 Sep Booking advisable Last arrival 22.00hrs Last departure noon
A 7.5-acre site with 36 touring pitches and 10 statics.
Basketball court.

LAHINCH

Lahinch Camping and Caravan Park
☎ (065) 81424 Signposted
►►►► **De-Luxe Park** ★ IR£8-IR£10 IR£8-IR£10 IR£8-IR£10
Open May-Sep Booking advisable mid Jul-mid Aug Last arrival 23.00hrs Last departure noon
A 5-acre site with 115 touring pitches and 12 statics.
Bicycle hire.

CO CORK

BALLINSPITTLE

Garrettstown House Holiday Park
☎ 021 778156 Signposted
►►►► **De-Luxe Park**
Open 19 May-16 Sep (rs Etr-18 May) Last arrival 22.00hrs Last departure noon
A 7-acre site with 60 touring pitches and 80 statics.
Disco, ceilidh, campers' kitchen

BALLYLICKEY

Eagle Point Caravan and Camping Park
☎ 027 50630 Signposted
Nearby town: Bantry
►►►►► **Premier Park** IR£9.50-IR£10 IR£9.50-IR£10 IR£9.50-IR£10
Open May-Sep Last arrival 23.00hrs Last departure noon
A 20-acre site with 125 touring pitches.
Credit Cards

BLARNEY

Blarney Caravan & Camping Park
Stone View ☎ 021 385167 & 382051 Signposted
►►► **Family Park** ★ IR£8-IR£9 IR£8-IR£9 IR£7-IR£8
Open all year Booking advisable anytime Last arrival mdnt Last departure noon
A 3-acre site with 40 touring pitches.
Mini golf.

CROOKHAVEN

Barley Cove Caravan Park
☎ 028 35302 & 021 542444 Signposted
Nearby town: Schull
►►►►► **Premier Park**
Open Etr & Jun-1 Sep (rs May & Sep) Booking advisable 7 Jul-17 Aug Last arrival 21.00hrs Last departure noon
A 9-acre site with 100 touring pitches and 50 statics.
Pitch & putt, children's playhouse

GLANDORE

Meadow Camping Park
Kilfinnin ☎ 028 33280 Off N71 at Leap or Rosscarbery. Take R597 to Glandore. For 5 Kms. Site is on R597 2kms Rosscarbery side of Glanmore. Signposted
Nearby town: Skibbereen
Town & Country Pennant Park ★ IR£7-IR£8
fr IR£7
Open 16 Mar-15 Sep Booking advisable Jul-Aug Last arrival 22.30hrs Last departure noon no cars by tents
A 1.5-acre site with 19 touring pitches.
Dining room.

CO DUBLIN

CLONDALKIN

Camac Valley Tourist Caravan & Camping Park
Corkagh Park ☎ 01 4640644
De-Luxe Park
Open all year
A 15-acre site with 163 touring pitches.

SHANKILL

Shankill Caravan Park
Sherrington Park ☎ 01 2820011
Family Park
Open all year Last departure noon
A 7-acre site with 82 touring pitches and 9 statics.

CO KERRY

CAHERDANIEL

Wave Crest Caravan and Camping Park
☎ 066 75188 Signposted
De-Luxe Park ★ IR£6.50 IR£6.50
IR£6.50
Open 17 Mar-12 Oct Last arrival 22.00hrs Last departure noon
A 4.5-acre site with 45 touring pitches and 2 statics.
Boat anchorage, fishing & pool room.

CASTLEGREGORY

Anchor Caravan Park
☎ 066 39157 Signposted
Nearby town: Tralee
De-Luxe Park ★ IR£8-IR£9 IR£8-IR£9
IR£6-IR£9
Open Etr-Sep Last arrival 22.00hrs Last departure noon
A 5-acre site with 24 touring pitches and 6 statics.
Camper kitchen.

KILLARNEY

Fossa Caravan Park
Fossa ☎ 064 31497
(2.5m SW on R562)
★ IR£9-IR£9.50 IR£9-IR£9.50 IR£8.50-IR£9.50
Open Etr-Sep (rs Oct & Mar/Apr restaurant & takeaway closed) Booking advisable Jul-Aug Last arrival 23.00hrs Last departure noon
A 6-acre site with 100 touring pitches and 20 statics.
Campers kitchens & bikes for hire.
Credit Cards

Flesk Muckross Caravan & Camping Park
Muckross Rd ☎ 064 31704 & 35794 (1m S)
Signposted
De-Luxe Park ★ IR£8-IR£8.50
IR£8-IR£8.50 IR£7.50-IR£8
Open mid Mar-end Oct Booking advisable Last arrival 21.00hrs Last departure noon
A 7-acre site with 72 touring pitches.
Bike hire.Bar/club, tennis, pool all within 50 mtrs.
Credit Cards

KILLORGLIN

West's Holiday Park
Killarney Rd ☎ 066 61240 (1m on Killarney rd) Signposted
►►► **Family Park** ★ IR£3-IR£3.50 IR£3-IR£3.50 IR£300-IR£3.50
Open Apr-Oct Booking advisable Last departure noon
A 1-acre site with 17 touring pitches and 48 statics.
Salmon/Trout fishing, volleyball.
Credit Cards

LAURAGH

Creveen Park
Healy Pass Rd ☎ 064 83131 (1m SE on R574) Signposted
► **Town & Country Pennant Park** ★ IR£8 IR£8 IR£8
Open Etr-Oct Booking advisable Aug bank hol Last arrival mdnt Last departure noon
A 2-acre site with 20 touring pitches.

WATERVILLE

Waterville Caravan and Camping
Spunkane ☎ 066 74191 1 Kilometre. N of Waterville just off main N70 "Ring of Kerry" road. Signposted
►►►► **De-Luxe Park** ★ IR£9-IR£9.50 IR£9-IR£9.50 IR£8-IR£8.50
Open Etr-Sep Booking advisable Jul-Aug Last departure noon
A 4.5-acre site with 59 touring pitches and 22 statics.
Playroom, cycle hire, campers kitchen.

CO KILKENNY

BENNETTSBRIDGE

Nore Valley Park
☎ 056 27229
Nearby town: Kilkenny
►►► **Family Park** ★ fr IR£9 fr IR£8 IR£5-IR£8.50
Open Mar-Oct Booking advisable bank hols & Jul Last arrival 22.00hrs Last departure 16.00hrs
A 4-acre site with 70 touring pitches and 4 statics.
Bread & farm produce, river walks, crazy golf.

KILKENNY

Tree Grove Caravan & Camping Park
Danville House ☎ 056 21512
► **Town & Country Pennant Park**
Open Apr-Oct Booking advisable
A 7-acre site with 30 touring pitches.
Campers kitchen & sinks.

CO MAYO

KNOCK

Knock Caravan and Camping Park
Claremorris Rd ☎ 094 88100 & 88223 Signposted
Nearby town: Claremorris
►►► **Family Park**
Open Mar-Nov Booking advisable Aug Last arrival 22.00hrs Last departure noon
An 8-acre site with 58 touring pitches and 8 statics.

CO ROSCOMMON

ATHLONE

Hodson Bay Caravan & Camping Park
Hodson Bay ☎ 01902 92448 Signposted
► **Town & Country Pennant Park** ★ IR£8 IR£8 IR£8
Open 9 May-Aug Booking advisable bank hols & last wk Jul-1st wk Aug Last arrival 22.30hrs Last departure noon
A 2-acre site with 34 touring pitches.

BOYLE

Lough Key Forest Park
☎ 079 62363 & 62212 Signposted
►►►► **De-Luxe Park**
Open 27 Mar-6 Apr & May-1 Sep Booking advisable 3 wks before arrival Last arrival 22.00hrs Last departure noon no cars by tents
A 15-acre site with 72 touring pitches.

CO SLIGO

ROSSES POINT

Greenlands Caravan & Camping Park
071 77113 & 45618 Take R291 (L16) NW from SLIGO 5m. Site golf club and beach. Signposted

De-Luxe Park ★ IR£10.50-IR£8.50 IR£10.50-IR£8.50 IR£10.50-IR£8.50
Open 21 May-17 Sep & Easter Last arrival 20.00hrs Last departure noon
A 4-acre site with 78 touring pitches and 12 statics.

STRANDHILL

Strandhill Caravan Park
071 68120 Signposted
Town & Country Pennant Park
Open May-14 Sep Booking advisable Jul-26 Aug Last arrival 23.00hrs Last departure 14.00hrs
A 10-acre site with 28 touring pitches and 12 statics.

CO TIPPERARY

AHERLOW

Ballinacourty House Camping and Caravan Park
062 56230 Signposted
Nearby town: Tipperary

De-Luxe Park
Open Etr-end Sep Booking advisable high season & bank hols Last arrival 22.00hrs Last departure noon
A 5-acre site with 58 touring pitches.
Mini-golf.

CO WATERFORD

CLONEA

Casey's Caravan Park
058 41919 Signposted
Nearby town: Dungarvan
Family Park ★ IR£9.50-IR£10 IR£9.50-IR£10 IR£9.50-IR£10
Open 2 May-7 Sep Booking advisable May-Jun Last arrival 22.00hrs Last departure noon
A 4.5-acre site with 108 touring pitches and 170 statics.
Crazy golf & games room.

CO WESTMEATH

BALLYKEERAN

Lough Ree Caravan and Camping Park
0902 78561 & 74414 Signposted
Town & Country Pennant Park
Open Apr-2 Oct Booking advisable bank hols
A 5-acre site with 40 touring pitches and 2 statics.

CO WEXFORD

KILMUCKRIDGE

Morriscastle Strand Caravan & Camping Park
Morriscastle 053 30124 & 01 4535355 (off-season) Signposted
Nearby town: Gorey
Family Park
Open Jul-27 Aug (rs May-Jun & 28 Aug-Sep shop, reception, games room, take-away food) Booking advisable Whitsun wknd & mid Jul-mid Aug Last arrival 22.00hrs Last departure 16.00hrs
A 16-acre site with 100 touring pitches and 150 statics.
Dish washing room, indoor cooking facilities.

LADY'S ISLAND

St Margaret's Beach Caravan & Camping Park
St Margarets 053 31169 Signposted
Nearby town: Wexford
Town & Country Pennant Park ★ IR£7-IR£9 IR£7-IR£9 fr IR£7
Open Mar-Oct Booking advisable Jul & Aug Last arrival 23.00hrs Last departure noon

contd.

A 4-acre site with 30 touring pitches and 20 statics.

WEXFORD

Ferrybank Caravan Park

Ferrybank ☎ 053 44378 & 43274 Signposted

►►► **Family Park** ★ fr IR£9 fr IR£9 ▲ IR£4-IR£9

Open Apr-Sep (rs Etr & Sep no shop) Booking advisable Whit wknd & Aug bank hol Last arrival 22.00hrs Last departure 16.00hrs

A 4.5-acre site with 130 touring pitches.

CO WICKLOW

DONARD

Moat Farm Caravan & Camping Park

☎ 045 404727 Signposted

Nearby town: Baltinglass

►►► **Family Park** fr IR£8 fr IR£8 ▲ fr IR£8

Open all year Booking advisable bank hols & Jun-Aug Last arrival 22.30hrs Last departure noon

A 2.75-acre site with 40 touring pitches.

ROUNDWOOD

Roundwood Caravan Park

☎ 01 2818163 Signposted

Nearby town: Bray

►►►► **De-Luxe Park** ★ IR£6-IR£7 IR£6-IR£7 ▲ IR£6-IR£7

Open Apr-Sep Booking advisable Jun-Aug Last arrival 11.00hrs Last departure noon

A 5-acre site with 45 touring pitches and 33 statics.

Campers kitchen & dining room.

Before You Go

This is the checklist compiled by one of our campsite inspectors to ensure that he leaves nothing behind when he sets off either from home or from park visits with a towed caravan. We thought you might like to share his handy hints, and save yourself from embarassment ... or worse.

- Check that all interior caravan items are safely stored, cupboards are closed, loos not full of moveable objects, all interior electrics set correctly. Remember that vase of flowers!
- Check roof lights are closed and windows secure.
- Corner steadies should be up tightly, blocks cleared away, steps stowed.
- Disconnect electric hook-ups to site and check that gas bottles are turned off.
- Make sure electrics to car are secure.
- Check that the tow-hook safety wire is clipped on, and, if used, that the anti-snake device is fitted correctly.
- Visually check that caravan number plate is secure - and that it reads the same as the one on the car.
- Using a second person to stand behind the caravan, check that all lights and indicators are working correctly.
- Move forward about 15 metres, then stop, get out and inspect your pitch for any items which have been left under the caravan.
- Check that the caravan door is locked and secure.
- Another useful and potentially life-saving tip is to travel always with a small fire extinguisher, fire blanket or both. Fires in caravans and tents are all too commonplace, and once started can take hold very quickly. By the time help has come, or you have gone to find the site's fire-fighting equipment, a tent in particular can already have burned down completely. Never treat fire lightly.
- If you use Calor Gas, they issue a free directory of stockists and dealers. Simply call free on 0800 626 626.

Useful Addresses

CAMPING AND CARAVANNING CLUB
Greenfields House
Westwood Way
Coventry CV4 8JH
Tel 01203 694995

CARAVAN CLUB
East Grinstead House
East Grinstead
West Sussex RH19 1UA
Tel 01342 326944

BRITISH HOLIDAY & HOME PARKS ASSOCIATION LTD
6 Pullman Court
Great Western Road
Gloucester GL1 3ND
Tel 01452 526911

NATIONAL CARAVAN COUNCIL LTD
Catherine House
Victoria Road
Aldershot
Hampshire GU11 1SS
Tel 01252 318251

Please write to: Campsites Editor, AA Camping and Caravanning Guide, Publishing Division, The Automobile Association, Fanum House, Basingstoke RG21 4EA

Use this form to recommend any caravan and camping park with good touring pitches where you have stayed which is not already in our guide.

If you have any comments about your stay at a touring park listed in the guide, we shall be grateful if you will let us know, as feedback from readers helps us to keep our guide accurate and up to date. Please note, however, that the AA only inspects and classifies parks for their touring facilities. We do not inspect or grade static caravans.

If a problem arises during your stay on a park, we do recommend that you discuss the matter with the park management there and then so that they have a chance to put things right before your holiday is spoilt.

Please note that the AA does not undertake to arbitrate between you and the park management, or to obtain compensation or engage in protracted correspondence.

Readers Report form

Your name (block capitals) ....

....

....

Your address (block capitals) ....

....

....

....

....

....

Comments ....

....

....

....

....

....

CAMPING AND CARAVANNING GUIDE 1998

CAMPING AND CARAVANNING GUIDE 1998

Readers Report form

Please write to: Campsites Editor, AA Camping and Caravanning Guide, Publishing Division, The Automobile Association, Fanum House, Basingstoke RG21 4EA

Use this form to recommend any caravan and camping park with good touring pitches where you have stayed which is not already in our guide.

If you have any comments about your stay at a touring park listed in the guide, we shall be grateful if you will let us know, as feedback from readers helps us to keep our guide accurate and up to date. Please note, however, that the AA only inspects and classifies parks for their touring facilities. We do not inspect or grade static caravans.

If a problem arises during your stay on a park, we do recommend that you discuss the matter with the park management there and then so that they have a chance to put things right before your holiday is spoilt.

Please note that the AA does not undertake to arbitrate between you and the park management, or to obtain compensation or engage in protracted correspondence.

Your name (block capitals) ....

....

....

Your address (block capitals) ....

....

....

....

....

....

Comments ....

....

....

....

....

....

CAMPING AND CARAVANNING GUIDE 1998

CAMPING AND CARAVANNING GUIDE 1998

PARKS APPOINTED JUST TOO LATE TO BE ENTERED IN THE DIRECTORY

SOMERSET, ENGLAND

Sparkford

LONG HAZEL INTERNATIONAL CARAVAN AND CAMPING PARK

High Stree, nr Yeovil, BA22 7JH
Tel 01963 440002

►►► **Family Park**

A very neat, smart park next to the Sparkford Inn, just off A303 bypass on A359. Facilities include a playground and EHUs

SUFFOLK, ENGLAND

Kessingland

HEATHLAND BEACH CARAVAN PARK

London Road NR33 7PJ
Tel 01502 740337

►►►► **De Luxe Park**

A well run and well maintained park with access to the beach and signposted from the A12. It has excellent toilet facilities, and amenities include a swimming pool, fishing lake, cafe, bar, tennis, EHUs and a laundry.

A 20 acre site with 106 touring pitches and 158 statics.

CHESHIRE, ENGLAND

Knutsford

WOODLANDS PARK

Wash Lane, Allostock, nr Knutsford WA16 9LG
Tel 01565 723307/722628

►►► **Family Park**

Open Mar - 6 Jan

An attractive park in the heart of rural Cheshire, set in mature woodland and with brand new facilities. Off the A50. Turn into Wash Lane by Boundary Water Park at Allostock and the park is quarter of a mile on the left. Amenities include EHUs, a laundry and a playground. A 165 acre site with 50 touring pitches and 130 statics.

GRAMPIAN, SCOTLAND

Craigellachie

Aberlour Gardens Caravan Park
Aberlour-on-Spey AB38 9LD
Tel 01340 871586

►►► **Family Park**

Pitch price from £7.75, from £6.50 for tents

Open Apr-Oct

A quiet walled garden park with very clean modern facilities, in a beautiful wooded setting. Signed off A95 between Aberlour and Craigellachie. Amenities include EHUs, laundry, shop, playground. A 3.5 acre site with 30 touring pitches and 26 statics.

Stop Press